Perversion, Pedagogy and the Comic

A Survey of the Concept of Theatre in the Christian Middle Ages

Perversion, Pedagogy and the Comic

A Survey of the Concept of Theatre in the Christian Middle Ages

Soumick De

Perversion, Pedagogy and the Comic: A Survey of the Concept of Theatre in the Christian Middle Ages
Soumick De

First Published 2021

ISBN 978-93-5002-689-2

Published by
AAKAR BOOKS
28 E Pocket IV, Mayur Vihar Phase I
Delhi 110 091 India
aakarbooks@gmail.com

Laser Typeset at
Sakshi Computers, Delhi

Printed at
Sapra Brothers, Noida

In memory of Vidrohi,
a nomad-poet who never really went anywhere
and
my father

Contents

PART 3

The Actualization of the Problem

Foreword

Theatre, philosophy, religion–how to distribute, configure and evaluate each of these, in their specificities and their points of contact, their historicities and their essences? How to trace their mutual alliances and repulsions, their complicities and their dissensions? Will we dramatize these scenarios and their protagonists/antagonists through strategies of rhetoric, that is, by painting *polemical* scenes of history, or will we place the value of truth on acts of thinking about their variations and relations and, if the singular name of the logic and historicity of such distributive scenarios is "politics" then is politics on the side of truth or is it a polemical affair?

With rare integrity and virtuosity, the book you are about to read will navigate you through sometimes the epically stormy, sometimes the deceptively calm waters of the above and several other questions and their attendant researches. It is true that the researches threaten to plunge any reader into the formidable if not intimidating depths of a history and an archive not frequently visited. But the scholarly threat is also the intellectual fascination of the project. But this promising equivocation I leave to the experience of the reader in the imminent encounter–I was going to say "duel"–to follow. However before that threshold, I will reiterate the three foundational names–theatre, philosophy, religion–and indicate the initial stakes of their vertiginous triangulation performed in this book. It is not unknown that with Plato, in the history of Western philosophy, and his paradigmatic deployment of the logic of mimesis, "theatre" (or more generally "poetry") is rendered into an *image of thought* evaluated and judged by the *truth of thought*–the measure of that evaluation being the mimetic distance of theatre, or poetry, from truth. However, at this very point of contact and repulsion between philosophy and theatre, a certain disjunctive wound is inflicted on thought. The wound consists of the following: while truth is the very apodeictic access of thought to being–an apodeixis without any need of the support of an *image*–the thought of theatre is already a disjunct "object" of thought–and the essence and discourse of that object pertain to *what an image is.* Can there be an "idea"–an *eidos*–of the image? That is the problem of the thought of theatre, an investigation which is the preliminary condition for propounding any "philosophy of theatre" or even a "philosophical theatre".

This is the point at which the philosophical blade cuts to the bone of the problem–a wound as sharp and fine as any. Philosophy retorts: how can there be an idea of the image when the very measure of an idea is its intrinsic consistency, its unicity and when the image is intrinsically multiple, inconsistent and a parasite of the apodeixis gathering thought unto truth? When the image is *not* ...? This is the monumental institution of philosophy's indictment of theatre. And yet...

And yet the canny and courageous researcher dares to ask: is there any ground of thinking about *another* institution, an inconsistent institution? An institution of the very logic of the image that philosophy pronounces errant? And further, is there some historical ground for such a "counter-institution"? The researcher comes up with a brief and shattering answer: religion. So a few remarks on the errant history of religion: it seems to me that in the space of ancient Greek religion a logic, a topology was obtained that allowed a grid of figural and affective transformations that were expressed in a strange form, which could be called the form of a "generic mixture" or "universal (or mutual) parasitism" The founding name of this paradoxical logic was not really "religion"; it was rather, what the great Hellenist Marcel Detienne calls, 'the name of "god"'[1]. The institution of "god", *whether in the singular or plural*, is already a multiplicity, a dizzying yet disciplined and coded space or *topos* of imagological transformations. One might even proffer a particular name of "god" as specific as that of Dionysus. But Dionysus, the great god of universal transformation–from animal to man, from man to woman, from nomadic to urban, from national to immigrant ... is the god of *theatre.* So when Plato philosophically indicts theatre and politically produces a virtual *fiat* against it, he could be as much effecting these founding yet interruptive moves vis-à-vis *religion*. This is a crucial point Alain Badiou, in his own way makes[2]. Though it follows from the above that the institutional knot tied between the threads of theatrical (or poetic) mimesis and religious figuration produces a double surprise. The logic of multiplicity and parasitism going by the name "god" on the one hand, fits well with the *particular* traits of pagan idolatrous polytheism and on the other, the essential topology, the logic is one of *universality*, of universal virtuality (or imagology). So it is not surprising that the sovereign claimant to universality, philosophy, should consider religion (or the "god") to be its privileged adversary though in theatrical disguise.

Second remark: while it certainly is a fact that Christianity unleashes the imperial gesture of banning the theatre, to begin with in Rome–an intriguing case of pre-Christian legal and liturgical organization moving into Christian *politics*–such an act of undisguised legitimized violence is also, through and through, a *theological* gesture. At this point of transformation of a kind of regional universalism of the Athenian "god" to Christian imperial theo-logic–a strange destiny of words because the Greek term "*theos*" twists around its own institution to create a movement from god as universal virtuality, as a generic topos-logic to a logic of god *as such* of the capitalized God. The institution of this theo-logic is usually called "monotheism", but it begs the question that if "god" is not a generic particular name any more–whether Dionysus or Jupiter or any other–but the name of Being or *all there is*, then how will such a name *function*, in the civic (from *polis* to *civitas*) sense (in the way say that Dionysus does in ancient Athens)? The answer is obvious: Christianity is not just a general theo-logic; it is a logic of incarnation. It is not merely a doctrine of the saturation of all there is, that is, a mere metaphysical theory of God; it is a phenomenology, an experience, a *history of God* broken and promised by the event of the Christic incarnation. So the institution of Christian "event" (of the birth, life and death of Christ) is not the simple abstraction of Being or all that there is but the doctrine of the singular "there is" of God *as image* (one can refer here to Marie-Jose Mondzain's exemplary analysis of iconicity in Pauline Christianity[3]). But suppose ...

But suppose the researcher doesn't blink at this enormous explosion on a world-historical and imperial stage of the most promising if not exhilarating, event; suppose the courage of immanent truth requires one to enquire whether the *function* of this Christic negativity, this redemptive brokenness, is still a measure of world-history's tragic failure to be adequate to the "there is" of all that world history is *not...* Suppose the "there-comes-into-existence" of Christ is as much a comic strategy of the theo-logic that must never stop measuring the "all there is" which is the "world" (*mundus*) against the "there is" of the actuality of a kind of surplus whose own intrinsic measure can appear in *this* world as the latter's negativity, its lack... So the strategy of Christ is comic because it is only meant to show the world's vanity, its hollow "being full of itself", its "being-nothing" appearing (as *eikon* or *imago*) as a garrulous empty vessel in contrast to God's "being surplus"—calling for a thinking of grace beyond being, *beyond* "all that there is" ... So measured against and by the originary surplus of a theo-logic of God or Grace, the world becomes a *metaphor* of "all that there is"; all imagology or iconology also becomes a "metaphorology".

I have no difficulty or hesitation imagining the thread of a metaphorology that passes through such exemplary and divergent researches as those of Hans Blumenberg and Jacques Derrida—and now of Soumick De. I also know all such research involves not immersing itself in some common rhetorical strategy called the "metaphor" but investigating and discussing *concrete* metaphors. And this is exactly what De's work performs with dazzling virtuosity. But before freeing the reader towards that "experience", let me supplement my structural and comparative remarks on the history of religion with a methodological observation: a metaphorology posits not that there are, to begin with, original documents to be rescued from the archive and then given a kind of secondary rhetorical and metaphorical treatment—but that the very status of a "document' demands metaphorological problematization. Nothing generates such a demand more insistently than the theological document. Its theological provenance lies in enunciating—in the particular interruptive sense indicated earlier—the disjunction between a topology of "gods" and a doctrine of God. Its documentary materiality, however, consists in the imagology or metaphorology which *performs* the "argument" of theology. This is the equivocation, even inconsistency internal to a theological document, its irreducible errancy. Let me, in the last part of this improvised foreword, try to correlate my earlier remarks on the equivocation of a christic theo-logic with at least one of Soumick De's exemplary metaphorological investigation.

The disjunctive wound at the heart of the history of religion consists of the following event: while the ancient Greek "god" was expressed by regions and neighbourhoods (for instance that of ancient Athens) to form a kind of universe of magical or imagological transformations, the Christian-monotheistic "God" was "said"—in the Bible, for example—to create, what could be thought of as the only and universal "world". From "god" as the institution of a civic (and mythic) *possibility,* one is doctrinally—and imperially—*decided* as a "believer" in a so-called monotheistic creator God, whose pure divine actuality becomes the ground, source and force of all that is *possible.* The notion of "*mundus*" or "world" is a negative notion of everything that divine actuality—is *not.* The sum of possibilities is "all' of being-possible, all that can be in so far as all that can be—is *not* divine, is emptied out of divinity to the very measure that the history of the world (*mundus*) is broken by this very "emptying-out" or *kenosis*—a word from Paul, which Mondzain mobilizes with remarkable results—of God's incarnation. But the christic event of incarnation is a wound—that is the crux of the above movement.

Soumick De's investigations, harnessing a repertoire of ancient and medieval texts, incessantly supplemented by methodological improvisations that create the trail of a new contemporaneity, seizes on a key, marginal and *impossible* concept of Christian Middle Ages: the "concept-problem"–in De's Deleuzist vocabulary–of the *theatrum mundus.* The author's references are not always the same as mine–but that is not relevant to the real matter of interest: the very concept-problem–its internal dissonance, its "inconsistent" force–of the "theatre of the world" arises from the undecidability that arises from the Christian "decision" of the in-carnation (the becoming-carnal or flesh) of the doctrine of pure divine actuality, or the doctrine of God. De's immense labours do not resolve this undecidability, they *articulate* it, in the canonical terms of a tragic and a comic theatrical discourse. According to me, this articulation has a singular ontological effect. A brief glimpse of this effect...

If all that there is, is *not,* if "world" is only a locus of possibilities, then it is, in its broken (and promising) unfolding, a world of images (*eikon*). Hence the concept of such a world is *not,* it is impossible. Or, the concept of such a world of vertiginous negativity, of productive virtuality forever carrying the trace of the "emptying, the kenotic negative of divine actuality–who is pure surplus and beyond being–is *metaphoric.* It is not that there is, or are, a metaphor or metaphors for the world (*mundus*); it is rather that the world *is* a metaphor. That is the scintillating- almost blinding- glimpse of a "metaphorology".

The historical transaction and compensations exchanged by imperial and theological Christianity are there for the reader to learn in Soumick De's dense–and lucid–genealogy from pre-Christian (Greek and Roman) to Christian usages of *theatrum mundi.* The obvious irony accompanying this genealogy is that while in the "pagan" logic, religion is the hidden institution under scrutiny, if not attack, at the hands of philosophy when the latter castigates theatre/poetry, the decision of imperial Christianity to ban the historical institution of theatre and the theological doctrine of God who creates the "world" (*mundus*) in the image of a "loss" (or emptying-out) of God's actuality leads to the return of the world in the image and as the metaphor of the *theatre.* The ontological wound is caused by the tearing off of the sovereign measure from the world, which can only be measured metaphorically.

The deepest enigma opened up above is the following: If the sovereign measure is beyond being, then such a God doctrinally pronounced as pure act(uality) is *not* subject to thought's evaluation. And the world created of this abyssal groundless ground (pure surplus over all ground) is also mere image, incessant "loss" or weakening of any proper thinkability. And if neither God nor the world is thinkable any more, then isn't the claim of any theo-logic (a *logos,* a conceptual survey of God's institution) already invalidated, and necessarily diverted and depleted into an (impossible) "metaphorology"? the diversion and depletion afflicting all truth-value of the "document" of research? This is the perilous edge on which Soumick De's research balances–and performs its virtuoso act of articulating the undecidability it encounters. It is undecidable whether the birth, life and death of God, that is, *the history of God,* is comic or tragic. This history of God is tragic if the subject of this history still cleaves to the *thought* of the sovereign divine actuality, a thought which paradoxically and tragically can only "lose' this actuality in its historico-human incarnation. The history of God is a comic, if not perverse spectacle if we *literally* picture divine actuality dying on the cross. Such a "letter" is the pure comic experience of *inconsistency.* In the history of theatre, this inconsistency is archetypically embodied in the figure of the *fool.* The christic event which breaks the mere cycle of "natural time'–after all, according to the Greeks, even political constitutions came and went like the seasons in cyclical rhythms–into a topologically articulated regional past and a world-historically open future, cannot despite its evental force, sustain its liberating temporalizing power. It re-inserts itself through a spatial and scenic metaphor–the *theatrum mundus–* into a territorial-imperial project. The trajectory from the earlier topological multiplicity of "gods" and "generic mixtures" to the territorial homogeneity of universal imperial history suppresses *historicity itself*[4].

It seems to me that the triangulation of theatre, philosophy and religion, once accelerated beyond a critical threshold, yields a kind of "vortex" whose force is nothing if not *political.* In the remote historical distance from where the documents of this book–errant, always errant!–signal to us, there exists already something here-and-now, absolutely contemporary–political, always political...

However it takes time, patience, humility and inexhaustible good humour to undertake the journey to one's present, to where we are, here and now. And it takes *others.* One such "other" that continues to make my own journey, not any less challenging but vastly more interesting, is Soumick De's book which the reader holds in her hand.

And all that I ask the reader is–to read.

New Delhi
2020

Soumyabrata Choudhury

NOTES

1. Marcel Detienne and Gulia Sissa, *The Everyday Life of the Greek Gods*, trans. Janet Lloyd (Stanford: Stanford University Press, 2000).
2. Alain Badiou and Nicholas Truong, *In Praise of Theatre,* trans. Andrew Bielski (Cambridge: Polity Press, 2015).
3. Marie-Jose Mondzain, *Image Icon, Economy: The Byzantine Origins of the Contemporary Imaginary*, trans. Rico Franses (Stanford: Stanford University Press, 2005).
4. It might be objected that this is too simplified a view of imperial territorialism. Isn't Christendom already a kind of christic globalization in the form of an iconological economy (*oikonomia*) rather than the homogeneous closure of territorial nations and empires? This is indeed true, particularly when the experience of capitalism is taken into account, whereby an economy of commodities is articulated with the christic economy of images and icons. However it might be pointed out that even as I write, we

are re-experiencing obsessive preoccupation with *theatrum mundi* that re-localize images and affects of national "love"–in vivid and terrifying memory of what medieval and crusading Christianity used to call "the love of Holy Land", of the *patria.* The general point which follows from this is that when theatre becomes a metaphor and the world becomes a theatre, a problematical affect–a problematical "love"–grips this theatre of the world. The concept-problem is problematically *subjectivized.*

Preface

At the very height of enlightenment Holderlin defined tragedy as the metaphor for intellectual intuition.[1] In the best tradition of German idealism the poet tried to capture through intellectual intuition a sense of unity and wholeness whose origin goes back to Kant. But what is perhaps more interesting in this definition of tragedy is the use of theatre as a metaphor for such a spirit of universalism. If for Holderlin intellectual intuition was founded upon an idea of arche-unity with everything living and divine then it was equally impossible for him to capture such totality within the finite realm of human reality *except as a metaphor*. Curiously enough the only metaphor worthy of such a spirit of universalism was taken to be theatre. Notwithstanding the intimate proximity speculative Idealism shared with the model of tragedy which was trying to produce a new theory of the Subject, of Art and of History, the use of theatre as a metaphor of universalism was nothing new. We find its echo in the idea of world theatre–a *theatrum mundi*–which in its different variations harks back to Plato. However theatre as a metaphor for the world has been historically informed by a double bind where the world acquires a theatrical image as much as theatre serves as a metaphor for a universal spirit. Moreover the relation between theatre and the world is also the fundamental basis of a

1. Holderlin in the essay titled "On the Difference of Poetic Modes" defined tragedy thus: "The tragedy, in appearance heroic poem, is idealistic in its signification. It is the metaphor of an intellectual intuition". (Holderlin 1988, 83)

relation between theatre and philosophy. In other words, behind the question of the metaphor of theatre lies the fundamental problem of representation *as such*.

Lets us imagine all the elements that make theatre possible (the actors, audience, props, costumes, lights, the theatre house and even the tickets distributed and the money exchanged, etc.) as a finite set or an assemblage which makes manifest something all together irreducible to any or all these elements of theatre. This irreducible theatrical substance can also be seen as the metaphorical foundation of a universalizing spirit which has to take into consideration the finite set of theatrical elements which is then transformed into an arche-totality. Hegel in this sense was right to point out that behind Greek tragedy was the question of representing the universal or absolute spirit though externally through enactment. Despite this relationship between Absolute Spirit and consciousness being enacted externally on the tragic stage, it did try to *imitate* the individual moment of self-consciousness which produced the universal spirit within itself. Moreover, Hegel argued that the entirety of the Greek consciousness historically was reflective of this aesthetic moment of the Spirit. Be that as it may, Hegel's speculative gesture did not disregard the actual material manifestation of the theatrical substance. On the contrary, such materiality was fundamental in actualizing that particular moment of the Spirit making it available for history. We can argue from such a Hegelian perspective that the theatrical substance did not lose its material concreteness in order to become a metaphor for world because the theatrical substance was an *imitation* of the universal substance.

However, we have a significant shift happening with Christianity when in a single gesture Christianity not only abolishes the theatrical substance but makes theatre a metaphor of the world which is alienated from its own universal substance. In some sense this is the inaugural moment of a modern sensibility of theatre when it gains access to the interiority of the subject who is alienated from his substance which resides in God. When theatre comes to represent this subjective moment of alienation it becomes a metaphor for the world in so far as it lacks any universalizing essence. The world becomes theatrical in so far as it is deceptive and treacherous because its true meaning lies elsewhere. Theatre as a metaphor of the world carries the same nothingness which informs the very theatrical substance. One can speculate that the idea of *theatrum mundi* which was so prevalent during the Renaissance, particularly in the plays of Shakespeare, carried in its heart this burden of alienation which becomes evident when we look at his tragic heroes who are not only alienated from the world but whose very alienation reflects the empty sound and fury of a world devoid of signification.

When Holderlin calls theatre the metaphor for intellectual intuition he therefore has both these moments in mind–unity and separation–which makes his definition of tragedy and by the same token his idea of theatre that much more paradoxical. Theatre becomes a metaphor for an arche-unity which must overcome itself and reflect upon itself in its moment of differentiation; while at the same time the differentiating part should feel within itself the intensity of a primordial unity because its essence is entirely present to itself. Holderlin argues that this can only happen in a world which is *becoming* a metaphor to itself, a world which is not *this* world or *that*, but a world which is becoming one world *in* another. This passage from one world to another is the sense behind the metaphor of theatre of the world and the essence behind the theatrical substance. It is in search of this metaphorical substance which is also to say a substantial metaphor that we embark on this research.

Acknowledgements

Strange are the paths of thought on which we walk silently while the world screams outside. Or perhaps it is the other way round. Clamours of ancient thoughts rage within us while the world around dims into the darkness of a thousand whisperless nights. To philosophize is to learn how to die. A lesson in dying only to be born again; to be born in the very act of dying. Socrates re-created in Montaigne who is more Socratic than Socrates. To begin anew, to become ourselves re-creations which would be more original than our beginnings, more primordial than our beings. But what creatures are we to become? In the words of a philosopher-poet are we to become "absolute creators"? "prototypes"? "An idea of humanity"? "An enormous hurricane"? "A beautiful witch"? "A great amnesiac"? To which dare we add–'an eternal student'? But then is that what a re-search is? To search where to start again? To search for the spot from where we can embark on another journey, always an-Other journey? Again and again along the straight line of Aion? .... But then what about a thesis? Is it the end of our imagination from which rises the gloomy towers of institutions? A university perhaps?

Perhaps not.

A life then?

Maybe.

Within such perilous uncertainty at least one thing is certain. To thank is nothing other than to praise the other to whom you are grateful. It is surely not to report an exchange of help and gratitude. Thanking cannot be anything less than the will to be worthy of the gifts which come your way. Gifts which are but signs of encounters with others. In praise of such encounters, I write this acknowledgement.

Firstly I would like to thank my supervisor, Dr. Soumyabrata Choudhury with whom everything begins... again! Naturally it is in the middle that I have always encountered him and continue to do so. Not only did he supervise this thesis in the middle of my PhD but since then he has always guided the work from a place between strictness and leniency, both intellectually and pragmatically. He evokes in us the belief that we do not learn from the books handed down to us by our fathers and teachers but through the torn pages we circulate among ourselves. He continues to inspire us to learn not under him but with him such that we can always begin again—begin to think again and perhaps also to live again in the spaces which separate us forever. I would like to thank Mr. K.K. Saxena, my publisher who took the risk of publishing this thesis as a book.

I would like to thank Dalip from our library for helping me out on those very rare occasions when I visited the place.

Dr. Saityabrata Das has presented some of us, who have had the pleasure of knowing him, with the rare gift of *philo-sophia,* the love of wisdom. From his relentless effort to *do* philosophy by creating such spaces of discussion as Agora to organizing conferences and talks on topics which were seminal to the development of this thesis, Saityabrata has inspired us to pursue philosophy like none other. But I would like to thank Saitya, more than anything else, for infusing in me the love of medieval philosophy which is perhaps his true gift.

Prof. Franson Manjali, Prof. Babu Thaliath, Achia Anzi, Dr. Anup Dhar and other members of Agora belong to that community of scholars that I was fortunate enough to know during my years of research which has had its effects on my thinking in more ways than one. Dr. Mohinder Singh in his immaculate tranquillity had read and offered his remarks on certain sections of this thesis in its early phase.

It is difficult to thank my friends because they keep reminding me of that ancient Aristotelian maxim: "O my friend, there are no friends!". But there is a certain insistence in them which forces you to consider new ways of dealing with them and in turn to deal with yourself. In a word they have all forced me to think of new and creative ways to construct relationships both intellectually and ethically. Rajat, the connoisseur of the void, Kunal, the always discontented social scientist, Sayeed, who I only meet in conferences. Then there are others. Like Prashant, the midnight political analyst who I also have to thank for helping me with editing and also for his valuable remarks. Agastha, the sleep-monger who is an old friend and a new accomplice. Monica, the trekker-philosopher who I hear likes to make poetry out of dust. She also helped me with the editing and gave her generous remarks. Amitanshu, the English-major who has a Dickensian strain of being what he is not. He too I have to thank for helping me with editing. Then there is Shatam, the cosmopolitan communist-humorist, the latter being an impossible combination these days. He too I have to thank for helping me with editing. One should not forget old friends. So there is Anirban, the now anarchist, erstwhile communist (or is it the other way round?) archivist who is singularly responsible for coining the term "revolutionary-academic vacation". I have to thank him for singing *The International* in his sleep and also helping me with the editing. And who can forget, Rakesh, the marathoner "food-fascist" who I suspect is a secret Terence Malik fan and who I miss the most when I feel the urge to be verbose. Oh yes he also helped with the editing. I think Debjyoti, the "Renaissance Man" as we all like to call him, needs to be thanked for the long hours he spent listening to me talking about my thesis long after I had submitted it. For those long hours of discussion I thank him as I do for helping me out with the cover design of this book.

Gauri and Anu are not exactly my friends and yet they are nothing but friends. With them I have to constantly invent categories of relationship. Gauri with her fragile and secret quest for life, love and knowledge, Anu with her tenuous contention with life, politics and art. Every day they prove me right that that life is way more than blood ties.

My brother and my parents have made my life as a student possible and they continue to do so even now. Everything begins from there.

Finally, I have to thank someone for which I have no words. To thank Vibhuti is to praise that encounter which continuously seizes me and brings me back to the reality of her presence. A reality which can perhaps be best exemplified through the metaphor of her too real smile. A smile not much unlike that of the Cheshire cat which Alice encounters in wonderland; a smile which lingers on while the cat disappears. So it is with these borrowed words from Lewis Carroll that I would like to thank her, words which best capture the sense of her place in my life.

Alice: Would you tell me, please, which way I ought to go from here?

The Cheshire Cat: That depends a good deal on where you want to get to.

Alice: I don't much care where.

The Cheshire Cat: Then it doesn't much matter which way you go.

Alice: ...So long as I get somewhere.

The Cheshire Cat: Oh, you're sure to do that, if only you walk long enough."

...the analogy between God's action and the world drama is no mere metaphor but has an ontological ground: the two dramas are not utterly unconnected; there is an inner link between them.

—Hans Urs Von Balthasar

Deeper than any other ground is the surface and the skin.

—Gilles Deleuze

Concept, Problem and Movement: A General Introduction

Section I

The English word 'survey' is but a poor translation of the French term *survol* which derives from *survoler* meaning 'to fly over' or 'to skim or rapidly run one's eyes over something'. More than anything what is lost in this translation is the sense of movement which is embedded in this visual metaphor. The French philosopher Raymond Ruyer[1] uses the term to describe the unity of the self while it is being subjected to the sensation of a visual field. While surveying a visual field from a distance, the sensation leads us to think, according to Ruyer of an 'I' which stands as an invisible centre outside the field. The whole field can then be surveyed from a point of view which is not only supplementary to the field but denotes a dimension perpendicular to it. Therefore the instantaneous survey of the different finite details which constitutes the unified visual field can take place completely *within* the visual sensation itself thereby becoming absolutely self-referential. Survey therefore becomes a kind of 'self-enjoyment' or an act of 'auto-eroticism' which gives the concept its moment of self-referentiality. But survey also gives the concept its speed because it is that conceptual point which refuses to stand still being identified only through its infinite displacement within a concept. Naturally the question would arise–what does such an infinitely displaced point traverse? What does it survey? Here we must introduce the idea of a multiplicity of a concept.

A concept never refers to a thing. Being completely self-referential a concept cannot be reduced to a discourse by itself. Therefore a concept is never simple but always complicated. Complicated in the sense that it is always a combination of components. These components are the finite singularities of the concept which can themselves become other concepts. The function of a concept is to maintain the internal consistency of its components. Each component of a concept being a concept itself, with its own components, which in turn are concepts themselves, a concept can be extended to infinity. However, what makes a concept distinct is the inseparability of its own components which though singularities themselves are brought together in their heterogeneity, to become a totality. This is the internal consistency or what Deleuze calls "endo-consistency" of the concept. However, a concept is never a complete totality but always a fragmentary one. This is because of the following reasons: a concept has a history which is never linear because it has components which are coming from other concepts or are concepts themselves. Hence from the point of view of history, a concept can belong to a number of planes of different temporalities. But a concept also has its own plane of *becoming*. Here the concept is always in the neighbourhood of other concepts all existing in the present moment. A concept can branch off towards other concepts in other regions of the same field. So a concept always builds bridges with other concepts on the same plane. This is what Deleuze calls its "exo-consistency". So, a concept has components which are heterogeneous singularities but which nevertheless can become indistinguishable from each other creating zones of indiscernability. Therefore a concept builds both connecting passages and zones of indiscernability. From this discussion we can come to the conclusion that a concept is absolute insofar as it is in a state of survey in relation to its components. The concept traverses its components moving in an infinite speed generating that side of it which is absolute in nature. And a concept is relative because it is in relation to its own components, to other concepts and to *problems* (to which they always pose solutions). As we shall see in a moment, it is through problems that an absolute and infinite concept is related to the finite field of historical discourses at any given time.

A concept is therefore an absolute instance of a self-referential creative event which is nevertheless relative and fragmentary at the same time. It is this paradoxical moment of the concept which is both absolute and relative, that perhaps explains the inconsistency of the title of this work: *A Survey of the Concept of Theatre in the Christian Middle Ages*. One can easily ask the following question: Being universal and absolute by definition, how can a concept be relativized to understand a particular sequence of history (even though it is such a long period as that of the Christian Middle Ages)? No matter how much we talk of the long *duree*, Christianity still remains from a historical perspective, a finite discursive phenomenon. Though the consequences of Christianity still pervade the modern world almost giving it a quasi-universal status, it is not our intention to analyse the universal implications of Christianity. Therefore from the perspective of a finite historical sequence–the question of a concept of theatre does pose an inconsistency which instead of being resolved should be taken as the constitutive paradoxical moment of the concept. Now the concept of theatre had a history before Christianity. At the same time, it also has its moment of becoming within Christianity. We shall come to this point later.

Let us at the beginning propose our first hypothesis: The concept of theatre in the Christian Middle Ages has at least three components which are that of pedagogy, perversion and the comic. According to our preceding discussion, we can then say that these three components are all singularities which are themselves concepts or components of other concepts. Pedagogy can be seen as part of a concept of Christian doctrine; while perversion can be analysed as part of a concept of Christian practices. Comedy itself can be a concept with such components as that of actor, acting and reality. One can have as many variations as one's imagination can invent. Nevertheless, these elements coexist as components of a single concept which is that of theatre where they are maintained as inseparable *variations* under the force of the following logic: Theatre can exist as a pedagogic tool being abstracted as a metaphor so long as it is identified as a perversion in its concrete reality. But this abstraction of the metaphor of theatre coincides with the negation of the sensation of theatre as perversion. Hence, theatre can become a pedagogic tool by becoming a *metaphor of perversion*. Now insofar as the pedagogic moment coincides with the speculative moment of abstraction and the moment of perversion coincides with the negation of the materialist moment of sensation, one can offer a dialectical understanding of the concept of theatre. Such an understanding of the concept of theatre would be that it is a negation of the material moment of perversion in order to be sublated into the speculative reality of abstraction. But it is the third element of the comic which challenges such a dialectical approach. Comic is the moment where the pedagogic/speculative moment becomes indiscernible from the perverse/materialist moment working together concretely at the level of material reality.

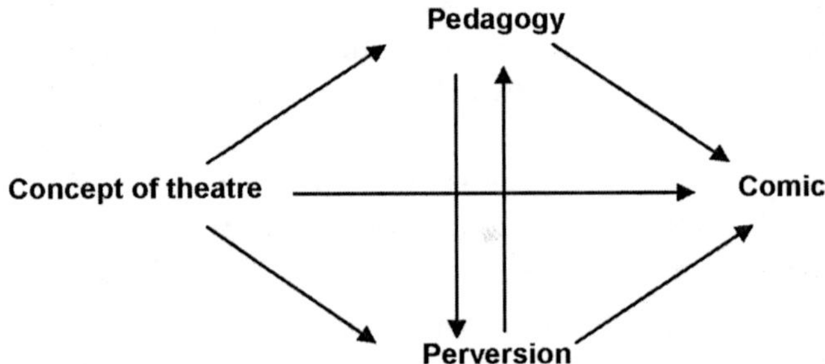

Comic is the diagonal that cuts through pedagogy and perversion making them coexist as a disjunctive synthesis without any moment of sublation. Comic therefore becomes the component which is not only indistinguishable from both pedagogy and perversion but itself starts defining the state of the concept of theatre. Having its essence in movement, the comic becomes that differential point which traverses the components of the concept of theatre including itself at infinite speed. However, comic also exists as a separate concept with its own variability. Hence it can be used to create a metaphysics of infinitude affirming a concept of dualism for the church fathers. But the comic could also be presented as a physics of infinity making the universal realize itself concretely in a material singularity.

The concept of theatre not only displays zones of indistinguishability between its singular components, but also builds bridges with other concepts. The idea of perversion which is an integral part of the concept of theatre becomes, for someone like John Chrysostom, indistinguishable from vainglory which in turn becomes inseparable from deception. Now, the idea of vainglory is an integral part of the concept of wealth in early Christianity and therefore any understanding of economy has to take into account the idea of false glory of man as against the true glory of god. Again the idea of deception is synonymous with the idea of female sexuality in Christian discourses of this period and the concept of female sexuality shares the common condemnation of being deceptive like the actors. Therefore we see that at least three concepts (and surely many more) are always in the neighbourhood of each other within Christianity: concept of theatre, concept of economy and concept of sexuality.

The concept of theatre being absolute and self-referential cannot be reduced to a discourse. The concept of theatre can only be understood through a perpetual digression where it always lands in some other concept. However theatre also belonged to the discourse of Christianity in so far as the concept was forced to become something like a proposition. Here perhaps lies the complex relation of the absolute and self-referential concept to the relative and finite sequence of history through something like problematizations. We have already implied that concepts are pure acts of creations, absolute and completely immanent to themselves which are nevertheless always produced in response to problems which in turn are relative to history. It is from the perspective of a history of problems that we try to understand the concept of theatre. In so far as the analysis of problems is outside the domain of analysis that tries to understand a set of representations beneath a behaviour, we are outside the purview of a history of ideas. Neither are we trying to understand theatrical attitudes which would explain certain theatrical mentalities during the Christian Middle Ages. What we would like to do is take a step backwards and try to analyse how theatre came to be an object of thinking before it became entangled (it does not matter whether positively or negatively) in Christian behaviour and conduct. Before searching for the theatricality of Christian rituals or the ritual presentation of theatre (depending on the point of view) we would like to analyse how theatre entered the Christian mind as an object of thought whose meaning had to be questioned, its conditions defined and its goals determined. Like any history of problems[2] our attempt is firstly to locate the moment when theatre becomes unfamiliar or disturbing enough to enter the realm of thought which would determine its practice within Christianity. We would try to argue that the particular historical juncture at which theatre offered a certain difficulty which made it unfamiliar or alien to Christianity happened quite early at the beginning of the Christian era when the emergence of Christianity was part of a significant social, political and cultural transformation. As a result of such concrete and finite historical provocations, theatre entered the Christian mind as a problem which generated at least two sets of responses. Firstly actual theatrical practices were severely denounced as perversion particularly because of its deceptive qualities and finally were legally prohibited. Secondly, theatre came to be used as a metaphor in sermons, homilies and other forms of Christian pedagogic literature and treatises. What our thesis sets out to examine is what makes them simultaneously possible. The problem of theatre is the point in which their simultaneity is rooted so to speak. To study the problem of theatre is to examine this point as a point of detachment of theatre from both the concrete historical realities that causes it to emerge as a problem and the equally concrete solutions provided for the difficulty it causes. In other words to analyse the problem of theatre in the Christian Middle Ages is to examine the general condition of thinking under which these practical solutions could be made possible.

We see therefore that the complicated question of the concept with its multiple components and infinite movement which makes it absolutely immanent to thinking itself—self-sufficient and total—nevertheless is relative to the problem which makes it possible for the concept to be connected to history. One can say that the concept always occupies the place between a historical difficulty and its practical solution being detached from both. On the one hand being a self-sufficient concept in itself it is nonetheless paradoxically but inevitably related to its own history both before and after the Christian moment. On the other hand, the concept of theatre moves in and out of other concepts in its own contemporaneity. The connections it creates to other concepts like the concept of economy or the concept of nature and the world is forced to belong to the single discourse of Christianity. Christianity as a discourse had to become a proposition attached to a reality which it had to maintain through concrete practices which in turn were forced to become homogeneous. At the level of the concept the figurative use of the theatrical idea was indistinguishable from the figurative imagination of the world as an illusion. But within Christian discourse such a metaphorical use of theatre was made a pedagogic tool to disseminate the Christian doctrine of *Civitas Dei* and its sovereign relation to our *civitas terrena*.

The comic can be seen as a possible threshold to this concept of theatre in the Christian Middle Ages. We have tried to argue that the comic is the concrete realization of the universal from the point of view[3] of an original difference. In opposing and subverting all figures of universal essence and substance, be it god man or nature, comedy affirms the concretely subjective. However, we examine how the subjective and contingent moment of comedy can be used in two ways. Firstly, it can function to re-affirm the universal by juxtaposing the finite subject against a universal infinite substance. Secondly, a more radical reading of the comic emerges when the subjective and the contingent itself becomes universal by revealing the emptiness of all essences and the vacuity of all substance. The work of the negative in comedy is the very threshold of the concept of theatre because in it the working universal is not only the transcendental moment of the concept of theatre but it is the substance of theatre which is revealed as completely void and contingent on the acting subject. Therefore the comic becomes the negative[4] power in and through which God does not merely vanish but becomes the acting flesh. It is this comic interpretation of the incarnation which places it at the threshold of the concept of theatre in the Christian Middle Ages.

Finally we would like to emphasize, even at this initial stage, that our 'survey' does not produce any subject of theatre which can represent or imitate the universal. Rather it tries to examine multiple instances of individuations–which are theatrical par excellence and which affirms the universal by putting it into concrete and free practice thereby 'incarnating' the theatrical substance in the assemblage of theatrical elements. It is not a concept of theatricality as an essence "which pre-exists its manifestation in the theatrical object, with the object then becoming the condition of its emergence" (Feral 2002, 95). According to Josette Féral, (though she rejects any privileged notion of the subject or thing which becomes vehicles of theatricality in theatre), theatricality in the final analysis resides with the spectator–the Subject of theatricality–who has the perceptual capacity to split "quotidian space" into an "other" space of fiction and thereby produce the effect of theatricality. The subject of theatre is a split subject who can assume the dual position of an actual "here" and an imaginative "elsewhere". But the condition or the power to cleave quotidian reality into a fictional space, a space where the other has a place, belongs to the transcendental nature of theatricality. Feral observes: "In Kantian terminology, we are confronted with the possibility of attributing a transcendent nature to theatricality, and thus defining stage-related theatricality as only one expression of a transcendent phenomenon" (Ibid., n.d., 98). A universal theatrical substance (pre-aesthetic theatricality) is therefore assumed to pre-exist the specific representations of theatricality which might be within or without the stage. All such theatrical statements are based on the subjective faculty of splitting quotidian reality into the "imaginary" space of the fictive other. An "other" space which the subject constantly doubts–Feral agrees with Schechner that the spectator is never truly duped during a performance–and can always recuperate because she herself is the distributor of signs. Therefore such a theatrical framework does not allow an event to be irreversible (like bodily violence or persecution on stage) if it has to be theatrical. As we shall see the intersection of medieval rhetoric with its dependency on torture and a medieval theatre of cruelty transgresses exactly this "law of reversibility" in order to produce a different concept of theatricality which is savagely finite.

It is our responsibility to seek from the history of Christianity a number of affirmations to the following hypothesis: when the problem of theatre comes up within Christianity in the Middle Ages or better during the Middle Ages when Christianity speaks of (and on) theatre it is already "a matter of theatre itself."[5] However, we continue to hold on to the position that the concept of theatre in the Christian Middle Ages, while being thoroughly theatrical at times, cannot be argued to be genuine theatre-ideas because it is the prerogative of philosophy to create concepts. This paradox of both belonging and not belonging to theatre is the subject of our examination. In a sense what we are saying is that though there is an element of theatricality in these texts that are texts of philosophy which in finding a certain alliance with theatre, and having theatre as its object introduces(or intervenes?) something akin to theatre. Ironically by the same token they are also at times texts of violence against theatre which are caught in a complex relation of power with the reality of theatre. There are occasions when these texts try to foreclose the possibility of theatre by setting up something like a philosophical theatre or a theological theatre (to be more historically precise). While at other times they help in setting up a mode of thinking–thinking as metaphor–which is equivalent to theatre and yet not being theatre in the actual sense, they invent a new mode of philosophizing.

Section II

From the above discussion we quickly derive the following three points which explains the task of our work.

1. A concept is always a multiplicity having components which can either be concepts in themselves or be part of other

concepts. To the extent that a concept is absolute it surveys its components making them completely indiscernible within the concept but also giving the concept its absolute status. But a concept is also relative not only because it has components which are fragments from other concepts but also because a concept is always created in relation to a problem.

2. A problem is that link which connects the concept to history by providing concrete historical difficulties to which the concept has to respond. The problem provides the general condition of thinking which eventually produces a number of discursive propositions as solutions to the problem. A concept does not provide any solution to historical difficulties but only responds to the problem.
3. Theatre emerges as a problem when it is detached from its practice and offered to thought as an object of thinking. But being detached it occupies a curious and paradoxical position of being both related and unrelated to actual theatrical practices.
4. Finally, in order to understand the concept of theatre as a problem, we would invoke the problem of the comic, particularly a materialist understanding of the comic to examine the question of a theatrical substance.

On the basis of this schema we have divided the work into three parts.

(a) In the first part we are going to take a step back historically to consider the nature of the problem of theatre in the Greco-Roman period. This is crucial for an understanding of the problem of theatre in the Middle Ages because it provides a trajectory of the development of a body of thinking which would eventually create the historical difficulties to which Christianity would seek practical solutions. Focusing on certain texts of Plato we would try to argue in the first chapter that problem of correct and incorrect imitation which gave birth to the concept of Idea in Plato also became a governing principle not to eradicate theatre but use it according to definite ethical imperatives founded on this constitutive principle of knowledge. At the same time such judgment regulating theatrical practices was challenged by an idea of cruelty in the tragic plays particularly in the Oresteia trilogy of Aeschylus which displayed an unworking of all judgments based on any universal model. In this idea of tragic cruelty we see a creative moment of violence which produces intensive forms of life. In the second chapter we see a clearer articulation of the problem of theatre in Roman society which would eventually be taken up by Christianity. The important place of theatre as part of Roman liturgical practices particularly that of euergetism only increased the contradictory treatment of actors who were branded as marginal figures, socially and juridically ostracized. This chapter tries to understand the logic behind this seeming contradiction by examining the hierarchical construction of Roman society from the point of view of ethical practices. The ambiguous status of the philosopher-citizen, who had to maintain a public life and yet dissociate himself from such distractions as theatre and other public spectacles, gives us an opportunity to examine the problem of theatre from a new perspective of what can be called a differential logic of subjectivation. We conclude the chapter with an introduction to the Christian interpretation of this social and juridical inconsistency regarding theatre through focusing on some of the writings of John Chrysostom. According to early church fathers like Chrysostom, such ambiguity is nothing other than symptomatic of deception. Theatre thus became the metaphor for deception, standing for the whole of Roman society. Hence theatre was not only denounced but it became a metaphor for the deceptive and illusive nature of life itself.

(b) Part two examines the extraction of theatre from its material practices and becoming an object of thought. The possibility produced by the problem of theatre awakens a whole series of movements from which the concept of theatre in the Christian Middle Ages takes its shape. The third chapter is devoted to an understanding of this movement of the concept which finds its way into certain theological ideas as that of glory and *oikonomia*. While the metaphor of theatre and spectacle take a number of shapes whose trajectory we try to establish, it is the use of the metaphor to understand the nature of divine and earthly glory as part of Christian *doxa* that we eventually concentrate on. On the other hand an examination of the problem of *oikonomia* in early Christian writings would offer us an opportunity to see how intricately it is linked with a doxological interpretation of Christianity. This in turn would give us a hint of the internal circulation and zones of indistinguishability that the concept of theatre creates within the discourse of Christianity. Our fundamental aim in this chapter would be to relate the disappearance and consequent reappearance of the theatrical metaphor to the paradoxical ontological split between transcendence and immanence undertaken by Christian theology in order to create two orders of reality. A transcendental reality of divine order which was completely self-referential and closed and yet functioned as the condition of possibility for an earthly economic order which was to be managed and governed. The fourth chapter narrows the focus of our examination to concentrate on the writings of St. Augustine for at least two reasons. Firstly Augustine provides the medieval world with some of the most developed and philosophically sophisticated arguments against theatre which are unevenly distributed in his works. But along with his polemics against theatre which moves from the domain of culture to that of semiotics and ontology, Augustine also uses theatre as a 'political' metaphor to analyse the question of Christian congregation thereby introducing it to a new meaning. Secondly, we attempt to develop a concept of *theatricality* from Augustine's' own theological writings particularly his early dialogues in order to come to, what we believe to be the heart of Augustinian philosophy: the problem of confession. Here we would wager the hypothesis that the problem of confession is essentially akin to the problem of theatre as an event. It is through expressing such an aleatory dimension of theatre where a finite theatrical element encounters the infinite theatrical substance that confession articulates the problem of theatricality within Christianity most prominently.

(c) Part three analyses the set of practices which developed in the way of practical response to the problem of theatre in the Christian Middle Ages. Starting with the controversies around the theatricality of Eucharist liturgy we move into the figurative and didactic use of the miracle plays which nevertheless frequently used a prevalent medieval rhetoric of torture to produce truth effects. We try to argue here that the fundamental reason for all these controversies and ambiguities could be traced back to the inability to reconcile the paradox of creating two separate orders of reality–namely the divine transcendental order and the mortal immanent order–while simultaneously arguing that one is the natural extension of the other. It is only in the force of the comic where instead of such a metaphysical (transcendental) basis of finitude (immanent) we come across an alternative physical and materialist force of thinking. Such a comic essence as we try to demonstrate never tires of putting the universal (and transcendental) right at the heart of all its activities which are otherwise finite and contingent. It is through such an idea of the comic as "universal at work" that we finally come across a radical departure from the effort to flatten out the problem of theatre by giving the very problem a creative counter-actualization.

Throughout this work we try to maintain that the concept of theatre always produces the sense of a disjunctive synthesis where contradictory moments remain inseparable but distinct within the concept. Such an understanding of a disjunctive synthesis can be thought best as a 'cut' which penetrates our given reality, penetrating and cleaving it into two. But the condition of possibility for such a cut does not lie somewhere else, in some other order but is produced from within that same reality. However the effect of such an intervention is always to produce something new and unknown. The immediacy of the effects of this 'new' and the infinite distance of the 'cut' are always held in a disjunctive synthesis, unable to be resolved, reconciled or even naturalized. It is clear that such an idea of theatricality runs contrary to any understanding of efficacy which is seen as the 'natural' attribute of all performativity in spite of all their internal cultural differences.

Today we are witnessing an anti-philosophical prejudice which can only be perhaps matched by the anti-theatrical prejudice to which history is a witness. But there is a curious and apparent contradiction between the two in the present. Today it is as 'natural' to say "Please do not philosophize such a simple point" as it is natural to remark "please be more forceful and performative in your presentation". We believe that it is only an apparent contradiction between the acceptance of theatre and performance and the suspicion of philosophy. We should not forget that our time is also witness to a proliferation of what can be called applied philosophy particularly that of ethics which traverses business and corporate sectors to media houses. While, on the other hand, honesty and truth are championed as if they are organical components of some people while others remain deceptive, dangerous, obsessive–all theatrical categories–and therefore to be marginalized and excluded. It is in this bio-politics of truth, that the theatrical with its phantasmagoric force to imagine other worlds finds its contemporary utterance. Therefore behind all these 'natural' utterances remain hidden a relation which has a complicated and long genealogy: a relation between philosophy and theatre. It would be our modest attempt to explore some of it.

NOTES

1. Raymond Ruyer, one of the key post war philosophers of France, uses the idea of survey to deconstruct the idea of a totalizing consciousness which he believes has been inadequately done

within philosophy. He takes the example of visual impressions to argue that we continue to believe in the 'totality' of the visual field which is in front of us and that we look at from a supplementary dimension. Ruyer argues this to be an error because sensations are brain achievements which cannot be synthesized by a brain behind a brain or an eye behind an eye. Ruyer argues that survey or absolute overview is the key to a subjectivity and consciousness which does not allow re-presentation of a single world but multiple worlds . This is part of what he calls *reversed epiphenomenalism* in his book *Neo-finalism*. (Ruyer 2016)

2. Michel Foucault in his later life spoke of such a history of problems as the analysis of freedom of thinking where thought detaches itself from behaviour to ponder on itself. Rather than providing a theory of what is thinking, Foucault wanted to analyse the concrete practice of such free acts of thinking from within history. The methodological approach of this entire thesis is unabashedly inspired by such a mode of thinking. See essay *Problematics*. (Foucault 1989, 416-422)
3. A point of view, according to Deleuze is always a closed totality which contains the universal immanently within itself being open to nothing but other points of view. The universal therefore works concretely within the point of view as an original difference. (Deleuze 2007)
4. In *Difference and Repetition*, Deleuze invites us to understand negativity or more particularly the idea of nothingness in Heidegger not in the sense of dialectical contradiction but as the affirmation of an original difference which is Being itself. (Deleuze, *Difference and Repetition* 2005)
5. Phillip Lacoue-Labarthe says this about Holderlin. He argues in an essay titled 'Holderlin's Theatre' that when Holderlin writes of (and on) theatre, it is already "a matter of theatre itself." (Lacoue-Labarthe 2000)

Part 1

Prelude to a Problem

CHAPTER 1

"The Bitch that Growls and Snarls at Her Master"[1]: Study of a Theatrical Relation in Ancient Greece

Introduction

Theatrical Crumbs: A Note on Methodology

In his *Life of Solon,* Plutarch tells us of the encounter that Solon had in his later life with the first actor in recorded history, Thespis. Plutarch writes:

> At this time Thespis was beginning to introduce the drama, and the novelty of his exhibition attracted people, although the regular contests were not yet introduced. Solon who was fond of seeing sights and gaining knowledge, and whose old age was spent in leisure and amusements and good fellowship, went to see Thespis, who acted in his own play, as the ancient custom was. After the play was over, he asked him if he was not ashamed to tell so many lies before so many people. When Thespis answered that there was no harm in saying and doing these things in jest, Solon violently struck the ground with his stick, saying "If we praise and approve of such jests as these, we shall soon find people jesting with our business." (Plutarch 1894/2004, 108)

Though the historical validity of Plutarch's narrative remains debatable and whether such an episode actually transpired or even if Thespis was a historical figure is contestable, the fact remains that a certain relation between theatre and polis is articulated in the Plutarch text. It would not be completely incorrect to say that it was an effort to demonstrate theatre as a political problem. The non-seriousness or the play element (*paidia*) of theatre which comes under scrutiny in this text, however has a more complex history in the ancient Greek discourse than being merely chastised for its inautheticity. Plato, for example, offers a more complex and ambivalent treatment of theatre/play which he acknowledges as only a type of *mimesis*. It has been often argued that Plato condemned the poets–a general term used for all those who were engaged with the mimetic art of producing plays–who according to him were involved in fabricating degraded translations of the Idea. Be that as it may–and we shall return to this question of Platonic condemnation in a while–it can be argued that Plato praises play when it is supervised and governed within the boundaries of ethics. Even more interesting is his use of the metaphor of play in the famous passage from *Laws* which evokes a close relation between *paidia* (play) and paideia (pedagogy/education):

> And I say that about serious matters a man should be serious, and about a matter which is not serious he should not be serious; and that God is the natural and the worthy object of our most serious and blessed endeavours, for man, as I said before, is made to be the plaything of God, and this truly considered is the best of him; wherefore also every man and woman should also walk seriously, and pass life in the noblest pastimes, and be of another mind from what they are at present... At present they think that their serious pursuits should before the sake of their sports, for they deem war a serious pursuit, which must be managed well for the sake of peace; but the truth is that there neither is nor has been, nor ever will be, either amusement or instruction in any degree worth speaking of in war, which is nevertheless deemed by us to be the most serious of our pursuits. And therefore, as we say, everyone of us should live the life of peace as long and as well as he can. And what is the right way of living? Are we to live in sports always? If so, in what kind of sports? We ought to live sacrificing, and singing, and dancing,

> and then a man will be able to propitiate the Gods, and to defend himself against his enemies and conquer them in battle. The type of song or dance by which he will propitiate them has been described, and the paths along which he is to proceed have been cut for him. He will go forward in the spirit of the poet (Plato, *Laws* 2006, 152)

Here we find all the possible complexities of a platonic treatment of theatre. We have an ironic inversion of human reality caught in the dialectic of serious/non-serious (*spoude/paidia*). By the same token we have one of the earliest uses of the idea of 'life as play' which would eventually develop into the medieval idea of *theatrum mundi*. But we have more. We also have, what Derrida calls "a dialectical confiscation" (Derrida 2016, 151) of play as it emerges into language, being metaphorized for a general purpose. When life itself starts coinciding with play such theological appropriation of play also becomes the condition of possibility of governing play (theatre). It comes to be seen as an activity to be supervised and controlled under a pedagogic order (*paideia*) determined to produce ethical subjects. Here we diagnose a relation between theatre and philosophy which is not merely a phenomenological problem (what is real and what is only appearance) but also becomes an ethical one. However the metaphorization of theatre or play can only take place through an ironic movement whose foundational logic remains *mythical*. Therefore in *Laws*, the foundational myth of Minos[2] serves to produce the condition where a city can be imagined–'logically'–to have the ideal laws. The emergence of play in language which erases the autonomous reality of play is an effect of the supreme platonic irony. But such irony–as we shall–comes as the voice of negation which takes us to the threshold of the Idea which can only be accessed *positively* through a foundational myth.

This ironic "play of taking play seriously" (Ibid., n.d., 151) becomes even more pronounced when further on Plato talks of the rivalry which exists between the tragic poets and the legislators who are also "poets" of a more serious and noble tragedy–which is that of truth,

> We also according to our ability are tragic poets and our tragedy is the best and noblest; for our whole state is an imitation of the best and noblest life, which we affirm to be indeed the very truth of tragedy. You are poets and we are poets both makers of the same strains. Rivals and antagonists in the noblest of dramas, which true law can alone perfect, as our hope is (ibid., n.d., 165)

In the final analysis the coming into being of play under the supervision of an ethico-political life is always already complicated by the ultimate stakes of "true law". Plato envisages the Dionysian horizon of constituting such truth when he talks of symposia which would serve as guardians of such law. True law is as much an invention as it is conditioned by the refusal of traditional values. Man who is born into madness can practise *parrhesia* (truth speaking) as much under the Dionysian effects of wine as when he joyfully participates in the affects of pleasure induced by singing and dancing. Laws which have to be invented rather than conserved have to wear the *mask* of tradition to be enforced but in itself such invention is possible only through the refusal of tradition. The ironic refusal of theatre and play through its metaphorization is always already theatrical, always already in the realm of the divine theatrical figure. This is the complexity that Plato brings to the problem of theatre in ancient Greece. And it is to the study of this problem that this chapter is primarily devoted.

The chapter is divided into two sections. In the first section we try to investigate the general problem of theatre in relation to ethics in the Greco-Roman period. Here, firstly the problem of theatre is analysed as a formal ontological problem in order to indicate its relation to the concept of ethics predominant in this time. Secondly, the question of ethics is elaborated from two points of views. A historico-ontological[3] understanding of ethics on the one hand, while on the other we concern ourselves with a more formal and universal understanding of ethics. The aim of this section is to find moments of conjunction between these two distinct methodological processes in order to inquire about the nature of their relation to theatre. Thirdly, we attempt to show another ethical moment emerging out of the margins of both these tendencies, which corresponds to irony and its relation to theatre. In order to illustrate this relation of theatre to irony we concentrate on the particular Greek case of Socrates, studying some of Plato's works where he talks about theatrical processes like Book III and X of *The Republic*, *Ion* and *Symposium* among a few others. This section thus offers a philosophical point of view of Socrates and his relation to theatre. We argue how in Plato's writings Socrates emerges as a figure who does not entirely exclude theatre (generally designated with the broad term 'poets'), as traditionally interpreted, but rather theatre under Socrates comes under the surveillance of the *Ideal* state ruled by the philosopher king. In other words, theatre cannot have a concept in and by itself but can only be reflected upon and conceptualized by the philosopher. Through an analysis of the Socratic concept of irony as an infinite negation (Kierkegaard), we show how this response towards the poets was part of a larger Socratic agenda of destroying a growing positivism within Greek culture particularly in the domain of knowledge and ethics, epitomized by the sophists. Negativity informs Socratic ethics in relation to which theatre and its function in the Greek life has to be analysed. At the same time, we show how the Socratic method of irony itself was performative in nature, expressed not only through the dialogic tradition but also having certain other performative elements.

The second section concludes our effort to understand the nature of this relation in the Greek period by

(i) A brief analysis of the liturgical elements in the theatrical activities around the 5th century BC. This includes the examination of theatre as a place of congregation of bodies and its relation to the state. A relation which is analysed from the perspective of a concept of debt and how it contributed to processes of incorporeal transformations and subjectivizations.

(ii) This concept of debt is further extended to analyse the three plays of the Oresteia trilogy–*Agamemnon, The Libation Bearers* and *Eumenides*–by Aeschylus. This section thus inverses our point of view twice, successively. First from the side of philosophy and ethics to that of theatre and drama, second from a logic externally relating theatre to ethics to an internal path of articulating the same. We conduct this investigation for a twofold purpose. Firstly, to identify certain ethical tendencies within the play which corroborate the dominant ethical conceptualization of the period. We try to show, through the problem of lamentation and sacrifice, that although occurring within the play text they correspond to the normative ethical standards of the day through producing a doctrine of judgement. Secondly, we try to illustrate how another system of justice inhabits the play in order to challenge this doctrine of judgement and the corresponding ethical order where a ceaseless revenge narrative captures finite bodies and spaces into expressing affects which are beyond the universal ethical order.

Section I

The General Problem Concerning Theatre and Philosophy

Study of a Relation

Now let us return to the relation between ethics and theatre as it unfolds in the Greco-Roman world. As we mentioned before it is evident from the Plutarch citation (at the beginning of our chapter), that what is at stake here is a consciousness which, though particular to the Greco-Roman period, points to the reality of theatre, or to be more precise, the reality of the actor as posing a problem to the business of the polis. So we can develop our argument further: So long as the concept of theatre, in its fragmentariness expresses itself through its relation to ethics, the consciousness or the disclosure of a concept of ethics considers theatre as a historical problem. Hence Solon who is conscious of the phenomenon called theatre as only an audience is nevertheless conscious of it as an ethical problem. And as a problem, such a conceptualization expresses a certain danger inherent to the experience of theatre. This chapter is a long detour to the ancient problem of theatre preciously from this perspective. We try to inquire into the origins of the processes of conceptualization of theatre in the Christian Middle Ages from the point of view of theatrical *experience.*

The inherent incompleteness of any attempt to conceptualize theatre at any period can very well be regarded as a problem. An attempt to conceptualize leading to a demand to problematize should not be confused with a chronological and evolutionary urge to trace the development of the concept. The latter involves an attempt to illustrate how the concept of theatre gradually moves from an incomplete expression to greater fulfilment and clarity from the Greco-Roman into the Christian period. It further argues how the concept finally fulfils and simultaneously exhausts itself some time in modernity with the arrival of dramatic studies or even theatre studies for that matter. Such is not our path. It is an implicit contention of this thesis that this process of conceptualization always remains incomplete not because of some world historical infancy which moves towards progressive maturity and development but because it is ontologically offered and authorized in the world historical reality as always already incomplete. Hence the imperative is to search for an *arche* or a principle which resides within the concept of theatre in all its variations but never discloses itself either as an element or even as the essence of the concept. The search for this *arche* which is the secret concealed within the variously disclosed concept of theatre is only given to us in the form of the problem.

Thus if the ethical consciousness of a period (the Greco-Roman) is also the disclosure of the fragmentary concept of theatre at that time, then it is through the problem that such a fragment is disclosed. And what the problem expresses is precisely that which needs to be concealed, forgotten and excluded. Yet in a more profound sense the problem remains the secret source of the concept. So the relation between ethics and theatre, in the Greco-Roman period is mostly articulated negatively. Theatre is something that ethics rejects as dangerous and difficult to assimilate within it as a positive element. But that does not mean that ethics disregards theatre as inconsequential. On the contrary, ethical conceptualization continuously takes theatre into consideration, studies it and tries to unravel the nature of its danger in order to either exclude it or render it inefficacious or better to re-construct and re-deploy it in such a way that it can be put to use for the very purpose of ethics. If we go back to Solon's supposed statement, we find this amply clear. The liar is determined as someone who enacts something which is shameful and ethically unacceptable. Whatever might be the intrinsic reason for this–and we shall come to the internal logic of the liar and the actor as a paradox and how it poses a danger to the polis–this much is clear that as an act it is not ethical for an individual to commit and particularly when it is committed within the business of the polis. So the ethical act which is related to the self is no longer confined within the self but becomes the condition for the self's relation to the other, to the polis[4]. If one is a liar or better, an actor, then one cannot be a ruler or participate in any matters of the polis; this seems to be the hidden injunction of the statement. This citation from the *Life of Solon* is immediately followed by an episode which is indubitably political in nature. Plutarch narrates that when Peisistratus wounded himself deliberately and sought sympathy from the citizens of Athens by claiming that he had been wounded by the enemies, Solon said, "Son of Hippocrates, you are dishonourably imitating Homer's Ulysses. You are doing this to deceive your fellow citizens, while he mutilated himself to deceive the enemy" (Plutarch 1894/2004, 108). Not only does this corroborate our earlier remark that the effects of acting are viewed to be deceptive and dishonourable endangering the management of the polis and hence condemned but the problem is also related to a question of will. The fact that actors are wilfully duplicitous and deceitful will become a major factor in the Christian discourse around acting. Here we have the distinction between wilful and unintentional deception obliquely hinted at when it is argued that Peisustratus was doing it by imitating Homer's Ulysses which is illustrative of the dangerous effects that poets can *unintentionally* generate.

The Liar's Paradox: An Ancient Political Problem

Now before we investigate the relation between theatre and ethics in the ancient world, which veritably exposes the relationship between theatre and philosophy, we need to clarify the relation between ethics as a mode of determining an individual act and the effect it produces and function it performs within the polis. But even before that we need to go back to the problem of lying as an unethical act and its danger when introduced within the business of the polis. One way of looking at it would be to identify the liar as simply an unethical subject whose lack of honour disqualifies him to be an ideal citizen subject. One might historically and culturally argue out the relevance of this point in the Greco-Roman society as something unacceptable. But when we analyse Solon's pronouncement, the problem of lying emerges as something more formal and structural which in no way diminishes its dangerous effects within polis. When Thespis defends himself by saying all *his actions were in jest or were part of a play*[5], Solon warns of the danger that such play might effectuate in the realm of the state. Why would a harmless act of lying in *jest* be taken so seriously and that too in context of the political? It is our hypothesis that lying even if it is merely a 'play' is treated as something akin to perjury here.

The ancient world was not ignorant of the intrinsic paradox of lying which was treated as a logical problem from Eubulides onwards. From Aristotle, Chryssipus up to Cicero the problem of this paradox finds its different articulation. Though there is no historical evidence that Solon or even Plutarch, for that matter, was aware of this logical paradox, it might be speculated that in our case the logical problem does find a resonance in the ethical, and more importantly, political domain. The proposition that "I am saying that I am speaking falsely" is both true and false at the same time. This in a sense corresponds to Thespis's confession that his lies are only in jest. Thespis not only lies but accepts that they are lies because they are only part of a performance or a play. Hence a play, like a lie, in being true to itself is determined by falsity. This is the ontological ambiguity of the play which can be only expressed performatively and not denotatively. What is at stake here, what Thespis the actor exposes is the internal paradox of all propositions, all meanings and definitions *including that of the polis*, which are judged to be true by being truthful about his falsity. The only way to solve this problem of the liar is to treat it as a performative utterance which constitutes the liar as a liar by uttering the same, just like the play constitutes itself by performing itself thus self-effectuating its own existence without the help of any external legitimacy. This is the performative efficacy of the actor as a liar which produces a counter efficacy within the polis where the polis itself is constituted on the basis of an oath, which is nothing but a performative utterance[6] in itself but once constituted it becomes the legitimizing principle behind all meanings and truths. Plutarch writes:

> To this Solon answered, that men keep covenants, because it is to the advantage of neither party to break them; and that he so suited his laws to his countrymen, that it was to the advantage of everyone to abide by them rather than to break them. (Ibid., n.d., 108)

The subjective emphasis of the oath comes out clearly here. The oath that men take is not only advantageous for the polis because it gives rise to a covenant which is what the polis is, but it is also an individual choice to suit one's own laws to that of the other. It is his subjective and ethical integrity that prompts him to abide by the oath, whereas it is this obedience which is the outcome of his personal choice that will constitute the polis as a covenant[7]. To that extent it is his integrity of maintaining the oath determined by his ethical rigour which constitutes the polis as a moment of pure efficacy sustained by a particular ethical turn. In other words the moment of transformation, where man becomes part of a covenant–the polis–is determined by something like an oath which in itself can only have a performative efficacy and not a denotative value. But such an incorporeal transformation is not merely a collective affair, though it is effectuated in the name of a common interest or an 'advantage of everyone'. It is also an obedience which one aspires for because it helps individual men to belong to a collective, a covenant. We shall explore this relation of an ethical choice to a political belonging from the point of view of incorporeal transformation again later on. Suffice it to say here that in such a state of affairs, the actor/liar not only implicates but challenges the performative efficacy of the polis as covenant by introducing a series of incorporeal transformation and counter efficacious moments. These moments of transformations and efficacies can become counter-productive to the function of the polis when not aligned to serve the common interest of the polis. Hence from an ethical perspective, theatre has to be either excluded or managed to serve not merely ethical requirements but also political. In *Laws*, when Plato criticizes a certain "theatrocracy" as an evil which threatens justice and law, theatre in the final analysis, is posed as a *problem* which expresses a "contempt of oaths and pledges, and no regard at all for the gods" (Barish 1981, 27) Rather than considering such "contempt" as a prejudice against the very 'nature' of theatre whose "anarchic" content threatens to upset the principle or *arche* of order which constitutes the republic, we need to perhaps analyse the question of theatre from the point of view of a relation of efficacy and power.

The Prejudice of Anti-Theatrical Prejudice

If we consider the oath as an affirmation of a certain political content in Plato, which is contradictory to the affirmation of a "theatrocracy" all we do is pose a counter theory where theatre serves to convey politically the idea of resistance to such a principle of order. This seems to be the entire project of such a theatre historian like Jonas Barish, in his book *Anti-Theatrical Prejudice* (1981). In spite of the importance and the brilliant scope of this study of the history of theatre, it nevertheless methodologically offers a certain "theory" of theatre trying to liberate its "anarchic" content from the ideological and idiosyncratic repression that such a concept, he believes, has gone through. Again one should not undermine the value of this study which in a rare moment of theatre scholarship unabashedly examines the relation between theatre and philosophy. Yet such an inquiry seems to propel towards unravelling the source of what he calls an anti-theatrical prejudice. The entire project is to analyse the different forms of this fundamental content that philosophy seems to have imposed on theatre. Thus it is Plato, who is identified as the chief architect of this "ontological malaise", this metaphysical degradation which puts theatre in a lower status or even permanently tries to exclude it from the domain of thinking. Barish in the introduction notes: "The fact that the disapproval of the theatre is capable of persisting through so many transformations of culture, so many dislocations of time and place, suggests a permanent kernel of distrust, waiting to be activated by the more superficial irritants" (Ibid., n.d., 4). It is Plato, who seems to have repressed the 'true' kernel of theatre, its theatricality by arbitrarily imposing upon it a 'distrust' which Barish analyses as a 'prejudice'. It is Barish's project to unravel the arbitrariness and self-contradictory nature of this distrust in order to pose it as nothing but a prejudice. The value ascribed by Plato to theatre as anarchic, according to Barish is nothing but the original articulation of this prejudice which finds its way into Western consciousness in various forms. Given that Plato's own work has a certain "theatricality" both in terms of their expression and substance–for instance, not only does he recognize the dramatic nature of the platonic dialogues but identifies the profound influence of the poets on Plato and a certain "aestheticization of politics" (Ibid., n.d., 14) in his imagination of *The Republic*. Barish explores this contradiction in order to argue that it points to nothing but an inherent prejudice towards theatre. This prejudice in Plato, he argues, is conditioned by a certain authoritarianism which is obsessed with an acutely limited idea of both art and politics. The entire thrust of his criticism against Plato leads to this idea of an authoritarian principle of order which, to use his term, is "monolithic" in nature. The main arguments are as follows:

1. The metaphysical degradation of theatre as a second order of imitation is inadequate when theatre is considered temporally that is in terms of action. Unlike paintings or sculptures which are determined only spatially, theatre is determined temporally and hence has a certain 'reality' of its own.
2. The criticism of theatre eliciting passion and desire in the audience by Plato is to be seen as a result of his arbitrary division of the psyche into rational and irrational faculties.

According to Barish, this dualism introduced by Plato is evocative of the censorship which Plato wants to impose where the lower faculty, to which the passion belongs (except for the passion of *thumos*, or courage), has to be governed by rationality. Theatre in affecting the sensate reality of this lower faculty cannot be trusted and has to be censored. According to Barish, while Plato accuses theatre of producing passions and emotions which divides the soul, he himself comes up with a theory of dualism of the psyche. Such arbitrariness contributes to the prejudice which in the final analysis is politically motivated and authoritarian.

3. Such surveillance translates itself into the collective domain of the political where the poets have to come under the purview of the philosopher-guardian who will not only censor the poets but govern them according to rational judgement of what could and could not be imitated. Theatre in imitating all aspects of life threatens to introduce anarchy into the republic, whereas the philosopher being the guardian of order governs the use of imitation justly.
4. Such justice, according to Plato, Barish argues is nothing but the monolithic idea of a form of life expressive of a single vocation. What theatre introduces is a possibility of multiple vocations and transformations which Plato himself unjustly excludes from his republic. The prejudice against theatre is conditioned by this authoritarianism which sees freedom of the individual as a curse of licentious diversity and hence disruptive. "Justice in sum means knowing one's place, acquiescing, in one's "natural limitations" performing one's allotted duties as prescribed by the authorities" (Ibid., n.d., 24).

Such an analysis gives a coherent and insightful idea as to what extent theatre occupies a central role in Platonic thinking. However, certain problems arise. It seems that the content of theatre which Plato identifies and negates becomes the very condition for understanding what Barish recognizes as his final purpose–to identify the "nature of the theatrical, and hence, inevitably of the human" (Ibid., n.d., 4). It is this "natural content" of theatre which is repressed and denied its place in thinking which needs to be liberated. Plato becomes the moment of the foundation of this repression (the first chapter is titled "Platonic Foundation") which is done in the name of an arbitrary and inconsistent logic or better a prejudice. Thus anti-theatrical articulations are seen to be derived from a fundamental and universal lack or prejudice. But what seems to constitute such lack is the desire for a 'natural freedom' assigned to the concept of theatre which it has been denied as a consequence of certain historical and political processes. For Barish, the prejudice in case of Plato definitely has a political condition, a mode of authoritarian thinking which alienates theatre from its radical and 'anarchic' nature of thinking diversity and individual freedom of expression. At the same time, according to Barish, and perhaps not without a slight irony, the best condition for the expression of such anarchic thinking of diversity seems to be a democratic spirit and a 'cult' of the individual. Against such 'freedom of the individual' Plato's republic firmly stands with an "anti-poetic austerity" (Ibid., n.d., 14). But what Plato betrays through his contradictions and arbitrary reasoning is the prejudiced nature of such an authoritarian political condition.

Methodologically this creates a confusion of categories where a certain universal theory of theatre, having such attributes as artistic freedom, diversity, transformative capacity, even an anarchic and disruptive quality, in a word "theatricality", is nonetheless negatively defined as a prejudice whose historical foundation, albeit as a lack, is laid by Plato. At the same time it is Barish's project, and here he seems to have set the tone for much of theatre scholarship in this area of theatre history, to reconcile theatre to itself, to the place it rightly deserves in the history of Western consciousness. Barish writes: "And Plato's hostility towards it (theatre) is destined to become the cornerstone of an anti-theatrical edifice, that is only now, after two and a half millennia, finally crumbling" (Ibid., n.d., 28) . The repression which the concept of theatre has gone through, whose founding father seems to be Plato, in the form of a prejudice is now to be exposed and overcome. It is in this overcoming that

Barish finds a logic for a 'true' idea of theatre, its natural theatricality, with all the attributes which hitherto engendered prejudice but will now contribute to a theory of theatre based on theatricality. Such a theory of theatricality will re-discover theatre's true nature and regain contact with its origin, this seems to be Barish's implicit claim. But this in a sense is nothing but ascribing a virtue to theatre where previously there was a prejudice. Interestingly, in the preface, Barish wants to distance himself not only from the detractors but also from the enthusiasts who see nothing but narrow-mindedness and fanaticism in such anti-theatrical prejudice.

The repressive hypothesis which is implicit in such theorization points to a continued thematic concern with *theatricality* which, according to Barish, was at the centre of such anti-theatrical expressions in the Greco-Roman world and which continued itself into Christianity. Instead of narrating the history of such a concept of theatricality as that which progressively moved from a certain prejudice to overcoming the same, gradually exposing itself as virtue (according to Barish this is still an ongoing process which has just begun)–rather than adopting such a theoretical project perhaps we need to evaluate the very *problem of theatricality.* To critically examine this concern for theatricality, its development from the Greco-Roman to the Christian period, one needs to perhaps see how this "theatricality" determined the concerned subjects' relation to themselves. Did reflection on theatricality allow them to discover the truth about themselves? What meaning did they attribute to the experience of such theatricality in relation to their own selves? In other words, how did an individual recognize himself as a subject of theatricality? It is evident that to ask this question is to examine not an "anti-theatrical prejudice" but the problem of theatre as moral problematization. This problematization can perhaps only be studied in terms of the relation between theatre and ethics, in the Greco-Roman period, where the subject of such "anti-theatrical" prejudice has to be asked the simple question: What is it that she recognized in the experience of theatre contrary to her ethical experience and what constituted such an ethical experience in this time? At the same time we cannot disregard the political aspect of this problem which we discussed in the context of oath and how theatre produced a danger of counter-effectuation which threatened the guarantee and assurance of the truthfulness and actualization of the political oath. The distrust for theatre has to be seen in relation to both these problems. The political problem of the oath which men take recourse to in order to maintain the stability and guarantee of the polis through a certain logic of efficacy. The ethical problem of self-mastery where the subject comes to recognize himself as a responsible citizen and the various meanings which can be ascribed to the truth of such a notion of self-mastery.

Two Modes of Ethical Subjectivization

The question of the ethical in the ancient world could be seen at least from two points of views. It can either be posed in relation to a theory of being, which not only makes it into an ontological question but at the same time a universal one. It is this Hegelian problem of the ethical which Kierkegaard so clearly identifies in his *Fear and Trembling* (1985) when he equates it to the universal such that it applies to everyone at every moment. This order of the ethical is not only the telos of everything outside but it is this telos which effectuates the dialectical overcoming of all particulars which must abrogate their immediate, sensate and psychic existences to express themselves in the universal ethical order. In the ancient world, particularly that of the Greeks, this movement takes the form of the objective dialectic of the tragic. This is our first approach to the question of ethical in this period. The ethical as the objective problem of the relation between the individual as particular and the ethical as universal necessitate a mediation. For the tragic world, such mediation is brought about through two elements: 1) The state or polis and 2) language.

We shall develop this problem of tragic mediation through language later in the chapter. Here we focus on the nature of this objective dialectic in relation to the state which becomes a condition for understanding the ethical from this point of view. As Kierkegaard notes that subjective freedom in the Greek context, in its authentic tragic expression was always guaranteed by a substance outside the subject–be it state, family or destiny. It is this fatalistic notion which the objective dialectics of the tragic effectuates in two ways. Firstly, the tragic guilt (*hamartia*) is never actively consumed by the subject through his action but always oscillates between guilt and innocence. It is this intermediary movement of the guilt, which never becomes completely subjective and reflective, but neither does the individual become completely absolved from it which gives the tragic its particular conflict and interest. This is what Kierkegaard calls aesthetic guilt. Secondly, the moment of *anagnoris* or what we call recognition corresponds to a moment of mediation, where the ethical realizes itself objectively not only through the disclosure of tragic knowledge but also through the resolution of this collision and recognition of the universal ethical order mediated through the state. The ethical as the universal order in the tragic sense thus gives rise to

1. An objective dialectic.
2. The subject though free is not completely autonomous in his action.
3. The ambiguity of his actions is the source of the tragic collision.
4. The conflict is resolved to establish the ethical as the objective order of the state or polis.

But such a universal objective idea of the ethical in the Ancient world, which we could call a tragic notion of the ethical, does not explain the experience of the ethical subject *per se*. In other words, in what way does an individual recognize himself as an ethical subject and evaluate his actions as governed by the same? The objective framework reduces the ethical to a sacrificial logic of sublation, where in the name of duty and responsibility the subject sacrifices his desires. We shall again dwell on this problem of sacrifice in a later section. But suffice it to say that such a sacrificial model of the ethical in case of the Greeks is inadequate for a number of reasons. Firstly, ethics was not merely a political pursuit but it was also a personal engagement. In case of the Greeks one can perhaps assume that the political question was *oriented ethically* rather than the other way around. Such a notion is corroborated by the fact that from a historical point of view, in Greece, of the 5th and 4th century B.C., the domain of the ethical was not juridically mediated, such that definite and universal codes of an ethical life were imposed on the subject. If the question of the ethical was brought in relation to that of the political it was not from an objective universal perspective but rather from a subjective point of view of the free citizen-subject where what was at stake in the ethical question was exactly the freedom of the subject. As far as the ethical problem of theatricality goes, it would perhaps be more effective to study this problem from this subjective perspective rather than following the objective point of view of ethics, because the latter can very easily lead to an understanding of theatre as detrimental and dangerous essentially from a political perspective. Hence the anti-theatrical prejudice at least in case of Plato, would be re-affirmed as a political prejudice. Alternately this leads to an understanding of theatricality as an aestheticization of politics in Plato. This, we would argue is far from the actual place ethics occupied in Greek life and the importance it exerted in their political activity.

In *The Concept of Irony* (1989), Kierkegaard was perhaps already aware of this subjective moment of the ethical as a relation of the self to itself. The dialectical relation of the subject-object constitutive of a speculative result is exactly what Kierkegaard critiques not only in this early work but all his life. Seen from this perspective, the ethical in case of Socrates, comes out in Kierkegaard as nothing but an "existence-relation to truth, just as negative as positive, (having) just as much humour as essentially he has pathos, and is constantly coming to be, i.e. striving" (Kierkegaard, *Concluding Unscientific Postscript to Philosophical Crumbs* 2009, 68). The contradiction–where the negative thinker in affirming his negativity, in his awareness of such negativity avoids being deceived or betrayed by the speculative illusion–becomes the ground for irony in Socrates. But such irony is at the same time the very knowledge of a self in which the infinitude and eternity of the spirit is both realized and betrayed because the self is always in life and hence in finitude. Thus the negative does not come in irony as the infinite nothingness in which the self is trans-appropriated (the sublated moment of sacrificial thinking) but rather the negativity in life has its ground in the subject's synthesis in the infinitude and eternity which being the only certainty is at the same time denied to the subject because he is in life. It is this "tremendous contradiction, that the eternal becomes, that it comes into being" (Ibid., n.d., 69) which serves as the condition for irony to become a mode of ethical existence in Socrates. We shall discuss the implications of this understanding of ethics as an ironical mode of existence in Socrates in a while. Suffice to say here that Kierkegaard in his concept of irony in Socrates does already introduce a subjective understanding of ethics and its relation to truth in ancient Greece.

Ethical Origins of Theatrical Knowledge

Nevertheless, it is Michel Foucault's seminal work on the history of sexuality which systematically brings into focus the ethical question in the ancient world from the point of view of the subject. This subjective turn in Foucault's own work also corresponds with a certain self-critique of his analysis of knowledge and power whose philosophical implication we cannot discuss here. The acutely precise and almost formulaic definition of ethics as "the self's relation to itself" which Foucault develops into a veritable concept of ethics in the course of his later works, starting from *The Use of Pleasure: The History of Sexuality*, Vol. 2 (1984/1992), testifies to a certain understating of sexuality as an experience intricately related to this 'formula'. As he writes in the introduction to this book, "It appeared that I now had to undertake a third shift, in order to analyse what is termed 'the subject'. It seemed appropriate to look for the forms and modalities of the relation to self by which the individual constitutes and recognizes himself qua subject" (Foucault, *The Use of Pleasure: The History of Sexuality*, Vol. 2 1992, 6). It is this emphasis on the subject as the nodal point of the investigation which Foucault pursues as further development to his genealogical examination of knowledge and power. We are aware of the fact that methodologically speaking, in Foucault's work three main domains of genealogy are visible

1. A historical ontology of modalities of being in relation to truth through which subjects of knowledge are constituted.
2. A historical ontology of modalities of being in relation to fields of power through which subjects of power are constituted.
3. A historical ontology of modalities of being in relation to ethics through which ethical subjects are constituted.

Though the problem of the subject remains central to Foucault's work throughout his life, it is in his investigation of 'sexuality' as a domain of experience–where the subject comes to recognize and hence constitute itself historically as a thinking being–that we finally find a convergence of all his earlier investigations into the relationship between subjectivity and truth. In case of ethics and its relation to sexuality, he suggests a general methodology of approaching the question, not from the aspect of sexual behaviour or even societies and ideologies, but from the point of view of what he calls "problematization" or a genealogy of problematizations. It is to examine a self's relation to itself in terms of the problem it confronts theoretically regarding the question of sexual experience and the concrete practices on the basis of which these problematizations are formed. Examination of such problematization lead to the recognition of an idea of morality not merely from the point of view of the moral values and sets of rules and their agencies of dispensation like family, educational institutions–in other words, 'moral codes'. It also points to the set of real behaviours of conformation or transgression vis-à-vis these codes which is termed as moral conduct or 'morality of behaviours'. But there is also a third aspect on which Foucault focuses, in his analysis of the problem of 'sexuality' which is the way one conducts oneself. The 'games of truth' one plays with oneself in order to give meaning to one's own experience of sexuality and the concrete forms of the practices that generate the necessity to give such meanings.

Four Features of a Single Relation: From Sexuality to Theatre

In Relation to Aphrodisia

Foucault identifies four aspects to this relationship to oneself. Firstly, what he calls the *ethical substance* concerns the material for moral conduct within the self; the part of oneself which needs to be 'worked over' by ethics in order to ethically constitute oneself. In case of the Greeks, Foucault recognizes this ethical substance as not merely desire or concupiscence from flesh which Christianity would take up later. Rather than questioning the forms or morphology of sexual behaviours, the Greeks, according to Foucault were more concerned with the dynamics of sexual acts themselves which included both desire and pleasure. This is what he identifies as the true meaning of the Greek term *aphrodisia*. Rather than a certain "elision" of pleasure during Christianity–where it was the meticulous decipherment of the nature of desire which was at stake as result of the injunction given in the preaching by the Christian clergy against the pursuit of sensual pleasure as a goal of sexual practice–*aphrodisia* constituted a dynamic chain of desire leading to the act, the act leading to pleasure which in turn leads to desire. As against an ontology of lack and deficiency which concupiscence would put forward, *aphrodisia*, for the Greeks, in Foucault's words "was an ontology of a force that linked together acts, pleasures, and desires" (Ibid., n.d., 43). It is crucial for our examination of the relationship between theatre and ethics in ancient Greece, to consider this idea of *aphrodisia* for many reasons. The dynamic ethical substance known as aphrodisia is analysed according to a quantitative variable where what is at stake is not the absolute eradication of this "substance" but rather a process of controlling the intensity of the practices. The ethical operation is conditioned by a division between lesser and greater. Thus the ethical consideration was oriented towards finding and determining a *perfect mean* to these practices. The ethical problem was not a question of studying and analysing desire in order to exclude or change its substance as in case of Christianity but in order to discern what is a moderate or excessive in the dynamics of aphrodisia which included desire, sexual acts and pleasure. Such analysis was oriented towards finding certain governing principles to control and master the problem. The problem of theatre, we would argue, was also analysed in terms of a force or an intensity whose excess or divergent use was to be curbed. That is to say, like the fate of the ethical substance of *aphrodisia*, the moral operation was not simply an injunction against the very presence of–what we might call–the "theatrical substance". In *Ion*, when Socrates/Plato talks of theatre as not a skill but a product of divine inspiration, he explains the nature of poetic inspiration as a divine power which constitutes a chain like a magnet which attracts scraps of iron which themselves get transformed and start attracting other iron pieces. The muse inspires the poet to compose as gods interpreter (*hermeneus*) while the rhapsode interprets this poetry and in performing attracts and transforms the audience. Plato writes, "well then, do you realize that your spectator is the last of those rings which I said received their power from one another, under the influence of the Heraclean stone? The intermediate one is you, the rhapsode and actor; the first is the poet himself" (Plato, *Early Socratic Dialogues* 1987, 57). What we call the "theatrical substance" on which ethics was to operate was not merely the idea of theatre as a form of representation. In fact it was not the morphology of theatre which was at stake in the relation between theatre and ethics but this dynamics where the text, performance and efficacy though understood separately was inseparable parts of the same process which we call the theatrical substance. It is with Christianity as we show in the following chapters that the argument shifted towards an examination of the morphology of the theatrical text. Like desire whose form had to be deciphered in its most intricate details so as to follow certain specific and clearly articulated codes of ethical conduct while sacrificing that part of the self which was the site of 'evil' and sinful desire while pleasure completely vanished. Theatre we later argue, at the beginning of the Christian world also vanished as a practice, in a sense was sacrificed because it was deemed sinful as an activity which produced pleasure. But, on the other hand, it remained as a problem within Christian discourse purely at the formal level which explains its frequent 'use' as a metaphor. In any case for the ancient world, the theatrical substance remained unified with certain clearly defined qualities where it again shares a remarkable resemblance with *aphrodisia*. The experience of aphrodisia was thought of as involving two actors, the active and passive, the one who performs the activity and one on whom it is performed. This feature finds an equivalent expression in the "theatrical substance" when we consider the role it was ascribed as a cultural practice in Greek society. First we have its passive nature, mentioned by Plato, which is again determined by the fact that it is not a skill or *techne* but divine inspiration. The role ascribed to theatre in its passivity corresponds to that of the world of women in Greek society while the active world of men was something equivalent to philosophy, which could ethically control and guide the theatrical substance in a "measured and opportune manner" (Foucault, *The Use of Pleasure: The History of Sexuality*, Vol. 2, 1992, 45). Thus philosophy in a sense was the only true *techne* or art which was in the hands of the active subject while theatre was an object-partner which had no say in its own game. Foucault observes that sexual activity was undergoing such moral differentiation and valuation not because it was deemed bad in its essence or related to sin (primordial fall from grace) as it would later be for Christianity. In general sexual activity was perceived as natural but at the same time acute in its intensity disposed towards excess. Foucault explains that of the two features which characterized the pleasure associated with *aphrodisia* the first was its natural inferiority. It was deemed ontologically or qualitatively inferior but nonetheless, and this is the second feature associated with sexual pleasure, this inferior was "extremely acute" (Ibid., n.d., 49). Again we find resonance with theatre considering Plato's explicit critique of poetry in *The Republic* as an inferior form of reality, ontologically distanced from the truth of the idea but nonetheless having acute power to affect people through imitation. More specifically, this problem of ontologically inferior but nonetheless highly efficacious function of theatre is primarily associated to its form of direct representation or mimesis.

In Relation to Chresis

The second feature that Foucault identifies in order to conceptualize the problem of sexuality is the mode of subjectivization or the way in which an individual recognizes himself/herself in relation to the ethical practices he performs. In other words, the principle he/she follows in order to participate in the acts in an ethical fashion. For the Ancient Greeks such a principle was oriented towards moderating and regulating the activity of sexual practices. Such regulation was directly related to the naturally acute efficacious function of the ethical material. As Foucault writes, "The goal of moral reflection on the aphrodisia was much less to establish a systematic code that would determine the canonical form of sexual acts, trace out the boundary of the prohibitions, and assign practices to one side or the other of a dividing line, than to work out the conditions and modalities of a "use"; that is, to define a style for what the Greeks called *chresis aphrodision*" (Ibid., n.d., 53). When we study the kind of remarks posed against theatre in the ancient world, the emphasis on finding a regularizing principle to govern theatre gains clear ascendancy over any outright prohibition or even systematic code to determine the boundary between what has to be allowed and what not. In Plato's *Republic* the regularizing principle has two aspects: First, regulations in relation to the content of poetry and second, regulations in formal terms. Plato's detailed analysis of what should or should not be the content of poetry in Book III of *The Republic*, in the final analysis is governed by a principle of use and not categorical injunctions. The principle of moderation remains central to Plato in this analysis as he censures poetry from showing the gods engaging in activities which are judged morally bad or showing deceptions or magical transformation. Plato writes, "Then of our laws laying down the principles which those who write or speak about the gods must follow, one would be this: God is the cause, not of all things, but only of good" (Plato, *The Republic* 2007, 73). Again "Do you agree that the second principle to be followed in all that is said or written about the gods is that they shall not be represented as using magic to disguise themselves nor as playing us false in word or deed?" (Ibid., n.d., 76). In both cases, rather than bringing categorical injunctions against theatre what is emphasized are two principles whose function is to ethically govern theatre. As Plato would go on to show a few pages later that aesthetic judgement has to correspond with ethical judgement.

Now if we follow Plato's argument as to what is a good action which poetry might be allowed to show in relation to the gods, we find that mostly those actions are judged inappropriate for the gods which upset internal harmony and which introduce immoderation. One ought not to portray Athena and Zeus prompting the breach of solemn treaty and oath by Pandarus, or to show strife between the gods or the misery of the house of Pelops or the Trojan War as caused by the gods. Thus such actions which cause a certain violent division between individuals, within a family or within the city or even between men and gods are deemed to be inappropriate and evil. The apparent theme of any violent disruption to harmony as being the cause of evil is obvious here. We would argue that this emphasis on harmony is related to the danger of stasis or civil war which causes internal division within the city or even the family. As Plato writes in this section: "Nor can we permit stories of wars and plots and battles among the gods; they are quite untrue" (Ibid., n.d., 70). Plato goes on to say that "quarrelsomeness is one of the worst evils" against which the guardians must always be protected in order to "persuade them that no citizen has ever quarrelled with any other, because it is sinful, our old men and women must tell children stories with this end in view from the first, and we must compel our poets to tell them similar stories when they grow up" (Ibid., n.d., 70). It is evident that the kind of strife being mentioned is not related to the protection of the city against an enemy. It is strife as stasis or civil war which remains implicit in these remarks which is a theme we will return to in a while. Suffice to say here that the first principle of showing good corresponds in this respect to the second principle of not showing deception or the gods enacting multiple roles or lying. It is interesting to note here that Plato distinguishes between true falsity of which the gods can never be accused and spoken falsehood which men perform on occasions "as a kind of preventive medicine against our enemies, or when anyone does something wrong from madness or folly" (Ibid., n.d., 70). The question of use and falsity becomes evident here as Plato introduces a kind of 'use' of falsity for men for a good purpose. The gods on the contrary cannot, by nature deceive because they are "without deceit or falsehood in action or word" (Ibid., n.d., 171). Hence he cannot change or transform in order to deceive or play multiple roles. Thus the action and words perfectly harmonize in the divine, becoming identical with each other. This is the structure of the oath, in which the gods speaks. The word of God corresponds to the oath which is seen as that function of language which does not produce merely denotative meanings but rather a certain performative efficacy. In this sense to portray the gods as lying or deceiving is a breach of this perfect harmony between word and action in God, or in other words the oath structure of all divine pronouncements and actions. There is a certain relationship here between the function of oath in language and the ethical subject. What is at stake in this absolute interdiction of showing the gods perform deception even in spoken words is, using another Foucauldian term, a problem of 'veridiction'. The words of god in being exclusively without falsity corresponds to an oath structure because rather than asserting something denotatively the words of god are identical to his actions which in turn coincide with his essence. Here the subject is not independent of the words he speaks because, in veridiction, "the subject constitutes itself and puts itself in play as such by linking itself performatively to the truth of its own affirmation"[8] (Agamben 2011, 57). It is this performative efficacy in its relationship to the subject which is not *solely divine*, but also operates in the domain of men but exclusively in the *realm of thought* "...surely when a man is deceived in his own mind we can fairly call his ignorance of the truth "true falsehoods". For a false statement is merely some kind of *representation* of a state of mind, an expression consequent on it, and not the original unadulterated falsehood" (Plato, *The Republic* 2007, 75).

What theatre unleashes, when not used appropriately is a form of deception which causes "true falsity" because it has the capacity of creating a division between man and that which constitutes him–his *thoughts*. So whereas in case of god, whose speech corresponds to his actions, the constitutive performative efficacy resides in language, for Plato, because the language of men provides no guarantee for 'truth', the only place for 'veridiction' is thinking itself. There is a certain performative efficacy, for Plato, in thinking through which the human subject constitutes itself performatively, bringing it into an essential relationship to itself which at the same time affirms the truth of his own existence. Whereas gods constitute themselves through language, or better in god, language, thought and action become identical, in men, action, language and thinking are separate operations but only in thinking essence corresponds to existence. This is also the moment of the constitution of the ethical subject in Plato, as someone who constitutes himself by inaugurating a relation to oneself. It is this relation of the self to itself (know thyself), which is breached in theatre when the gods are shown as deceptive or lying. It needs to be understood here, that in simple language, false statements only *represent* "true falsehoods". But there is a certain variation or abuse of language, like in poetry where through the representation of lying gods, a breach is produced not only in the realm of divine speech and divine action (the structure of oath). A scansion can also be produced, through poetic use of language (and not through ordinary language) between the self and its relation to itself. Thus though human language as such cannot harbour true falsity but merely its representation, poetic language, through its representation of deceptive gods can achieve this thus producing a logic of counter-efficacy which first affects the domain of ethics before anything else.

This highlights two aspects; one related to theatrical/poetic language and the other related to ethical conduct. Firstly, we realize, that in Plato, poetic language, or more particularly the language of theatre is not merely representation. Theatrical language or better the poetic language particularly of the tragedies and epic poetry which employs mimesis and talks about the gods, has the capacity to affect that part of the soul which remains unaffected by ordinary use of language–namely, thinking. The second point concerns the performative efficacy of such ethical subjectivization itself. It is because a relation of the self to itself produces a certain transformation through the actualization of certain transformative powers that such processes of ethical subjectivization have to be guarded from other forms of transformations or counter-actualizations of power. It is against this counter-efficacy which poetry/theatre produces that Plato censures the poets and not against a certain use of deception or falsity in spoken words. In a sense such falsity in language is necessary to a certain extent. It is the excess of this 'use' when it extends to the gods and the nature of oath in which the gods speak, that poetry becomes morally unacceptable.

Similarly, in the formal engagement with poetry, it is mimesis or direct representation which is primarily the domain of tragedy and comedy (though epic also employs mimesis but not exclusively like tragedy/comedy, while lyric exclusively employs the narrative mode of expression) that is censured because though ontologically inferior, this type of imitation produces the greatest effect on the mind of the audience. At the same time, such representation produces multiplicity of roles in a society where everyone is ascribed his or her specific role of either being an active subject or passive object-partner. But even here, Plato's analysis does not lead to an absolute injunction against theatre. In *The Republic*, Book III, he writes, "'I suspect', he replied, ' that you are wondering whether we should allow tragedy and comedy in our state or not'. 'Maybe', I replied, 'or maybe the question is more far-reaching, I don't know yet; we must go wherever the wind of argument carries us'" (Ibid., n.d., 88). The implicit irony exposes not an ambiguity in Plato's supposed prejudice against theatre thus making such prejudice irrational and invalid in his own terms. Rather the irony exposes the possibility of extracting a certain use of theatre based on moderation and harmony or, in other words, following an ethical choice which leads to freedom.

Dramatic representation because of its peculiar quality of acute efficacy, though ontologically inferior, can produce when indulged in without any regulative principle, habits or second nature "of physical poise, intonation and thought" detrimental to the ethical pursuit of freedom. That the problem of this use of theatre is strictly associated with that of moderation becomes evident when we consider how extravagant acts are not to be represented like that of excessive indulgence in food or sex. Thus the poet saying "death by starvation is the most miserable end one can meet?" (Ibid., n.d., 81) or when Zeus "stayed awake, when all the other gods and men were asleep, with some plan in mind, but forgot it easily enough when his desire for sex was roused; he was indeed so struck by Hera's appearance that he wanted to make love to her on the spot, without going indoors," (Ibid., n.d., 81)–such scenes need to be censured according to Plato. However, the scene, where Odysseus screams, "Patience my heart you have put up with fouler than this" (Ibid., n.d., 83) needs to be illustrated because it portrays endurance. Thus we see that the 'use' of theatre/poetry is explicitly related to the question of mastery over the self.

In Relation to Enkrateia

The third aspect which concerns Foucault in his conceptualization of ethics is what he calls the elaboration of the ethical work (*travail ethique*). It is this self-forming activity *(pratique de soi*) which in the ancient world takes the form of *enkrateia*. The form of relationship that one ought to establish with oneself which would determine the proper use one made of pleasure was encapsulated by this term *enkrateis* which though close to an idea of moderation (*sophrosyne*) was not entirely exhausted by it. *Enkrateia* designated a more active form of self-mastery which was seen more in the sense of *agon* or a struggle that one part of the self was engaged with against the weaknesses and extravagances of another half. It is this active form of maintaining control over pleasures and desires which was captured by this term. Now in order to conquer (*kratein*) over desires and pleasure so as to bring it under the rule of the self, the rational and stronger part of the self had to take up a combative attitude towards oneself in order to reach ascendancy and dominion. Thus *enkrateiae* was a process to settle a state of crisis within oneself where the self was always at risk of being enslaved by desire and pleasure. It was not the complete rejection of desire and pleasure which was natural but a victory over them that defined the activity of *enkrateia*. It is this polemical (*polemos* as combat) attitude with respect to oneself which was associated with the idea of moderation. If moderation was a stable and harmonious state of self-governance which came to light, then *enkrateia* was its dark underbelly where a state of 'civil war' (*stasis*) was unfolding within the self. But such a state of combat within the self was always oriented towards finding a stable government of the self. Sometimes it called for a complete rejection and expulsion of desire though "much more often, it was defined by the setting up of a solid and stable state of rule of the self over the self; the intensity of the desires and pleasures did not disappear, but the moderate subject controlled it well enough so as never to give way to violence" (Foucault, *The Use of Pleasure: The History of Sexuality*, Vol. 2, 1992, 69). As Foucault correctly points out, in Plato particularly, the civic model was designed corresponding to this state of the ethical subject. The political structure which corresponds to this ethics of pleasure will thus have the arche, that would allow the defeat of rebellious hedonism of the masses, to rule over (*kretein*) these inferior powers so as not to be enslaved by them. In order to define this immoderate (*akolasia*) attitude, Plato constantly compares uncontrollable desire to a low-born populace "that will grow agitated and rebellious unless kept in check". Plato points out at the end of *The Republic* (the next to last book of *The Republic*) after setting up his model city that although it is almost impossible for the philosopher to find such a 'paradigm' of the city, it is nevertheless laid up in heaven for him who wants to contemplate in order for the philosopher to "set up the government of his soul" (Ibid., n.d., 71). Now this comparison of the ethics of the self to a civic model immediately brings into focus the problem of theatre and its relation to democracy. Firstly, from the ethical perspective, theatre produces this crisis of immoderation through not only its portrayal of desire and pleasure but being a site of the production of the theatrical substance which like the ethical substance of *aphrodisia* has to be worked upon in order to control and rule over it. Of course this attitude of governance is not limited to theatre but extends to all art. In Book III of *The Republic* Plato writes: "It is not only to the poets therefore that we must issue orders requiring them to portray good character in their poems or not write at all; we must issue similar orders to all artists and craftsmen..." (Plato, *The Republic* 2007, 97). This notion of good character in Plato is immediately related to beauty and idea of good. While ugliness of form corresponds to bad character, good characters are by definition beautiful in their form. However, the rule of the guardians over the poets immediately corresponds to the ethical concept of *enkrateia* because in the ideal city, the theatrical substance which like aphrodisia is ontologically inferior but with acute effective power has to be combated against and brought under the rule and constant vigilance of the guardians. The extravagance and excess of theatre can be compared to that of democracy. For Plato, being born out of oligarchy (excess of wealth), democracy logically leads to tyranny because what democracy and the democratic citizen epitomizes is an excess of liberty and self-indulgence by everyone which can only lead to a usurpation of power by an unworthy leader.

In Relation to Freedom

This brings us to the final question of *telos* which Foucault identifies as the fourth aspect of his ethical conceptualization. In the ancient world the telos for such ethical transformation was what Foucault calls the pursuit of freedom and truth. It is ironical that the idea of ethics which according to Foucault is the expression of a sense of freedom for the Greeks, in Plato finds liberty itself–when practised immoderately–as the cause of servitude and enslavement. Jonas Barish has attacked Plato for his curbing of individual freedom of expression and policing of art. But we need to understand here, and Barish's method perhaps prevents him to do so, that where Barish sees individual freedom of expression, Plato senses self-indulgence and while Barish critiques Plato for his authoritarianism and lack of a democratic idea of freedom, Plato cautions against democratic freedom leading to enslavement precisely from an ethical perspective of moderation and immoderation. Plato writes: "So from an extreme of liberty one is likely to get, in the individual and in society, a reaction to an extreme of subjection" (Ibid., n.d., 301). It is this irony of democracy which Plato compares with theatrocracy, precisely from this perspective of excess and immoderation. One needs to take this into consideration in order to *distinguish* between the Foucauldian concept of ethical subjectivization in ancient Greece which evokes an idea of freedom *from* a democratic idea of an independence of free will. According to Plato, liberty which democracy practises in excess comes in the first place as a response to a stagnation and crisis of an earlier relation of power, namely oligarchy. This liberty when practised immoderately leads to subjection and enslavement. Here *liberty* is also treated as an 'ethical substance' where the *desire* for freedom and its actual enactments and fulfilment in pleasure becomes excessive within democracy. The desire for freedom which remains repressed in oligarchy as singularly the desire for wealth becomes liberated but at the same time leads to self-indulgence in democracy. Whereas the platonic idea of freedom, drawing from Foucault is that ethical freedom which has as its polar opposite, the danger of being enslaved to an excess of desire, pleasure and even freedom itself when practised immoderately. *This ethical freedom has to be practised constantly rather than in moments of political stagnation and crisis.* Thus one needs to clearly distinguish an idea of liberation in Plato which comes through the democratic moment as a response to existent political blockage and stagnation of power relation in oligarchy. This idea of liberation when practised immoderately leads to enslavement and tyranny. While practice of freedom operates at the ethical level and leads to truth and needs to be practised constantly as self-mastery.

From Theatre to Philosophy and Back: On the Use of Theatre and Performance of Irony

We are aware that at the end of Book X of *The Republic*, Plato famously proposes to banish the poets and the tragedians on grounds which he had argued hitherto. He adds that this is not something new but a reiteration of an "old quarrel between philosophy and poetry" (Ibid., n.d., 351). But like the true dialectician that he is, Plato continues to speculatively argue that if condemned for being insensitive and ill mannered, he would make a case for the return of poetry if "she can make her defence in lyric or other metre" (Ibid., n.d., 351). What is interesting and perhaps crucial for our own understanding of the relation between theatre and philosophy is what he says immediately next. Plato writes, "and we should give her defenders, *men who aren't poets themselves* but who love poetry, a chance of defending her in prose and proving that she doesn't only give pleasure but brings lasting benefits to human life and society" (Ibid., n.d., 351). We encounter a similar line of argument in Book III, where the education of the guardians is discussed in relation to what kind of poetry should or should not be allowed in the Republic. There Plato argues that it is the philosopher-guardians who should have the skill to recognize not just good poetry which is beautiful and portray ethical characters but also the bad ones which are ugly and portray characters of low moral value. Plato writes:

> Then I must surely be right in saying that we shall not be properly educated ourselves, nor will the guardians whom we are training until we can recognize the qualities of discipline, courage, generosity, greatness of mind, and others akin to them, as well as their opposites, in all their many manifestations, we must be able to perceive both the qualities themselves wherever they occur and representations of them, and must not despise instances great or small, but reckon that the same skill and training are needed to recognize both. (Ibid., n.d., 98)

If the poets themselves are incapable of defending poetry then it is obvious that they lack the skill and training required to recognize which is beautiful and good and which is its opposite on the basis of certain criteria which, as discussed before, are essentially ethical in nature. In *Ion*, Plato already clarifies this problem of skill, when he argues that poetry is not the product of skill but of divine inspiration. But what exactly is the consequence of this line of argument can perhaps be clarified when we examine this problem of skill in relation to poetry and theatre. While making his case *against* poetry as a form of skill, Socrates argues that each specific skill leads to a body of knowledge such that the two are inseparable. It is through the skill that one recognizes and understands the knowledge one possesses but at another level, certain skills like charioteering, itself is knowledge. So technical skills are different in so far as each skill leads to a specific body of knowledge from which it is inseparable. But in case of the rhapsode, his skill does not lead to a specific body of knowledge which it saturates but leads to all kinds of false knowledge. So the rhapsode has the skill to talk about the charioteer, the doctor and the general. Yet he has the knowledge of none. So surely when Socrates says that the rhapsode is conditioned by no skill but divine inspiration what he means is that he has no *skill that will lead to recognition and judgement of knowledge*. But nonetheless he has a skill, which is that of the rhapsode. Thus Socrates can differentiate between the skill of a general and that of a rhapsode when he says, "And when you make a judgement about military matters do you judge in virtue of your skill in generalship, or in virtue of the skill that makes you a good rhapsode?" (Plato, *Early Socratic Dialogues* 1987, 64). In *The Republic*, this problem of skill or technique (*techne*) in relation to poetry and art is clarified most vividly. In Book X, Plato distinguishes between three types of techniques–use, manufacture and representation. Plato explains that the quality, beauty and fitness of any implement or creature or action is always judged by reference to the use for which man or nature produce it. Hence it is the one who uses something who has the true knowledge (*logos*) to judge. While the one who manufactures–the craftsman–only has what Plato calls belief (*pistis*) about something's merits and defects only through associating with and listening to someone who knows, i.e. the relevant user. However, representation as a technique is neither conditioned by the user's knowledge nor the manufacturer's correct opinion. Hence the "poet too, as artist, will be beautifully ill-informed about the subjects of his poetry" (Ibid., n.d., 344). It is the philosopher-guardian who has the skill to recognize the subjects of poetry on the basis of the knowledge he possesses, a knowledge which is intimately related to a certain ethical way of life based on moderation and self-mastery. It is on the basis of this knowledge that the philosopher-guardian will 'use' poetry, passing judgement on both its content and form. We see that though there is talk of banishment of the tragic poets, the orientation of the problem regarding theatre is not simply connected to political censorship. A deep relation exists between ethics and politics in Plato, in light of which *the problem of theatre appears in terms of its use, both ethical and political.* In the final analysis, the problem of theatre is posed as a problem of knowledge so that its transformative powers could be harnessed ethically and politically by philosophy. In other words, it is perhaps here that we find the original principle of separation between the critical skill to theorize theatre and the skill of theatrical performance itself, the skill of the philosopher-guardian being praised while the skill of the rhapsode being derided by Plato in *Ion*. At the same time it is here that we find the clear relationship between theatre and a certain politico-ethical usage based on its transformative possibilities. In Aristotle this division between theory and practice, between critical conceptualization of theatre and theatre's own transformative possibilities would get a much more systematic expression through his concept of *Katharsis*, and its relation to poetics as such[9].

Meanwhile, in Plato we find that the technique of representation or mimesis generates no knowledge or even correct belief but has the acute power to transform individuals. Hence it has to be used with utmost care and moderation but even more importantly with reason and not according to the pleasure it generates. In fact for the guardian-philosopher it ought not to generate immoderate pleasure like it does for women and children. But Plato goes on to write in *The Republic*, "the combination of the two styles (narrative and mimetic as in the case of epic poetry) is very pleasant, and the opposite style to the one you have chosen (here what is hinted at is the unmixed style of representation or mimesis as in the case of tragic poetry) gives most pleasure of all to children and nurses and the general public" (Plato, *The Republic* 2007, 92). It is not surprising that in a hierarchically arranged society like Greece, where women and children were categorized as belonging to the lowest social strata, their corresponding pleasures would also be deemed inferior. It is even more interesting to note here that Plato distinguishes theatre in this light of being a skill which can generate incorporeal transformations among the *general public* without the authority of logos or knowledge. It is this mass appeal of theatre that induces Plato to compare it with the problem of *public opinion.* In *The Republic* while presenting a case for the philosophers and the reasons for their corruptions in the hands of public opinion, Plato presents theatre as one such public place–along with the law courts and assembly–where mass opinion corrupts the fertile minds of the would be philosopher (Ibid., n.d., 215). But for both Plato and Socrates if there was one group which epitomized this tendency of providing false knowledge in the name of science it was the *sophists.* The relation between sophistry and theatre is based on this problem of knowledge, where the poet is identified with the sophist as a maker of counterfeits that looks like the truth. But the problem with sophistry is not simply that it imparts false knowledge but that it is able to pass mass opinion as knowledge and truth. In *The Republic* Plato points out, "All those individuals who make their living by teaching, and whom the public call "Sophists" and envy for their skill, in fact teach nothing but the conventional views held and expressed by the mass of the people when they meet; and this they call science" (Ibid., n.d., 215). It is this production and dissemination of a "universal culture" in the name of science that Socrates and Plato attack. Theatre needs to be identified as part of this universal culture whose technical credibility is being questioned by Socrates and Plato.

Kierkegaard, in his development of the concept of irony through the personality of Socrates, identifies this universal culture of the sophists as the positivist tendency of the Greek society which had outgrown its aesthetic stage. According to Kierkegaard, Sophistry was a response to the ability of the Greeks to become sufficiently reflective and self-conscious to identify the contradictions inherent to existence–contradictions arising out of erstwhile determinate factors handed down by law and custom. He writes, "it discovers that what is supposed to be absolutely certain, determinative for men, places the individual in conflict with himself; it also discovers that all this is something external to a person, and as such he cannot accept it" (Kierkegaard, *The Concept of Irony: With Continual Reference to Socrates* 1989, 204). It is this reflective revelation of sophistry that echoes itself in the tragedies as we shall examine in the next section. Suffice to say that like sophistic reflection, poetic inspiration also exposes these existential contradictions of man, for which Socrates compares the poets to a winged creature who reveals the truth as in a dream or being possessed (Plato, *Early Socratic Dialogues* 1987, 55). But the sophists also provide answers to these contradictions in a fashion that Socrates attacks most vehemently. They teach how to give reasons for everything such that instead of examining the truth what they provide are general positions about particular instances, observation and expert knowledge of everything without treading on the difficult path of self-knowledge. It is this adroitness which deviates their reflective capacity from the path of reason and reduces it to nothing but finite empiricism. In the case of poetry, which employs representation, and is divinely inspired, reflective capacity is altogether absent. But nevertheless, and this is Socrates' main point of attack in Ion, the poet and the rhapsode *claims knowledge of everything.* In case of both the sophist and the poet/rhapsode, the problem is not that they fabricate false knowledge but they introduce a universal culture of positivism under the principle of an arbitrary finite subjectivity. Like the sophists, the poet could by some divine inspiration or "bacchic frenzy" discover the contradictions of existence but instead of having a comprehensive and universal approach (the good, etc), both sophistry and poetry are absorbed by the present moment of the finite subject and his propensities and desires. For Plato/Socrates they both represent the existent Greek culture that everything is true and man is the measure of all things.

It is against this finite subjectivity based on a positivist culture that Socrates introduces a concept of irony and a new subjectivity based on a concept of infinite negation. We extend this in order to argue, that what irony introduces is a new *techne* or skill of dialectics which finds an equivalent of theatre within philosophy. In order to argue this point, we need to understand the concept of irony itself. When Kierkegaard identifies the concept of irony in Socrates as that of infinite negation which is always at work he does not have in mind the abstract relation of the particular to the concept in general. What is evident from Kierkegaard's unfolding of the concept of irony is the true relation of the singular (the personality of Socrates) and the universal in the Idea. The negativity that Socrates unleashes through irony does not dissolve the substantial reality in order to be sublated and trans-appropriated in the objective order of the idea. The ironic does dissolve the immediate substantiality but not in order to arrive at its telos in the idea. Neither does the ironic as infinite negation start at the idea as the condition for the possibility of negating substantial reality. The infinite negativity of Socratic irony, according to Kierkegaard neither beings nor ends in the Idea. It rather establishes a (non)relation with the idea where the Idea serves as its boundary, as the limit which irony must never actualize in itself but keep as a pure possibility. The sophistic claim to have the answer for everything saturates reality by rhetorically responding to each particular case and thus betraying its own positivity. But at a more profound level, in deciphering the contradictions of existence, it is ultimately negative. Conversely, irony dissolves the finite reality with the force of infinite negativity but at the same time it signifies the "eternal self-positing infinity" in which all reality is encompassed. As Kierkegaard notes about Socrates, "he is positive to the extent that the infinite negativity contains within itself an infinity; he is negative because for him the infinity is not a disclosure but a boundary" (Kierkegaard, *The Concept of Irony: With Continual Reference to Socrates* 1989, 209).

The new subjectivity that Socrates inaugurates through his concept of irony determines itself through a certain ethical force which helps him to determine himself through negative qualification. Here subjectivity lacks its intrinsic freedom because there is no higher objective order which enlarges the boundary of subjectivity to universally encompass everything. The point that subjectivity reaches in relation to the idea is only the self-consistency of infinity which its grasps only as abstraction. But nevertheless it is sufficiently equipped to efface the substantial world of positivity and its principle of unwarranted subjectivity with the force of "the infinite, nonchalant freedom of subjectivity that we see in Socrates, but this is precisely irony" (Ibid., n.d., 211). Thus the new principle of subjectivity on the one hand must combat against the old principle of positivism and the subjective arbitrariness it generates. The new subjectivity captured in the infinite negation of irony thus comes as a demand, like a law. But at the same time it is not Socrates who brings this new principle to its fullness because "in him it was only cryptically present" (Ibid., n.d., 211). The new subjectivity inaugurated by irony advances the demand for absolute abstraction but itself never realizes it because it is an intermediate stage between the old principle and the new, where the new expresses itself potentially, not actually *(potential, non actu)*. To that extent irony is the very incitement of subjectivity which in the case of Socrates comes as a world-historical passion. In Socrates it is this demand for ideality which was the "judgement that judged and condemned Greek culture" (Ibid., n.d., 214). But at the same time, as Kierkegaard notes, his negation was so radical because he did not possess the idea. Ideality was only a boundary, a condition for possibility of the demand to exist, but in itself, it was purely abstract, virtual. Kierkegaard notes:

> But irony is the beginning, and yet no more than the beginning; it is and it is not, and its polemic is a beginning that is just as much an ending, for the destruction of the earlier development is just as much the ending of this as it is the beginning of the new development, since the destruction is possible only because the new principle is already present as possibility (Ibid., n.d., 214).

Socratic irony as a concept for a new subjectivity is nothing other than being placed in this focal point which orients itself negatively to a past on the condition of an affirmation of a future which is both there and not there. Ironic subjectivity orients towards and yet does not orient towards a point of view. It is this paradoxical place of non-orientation, topologically inhabiting a *point of either/or* which makes the ironic subject a mere beginning. In so far as it is the possibility of a beginning, it affirms newness. But at the same time it is *merely* a beginning and not *the* beginning in this or that concrete fashion. To all beginnings, such a mere beginning is related only negatively. But at the same time it is real, in so far as it is immanent in the world as a real possibility for newness. Socratic irony captures the disjunctive synthesis of this paradox which becomes the condition for the possibility of a new subjectivity.

It is this paradox which is summarized in the Socratic ignorance of knowing that one does not know. But such ignorance, far from being empirical (Socrates was otherwise a very learned man) in its philosophic sense inaugurates a relation with oneself based on this concept of infinite negativity. But this nothingness is not the pure emptiness but the nothingness of the substantial content of the world as it is. The Socratic wisdom is the human wisdom of the negativity of all finite content. But it is because of this wisdom that Socrates is drawn to himself, his exploration of himself (know thyself) is what he declares to the world as his absolute goal. "It is the beginning of infinite knowledge, yet merely the beginning, since this consciousness has not been consummated but is only the negation of everything established in a finite sense" (Ibid., n.d., 174). Hence from an ethical perspective, discussed earlier as a relation of the self to itself, 'know thyself' becomes a condition for separating oneself from others. But such a folding[10] back of the self within itself which seems to be the Socratic task of thinking par excellence also becomes the condition for opening up the self to the infinite Other. However such unfolding of the self onto the Other comes only as pure abstraction rather than a concrete historical reality. In one sense the self's relation to itself inaugurated by such negation denies all possibility for a finite relation with the other. To that extent, the self through such an ethical relation, frees oneself from grids of knowledge and power which always operates as relations with the other. But at the same time in opening a place within oneself where one enters into a relation with an infinite other though always sustained negatively provides the subject an infinite freedom. In teaching others not the virtues but a way to know themselves, Socrates "admittedly freed the single individual from every presupposition, freed him as he himself was free" (Ibid., n.d., 211).

The Concept of Irony sustained by a logic of negation which informs the life of Socrates comes as a gift of the absolute. (In Apology, Socrates says he is a gift to the state of Athens). Here the virtue of ignorance comes unexpectedly where the human participates in the divine, through establishing an absolute relation to the absolute. But in Socrates such a relation is realized only negatively. Again it is this relation which is expressed in the Socratic idea of the *daimon*, a voice from within the self which warns Socrates unexpectedly at different moments in his life. The *daimon* triggers decision in Socrates which is neither completely divine, hence external to the self and imposed upon it, nor is it the human consciousness of his self mediated through reason. The *daimon* directs him *minimally* to enter upon a life of irony and negation by warning him unexpectedly of what not to do. This unexpected *daimonian* gift when compared with the divine gifts imparted upon the poets (as Socrates argues in *Ion*) reveals a considerable difference. When poetry comes as a divine gift it comes without the knowledge of the one on whom it befalls. Hence the poet/rhapsode mistakes it as a skill; While Socrates is aware that his power to participate in divine knowledge (even if it is through ignorance) comes as a gift. Hence while the gift of the poets distorts into false knowledge which gives rise to unwarranted subjectivity, in the case of Socrates the recognition of his ignorance coincides with his suturing himself to the unknown which becomes the condition of possibility of a new subjectivity to unfold. The ground of such subjectivity is not the ground of any knowledge but the groundless contingency of the gift. But at the same time it is a process of subjectivization because there is enough knowledge to recognize that no knowledge can explain this process. Suffice to say here that the constitutive inconsistency of the affirmation that 'one only knows that one does not know' is related to this movement of the *daimon*, this secret movement of the self within itself. The undecidability of knowing anything becomes the very condition for the possibility of the decision that 'one knows that one does not know' through the movement of this power of the self.

If irony is a world-historical passion in Socrates which induces a new subjectivity, then the method which sustains such irony is dialectic. But here Kierkegaard shows the different use of dialectic which is never completely accomplished for either Plato or Socrates. In Socrates, dialectic leads to a progressive hollowing out of the world–an operation which uses the famous Socratic conversation or the art of questioning. It is through conversation Socrates manages to vacuum out all modes of substantiality leaving only the trace of the idea as its boundary in which everything disappears. The speculative also utilises the dialectic but in order to rarify thinking such that it becomes more and more purified, existing beyond the substantial reality but nonetheless in plenitude which ought to be made visible. If the point of presupposition from where the philosopher begins is exactly where he ends up, then for Plato it is the purity of the idea from where he begins and where he finally arrives though in a fashion which would remain incomplete[11]. While for Socrates, who begins with nothing arrives nowhere because the irony only bears the trace of the ideal as a possibility but never actualizes it. Thus Kierkegaard distinguishes two methodological tendencies in Socrates and Plato which becomes the line of separation between the ironic and the speculative personalities. It is the distinction between the exclusively dialectical method of Socrates and the dialectical which alternates with the mythical at least in Plato's later constructive dialogues.

The mythical is not simply the reference to a myth but to put myth to a use which already indicates that one is beyond the mere realm of mythical presentation. When in the earlier dialogues, as Kierkegaard points out, the mythical is held in contrast to the dialectical, it is because myth gives the task of dialectical thinking that flourish of an embrace where it can stand still and experience the idea if only through imagination. Thus according to Kierkegaard, the mythical is nothing but the idea in a state of alienation, i.e. externalized in space and time. When dialectic fails to accomplish the speculative fulfilment trying to clamber up to the idea, the imagination reacts. Thus the myth is not to be confused with the historical because any attempt to explain it historically already proclaims the death of the myth. Hence the myth remains purely in the twilight of imagination, as in a dream. In Plato's later constructive dialogues, the mythical is not in opposition but alternates with dialectic because as Kierkegaard indicates it has gone through a metamorphosis. As the passion for speculation displaces the ironic restlessness, the mythical is transformed and put to use as a metaphor in the service of speculative dialectics. While in the earlier dialogues the myth betrayed the failure of speculation and the restlessness of irony which could only contrast dialectic against the mythic, now myth metamorphosed as metaphor adds to the insufficiency of dialectic to fulfil itself. As a metaphor the idea is held under the qualification of time and space but nevertheless understood *ideally*. Metaphor comes as a response to the temptation to maintain something which actually is not. It is the temptation to represent that which cannot be represented and hence has to come into being taking into consideration the infinite distance that separates itself from the essence of ideality. But at the same time it finitizes the infinitude of the idea in alienating it into time and space. We shall try to develop this problem of use of the metaphor and its relation to the infinitude of the idea in the later chapter. Suffice to say here that when, as in *Symposium*, myth is used to make visible the purely negative problem of desire, there is always a desire to behold that whose only access through irony is purely negative. This is a movement of philosophy where an equivalent of theatre is found such that within a philosophical work, instead of the mediating movement of representation, metaphor or, more importantly, the mythical carries out an immediate act of affecting the mind beyond all representation. The myth here becomes a *direct sign*, where imagination reacts in the incapacity of reflection to find any representation to mediate the idea.

In *Symposium*, Diotima'a story unravels the presence of the mythical. Eros having been born of wealth (*Poros*) and poverty (*Penia*) inhabit an intermediary state of neither being rich nor being poor. But here the characterization of Eros still remains negative. Eros expresses the infinite negativity of desire which can only become the condition for love and knowledge, propelling love and thinking alike through its restless resourcefulness. But thinking cannot get hold of its own propelling element, this negative agent which is always in a state of flux. Herein resides the mythical. It is through the mythical that this pure state of flux, this original movement is captured and put to rest in the sign which becomes the metaphor. Here the metaphor is not the representation of the Idea because irony is incapable of realizing the idea objectively and keeps it as a boundary or limit against which it negatively maintains itself. Nevertheless imagination intuitively captures the trace of the idea such that the sign which actualizes it, rather than mediating, becomes a place where forces pass into each other. The restlessness of the negative pass into the enthusiasm of the speculative while the intuitive tries to externalize or express the infinite distance that separates it from the Idea. In the absence of any dialectical resolution which can phenomenalize the spirit, it is the myth or the metaphor which operates as the sign that captures the dialectical struggle of the ironic. To that extent it is positive because it actualizes or expresses what ironic reflection only keeps negatively at infinite distance. But at the same time, it is through the sign and its interpretation that the Idea is repeated, where instead of a theatre of representation availed through opposition and mediation, we have the force of the metaphor which captures the restlessness of the negative, the original infinite distance that separates the ironic from the ideal and throws it back into the world through "dramatizing Ideas" (Deleuze, *Difference and Repetition* 2005, 11).

At the same time the ironic method reveals itself in the personality of Socrates as nothing but the play of masks which comes before faces. As we discussed earlier, in *Symposium*, love is defined negatively as desire for something one does not have. Apart from being a most abstract definition it is this desire, longing which becomes the infinite subjectivizing impulse of love which lacks any content. This abstraction is thus neither deductive nor inductive and does not have its ontological validity in the speculative. It is a practical abstraction which has its negative validity in the ironic. Nevertheless it is this infinite negativity which draws not only Alcibiades, but all the rest (Charmides, Glaucon's son and Euthydemus, the son of Diocles and many others) towards Socrates.

If we consider the nature of these love-relations, epitomized by the relation between Alcibiades and Socrates, we find that rather than the calm yet profound serenity of the idea we have the restless agitation of the negative. It is like Alcibiades has been "bitten by a snake"—"he avoids him as if he were a Siren, plugs his ears least he remain sitting at his side and grow old—indeed he often wishes that Socrates were dead" (Kierkegaard, *The Concept of Irony: With Continual Reference to Socrates* 1989, 48). Now this is not the love-relation inaugurated by the rich exchange of ideas, by the abundant offering of knowledge on one side and the grateful reception on the other. In other words, it is not a relation which finds its fulfilment in a third element—namely the idea. Rather it is the torment initiated by an impassioned longing for the personality of Socrates which means that it is a longing induced by the ironic. Hence Kierkegaard writes "... precisely because it is the nature of irony never to unmask itself and also because a Protean change of masks is just as essential, the infatuated youth must inevitably experience so much torment" (Ibid., n.d., 48). It is this play of masks which reveals not an original face but the original distance between two masks and the flux that informs the activity of taking one off to reveal another that defines the ironic.

It is from this sense also that the ironic introduces a theatre of repetition which directly affects the spirit as a pure force. In Symposium, Alcibiades emphasizes this Silenus side of Socrates. "Your view of Socrates is of someone who fancies attractive men, spends all his time with them, finds them irresistible—and you know how hopelessly ignorant and uncertain he is. And yet this pose is extremely Silenus-like. It's the outward mask he wears, like the carved Silenus. Open him up, and he's a model of restraint—you wouldn't believe it, my dear fellow-drinkers" (Plato, *Symposium and the Death of Socrates* 1997, 51). Alcibiades goes on to say that Socrates "treats his whole life in human society as a game or puzzle." Alcibiades points out that Socrates very seldom opened up to reveal all this, but he—Alcibiades—saw him thus only once. "I saw it once, and it struck me as utterly godlike and golden and beautiful and wonderful" (Ibid., n.d., 51). And yet as Kierkegaard suggests that this says nothing more about Socrates than what can be said about him as an ironist. The ironist persona which reveals itself discloses nothing but the emptiness which he fills with the masks and the signs through which, like an actor he plays a role of playing other roles. It is this insufficiency of the idea, the original difference which is dramatized in this play of masks which looks god like and beautiful and wonderful for Alcibiades.

The sign and the mask are the two ways through which a theatre of representation is replaced by a theatre of repetition in Plato and Socrates. They come separately in the use of mythical-metaphorical in Plato and the ironic in Socrates. But they can also arrive together because irony is just one step behind the speculative. More importantly, they introduce a theatrical equivalent in philosophy before a logic of representation and the "false movement" of dialectical mediation can usurp this theatre of repetition by a philosophical theatre of representation.

Section II

The Particular Problem of Theatre and the Tragic

A View from Above: The Inaugural Problem of Theatre and Debt

Till now we have tried to look at the relation between theatre and ethics from the point of view of philosophy in Socrates which was determined by a certain understanding of irony. We have tried to show that the problem of theatre in Socrates was not simply an ethical problem related to the mastery of the self and its implications for the polis as it apparently seemed. That this problem of the self, in Socrates was profoundly related to his response to a certain Greek culture of positivism, epitomized by the sophists of which theatre was a part. What is important to note here is that if we draw a parallel between a Socratic critique of the sophists and his critique of the poets as both being informed by a universal culture of positivism–which according to Socrates lacked any true totalizing spirit of eternity which only comes negatively–we must also acknowledge that for him both these moments served as surrogates for the state. As Kierkegaard writes, "against the established order of things, the substantial life of the state, his whole life was a protest" (Kierkegaard, *The Concept of Irony: With Continual Reference to Socrates* 1989, 218). This idea of the "substantial life" of the state as higher than the individual made possible the objective dialectic of the ethical order, as noted before. While at the same time to participate in this objective order was to be achieved through a set of practices and techniques of self-mastery which were transformative in so far as in giving oneself up to a higher order one transcended the immediate sensate level to participate in the universal ethical order, embodied in the *polis*. This was the mode of ethical subjectivation which we discussed in the first section.

In his book *Theatre Number Event : Three Studies on the Relationship Between Sovereignty, Power and Truth* (2013), Soumyabrata Choudhury provides another circuitous but vivid path into the liturgical origins of sovereignty to show a process of subjectivization at a more collective level during 5th century BC Athens. This process of subjectivization, according to Choudhury is related to what he calls, drawing from Marcel Detienne, *systems of transformations* in bodies and congregations which implies their liturgical origins in Ancient Greece. According to Choudhury, the relation of such modes of subjectivization to logics of constitution, dissemination and exercise of sovereign power is on the one hand dependent on the locus of "god" in Greek history. On the other hand, in order to perpetuate and exercise the sovereign judgement in the *polis*, a "common interest" has to be discerned and articulated which becomes the liturgical element of congregation. The reason for this operation of power, Choudhury analyses through the nature of the theo-logic in ancient Greece, where the gods are living in the creaturely sense *and* are immortals. Hence the constitutive logic of sovereign power as indivisible and imprescriptible has to be determined through a set of relations and strategies between the eternal and the temporal, strategies which express a certain cunning of the gods in assigning to men particular *forms* to ascribe to or what Choudhury calls *multiple logics of situations.* One such situation that is analysed in great depth is that of theatre and its relation to the polis. Here one needs to underline the point that the logic of a situation, in this sense is never the isolated designation of an element like that of theatre or the *polis,* but a relation which expresses this logic. This relation is articulated by Choudhury through an original concept of debt applied to such historical context. Without going into the historical details of how this debt logic operates in the context of citizen participation in theatre and how the state provides a certain "dole" which the citizen pays in order to participate in the congregation of theatre, we will take for our point of departure some of the conceptual consequences of this debt logic. Choudhury argues that what this liturgical dole expresses is the capacity of an individual to be transformed into a citizen who will be indebted to the *polis* in taking this dole. But this indebtedness is the very condition for the possibility of an ordinary man to become an ordinary citizen. Here what the debt marks is the *extraordinary* capacity of being in debt which paradoxically is the marker of an ordinary citizen. The extraordinariness of the situation becomes evident when we realize that the operation is illustrative of a process of exclusion where the slaves, women and children are denied any such transformative possibilities which are required to become an ordinary citizen. The debt becomes the condition for the possibility for what Choudhury calls "incorporeal transformation" which at the same time articulates the relation between the immemorial polis and the particular cultural expression of theatre in 5th century BC Greece. At the same time, if we view this thesis from an ethical point of view, then a mode of subjectivization becomes discernible where a certain relation between the self and the other, the citizen and the polis is also articulated. Seen from the point of view of the polis, to produce these conditions of indebtedness becomes in turn the condition for constituting a citizen subject. But from the point of view of the self, to be indebted to the polis can be seen as an ethical imperative that one has to voluntarily pursue in order to express one's capacity to be indebted. This capacity involves the overcoming of one's immediate and creaturely response to *transform* oneself into a responsible citizen who can now participate in the universal order mediated by the state. The logic of mediation is central here, where the *polis* becomes the locus of this mediational logic between the temporal order of the citizen and the universal and eternal order of the *polis*. This line of argument perhaps brings together, the two modes of understanding ethics in the ancient world. The historical ontological mode of the self's relation to itself as a form of self-mastery and the tragic mode of giving oneself up to the universal ethical order. The incorporeal transformation brought about through a process of indebtedness alludes to a process where the individual aspires for a particular form of life which identifies a common 'lot'. The problem of ethics can then be posed as a search for 'knowing' if the personal choice for a particular form of life corresponds to the common 'lot' to which one is "condemned". It is this condition to be indebted to something which is outside the sensate reality of the individual self, in this case a common substance which is the *polis* which presents the ethical problem as a problem of *dialectic* in the Greek world between ethics and politics. The process of transformation is embedded in this *dialectic* of the self and other, of the individual citizen and the political substance of a 'common interest'. This is reflective in so far as it indentifies this contradiction but at the same time, unlike the Socratic moment, it is positivist because it presupposes a 'common substance'–the *polis*–towards which one chooses to be indebted. Here the ethical moment–as a relation of the self to itself–is articulated from the perspective of knowledge as the reflective capacity of judging or recognizing oneself as being capable of being in debt and hence being judged. Thus we have an economy of judgement at work in the *relation* of ethics to politics. As Choudhury informs us, in the Greek case, this creditor-debtor relation as logic of sovereignty is not an infinite, absolute 'adventure' but a finite process which even beyond the Greeks, suffers a "series of ricochets and false starts, of leaps and fabulous turns as well as awkward, almost embarrassing falls" (Choudhury, *Theatre Number Event: Three Studies on the Relationship Between Sovereignity, Power and Truth* 2013, 7). It is left for us to turn our point of view to the other side, to see if such an economy of judgement is not only at work on the galleries of the amphitheatre where as the dust settles, the slave, the woman, the citizen and the philosopher-critic take their respective seats; each aspiring for their own incorporeal transformations to take place which range from the creaturely and cathartic to the sublime and reflective[12]. In other words, each waiting to be judged according to his/her lot. We will now turn our attention to the orchestra where unfolds the very 'substance'[13] of the theatre–the tragic plays–to see what kind of judgements awaits the tragic 'heroes' and the demonic 'villains'.

A View from Below: The Problem of Debt Continued in Aeschylus' Oresteia

In Aeschylus' *Agamemnon*, right after she has murdered her husband and king, when the chorus accuses and condemns Clytaemnestra of both mariticide and regicide, Clytaemnestra responds thus to the chorus:

> Clytaemnestra: And you,
> You try me like some desperate woman.
> My heart is steel, well you know. Praise me,
> Blame me as you choose. Its all one.
> Here is Agamemnon, my husband made a corpse
> By this right hand–a masterpiece of justice.
> Done is done
>
> Chorus: Woman!–what poison cropped from the soil
> Or strained from the heaving sea, what nursed you,
> Drove you insane? You brave the curse of Greece.
> You have cut away and flung away and now
> the people cast you off to exile,
> broken with our hate.
>
> Clytaemnestra : And now you sentence me?–
> You banish *me* from the city, curses breathing
> Down my neck? But *he*–
> Name one charge you brought against him then.

He thought no more of it than killing a beast,
And his flocks were rich, teeming in their fleece,
But he sacrificed his own child, our daughter,
the agony I laboured into love
to charm away the savage winds of Thrace.
Didn't the law demand you banish him?–
Hunt him from the land for all his guilt?
But now you witness what I've done
And you are ruthless judges.
Threaten away!
I'll meet you blow for blow. And if I fall
The throne is yours. If god decrees the reverse,
Late as it is, old men, you'll learn your place (Aeschylus 1996, 163)

Here as elsewhere in the entire Oresteia trilogy, the central conflict remains between two forms of justice. In the play *Agamemnon*, the conflict is between whether the act of sacrificing Iphigenia is a just act of Agamemnon or whether it is a murder which anticipates the avenging punishment of Clytaemnestra. Causally related yet posed against this is the question whether Clytaemnestra's act of killing is merely the insane action of a murderous and vengeful woman or whether it is justified as an act of revenge on Agamemnon for the heinous crime of filicide. Similarly, the remaining two plays, *The Libation Bearers*, and *Eumenides* revolves around the conflict of whether Orestes' killing of his mother is to be taken as a matricide and condemned or a just act of punishing a murderess who has committed regicide. These conflicts express two parallel yet distinct understanding of justice which themselves are placed against each other. One is an idea of justice as seen from a point of view of a doctrine of judgement which presupposes the ethical order as the universal form of the *polis*. Agamemnon sacrifices Iphigenia in the name of the state, while Orestes embodies the ethical judgement which the gods assign to Orestes for the crime of regicide. The other form of justice is imagined through a series of violence which is displaced among the families of Atreus and Thyestes where individuals participate in a ceaseless dialectic of blood.

On Tragic Guilt

In *Fear and Trembling*, Kierkegaard interprets the act of Agamemnon as the quintessential action of the tragic hero. Here the ethical life as the universal *telos* applies to the hero, who resigns his immediate and sensate desire in order to belong to the universal. The tragic hero begins from the self-assurance that "the ethical obligation [his son, daughter] is totally present in him by virtue of the fact that he transforms it into desire" (Kierkegaard, *Fear and Trembling* 1985, 105). Hence Kierkegaard explains that Agamemnon can point to his duty to Iphigenia as his only wish. Here desire and duty perfectly coincide. The structure corresponds to a particular form of life in accordance to the 'lots' given to men by the gods. We shall return to this problem of a form of life and the 'lots' assigned to men by gods in the tragic context in a while. Suffice to say here that the tragic hero faces a dissonance between his form and the lot to which it must correspond. This crisis which introduces this contradiction and becomes the condition for the tragic dialectic to unfold on stage is concealed as "an epic survival based on a fate in which the dramatic action disappears from view, and from which it acquires its obscure and enigmatic origin" (Ibid., n.d., 111). It is in another essay titled "Ancient Tragedy's Reflection in the Modern" in his book *Either/Or*, that Kierkegaard had already hinted towards the enigmatic nature of tragic action and the place of monologue and the chorus which rather than expressing the exhaustive reflection of the hero, is absorbed in the excess of a concentrated lyricism which Kierkegaard terms "epic". This extra or excess which the lyricism of the monologue and chorus expresses is for Kierkegaard the 'inappropriate' nature of action in ancient tragedy, where action and situation is always impregnated with sorrow. That which gives momentum to the tragic sensibility is this oscillation between the action of the individual and the event of the existence of the hero, determined by fate. Kierkegaard notes:

> In ancient tragedy the action itself possesses an epic feature; it is just as much event as action. The reason is of course to be found in the fact that in the ancient world subjectivity was not fully conscious and reflective. Even though the individual

> moved freely, he still depended on substantial categories, on state, family, and destiny. This category of the substantial is the authentically fatalistic element in Greek tragedy, and its true peculiarity (Kierkegaard, *Either/Or: A Fragment of Life* 1992, 142-143)

If thought and character (*dianoia* and *ethos*) are the source of action in tragedy, as Aristotle believed, then this action, which is the *telos* of tragedy has to be seen as not generated from the character but inversely the character comes into being for the sake of action. At the same time this action, which is also the unfolding of the event of the tragic can only come about through something like lamentation which either the monologue achieves through approaching the epic or the chorus anticipates though its lyrical exaltation. Kierkegaard further notes that since the tragic guilt always oscillates between the immediate domain of the aesthetic and the objective domain of the ethical, hence before its appropriation into the ethical order or even after it, lamentation is the true expression of the sorrow which is not the reflective pain of the modern hero. Neither is it the anxiety which has as object something on which it can reflect. Rather than be anxious about something, lamentation evokes the very sorrow of the hero's existence, a sorrow which saturates his life such that he becomes extraordinary but at the same time this extraordinariness can be comprehended and shared as a common goal, as an exemplary moment in the life of the polis. As against anxiety and pain, which has a relation to the past and the future, sorrow always belongs to the present. Lamentation is always present in Greek life which perpetually transforms myth into history. Kierkegaard notes, "Greek sorrow, on the contrary, like the whole of Greek life, is in the present tense, and therefore is deeper and the pain is less" (Ibid., n.d., 153). The problem of lamentation and its relation to tragedy from the temporal point of view of a putative present tense becomes indicative of its political purpose.

From Myth to History

In his book *Hamlet and Hecuba*, Carl Schmitt draws a distinction between a tragic play like *Hamlet* which raises the stakes of a mourning play to make it into what he calls "a genuine myth" (Schmitt 2006) and a tragedy like Oedipus which uses myth[14] as a common knowledge or a historical reality. Schmitt writes that in case of the Greek tragedy, the tragic events, which in the case of *Hamlet* where historical, becomes mythic. Thus here history offers a common mythic knowledge and a collective, living and hence historical reality which tragedy makes use of in order to make it all embracing for both the poet and the audience. Thus a contemporary external source of knowledge which in this case is a "live myth" is introduced in the tragedy. But here he also makes a very important distinction between the Greek tragedy which *uses myth as a historical reality* and a tragic play like *Hamlet* which *uses historical events in order to produce myth*. Thus we sense a difference between 'living myth' and 'making myth' in Schmitt. While the later makes myth out of history through its tragic use, the former historicizes myth. In the latter, history becomes mythical while in the former myth becomes historical. The tragic mythologization of history in Hamlet is akin to opening history to its own possibility and infinite interpretations. Thus one can say that in the case of Hamlet, the tragic source is made *virtual*. While in Greek tragedy as Schmitt argues, "In its performance an element of reality, which is no longer pure play, consistently sneaks in, from the actual knowledge of the audience about the myth" (Ibid., n.d.). Hence somewhere the process of "recognition' which Aristotle guards as the fundamental moment of Tragedy seems to operate here which makes myth repeat itself historically (but not as history) in the performance space only to be recognized as the destinal knowledge or fate of a tragic race. If fate operates within tragedy as a moment of recognition or repetition of a knowledge which has been suppressed, which legitimizes the future in the name of the past, then a corresponding recognition seems to operate outside in the amphitheatres where the tragic tradition and knowledge of myth is recognized as the determinant markers of a race.

On Tragic Lamentation

We argue that lamentation in the Greek case has this political purpose of translating myth into historical knowledge, where the tragic hero in being the extraordinary 'figure' of a 'living myth' serves as the model for Greek life as such, a life which not only tries to absorb the past and the future in the present tense but expresses that eternal present in the universal ethical order which the polis embodies. The destinal logic constantly feeds the present moment through the mediation of the polis which is saturated with fate but at the same time it belongs only to the present moment. Through lamentation, the constant threat of a present crisis could be recognized and negotiated. Lamentation, which is the expression of the sorrow, discloses the constant oscillation of tragic guilt between the immediate and the destinal. Lamentation like tragic guilt is always ambiguous, impregnated with both individual action and the tragic event. However it *exposes* this ambiguity to the universal ethical order which appropriates the crisis, transforming the tragic situation into a condition for the possibility of the polis to exist. In lamentation the crisis is given a voice in language. Language offers a resolution to the crisis by the very fact that the crisis is lamentable and hence recognizable in language. The oscillation between the immediate aesthetic order and the ethical universal order inevitably orients itself to the ethical through the language of lamentation in Greek tragedy. Thus Agamemnon laments:

> And I still can hear the older warlord saying,
> 'Obey, obey, or heavy doom will crush me! -
> Oh but doom will crush me once I rend my child.
> The glory of my house–
> A father's hands are stained,
> Blood of a young girl streaks the altar.
> Pain both ways and what is worse?
> Desert the fleets, fail the alliance?
> No, but stop the winds with a virgin's blood,
> Feed their lust, their fury?–feed their fury!–
> Law is law! – (Aeschylus 1996, 110)

Agamemnon has to sacrifice Iphigenia in the name of the state to appease the gods. This is Agamemnon's duty in front of the *present* catastrophe. This is the ethical order to which the tragic hero must abandon himself because as the universal *telos*, it demands this obligation out of the hero under its doctrine of a justice. Hence the tragic hero has to make the (infinite?) movement of resignation, renouncing what he desires in order to fulfil his duty. Kierkegaard writes, "the tragic hero stays within the ethical. He lets an expression of the ethical have its *telos* in a higher expression of the ethical; he reduces the ethical relation between father and son, or daughter and father, to a sentiment that has its dialectic in its relation to the idea of the ethical life" (Kierkegaard, *Fear and Trembling* 1985, 87). This movement of the hero from the immediate and particular order of desire to the higher level of universal *telos* realized in the ethical life of responsibility is a movement of resignation. However being universal, such a tragic movement is always mediated. The two moments of such mediation which also renders the infinite movement of resignation of the tragic hero recognizable and comprehensible are, as indicated before i) the polis and ii) language. It is in the name of the 'higher substance' of the state that Agamemnon sacrifices Iphigenia, and because of this very fact he can lament his loss and make it comprehensible. Kierkegaard observes, "it is a simple enough matter to level the whole of existence down to the idea of the state or to a concept of society. If one does that one can no doubt mediate" (Ibid., n.d., 91). However we see that such an act of mediation, which demands the sacrifice of 'someone' to 'something' nonetheless produces a transformation which in case of the tragic hero is not sustained spiritually and reflectively like the Kierkergaardian "knight of resignation" who expresses the infinite or impossible movement of resignation spiritually or reflectively. Thus the tragic sacrifice in *Agamemnon* is not self-sacrifice but one rendered on to someone. The former is purely an inward movement inaugurating dialectic of the subject while the latter is an objective *dialectic* where the self offers as sacrifice the finite possession of something that he desires to something outside himself as a tribute or a debt. The self-sacrifice of what Kierkegaard calls the knight of resignation is something the tragic hero knows nothing of. For the knight of resignation the sacrifice is identical with a self-sacrifice while the transformation coincides with a transfiguration of the self in the infinite negativity of the Other. It remains in the fullest sense of the term, and in both senses of the genitive, a problem *of the subject.* As Kierkagard observes, "(for the knight of resignation) the desire which would convey him out into reality, but came to grief on an impossibility, now bends inward but is not lost thereby nor forgotten. ... for one who has infinitely resigned is enough unto himself. The knight does not cancel his resignation, he never lets it go, simply because he has made the movement infinitely..... it is only lower natures who have the law for their actions in someone else, the premises for their actions outside themselves" (Ibid., n.d., 73). Through making the movement of resignation, the tragic hero has to mediate. All he can do is "surrender an immediate finitude, in the sense of my testifying that the finitude ought not to be my own possession and that I do not want to keep it for myself" (Ibid., n.d., 73-74)

As we had argued before, the real challenge lies in finding a passage where the eternal order becomes aligned with the temporal in such a way that even though he cannot make the infinite movement inwardly, the tragic hero nonetheless can belong to the 'common substance' of the polis which is universal and eternal. The objective dialectics of the tragic offers this possibility where the incorporeal transformation of the subject anticipates the absolute sacrifice of the 'knight of resignation' even though here the movement is from the self to the other. We take this Hegelian argument as our point of departure that before depths of mind and heart are realized, i.e. before sacrifice is determined inwardly in a "figurative sense" which also coincides with the time of the tragic, a process of actual sacrifice is at work. According to Hegel, this process of actual sacrifice of the ancients is nothing but the expression of the "the negativity of the infinite which can only come about in finite fashion" (Hegel 1984, 384). Nevertheless the relation of the finite and infinite, the eternal and the temporal, the self and the other, man and god at this stage is maintained through a constant process of mediations, negotiations, of assigning 'lots' and *multiple logics of situation.* The ethical task is thus to recognize what is the form one has to endure, so that a relation of creditor-debtor can be established with the state, which determines the ethical. We shall come back to this point of the economy of exchange and the sacrifice in a while.

On the Question of Sacrifice

Meanwhile let us inquire about the problem of sacrifice in general which not only haunts the entirety of the Oresteia trilogy but is fundamentally related to the question of justice which is our inaugural point of entry into the text. At the same time this "allure of sacrifice" in the Greek context also corresponds to, what Nicole Loraux calls the city of the anthropologists as against the city of the historians which is based on conflict and crisis. The polis not of conflict (*neikos*) but maintained in the repetitive time of social and religious practices–of marriages and sacrifices. As the centre of repetitive human activity, Loraux points out how this polis determines its own boundaries, of what lies at its margins and what is defined as the outside. This spatialization which leads to the question of who belongs to it and in what way comes as a consequence of the polis being constituted as a human society which makes it "possible to situate it in relation to an elsewhere" (Loraux 2006, 17). In determining and constantly reproducing the centre, as the place of the mimetic repetition of sacrifice, the polis "proclaims the distance of this elsewhere, be it the time of gods or the untamed world of animals, in order to integrate it more fully. The city has absorbed the outside, and sacrifice founds the polis" (Ibid,. n.d., 17) And because from this anthropological point of view the *polis* is founded on this empty time of repetition, this suspended temporality of the sacrifice in which the city is endlessly born and reborn, Loraux argues, always presents the temptation of giving in to the idyllic illusion of the slow gestures of ritual. Thus effectively concealing or masking the conflict (*neikos*) and internal strife (*stasis*) as the original moment of the political so that "the political thus constructed looks very much like the myth of the political" (Ibid., n.d., 18).

In his essay "The Unsacrificeable" (1991), Jean Luc Nancy proposes to deconstruct the fantasy for sacrifice that Western thinking holds at its heart. The sacrificial core of Western thinking, according to Nancy, constitutes itself in a paradoxical moment of a rupture, which proposes to break away from an ancient idea of sacrifice as mimetic repetition but nonetheless transforms itself into a form of thinking which articulates the truth of sacrifice. This is what he calls the "mimetic rupture of the West's sacrifice" inaugurated by Socrates and Christ which proposes a new sacrifice with at least four aspects:

1. Sacrifice as self-sacrifice where the event of sacrifice no longer punctuates life in order to understand and resolve a crisis but unfolds a truth of life, where "what is involved is a life that would be in and of itself, wholly a sacrifice" (Nancy 1991, 22).
2. Sacrifice as a unique event which nonetheless embraces everyone in its fold because it is accomplished for all. In this sense it is a particular moment which is offered to the universal, thus becoming universal in character.
3. Sacrifice as the disclosure of its own truth, thus standing for all other sacrifices. Sacrifice becoming the truth of all sacrifice in general.
4. The truth of sacrifice sublates, thus negating the sacrificial moment of its own sacrifice. In negating itself, or in other words, sacrificing sacrifice itself, the new sacrifice becomes infinite and figural at the same time, operating spiritually and reflectively through this *dialectic* of sacrifice in the self.

It is this last point which is crucial for us to understand because in this moment of transgression of the finite moment of sacrifice, the self is appropriated in its own negativity. This is what Nancy calls the "trans-appropriation" where the finite functions and the exteriority of the sacrifice becomes sublated and absorbed in the infinite and absolute negativity of the self. It is transgression because the finite is annihilated and thus the law of self-presence is transgressed. In the case of Socrates' death we can easily understand the relevance of this mimetic rupture of an earlier understanding of sacrifice, where his whole life bears witness to this sacrificial "process". One can explore the meaning of philosophy as this sacrificial process of dying in the life of Socrates. But as we tried to show in our section on Socrates, the relation of death and life takes a new sense when analysed through the lens of irony, where any sacrificial transfiguration is rendered inoperative in the abstract indifference that irony unleashes into the philosopher's life. Here the absolute negativity does not come through the speculative moment of a sacrificial sublation even though an absolute negativity operates in this new sacrificial logic. In the case of Socrates as we saw, the absolute negativity is achieved without an infinite appropriation of the finite but rather through an infinite *displacement of situations*, where the absolute negativity comes only as a demand of an infinite absence of all meaning, of all appropriation. It is merely a technique, a *techne* which renders all appropriation "immanent" because what the Socratic irony unfolds is nothing but the infinite horizon of ideality which holds existence always at a infinite distance. It is not a disclosure of the absolute infinity where the finite finally comes to rest. Rather irony discloses this infinity only negatively, in its concealment, in its infinite regression. The absolute negativity of irony is not the absolute negativity of self-sacrifice because the horizon of ideality is held in infinite negation which does not allow for any sublation to take place. There is no trans-appropriation because the finitude of life is exposed through irony only to itself and nothing else. It is thus an ontological affirmation where the essence of existence lies only with existence.

But in the case of this sublated sacrifice, the infinite negativity is where the self transfigures and comes to rest. It is the figurative form of sacrifice *par excellence* because it is spiritual/dialectical and it rejects the earlier violent actualizations and reproductions of mimetic sacrifice. Hence, according to Nancy, this process of a new sacrificial thinking, in being a rupture from the old mimetic repetition of sacrifice, criticizes such an archaic sacrificial form whose truth it nonetheless wants to appropriate. The two aspects of this criticism become *economism and simulation*—the debit-credit structure of this earlier mimetic form and its simulatory and reproductive aspect. Though Nancy points out the inadequacy of such criticism in identifying new forms of subjectivity based on a new absolute economy it is impossible to discuss it in detail here. Rather it is more relevant for our inquiry to shift our focus to another consequence of this fantasy for sacrificial thinking in the Western consciousness.

In his critique of Bataille, Nancy points out that Bataille's obsession for a sacrificial thinking could be traced back to his effort to question this apparently innocuous theatre of sacrifice which had lost its system of cruelty. In other words, though he wanted to overcome sacrifice, he affirmed it more vehemently than ever. Bataille's effort to supplement sacrifice by art, was an effort according to Nancy to find a way out of this impasse between two modes of sacrificial thinking. An 'old' sacrifice which in its mimetic repetition was never able to truly destroy the subject rendering it equivocal; and a new idea of self-sacrifice which destroys the subject and resolves the equivocity but leaves nothing. According to Nancy, what Bataille wanted to introduce was a realization of this impasse as a momentum for art, where his formula of "ravishing without repose" would inaugurate a new dialectic of expressing the void through a new idiom of sacrifice in art which will now simulate the void by making it into an "apparent cruelty". This, according to Nancy, is singularly ambiguous because cruelty can only be efficacious when it is not a simulation, when it unleashes certain horrors which come as a force. While in the case of Bataille it comes about only through the simulation of art. Though one can recognize Bataille's intention of introducing a logic of efficacy into art through this type of thinking about an effective cruelty, Nancy identifies a sacrificial mode rather than the overcoming of a sacrificial thinking in such a conceptualization of art. He notes that in the case of Bataille, "art thus matters only if it still sends us back to the sacrifice it supplants. It cannot sacrifice except by still sacrificing to sacrifice" (Ibid., n.d., 29).

From this perspective of a sacrificial violence which perpetuates by reproducing itself through a certain logic of economism, Agamemnon's act can be read as an example of the 'old' understanding of sacrifice as mimetic repetition. As we discussed earlier this economism can be explained by a certain process of creditor-debtor logic, where the polis constantly mediates a system of exchange, appropriating the tragic hero into its fold of a universal ethical order. The tragic sacrificial thinking is not the sacrifice of the self which sublates itself, annihilating the very finite function of the sacrifice. The finite repetitive structure of sacrifice, in the tragic sense of Aeschylus has to be seen as an enactment of violence within the polis. But this violence displaces the internal strife (*stasis*) within the family outside the borders of the city. If the putting to death of Iphigenia by Agamemnon was the inaugural moment of this stasis within the family, then by the end of *Eumenides*, this putting-to-death has to be justified and the internal strife it inaugurates has to be displaced on to the outside as war against the enemy of the polis which brings about glory. As Nicole Loraux points out "... at the end of the *Eumenides*, Aeschylus opposes war against a foreign enemy, in which one may win fame—the only good war, because it is the only war that brings glory to the polis—to the scourge of internal war" (Loraux 2006, 22). The peaceful city of marriages and sacrifices can only be prepared to wage war against its enemy and win victory (*kratos*) and glory. This is the duty and ethical responsibility of its citizens. "It is not death the destructive that presides over this kind of war but the "beautiful death" of citizens for the sake of the fatherland" (Ibid., n.d., 23). As the internal war is displaced into the war against one's enemies, the peaceful city and the warring city is brought together under a logic which has sacrifice as its foundation. Here we find the cruelty and horror of a sacrificial thinking operating as a mediating logic which brings about peace and prosperity to the polis and at the same time binds the citizen subject into a form of life which is sacrificial to the extent that it extracts this sacrifice as the debt to be paid for the safety and maintenance of this immemorial city. The furies transformation into the Eumenides, the guardians of the city is based on this logic of sacrifice. As Athena speaks at the end of *Eumenides*,

> Neither anarchy nor tyranny, my people,
> Worship the Mean, I urge you,

Shore it up with reverence and never
Banish terror from the gates, not outright,
Where is the righteous man who knows no fear?
The stronger your fear, your reverence for the just,
the stronger your country's wall and city's safety,
stronger but far than all men else possess (Aeschylus 1996, 262)

When Nancy criticizes Bataille for his inability to separate himself from the sacrificial thinking, it is perhaps this mediation that he warns us against. The tragic mediation though sustains the intensity of a certain cruelty, nevertheless cannot but be appropriated under the sign of sacrifice. What Bataille was looking for in the "effective exercise of an effective cruelty" was an affective access to the entire possibility of thinking. But as Nancy points out, not without sufficient reason, such an "'opening to the entirety of the possible" is appropriated as soon as it is placed under the sign of the sacrifice" (Nancy 1991, 30). The tragic is saturated with the inadequacy of this cruelty, which constantly gets appropriated by the polis and the doctrine of judgement which the gods enunciate through the form of the polis. If the polis is that obscure place which founds itself on sacrifice, where its originary constitutive crisis of stasis becomes masked and forgotten through the repetitive and mimetic possibility of sacrifice, then such a transformation can only be brought about through logic of mediation. Greek life, like the Greek polis is thus saturated by the tragic, which not only affects the mythic life of the tragic hero but constantly transforms itself into a historical condition. Ian Kott calls this the *trageme*, the smallest structural unit of tragic opposition:

> The tragic hero is a scapegoat. A scapegoat is a sign, a symbol and a figure of mediation. The tragic opposition exists between suffering which does not justify anything, and myth which justifies all. In that mythical theophany there takes place a transformation of the cruel God into the just God, and of time which devours everything into history achieving its aims. In tragic anthropology it is only the scapegoats' names that keep changing; the myth of mediation remains the same. The road from exile out of paradise to the new paradise, which has

> been promised, is littered with corpses. Tragedy is a spectacular exhibition of these corpses (Kott 1970, XVIII).

At the same time, Kott goes on to argue that the tragic is also the annihilation of myth because its call for mediation constantly faces forces, affects and bodies which cannot be mediated. It is here that we identify a whole system of justice, writing in blood which is opposed to judgement and the book. It is a system of cruelty which not only resists judgement but meets such a doctrine "blow for blow". This system of justice, opposed to judgement, never mediates through sacrifice into a higher order but constantly displaces itself from one finite act of cruelty to another, such that it establishes an entire system of cruelty which is separate from sacrifice. It is here that we find a certain other imagination of cruelty, outside the sign of sacrificial terror which, posing the problem of cruelty in terms of force, "already surpasses all subjectivity" (Deleuze, *Essays Critical and Clinical* 1997, 135). Gilles Deleuze in the essay "To have done with judgement" (1997), schematizes such a system of cruelty which opposes all doctrine of judgment. Deleuze introduces and develops this problem of cruelty as a response against what we have been calling a sacrificial thinking, and in doing so he presents us with a theory of cruelty as vitally creative. Beginning with Spinoza, Deleuze, identifies four such figures, Nietzsche, D.H. Lawrence, Kafka and Artaud who, according to Deleuze not only critiques this alignment of thinking to the tragic but offers a way of thinking which is not under the 'sacrificial' sign of judgement but creative and vital in its unfolding. As Deleuze writes, "What is tragic is less the action than judgement, and what Greek tragedy instituted at the outset was a tribunal" (Ibid., n.d., 126). We cannot go into the details of how each of these figures invents for themselves new ways of thinking under the condition of cruelty separate from the sacrificial. However it would be instructive for us to inquire through Deleuze's schema another understanding of justice which coexists with an ethical judgement in the Oresteia trilogy. Deleuze's treatment of the problem of cruelty as a condition for thinking perhaps also offers a 'way out' of the impasse of sacrificial thinking which Nancy urges us to overcome in Bataille. This impasse either leads to mimetic repetition of a continuous process of subjectivization under the sign of an 'old' sacrificial logic or the modern sacrificial mode which leads to a 'will to nothingness'. What Deleuze offers is an 'escape', a 'line of flight' from all tragic and sacrificial thinking by making *cruelty* not a disclosure of sacrificial thinking but a *hidden condition* for a new mode of thinking. Against Bataille, who saw cruelty as a dialectic between simulation and violence, Deleuze conceives of cruelty as nothing but the intensification of forces which conditions the becoming of the meaningless but affective symbol. Rather than the sign which bears the sublation of cruelty as an 'apparent cruelty' in the domain of art, Deleuze inverses art as the very place where cruelty reveals itself as coming into being. Unlike Nancy, who criticizes the paradox of simulated cruelty as betraying a sacrificial core, Deleuze, like Artaud, embraces this paradox as the very condition for the possibility of cruelty to exist. It is in the words of Artaud what "frees the repressed unconscious, incites a kind of virtual revolt (*which moreover can have its full effect only if it remains virtual*), and imposes on the assembled collectivity an attitude that is difficult and heroic" (Artaud 1958, 28). In the Deleuze essay, this 'heroic' tendency of *becoming-minor* is impossible to disregard. And as we try to argue, this becoming-minor, becoming-rooster, becoming-scylla is an ever present movement within the Oresteia trilogy, particularly in context of the non-heroic figures like Clytaemnestra, and the non-deific gods like the furies.

From the Doctrine of Judgement to a System of Cruelty

Drawing from Nietzsche, Deleuze very early on in the essay identifies the condition for such judgement "the consciousness of being in debt to the deity". It is this "adventure of debt" that Deleuze traces in infinite speed over the next couple of pages by analysing the problem of debt as it moves from–finite creditor-debtor relation which always involves 'incorporeal transformation' in both the parties involved to–something like the very horizon of this relation, where the debt becomes infinite and unpayable, which following Nietzsche, Deleuze identifies with the emergence of

Christianity. But the condition remains this debt relation which in case of Christianity, rather than being constantly displaced, (as we see happening in ancient blood feuds, like in the Oresteia trilogy), follows the logic of 'unlimited postponement'. "It is not as if judgement itself were postponed, put off till tomorrow, pushed back to infinity; on the contrary, it is the act of postponing, of carrying to infinity, that makes judgement possible" (Deleuze, *Essays Critical and Clinical* 1997, 129). But even this doctrine of judgement as infinite debt, according to Deleuze, originates through many circuitous paths, through many modalities and numerous movements. Deleuze distinguishes a fundamental difference between the infinite debt of a Christian judgment and its precursor, the soil on which judgement first appeared. We can easily sense what he has in mind is the tragic movement of judgement. Instead of a debtor-creditor relation which flourished under a constant flux of incorporeal transformation and affects, judgement even in its earlier stage had to fix this flux to a definite body, a form. This according to Deleuze is the passage from a "prejudicative" system of debtor-creditor relation which gave rise to a system of affects to a reversal (not disappearance) of such a system of affects. The latter enunciates the Christian understanding of a doctrine judgement as infinite debt where "we are no longer debtors of gods through forms or ends, but have become in our entire being the infinite debtors of a single god" (Ibid., n.d., 129). While the former, according to Deleuze is nothing but a system of cruelty where justice is infinitely displaced, marking finite bodies that circulate within a given territory. This constant state of flux determines not an immobile and eternal law but justice which is evinced through being "ceaselessly displaced among families that either draw blood or pay with it" (Ibid., n.d., 128). But between the two, one had to envisage a passage, where these 'finite blocks' had to be fixed according to the infinite demands of the gods. "The debt had to be owed to the gods, it had to be related, no longer to the forces of which we are the guardians, but to the gods who were supposed to have given us these forces" (Ibid., n.d., 128). It is here that Deleuze introduces the concept of the gods assigning lots to men. In order for men to become both judges and capable of being judged, the relation of hierarchy had to be established between men and gods, instead of gods being passive witnesses or plaintive litigants who could not judge. This movement from being passive witnesses to active judges offers a clue of how in *Eumenides* the problem of a family feud and a system of justice which is finite and drawn in blood and where the gods are only instigators or witness gets transformed into Athena being the supreme judge. Deleuze illustrates this movement when he notes that this transition was brought about through the exercise of power where the gods give lots to men and depending on their lots, men have to choose a particular *form* (of life) which corresponds to his lot which is his organic end or *telos*. Deleuze further argues that, this exercise of power through assigning lots, explodes into the world when man is mistaken about his lot and the form he/she takes is antithetical to the judgement of god. We find an almost exact corollary to this movement in the Oresteia trilogy, when in *Eumenides*, Athena finally declares:

> My work is here, to render the final judgement.
> Orestes,
> I will cast my *lot* for you.
> No mother gave me birth.
> I honour the male, in all things but marriage.
> Yes, with all my heart I am my father's child.
> I cannot set more store by the woman's death—
> She killed her husband, guardian of their house.
> Even if the vote is equal, Orestes wins (Aeschylus 1996, 264)

What this judgement unravels is not simply the passage from a system of justice which being constantly displaced in the family produced a debt-creditor relation based on a system of affects to move on to a counter-utterance, where a final judgment is rendered which establishes the final debt to the god. The passage bears a judgement far more effective and far-reaching, extending back to the very first act of killing. The judgement is self-constitutive in the sense that by casting her vote in favour of Orestes, she in a sense votes for herself or at least for the gods who embody justice. Apollo instigating Orestes into murder, seen from this point of view is no longer a mere provocation for vengeance but also a just act. By not punishing Orestes, this final judgement clearly differentiates between acts of sacrifice and murder for the entire trilogy. Again the entire madness and delirium of wrath, the theatre of blood, is now given a meaning as nothing but the inability of certain individuals like Clytaemnestra, Aegisthus–to mistake their forms of life as antithetical to the lot assigned to them. For Clytaemnestra it is her inability to conform to the duties of a queen and wife, hence it is merely a problem of false judgement. Whereas Orestes, even though he commits matricide, is pardoned because it is seen as conforming to his lot which is not simply that of a son avenging his father, but justice rendered for the assassination of a king. Thus the forms of lives that one needs to choose according to the lots assigned to them, in the trilogy converge on the idea of *polis*. In the last analysis it is the city which corresponds to the lot assigned to men by gods. We again see here a reiteration of *multiple logics of situation* that we discussed earlier regarding the liturgical function of theatre which is being articulated again though strictly in the tragic sense.

As against this doctrine of judgement which has its origin in the tragic, Deleuze enunciates a system of thinking which is not merely opposed to judgment but which affirms a certain vital creativity through a confluence of forces which overcomes all forms of subjectivity. He identifies at least three aspects of this life, which plays out a theatre of cruelty rather than a tragic drama.

1. According to Deleuze, unlike the debilitating forms of dreams, the system of cruelty functions like the Dionysian intoxication which always escapes judgement. The dream according to Deleuze, urges us to conform to nothing but shadows, forms which are rendered through judgements. This relation could perhaps be illustrative of the fact that Apollo, the god of both judgement and dream provokes Orestes to kill his mother. The second play *Libation Bearers* is nothing if not an illustration of the effects of a judgement which comes in a dream. The form of life assigned to Orestes,

its organic end of avenging a father and a king not only imprisons Orestes but is the moment of actualization of a judgement. Counter to this we have what Deleuze calls the "dreamless sleep of the insomniac" which characterizes the furies and Clytaemnestra. The avenging spirit of the furies which resonates in Clytaemnestra's own wrath does not belong to the world of dreams but to the sleepless vigilance of the vengeful. The desire of killing Agamemnon is not the illusive proposition of a judgement which erects walls and imprisons life to a code like that of Orestes. Clytaemnestra explicitly says, "No one takes me in visions–senseless dreams" (Ibid., n.d., 113). The desire of killing Agamemnon is where the dream is re-discovered like a lightning bolt that pierces and screams through the night. At the beginning of *Agamemnon* we hear of the "god of fire–rushing fire from Ida!"–the signal fire that pierces the night sky to bring to Clytaemnestra, the insomniac sitting in Argos, the news of the fall of Troy and the return of Agamemnon. This is the moment of the re-discovery of the dream to kill Agamemnon–"the new dream has become the guardian of insomnia" (Deleuze, *Essays Critical and Clinical* 1997, 130). Clytaemnestra does not desire revenge in her sleep, but eternally wakeful, she dreams of vengeance alongside her insomnia. Vengeance functions as intoxication, in both Clytaemnestra and the furies, who are rudely awakened from their sleep by Clytaemnestra's ghost to pursue Orestes. Vengeance is the dream of the insomniac which coexists with the dream of judgement in the trilogy.

2. The second feature that Deleuze indicates to distinguish between a theological doctrine of judgement and a system of cruelty concerns the body. The act of judging and being judged always involves a certain organization of the body, both externally and internally. We can immediately trace this logic back to the problem of liturgy and congregation on the one hand, where bodies assemble and are collectively brought into a debt relation within the polis through

participation in something like theatre. But the organization of bodies are also internal where the tragic hero organizes himself according to the form assigned to his lot. Here we find an *embodiment* of the ethical order which the tragic hero voluntarily assumes. Such embodiment is not without transformation, which though incorporeal affects the body. But such affects do not destroy the body but organizes it in a particular fashion, aligning it to a higher order. Hence the heart and the suffering it endures becomes the sign of such organization which is not without emotions. But here the affects instead of creating a new system of cruelty becomes subject to the higher ethical value. In the organized body of the tragic hero, the organs are never separate, never divided. Hence the frenzy of the brain is mediated through the suffering of the heart. There might not be any available language for such madness but there is always the language of tragic sorrow which comes through lamentation. The embodiment is also a transformation but such that the body is discovered instead of being invented. There is a disclosure of the body in the logic of ethical embodiment, a suppliant body like that of Orestes when after he kills Clytaemnestra and Aegisthus, Pylades gives Orestes a branch of olive and invests him in the robes of Apollo, the wreath and insignia of suppliants to Delphi. But at the same time the body is concealed, the frenzied body of the killer who has just murdered his mother. This simultaneous concealment and discovery of the body is intrinsic to the ethical embodiment of the tragic hero which corresponds to the concealment and discovery of the body-politic as the place of crisis and internal strife which is concealed in order to disclose the peaceful and stable body of the city. But coexisting with this process of embodiment and organization is the notion of a body which is the site of encounter of forces and affects. A body divided, ripped apart and saturated by desire. A site where scattered organs float in indeterminate but violent precision. The body which invents itself *in cruelty.* For

Artaud and for Deleuze this is the idea of a "body without organs" which "is affective, intensive, anarchist body that consists solely of poles, zones, thresholds, and gradients. It is traversed by a powerful, non-organic vitality" (Ibid., n.d., 130).

In the trilogy, we find this idea, in certain corporeal motifs which are separated from the actual organic institution of the body. These are organs which seem to function separately, emanating nothing but the forces and intensities they carry and constitute at the same time. Such that through them cruelty comes into existence for the first time which recalls Artaud's idea that "cruelty is nothing but determination as such, that precise point at which the determined maintains its essential relation with the undetermined" (Deleuze, Difference and Repetition 2005, 37). Blood and brain seems two such examples of "organ without bodies" in the trilogy. Insanity, madness affects these two 'organs' more than anything in the play. Thus the furies scream in *Eumenides* "the reek of human blood–its laughter to my heart" (Aeschylus 1996, 242), or in *Agamemnon*, Cassandra evokes the furies and their orgy of blood in the house of Atreus "Flushed on the blood of men, their spirit grows and none can turn away, their revel breeding in the veins–the furies! They cling to the house for life. They sing, sing of the frenzy that began it all" (Ibid., n.d., 150). The blood with which the system of debt is infinitely displaced and which transforms bodies each time is not merely the connecting element running within the family. The blood which flows in the veins is the symbol of an infinite flux which affects and is affected. It is an intoxicated blood, raging with vengeance which dissolves the body in affects retaining nothing but the intensity which it carries. The blood restores the body to nothing but itself, where wrath and vengeance surges up in a fever, provoking acts without judgement or profit. It is something which is both "victorious and vengeful" (Artaud 1958, 27). Similarly the brain is also an organ which functions outside the body in being affected and affecting in return. As the chorus cries in Agamemnon about Cassandra whose soothsaying power induces nothing but her own madness and destruction "Never to ravel out a hope in time, and the brain is swarming, burning" (Aeschylus 1996, 142) or the chorus accusing Clytaemnestra after her crime–"mad with ambition, shrilling pride–some Fury, crazed with the carnage through your brain" (Ibid., n.d., 163). If blood is the organ for wrath and vengeance, then the brain is the organ for madness and delirium. But such delirium is not excluded by giving it the meaning of a false interpretation of the form of life and the lot assigned to it by the gods. Clytemnestra has not misinterpreted 'the signs' to act on false judgement. Like the hand which acts as another organ without body, she individuates herself as a hand of justice. "By this right hand–a masterpiece of justice". Here we find a "will to power" which is separate and opposed to the doctrine of judgement and the sovereign power of the gods. It defines a body in its *becoming* as a power to be affected and affects in return. But at the same time this "organ without body" is absolutely free to act on its own like the furies who before their transformation into Eumenides, utters "the fates who gave us power made us free" (Ibid., n.d., 246).

3. The third point that Deleuze makes regarding this system of cruelty is its constant combative nature. This system of cruelty which is also a system of justice opposed to judgement combat against judgement everywhere. But the movement is not singularly negative. There is also, and more importantly, the generative feature of the combat. The combat is also *between* the forces that constitute the becoming of this system of cruelty. As Deleuze explains "the combat-against tries to destroy or repel a force, but the combat-between, by contrast tries to take hold of a force in order to make it one's own" (Deleuze, *Essays Critical and Clinical* 1997, 132). At the same time, Deleuze distinguishes this combat against war. War is always a "will to nothingness", a will

to destruction, "a judgement of God that turns destruction into something just" (Ibid., n.d., 133). Combat on the other hand is a powerful non-organic vitality that individuates, creates becomings, it is a centre of metamorphosis.

Nicole Loraux explains how at the end of *Eumenides*, a process takes place where stasis or internal strife is transformed into 'just' war against the enemies. This is perhaps an *inversion* of a system of cruelty being appropriated and made into a condition for a doctrine of judgement to take place. Loraux explains that when Athena, at the end of *Eumenides* compares stasis, or internal strife within the polis with roosters, the metaphor has relevance to a certain desire for combat not for the sake of country or fathers, but for a certain *eros*, desire for combat itself. Loraux notes "there is only one reason left, which is desire, the desire to defeat for the sake of defeating, which the discourse of war usually tries to hide, but which the Greeks detect and condemn in stasis" (Loraux 2006, 36). While stasis is turned into the 'just' war against the enemies of the city, Athena transforms the furies into the Eumenides, protectors of the city, who rather than threaten the city with internal strife would guard it against all outside enemies by waging glorious war to satisfy the desire of the polis. "let our wars rage on abroad, with all their force, to satisfy our powerful lust for fame, but as for the bird that fights at home–my curse on civil war (stasis)" (Aeschylus 1996, 269). Combat for Clytaemnestra is not war but follows this logic of cruelty, which is also a system of justice. Hence it is not a will to nothingness but a will to power. Like Annabella, who Artaud evokes from Ford's *'Tis Pity She's a Whore'*, who acts with "vengeance for vengeance, crime or crime" (Artaud 1958, 28), Clytaemnestra reveals herself in rendering "destiny threat for threat and blow for blow" (Ibid., n.d., 28). She screams "Threaten away! I'll meet you blow for blow" (Aeschylus 1996, 163). But while her combat is against this doctrine of judgement, "But *he*–Name one charge you brought against him then" (Ibid., n.d., 163)her combat is also *between* the forces, where combat does not qualitatively define her conduct but she herself becomes the combat. Clytemnestra expresses the relation of these forces, which are subjugated or subjugates. (After the murder, she quickly changes her position and tries to offer libation and end the dispute but again rises in vengeance literally as a ghost, in *Eumenides*). The spectral presence of Clytaemnestra is nothing but a *symbol* of her numerous becomings, a becoming viper, becoming schylla, where the forces of rage, vengeance, and justice seize the body, making it into a compound, passing into each other and creating a new ensemble. Here we do not have a theatre playing out the "leniency" of tragic guilt which sublates itself through lamentation. It is a concrete conception of an abstract double, a victim who creates a metaphysic of gesture, by holding her right hand out as a "masterpiece of justice" which is perhaps akin to the victims that Artaud evokes, burning at the stake signalling through the flames.

FOOTNOTES

1. At the end of Book X of *The Republic*, Plato remarks on the ancient feud between philosophy and poetry. In order to substantiate the ancient nature of this conflict he offers a number of old proverbs which capture this antagonism. For example, "the bitch that growls and snarls at her master", "a reputation among empty-headed fools", "the crowd of heads that know too much" (Plato, *The Republic* 2007, 351)
2. The Cretan laws which are taken to be the best were given by Minos who was not only a son of Zeus but the only hero to be educated under Zeus' guidance. Minos however is regarded as an enemy of Athens because he had waged victorious war against Athens. So the best legislator is not only an enemy to Athens, but the Athenians have to transcend the laws of Athens to become pupils of an enemy–an act which would appear to be unpatriotic.
3. A historico-ontological perspective would elaborate how a particular ethical structure develops at a particular moment in history which goes through modification adding or subtracting elements, accenting or subduing emphasis, all relative to the particular sequence of history. While a formal understanding of ethics would be seen as universal and always already given as part of a sovereign ontology.

4. We have to take into consideration that this is one way of understanding ethics in the ancient world as a relation of the self to other, while the other distinctly Foucauldian method is to pose it as a problem of the self's relation to itself. The chapter in dealing with the problem of ethics would vacillate between these two methods while clarifying them according to the context. Yet one needs to be aware of the overlapping nature of their use which implies a deep and complex philosophical relation that cannot be properly articulated here.
5. The two translations of the *Life of Solon* have two different words designating this playful nature of using lies. While Aubrey Stewart uses "jest", John Dryden in his translation uses the more 'theatrical' word "play".
6. For a detailed understanding of the oath as a performative utterance refer to Giorgio Agamben's detailed study of the archaeology of oath. (Agamben 2011)
7. In *The Republic*, Book III, Plato would argue that the best ethical act pertaining to moderation, suitable for a citizen is to obey the rules and regulation of the guardians.
8. Agamben proposes an interpretation of the concept of truth telling from a linguistic point of view, identifying it as a performative speech act. This is a key aspect of Agamben's thinking where he tries to re-interpret the relation between subjectivity, truth and law from a certain philosophy of language, particularly influenced by the works of J.L. Austin and Emile Benveniste. See (Agamben 2011)
9. For a detailed analysis on how the problem of catharsis becomes central to create a hierarchic division among the citizen-critic who in leisure contemplates about theatre overcoming its base transformative powers and the lower groups like women, children and slaves who are overwhelmed by such transformative possibilities. See Andrew Ford's "Katharsis and Ancient Problem" (Ford 1995). Also to understand the hierarchic division of Greek society and its relation to an idea of graded sovereignty see the essay "Caste and Debt: The Case of Ancient Greek Liturgies" by Soumyabrata Choudhury (Choudhury 2012).

10. The folding of the self on to itself and its unfolding on to the other is the 'double' movement which informed Foucault's later work on truth and subjectivity as so perceptible pointed out by Deleuze in his book on Foucault. See (Deleuze, *Foucault* 1999)
11. Kierkegaard a more evolved triadic structure of dialectical movement in Hegel caught in thesis-antithesis-synthesis. However a more basic dialect structure of thesis-antithesis which is presented through the form of questions and answers makes Socratic dialectic less systematic and therefore more improvised. This improvisational quality of an earlier dialectical mode is identified by Kierkegaard as the key to Socratic irony. See (Kierkegaard, *The Concept of Irony: With Continual Reference to Socrates* 1989)
12. See Note 6.
13. Here the idea of a substance of theatre denotes the dramatic plays and is not to be confused with the notion of a theatrical substance analysed in the previous section which implies the inseperability of text, performace and performative efficacy of theatre in Ancient Greece.
14. We should not confuse this idea of the mythic as discussed by Schmitt which is mediated through history with the earlier Kierkegaardian notion of the mythic in the context of Socrates and Plato. The later idea of the mythic as interpreted in the earlier section of the chapter is more in terms of a sign which expresses the deployment of forces and is not mediated through representation. While in Schmitt, myth becomes the vehicle of representation of a certain historical knowledge. One might rather draw an interesting distinction between the relation of myth to philosophy against its relation to tragedy along these lines.

CHAPTER 2

"The Artist is Branded While the Art is Extolled"[1]: The Differential Reality of *Persona* and the Question of Theatre in Ancient Rome

Introduction: Two Modes of Inconsistency

When we consider the movement of the concept of theatre from the late Roman antiquity to the time when the 'world became Christian'[2], we cannot but be amazed by the continuities of certain discursive elements. Theatre was a prominent social and cultural reality of the pagan world at the time of this 'transformation'. However, the moral condemnation brought against theatre by early Christian scholars also shared its tonality with some of the pagan moralists. The tendency to disparage theatrical shows for being deceptive, licentious, anti-social, vulgar to the level of being indecent and distastefully crude, continues from Cicero to Augustine. Hence it would not be completely wrong to assume a continuity in the relation between theatre and ethics which was the concern of our last chapter. This relation which we examined in some detail was based not simply on articulating the conditions for a possible censorship of theatre. The relation of theatre to ethics and in turn to philosophy, as we saw, was informed by a complex set of problematizations, fundamentally ethical in nature, which sought to govern "the theatrical substance"[3] in order to *use* it for ethical ends. Such a method was intimately related to logics of moderation and self-mastery. Thus we tried to examine the relation of theatre to ethics from the wider perspective of a relationship between the subject and truth. By the same token we also examined the results of such modes of subjectification where a mastery over the self effectuated a mastery over the other which opened up its political dimension. In a closely determined socio-political space like the 5th and 4th century city state of Athens, such ethical practices had direct political consequences. Therefore, the ethical imperative behind the government of the self and others became the condition for determining the role of theatre in the Greek polis.

When we survey the pagan world of Rome in late antiquity, starting from the end of the Republic till around the end of the 3rd century CE, we discover that many of these elements continue to function as part of the relation between theatre and ethics. On the one hand, theatre is still considered a problem which is fundamentally moral in nature, while on the other hand it continues to be part of liturgical processes, in this case, related to forms of Roman *euergetism* with its complicated socio-cultural and political consequences. And yet the discontinuities too come into prominence. The ethical problematization of theatre is no longer determined by *dialectical* investigation of its relation with the development and government of the self. The examination of the "theatrical substance" is no longer part of the deeper existential and philosophical question of "know thyself" (*gnothi seauton*) which attempted to see if the "theatrical substance" could contribute to the process of giving meaning to the self (which was the primary quest of Socratic philosophy). Now, the problem of theatre seems to have broken out of its philosophical boundaries in order to inhabit a more general discourse related to practices, modes of behavior and logics of social and cultural exchange which defined Roman politics. But this dispersion of the 'theatrical substance', which is now embedded in discourses around ways of living, does articulate itself as a problem revolving around the question of whether it is part of the "Roman persona" or whether it is alien, degenerate and dangerous. Of course, even here we decipher a relation of theatre with ethics when we consider the problem of Roman persona as a constant struggle, caught within a field of discourses comprising of law and culture on the one hand and ethics and politics on the other. At the same time, theatre was already accepted as part of Roman culture and politics in view of its liturgical involvement which in turn, as we shall see, had particular ethical implications.

However, whether it is the Greek case, which we studied before, or the Roman world, as we shall examine in a while, the problem of theatre, though posing a complex ethical challenge, is never viewed as something which is inconsistent with the 'truth' of its historical reality. It would be the argument of this chapter that the significant shift in relation to the problem of theatre from the Greco-Roman to the Christian world was to view theatre as inconsistent with the Christian reality. This inconsistency was both internal to theatre–it was a site of falsity but nonetheless, as Augustine would argue later, a 'true' manifestation of such falsity–and external insofar as theatre was seen as a paradigm for the inconsistency of pagan culture as such. The nature of this 'external' inconsistency as defined by Christianity at the time is as follows: although the phenomenon of theatre is such an integral part of Roman culture and religion, the actors continue to have low status such that, according to Roman law, they are considered below the level of citizens, dishonourable and infamous. As early as the second century, Tertullian identifies this supposed duality in the Roman response towards theatre:

> The characters and actors of such spectacles, the charioteers, stage heroes, boxers and gladiators of which people are so fond, to whom men submit their souls and women even submit their bodies ... are at the same time despised and exalted; they are even condemned to infamy and denied the rights of citizens .... what perversity! People love them and do them harm, they dishonour them and applaud them, the artist is branded while the art is extolled (Balthasar 1988, 95)

This is not an isolated remark induced by an individual point of view on these theatrical shows. By the end of the 4th century, Augustine would pose the same problem. In the *City of God* he writes, "By what consistent principle can dramatic performers be excluded from all right to honour, if drama is included among the honours paid to the gods?" (Edwards 109). We see this argument shared by many of the church fathers of the time, which in a sense can be seen as not simply an innocent attempt to recognize a socio-cultural inconsistency. The entire project of patristic scholars writing against the pagans at the time was to examine, discover and identify elements within pagan culture which would exemplify the nature of the pagan culture and religion as not merely culturally inconsistent, but *ontologically incongruent.* This ontological incoherency would become the condition for their being recognized as perverse and thus sinful in nature. So it was not merely a cultural harangue but a profound onto-theological critique made possible by a method of investigation which included the examination of a phenomenon in order to not simply attribute a meaning to it but to disclose what meaning it holds at the depth of its heart in spite of appearing otherwise. It is this hermeneutic process of investigation which, we would argue, lies at the heart of the early Christian conception of theatre, which becomes responsible on the one hand to abolish theatre as it was understood then, at least theoretically, from all Christian modes of life. On the other hand, as we shall see, it was on the basis of this negation that a new form of theatrical thinking comes into being within Christianity which was called divine/world theatre. At the same time, the liturgical function of theatre also transformed itself from the pagan to the Christian world which inaugurated the fundamental contradiction or 'inconsistency' within Christianity. It is this conflict over the 'truth' of Christianity, sought either through the sacramental participation or through individual faith, in other words, through the mediation of the Church liturgy or through the singular and absolute relation to God, which rearticulates the problem of theatre within Christianity. As we shall try to show in the coming chapters, a new problem of theatre articulating a *new* relation between theatre and religion replaces the earlier concept of theatre determined by its relation to ethics. Although ethical considerations play a crucial role in this new process of conceptualizing theatre, just as religion played an important role in conceptualizing theatre in the Greco-Roman period, it is no longer the focal point of the problem of theatre. The following chapters try to develop the new problem of theatre and its corresponding conceptualization which can be identified by a new mode of theatrical thinking aligned to a new inconsistency opening an inner tension within Christianity.

But before we start examining this new relation between theatre and religion, we need to understand the nature of its earlier relation to ethics and politics in the Roman world against which it established itself. It is primarily to this purpose that we devote this chapter. In order to do so, we need to ask ourselves the following question: if the importance of theatrical shows as an integral part of Roman liturgy appears contradictory to the reaction towards actors, particularly the juridical response to actors in Roman society which exemplified the inconsistency of the entire pagan consciousness for the early church fathers, what was the corresponding response within the Roman world for this supposed discrepancy? In other words, how did the Romans conceive of their ambiguous relation to the theatre internally, in their own discursive practices? What value was attached to theatre such that, to paraphrase Tertullian, the artist was branded while the art was extolled?

Section I

Persona

Laying Out the Problem: A Topological Consideration

The least one can say about the ambiguous status of theatre in the Roman world is that it posed a problem to the Roman way of life. By problem we mean a particular situation where opposing forces gather together as if on a threshold. *Problema,* the Greek word carries the meanings of both protection and projection[4]. Here problem connotes the idea of sheltering something, marking out the boundary within which something is protected, a place which comes 'before' the thing marking it out and even disavowing or hiding it within its folds. But problem also refers to the idea of being thrown or projected outside and transgressing a border or a threshold thereby being discarded or made into something else, elsewhere. So implicit in the idea of a problem is the topological notion of a border, a place whose boundary is marked. In the same semantic spirit, the general idea of a problem being nothing other than an obstacle carries this play of forces–a force which seeks to enclose upon itself or close down its boundaries by making it impossible to pass, thereby marking the place clearly by fortifying it, and an opposing force which wants to overcome the obstacle and open up to an elsewhere. This topological ambiguity marked by a play of opposing forces is something which theatre seems to represent in the Roman world.

We know that in 67 BCE, a tribune of the *plebs* proposed what is known as *les Roscia theatralis* (Roscian law on the theatre) under which the first fourteen rows of seats in the theatre were to be reserved for the senators and equestrians (Edwards 2002, 111). This was later reiterated by Emperor Augustus in his *lex Iulia theatralisi* (Julian law on the theatre). According to Suetonius, Edwards notes, it contained the following provisions:

> The resulting senatorial decree provided that at every public performance, wherever held, the front row of seating must be reserved for senators. At Rome, Augustus would not allow the ambassadors of independent or allied states to sit in the orchestra, when he discovered that some were only freedmen. Besides this, his rules included the separation of soldiers from civilians, the assignment of special seats to married common people, to boys not yet of age and, close by, their tutors; and he refused to allow those in dark cloaks to sit anywhere but the black rows. Also, although until then, men and women had always sat together, Augustus made women sit behind, even at gladiatorial shows. (Ibid., n.d., 112)

On the one hand, this law is a testimony to the class and gender divisions which marked Roman society. But even more than that it illustrates other social divisions based on relations of power and even ethics like the relation between student and tutor. On the other hand, such prescriptions on seating arrangements are also indicative of the topological organization which not only clearly demarcates and makes visible the socio-political hierarchy of Roman society, but also enframes, within the boundary of the theatre space, this hierarchicized *unity* of Roman society itself. In other words, topologically speaking theatre not only marks out and represents the social and political divisions *within* Roman society but symbolizes that society as a unified whole. Theatre in this sense anticipates the desire for making visible and hence strengthening and protecting social and political cohesion where everybody is assigned respective places according to their roles in this hierarchy. The assignment of such roles is dependent on a number of factors based upon *naturalized* power relations which in the final analysis are historically determined. This enframing procedure which marks theatre as a paradigm or an example of Roman society is merely a topological analogy to other instances which mark the importance of theatre in the Roman world. For example, theatre as a place of public opinion or theatre being an integral part of Roman liturgical practices all re-affirm the significance of theatre in Roman society.

Now for our second topological example from a contrary perspective.

It has been pointed out by scholars that unlike Greek cities, there were no permanent theatres in Rome–though plays were performed at least since the middle of the 3rd century BCE–till one was built in 55 BCE by Pompey. This reluctance to build a permanent theatre within the city walls is testified by Tacitus' spiteful remarks while discussing Nero's interest in theatre.

> Some remembered the reproaches made against Pompey by his elders for building a permanent theatre, while previously performances had been held using an improvised stage and auditorium or (in the remoter past) spectators had stood since it was feared that seats would keep them idle for days on end. (Ibid., n.d., 122)

These remarks not only highlight the moral suspicion against theatre but also a reluctance to shelter theatre within city boundaries. Catherine Edwards points out this difference between Greek and Roman cities when it came to the questing of housing a theatre. "In Athens the theatre was situated on the slopes of the Acropolis, within the precincts of the god Dionysius, in the heart of the city. When Pompey's theatre was built in Rome, it was constructed in the Campus Martius, that is, outside the city of Rome" (Ibid., n.d., 122). Theatre was not merely marginalized morally but was thrown outside the border of the city. The two theatres constructed under Emperor Augustus were both outside the *pomerium,* the religious boundary of the city, while Emperor Constantius in an edict described theatre as being "outside the wall". (Ibid., n.d., 123). Clearly we have two opposing topological aspects here which quite literally embodies the *problema* of theatre–as being expressive and protective of the boundary of the Roman society and being projected outside the boundary of the Roman city. This threshold position of theatre becomes all the more obvious when we consider it from a diverse set of perspectives starting from the legal status of actors (as we shall discuss in a while) to the moral attitude towards the actor's voice.

Our hypothesis is that this ambiguity regarding the theatre in Roman society can be traced back to a certain crisis of the relation between the public and private, which in turn points to a problematization of the process of subjectification at work in the Roman world. Without going into the historical details, we can briefly summarize the problem as follows. With the gradual disintegration of the city states due to a number of social, political and economic reasons, the nature of politics underwent a shift from the Hellenistic period onwards reaching its apex in imperial Rome during the first few centuries of the Common Era. The structural transformations that took place politically during this period saw the emergence of a cult of monarchy which was neatly blended with the administrative and municipal functions of the aristocracy. On the other hand, there was also a counter tendency of dissociating oneself from civic activities and socio-political obligations to withdraw into the isolation of the self for definite ethical purposes. Politics was finely balanced between the choice of activity and retreat which is also to say that the relation between politics and ethics was inextricable. As Foucault insightfully notes in this context, "it was a matter of elaborating an ethics that enabled one to constitute oneself as an ethical subject with respect to these social, civic and political activities, in the different forms they might take and at whatever distance one remained from them" (Foucault 1990, 94). While public obligations and popular imagination maintained a deep relation to theatre, personal attitudes particularly as part of an ethical imperative sought to dissociate oneself from the clamour of such popular pursuits in search of an inner citadel. But almost inevitably these two moments not only struggled with each other giving rise to what we call the problem of theatre in Roman society, most often they became inextricably entangled with each other. At such moments there was nothing less than a theatricalization of one's inner self while on other occasions a spectacular display of public approbation was necessary to seek individual virtue.

Development of the Problem: *Romanitas*

When we talk of an inconsistency which informed the discursive practices of the Roman world what exactly are we hinting at? There was a clear discrepancy between how theatre actors were socially and legally maltreated on the one hand, and on the other hand, the importance of the phenomenon of theatre and its cultural, social and political efficacy. But if we look more closely, we can narrow down this ambiguity to two general domains: the domain of action and the domain of being and the intricate and complex relation between the two.

Certain scholars, both modern and ancient, consider the Roman ambivalence towards theatre as being induced by its foreign origin. Among Roman scholars, the alien root of theatre was given as the basis for its un-Romanness. Theatre was considered as something imported from outside, hence not belonging to the 'persona' of being Roman. Catherine Edwards points out that it is this motivation that prompts Livy to explain the beginnings of the theatre in the following way:

> Among other efforts to placate the angry gods, they are said to have instituted dramatic entertainments. This was a new departure for a warlike people, whose only spectacles had been those of the circus; but indeed, it began in a small way, as most

> things do, and besides was imported from abroad. Without singing, without imitating the action of singers, players who had been brought in from Etruria danced to the music of the flautist and performed graceful movements in the Tuscan manner (Edwards 2002, 100).

We find variations of this 'theory' of Etruscan origin of theatre articulated in many later scholars of antiquity, both pagan and Christian, like Valerius Maximus, Tacitus, Tertullian and Augustine. But, as we shall see later, the Christian intention for finding such a theory of origin of pagan theatrical practices was motivated by completely different reasons, even inverse ones, though they frequently cite Roman scholars like Livy and Varro[5]. However, for the Roman scholars, the alien nature of the origin of theatre was rather induced by the urge to define the contours of the figure of the Roman citizen. The deeper ethico-political and juridical implications of this discourse become clearer when we consider the way theatre was marked as a Greek cultural practice as distinct from its Roman status. Edward cites from Cornelius Nepos when in the preface to his *Lives* he marks out some of the fundamental contrasts between Greek and Roman Culture:

> Almost everywhere in Greece, it was thought a high honour to be proclaimed victor at Olympia. Even to appear on the stage and exhibit oneself to the people was never regarded by those nations as something to be ashamed of. Among us, however, all those acts are regarded as disgraceful or base and inconsistent with respectability. (Ibid., n.d., 98)

Again we have a distinction made between Roman respectability (*dignitas*) which was synonymous with being Roman (*romanitas*), and the theatrical practices which according to Nepos, are essential attributes of a different culture, namely Greek. Of course, the relation of Roman identity with Greek culture is fraught with contradictions. On the one hand, Greek practice of philosophy and literature was held in high esteem, among the Roman elite as a mark of their superiority. But at the same time, this culture was denounced by another group of Roman statesmen, literati and philosophers for unleashing moral degeneracy upon the Romans by making them too 'cultured, meek and passive' while true Roman nature dictates one to be energetic, virile and active. Thus, Cicero, though praising the high philosophic value of the Platonic canon, would nonetheless evoke Roman figures (sometimes fictive) in his dialogues as models for behaviour. Idealized Roman forefathers not only gave authority to the moral precepts but also helped to distinguish the Roman spirit of praxis against the Greek spirit of theorization. In *Pro Caelio,* Cicero categorically observes that though achieving success and brilliance in their speech and writing[6], the Greeks fell short of actualizing this possibility in their actions—unlike the Romans.

The Ethics of Praxis

This logic of action which, according to Cicero, was the distinguishing feature of being Roman would be elevated to the status of being a 'natural' attribute of the Roman persona. Thus, action would become an inescapable feature of being and praxis would gain an ethical status while its absence or falsification would tantamount to immorality. This was the complex setting in which the problem of theatre surfaces in the Roman world. The question of action was implicit in much of the moral disapproval against theatre. The sexual allure of actors attributed to their effeminate nature was also interpreted as passivity which overturned the distinct gender roles ascribed to men and women in Roman society as being active and passive respectively. Certain moralists would condemn the theatre as a place of idleness where the degenerate elite would indulge their habits of indolence and laziness. Perhaps most interestingly, it was the nature of the action displayed on stage which was brought under scrutiny. Hence comedy, particularly the comic mime gained considerable notoriety in late antiquity. Catherine Edwards notes: "It is comedy of which Horace is most scornful in his attack on Roman Drama. Juvenal is horrified by the appearance of a Roman noble in a farce, where his antics will be a source of amusement to the common people." (Ibid., n.d., 106) Edwards goes on to correctly remark that the elite had to distinguish itself according to its own manners and cultural preferences. But if we examine this problem more deeply, we find that the elite's reaction to comedy was not simply a question of aesthetic taste and cultural snobbery. The problem with comedy was on the one hand an offshoot of an ironic tendency of Roman literati to disparage spectacle while belonging to a culture of spectacles. This seemingly paradoxical tendency will be discussed later. What we are more interested in at the moment is the connection between the problem of laughter and the more general problem of persona. Comedy could easily be disparaged because the actions it portrayed were identifiable with the *levitas* of the players. But when it came to serious theatre, particularly tragedy (though tragic plays were not nearly as popular or important as they were in the city states), the response becomes more and more ambiguous. "Seneca suggested there was little difference between those who held power in real life and those who played the part of rulers on stage" (Ibid., n.d., 127).While Cicero points to the similarity between oration and acting, though cautiously maintaining their difference, Quintilian, in his treatise on education of the orator, repeatedly emphasizes that the good orator should proceed with extreme caution so that he does not resemble the actor. It is in this domain of 'serious' acting, where ambiguity reigned supreme, that we find some interesting overlaps. We know that actors faced a string of legal disabilities ranging from social ostracism to legal disadvantages in Roman antiquity. They were legally branded as *infames*, along with gladiators, slaves and prostitutes who could be beaten up or even killed under extraordinary situations with impunity. We shall return to this legal question in a while. But as Catherine Edward points out from Livy's history, it seems that the actors of the Atellan drama were exceptions to these disabilities. "Those who performed in this form of drama, he claims (Livy), were the only performers in *artes ludicrae* not to be subject to legal disability" (Ibid., n.d., 126). The reason for this exception seems to originate from the fact that Atellan plays were viewed as a distinctly Roman kind of theatre which is described by Valerius Maximus as *sever or* stern. We find a similar approval of the tragic actor

Aesopus by Cicero in *De Officiis*, where he affirms that Aesopus (who Cicero notes was not only an actor but a great supporter of the senatorial party *both on and off the stage)* could make manifest the genius of a great dramatist not only by his art but also by his *dolor* or grave demeanour. (Hence he did not often take the role of Ajax because it required certain strenuous exertions unbecoming of his serious demeanour). Now, if we return to the exceptional status of the Atellan actors, we find another interesting observation made by the grammarian Festus. Festus observes that the actors of the Atellan plays were the only ones permitted to keep their masks on throughout the performance. Now we know from Livy's account that the Atellan actors were the only ones allowed to become soldiers and maintain certain social dignity and juridical advantage. Hence, the usual implication of Festus' comment as endorsed by Edwards is that "masks were seen as protecting the performer's social status by concealing his identity." We, however, will follow a different trajectory of argument and speculate that on the contrary, the wearing of masks (*prosopon*) by the only category of actors whose actions were accepted as severe or stern enough to be called Roman is related to a far more complex relation. This relation which existed between persona as an ethical category of determining conduct and a juridical category of identifying the *paterfamillia*, has to be examined in the light of a growing tension within the senatorial class, particularly between the *patres auctores* (the group of senators who belonged to the consular family) as opposed to the *patres conscripti* (the conscripted fathers/senators who like Cicero did not belong to the consular family but rose to the senatorial class). We will examine this relation in a while. Suffice it to say here that the persona of being Roman was not always seen as 'natural' (metonymic) to oneself but treated like a *prosopon*, (the Greek origin of the Latin term 'persona' meaning mask) external to oneself like a mask (metaphoric) where one needs to play the role 'correctly' which is assigned to oneself by circumstances. To play one's role correctly in this ethical context implied a life of praxis governed by certain principles determined by reason and good judgement.

From Ethics to Rhetoric

The problem of defining 'authentic' action which would become a genuine attribute of a persona was a crucial task of Roman thinking while at the same time action also had to be 'proper' to one's persona. To align one's action or conduct to one's persona was the quintessential ethical problem, while to determine which action is authentic and which is merely an imitation was an ontological quest. Thus, Cicero could on the one hand try to align philosophy with rhetoric while on the other hand, distinguish rhetoric from acting arguing that the former is a true guarantor of actions, particularly ethical actions. Again and again, Cicero returns to the parallelism of the profession of acting to the orator's profession. Nevertheless he clearly maintains their distinction insofar as the actor is concerned who is engaged with reproducing 'verita'–truths of life in the likeness of life. In the final analysis such reproduction is only an imitation. While the orator is immediately concerned with the actual life of courts thus attaining something more: the force of truth in itself. The action of the orator in terms of its success or failure to persuade the jury is merely its legal goal. The profession of the orator serves something beyond its success or failure to persuade in a court of law. It is an action which carries its own authority in being true. It is thus an end in itself while the actor's action is a mere imitation of truth. The orator needs much of the technique of the actor, the gestures and grace of the actor, but his goal lies not in acting out that which is made by the poet but taking the responsibility for disclosing the truth, taking it upon himself the responsibility of another life. The orator who carries the authority of truth, is burdened by it while the actor merely translates the fictional emotions of the character onto the stage as an imitation of truth. Therefore, Cicero speaks of actors as '*veritatis impious actores*' but of orators as '*imitatores veritatis*'[7]. So a culture of rhetoric, ironically inspired by both philosophy and theatre would nonetheless be identified with neither because it would refuse to be simply a potential for reality (philosophy) or an imitation of actuality (theatre).

Ethics and its political manifestation in rhetoric comprised 'a culture of praxis' which would challenge but also negotiate with existent juridical and political structures. The problem of immorality can be traced to this re-definition of the Roman persona as not determined exclusively by property or ancestry but by one's actions. Persona was, as we shall see later, not simply a juridical and political category but also an ethical one which was desperately trying to seek political legitimacy. Rhetoric was perhaps the techne *per excellence by* which it manifested itself. The challenge to ancestry and patria as constitutive features of the senatorial class by such statesman philosophers like Cicero was perhaps part of this culture of praxis where they sought to define the persona of being Roman as not determined by one's class but by one's actions.

The Question of Ethics Reconsidered

Cicero begins the fifth book of his treatise on the ideal state (*De Republica*) with a quotation from *Ennius*, regarded as the first Latin poet whose composition dates back to the early second century BCE: "*Moribus antiquis res stat Romana virisque*", "The Roman state is built on ancient mores and on men". Ancient mores (morals or customs) and Roman men together form the foundation of the *res Romana* (Romanness). Of course, one could easily distinguish in this definition the complicity of the male figure whose self-mastery announces his superiority over others with his wealthy status, military achievements and elite ancestral roots. In most of the cases the self-regulation and virtuous behaviour were naturally assumed to belong to the republican elite. *Dignitas* or *Romanitas* were, to a large extent, the prerogative of aristocracy in the public domain and the *pater* or father in the private domain. The eldest male ascendant in the family, the paterfamilias was taken as the source of moral and legal authority. We will come to the legal issue in a while. Suffice to say here that Romanness, ethical behaviour and material wealth, social status and familial ancestry went together in the Roman world.

Yet there was a tendency among the philosophers, particularly the stoics, to define virtue not from the point of view of external factors like social and political markers but from one's relation to oneself. We are indebted to Michael Foucault to underline this trajectory of Hellenistic and Roman thinking. This line of thinking, unlike traditional scholarship focusing on the Roman world as the source of the legal heritage of the West, argued about the complex relations of such 'culture of the self' to a legal and political reality. In his *History of Sexuality Vol 3: The Care of the Self,* Foucault argues that the dissolution of the city states and the breaking up of the Hellenic world into monarchies and later the municipalisation of Rome, both under the Republic and later the empire, did not obliterate the relation of the government of the self and others but introduced in it a complex set of changes. Unlike an ethics of self-mastery directly translated into a mastery over the other which dictated the relation of ethics with politics in the Greek city state, Hellenic and later Roman ethics, according to Foucault, reflected a crisis of subjectification which gave rise to a number of complex strategies and modifications in the subject's relation to truth. However Roman law, as we shall see later, perpetuated and tried to generalize action by making law immanent to life while inducing a crisis of subjectivity which was responsible for ethics to be placed in a relation to politics and law. As a result, ethics simultaneously tried to distance itself from the public sphere while being keen on gaining legal and public legitimacy. It is this double movement of truth seeking legitimacy in itself, in its very coming into being, but also seeking legitimacy elsewhere (like in the given juridical or political order) which perhaps best captures the problem of persona and its double meaning of being a face and a mask.

Relativization of Power: The Fold

On one hand, we have the various strategies of relativization which made one's action, even political action independent of one's status and a direct consequence of a personal act of choice. Foucault writes citing Plutarch that in his treatise where he addresses Menemachus, Plutarch condemns the attitude that would make politics into an occasional activity and does not treat it as a necessary consequence of a status. This tendency is also reflected in the Ciceronian definition of persona in *De Officiis* as an ethical category not simply determined by one's necessary conditions but through a complex relation of choices and circumstances. We will return to this point in a while. Coming back to the relativization of the exercise of power in Plutarch, Foucault writes:

> One must not, he (Plutarch) says, regard political activity as a sort of pastime (schole) in which one would engage because one has nothing else to do and because circumstances are favourable, only to abandon it when difficulties arise. Politics is "a life" and a "practice" (bioskai praxis). But one cannot devote oneself to it except by a free and deliberate choice. (here Plutarch employs the technical expression of the Stoics: proairesis) And this choice must be based on judgement and reason (krisiskai logos) (Foucault 1990, 87)

At the same time the efficacy of one's action is relative in so far as its political power is concerned. Authority is always relative because one is always governing and governed at the same time. Hence it is not supreme authority (*imperium*) but the delegated power of a *procuration*, the limits of which are always determined, that Seneca advises Lucilius to exercise while enjoying the pleasures (*delectare*) of leisure. As we shall see later, *imperium* is not the source of authority in Roman law but *actoritas* which manages to intensify and homogenize this heterogeneous relativity of power to such a degree that the entire field of relations can no longer function in its *different modes of intensities* but has to rely on a maximal point which is that of a state of exception. That this authority (*actoritus*) in Roman private and public law remained with the father (*pater*) re-establishes the logic of status and *persona* back into the domain of politics. The problem of the actor, we would argue, counter-effectuates another heterogeneous logic into this effort to homogenize the relativity of power. But all that for a later discussion. We are now concerned with the different modalities of power and its relation to ethics defined as the self's relation to itself.

Foucault identifies two other modalities of the relation of ethics to politics in the Roman context. Individual actions and conduct, governed by a certain rational principle become the condition for governing others not simply because self-mastery anticipates mastery over others, but because good government from a managerial and administrative point of view of curtailing excesses is conditioned by the administration of the self and its actions when confronted by the excesses and vicissitudes of life. Moreover, like the relativization of power, this administrative logic of ethics is also not determined by one's legal and social persona but applicable to all according to their capacity to apply the principles of reason. Thus Seneca observed, "Each man acquires his character for himself, but accident assigns his duties" (Ibid., n.d., 93). This leads us to the third modality of the relation between ethics and politics where personal destiny was involved. Because in politics a crisis might befall any time which could reverse the relations of power, the ethical subject is required to maintain a limited degree of intensity of relation with the public domain. In other words, one should not be over ambitious such that one is ruined if there is a reversal of fortune. This moderation of one's political ambition actually comprises an ethical practice which is also associated with a certain idea of freedom. Foucault notes:

> And if the occasion presents itself, it is good to withdraw from these activities (political) when they become disturbing and prevent one from attending to oneself. If misfortune strikes, if one falls from favour and is exiled, one ought to tell oneself–this is the advice Plutarch addresses no doubt to the same Menemachus whom he had encouraged, several years before to enter politics "by free choice"–that one is finally free from obedience to government, from liturgies that are too costly, from services to render, from ambassadorial missions to accomplish, and from taxes to pay (Ibid., n.d., 93).

Of course, such lines of flight which encapsulate the subjectivation of the free man exercising his ethical choice in terms of the self's relation to itself in every mode of life including politics, can be re-appropriated by institutionalized hierarchy of power. This is what Deleuze anticipates as the fate of the fold, which again is unfolded "and the subjectivation of the free man is transformed into subjection" (Deleuze 1999, 103)[8]. Again ethics (and more generally philosophy) is brought into the realm of law and the ethical definition of persona is unfolded in the homogenized field of juridical power. Here ethical action no longer seeks detachment but legitimacy of being approved as the true criteria for being Roman. The culture of praxis cannot simply remain a culture but has to become the legitimate culture of the Romans. It is this re-manifestation of the folded ethical persona in the public and legal domain that we see in Cicero and his championing of sceptic philosophy.

Folds Unfolding: Socrates to Cicero

One can already sense that there is a certain "pedestrianism", a certain utilitarian logic to Cicero. The infinite and interior art of questioning in order to empty out existence, where the interlocutor not only participates externally in the act but internalizes it in order to question his own self, is displaced or rather externalized into the art of question and answer which leads to speech and rhetoric in order to standardize a class of subjects who would now be prepared to participate in the affairs of the state wearing the mask of reason and virtue. The dialogue thus becomes a tool, the most useful and rational as far as philosophic methods are concerned, in order to paint the glorifying image of philosophy itself as the noblest and highest of all activities, the "most honourable delight of leisure" (Cicero 1993, 413). It is this persona of the philosopher, as the figure of wisdom and hence superior to all, that becomes the heart of the problem in Cicero, even if the wisdom is the suspension of all wisdom. Cicero remarks in Book I of *Academica*:

> The method of discussion pursued by Socrates in almost all the dialogues so diversely and so fully recorded by his hearers is to affirm nothing himself but to refute others, to assert that he knows nothing except the fact of his own ignorance, and that he *surpassed all other people* in that they think they know things that they do not know but he himself thinks he knows nothing, and that he believed this to have been the reason why Apollo declared him to be the wisest of all men, because all wisdom consists solely in not thinking that you know what you do not know. (Ibid., n.d., 425)

Whereas in Socrates, the absence of wisdom makes one wise *minimally,* which is what human wisdom amounts to[9], in Cicero this fragile interiority of a realization which makes one wise has to be given a face, a personality quite distinct from others in its glory and superiority. In Socrates we have the expression of a personality which in being the location of truth is also and immediately the location of simulation because it exposes the emptiness of all faces, of all personalities–be it the orator, or the poet or the craftsman. What Socrates shows, in hollowing out all faces, all personalities, is the human and finite predicament of having no knowledge, possessing no truth except the minimal knowledge of this negation. If we follow Kierkegaard's concept of irony as negation of the phenomenal world in Socrates, then what Socrates shows through such negation is perhaps this: that behind all appearance (be that of the orator or the poet, of *Lycon* or *Meletus*) is hidden nothing but the emptiness of all such appearance[10]. It is not simply that the face of the poet or the craftsman hides some other truth about their existence. But insofar as they all fall into the same abyss of the emptiness behind their respective faces (which is also their mask) they bring into the phenomenal world nothing but their resemblance to each other, their simulations of each other which include Socrates himself. This is the infinite interior movement of the self, caught in irony vis-a-vis the phenomenal world, which minimally realizes itself through this infinite interior dialectics.

In Cicero we find no such interiorization of truth which leads to anonymity. What we find is the public display of this very subjective decision of acknowledging that one does not know. But even this exposition is not done nakedly, never absolutely. (The nature of Ciceronian decision is that it has to be mediated or masked in order to make it more utilitarian. It is here, as we shall see in the following section that the concept of probability comes in). The exposition thus transforms itself into a *value* in the name of the truth which till now was infinite but accessible to all. The figure of the philosopher now comes into the public stage as the face, the *persona* who possesses the truth and who controls it. Thus, the finite personality of the philosopher in possessing truth gives it a value which can now be distributed according to the order of the state and the hierarchy and status of personas. Thus, the elite erstwhile statesman possess more wisdom than the statesman immersed in public life though he, in his turn, possesses more truth than the ordinary citizen and so on and so forth. This is the *politics* of the persona which Cicero explains in the first book of *De Officiis*[11]. The problem of persona as an ethical problem of the self's relation to itself, of how best to conduct oneself so that one comes into being or makes oneself manifest as an ethical subject is now concerned with taking possession of the face, of making it into an attribute which could be legitimized as true.

Interestingly, by the same token of assigning a value to it, the infinite interiority of the Socratic truth is made finite, pedestrian. If for Socrates the task of the philosopher was to expose the truth in spite of himself, in which all, including the figure of the philosopher himself, would be anonymously dissolved, for Cicero the task of the philosopher seems to turn truth into "his own proper truth"(Agamben, *Means Without Ends* 1996, 97). A value which, when assigned to truth, which till now was free and accessible to all, is then accumulated in images, personas of different degrees and levels of truth accessible to each according to his persona but always jealously guarded by the highest of all personas , which is that of the philosopher. It is this externalization of an interior movement, to give a recognizable face to the anonymous figure of the philosopher which, we would argue informs the nature of Sceptic philosophy itself.

Two 'movements' are thus at work here in the context of Ciceronian appropriation of Socratic dialogues.

1. An exteriorization and exposition of the Socratic interior movement of irony (through negation) in order to make such philosophical 'movement' useful for the state. This makes the Ciceronian 'movement' *mimic* the Socratic movement but also makes an infinite interior movement finite by assigning a value to it. This is the "pedestrianism" of Cicero which this section has tried to demonstrate.

2. The concept of probability is devised in order to disseminate and make philosophy useful for the public, while maintaining the value of wisdom and truth ascribed to it in the name of negation of the phenomenal world. On one hand, this disseminates wisdom while on the other hand, it dissimulates wisdom in order to retain the value ascribed to the *persona* of the philosopher who acknowledges his ignorance

A Further Elaboration of the Problem: Folding Back and Unfolding Again

In his book on epistemology, titled *Academica*, Cicero explains the problem of dogmatic knowledge which informed the peculiar state of philosophy in his time. As Foley notes, "Cicero had competition: unlike Plato he had to contend with many well-developed and well known schools of thought, some of them promoting themselves as the true heirs of the Socratic legacy"(P. Foley 1999). *Academica* is thus structured as a dialogue between the representatives of these 'decadent' forms of philosophy and his own conviction that it is only through the philosophy of the New Academy which he championed that the classical model of Socrates and Plato could be saved. Here his main opponents were the Stoics as represented by Varro and Lucullus in Book I and Book II respectively.

The Stoic School, presumably founded by Zeno, claimed to be a modification and not a rejection of the philosophy begun by Socrates. The fundamental critique of the sceptics against this school was in the domain of knowledge or logics, which then led to further criticism regarding physics and ethics, the two higher domains of philosophy in the classical world. This criticism came in view of the Stoic idea of sense perceptions or *catalepsies*. According to the changes made by Zeno in the domain of Logic, Cicero informs us, sensation was triggered by a combined operation of some sort of impact offered from outside which are received by the senses, termed *phantasia* (presentations), conjoined with the act of mental assent or *syncatathesis* which he made out to reside within us and is thus a voluntary act. This process of reception and approval of the phenomenal world was jointly called *Catalepton* or "mental grasp". It literally translates to the idea of grasping or gripping between the hands an object whose existence cannot be refuted. The question of assent is crucial here because in order for free presentations or *phantasia* to become 'manifestations' or truthful sense-presentations they have to naturally offer themselves for approval or assent. Zeno further elaborates, again according to Cicero, that true things are naturally graspable, where the truth is inscribed or marked into the object. "They are recognized by a mark that belongs specially to what is true and is not common to the true and the false." (Cicero 1993, 511) Here the relation between reason and *catalepton* is negative, where reason cannot remove the truth of what is naturally grasped and thus approved by the senses. It is against this idea of sense-presentation embodied in the idea of *catalepton* that Cicero forwards the concept of probability. The sceptic, Cicero asserts repeatedly, is not against the idea of truth. Rather the sceptic considers himself the most vigilant guardian of truth because he is guided by reason and not authority. And it is this reason which makes him doubt the nature of appearances *as such,* both true and false. And since there is always the possibility that false sensations can appear exactly identical to true sensations, all perception which is based upon the inherent quality of a sensation which offers itself for approval, has to be rejected. And since no perception is possible, sense-presentations can only be judged, according to true reason, on the basis of their appearances only partially. This leads 'the wise man to withhold assent' which the sceptics expressed through the doctrine of *epoche.* But to 'withhold assent' does not lead to inactivity and confusion of duty, which the stoics accuse the sceptics of. Rather, according to Cicero, it leads to proper action without judgement being clouded by dogmatism. According to Cicero, the Academics hold that there are dissimilarities between things such that some of them seem probable while others do not; but this is not adequate ground for saying some things can be absolutely perceived and others cannot, because many false objects are probable but nothing false can be perceived and known. Thus Cicero writes:

> The 'wise man withholds assent' is used in two ways, one when the meaning is that he gives absolute assent to no presentation at all, the other when he restrains himself from replying so as to convey approval or disapproval of something, with the consequence that he neither makes a negation nor an affirmation; and that this being so, he holds the one plan in theory, so that he never assents, but the other in practice, so that he is guided by probability, and whenever this confronts him or is wanting he can answer 'yes' or 'no' accordingly (Ibid., n.d., 601).

On the one hand such a strategy of 'withholding assent' can be seen as the perfect modality of being which reveals a dimension of subjectivity derived from power and knowledge without being dependent on them. If such a probabilistic theory of knowledge is applied to form a relation of self to itself, then we have a mode of self-mastery which will always keep the politics of persona at a distance both participating in the face and yet not being subjected by it because of its (probabilistic theory of knowledge) refusal to possess it (persona). The relation with others will in this case always have the double gesture of the self's relation to itself. Every decision in the external world would also be an internal affirmation of an impossibility to decide. The necessary rules of knowledge and power would empty themselves within the self, so that an empty double would be created which would detach itself from every obligation, every principle of knowledge and power but nonetheless be governed by 'facultative rules' which are independent from all forms of social and juridical codification. In this sense, probability would provide the necessary epistemological tool for an 'aesthetic existence', a face whose coming into being would be free from the subjection of persona. The problem of persona as an ethical question *par excellence* that Cicero elaborates in *De Officiis* could be understood from this point of view as not a question of appearance or making oneself manifest in terms of one's definite and necessary attributes but in terms of *becoming detached* from the necessary logics of appearance. Stoic ethical doctrine from which, according to De Lacy, Cicero draws his concept of the *persona* in the first book of *De Officiis* differentiates four conditions which need to be considered when we talk of personae. 1. The nature we share with all human beings. 2. Our individual natures. 3. The persona arising from circumstances which are imposed onto us by chance and time and 4. Those which pertain to our choices resulting from the judgement arising from the kind of life we wish to live. Thus, we see that as an ethical doctrine, Cicero does not evoke a theory of identity. It is not simply a question of possessing the role which is assignéd to one under the *debt* of playing it perfectly. It is never one persona, but personae, a multiplicity of masks, some natural, others circumstantial, whose ultimate function is to determine the modality of one's existence according to the free exercise of reason. Persona in this sense is not a definite and necessary attribute, it is not simply one's *ergon*, his distinctive nature, but the force of truth which raises the face hidden beneath the mask to come to the surface so that nothing is left of the face and yet it is nothing but the face which is also the mask. It is the becoming mask of the face which has the force to detach itself from the codes and regulations of knowledge and power and yet be regulated and governed by the rules of ethics. This is the ethical possibility of a fold arising out of a concept of persona which is quickly unfolded and reabsorbed into the homogeneous field of power.

Hence, on the other hand, what such a distinction does to the concept of knowledge is to first and foremost de-radicalize the dialectical intensity of negation. This dilution of the intensity of negation still functions by opposing categories (probable and not probable), hence *mimics* the infinite interior dialectic of Socratic dialogues. However it is no longer able to produce a concept of irony which hollows out the phenomenal world through a conception of absolute negation. And hence hierarchies are now established in the world of phenomenal knowledge, categories on the basis of which one can take finite decisions in the finite realm of appearances. Cicero writes: "Thus he is not afraid lest he may appear to throw everything into confusion and make everything uncertain" (Ibid., n.d., 609)[12]. But according to Socrates, it is exactly this uncertainty which makes the philosopher wise because he can put anything and everything under his ironic vision, questioning and dismantling the established order of things within the state, so that he can fulfil a higher duty outside the state, which is the private or subjective obligation to serve truth and justice. This distinction of the private from the public is crucial to Socrates whose teachings are always a private affair[13], a pedagogy which is not allied to the state. Thus the Socratic sense of duty is different from, the Ciceronian sense. Cicero further writes:

> For if a question is put to him about duty or about a number of other matters in which practice has made him an expert, he would not reply in the same way as he would if questioned as to whether the number of the stars is even or odd. And say that he did not know. For in things uncertain there is nothing probable, but in things where there is probability the wise man will not be at a loss either what to do or what to answer (Ibid., n.d., 610).

From the political (public) perspective the Ciceronian *persona* of the wise man is based on two fundamental principles. That in matters of public affairs that correspond to matters regarding the state he will be dutiful according to the distribution of his senses, judging and affirming according to the demands of the phenomenal world. This is his public persona which is immediately mediated by his modesty of not assenting to anything, of affirming that he does not know. This is what makes him wise because he now privately possesses the truth which is the condition of possibility of all his worldly freedom of judgement. The theory of probability not only mediates this state of public practice of philosophy with the realm of private practice of theory but also gives a certain value to theory which makes it superior to practice. To dissimulate truth through a concept of probability is also to give truth the value it requires in order to have the scholastic status it requires in Roman society to become an effective political tool. With Cicero we see the emergence of a culture of praxis which nonetheless depends on the value of theory to give it its desired efficacy. At the same time, it succumbs to the temptation of legitimizing truth such that one can legitimately claim to be a master of truth. For Cicero, the struggle between the persona of the statesman-rhetorician and the persona of the philosopher attest to nothing but this struggle.

Section II

Liturgy

According to scholars one of the major shifts in the theatre of late antiquity was the replacement of tragedy with pantomime. Though the majority of the plots still came from mythology, most scholars seem to believe tragic plays were no longer staged in their entirety. Rather the most famous scenes, which also happened to be the most sensational ones–Thyestes banqueting on his own children or Heracles butchering his family–were simply performed as dramatic interludes. Such sensationalism prevailed even when it came to comedy where apart from the predominance of a certain mythological burlesque, a certain burlesque of Christianity seems to have been quite popular. Blake Leyerle informs us, for example, that among the favourite topics related to Christianity seized upon by the comic stage of late antiquity was the humorous representation of the baptismal rite, where an actor would be dipped in a tub in order to emerge proclaiming his transformation[14]. But such a caricature of Christian processes of transformation and individuation did not prevent this theatre to participate in modes of cultural and political subjectification in the late antique world of Rome. Hence the predominance of mythological plots did not merely serve to cater to the popular desire for sensationalism, but such spectacular form of display was equally effective to produce a popular pedagogy of a truly democratic nature. Libanius, we learn from Leyerle, who was otherwise not very fond of theatre speaks of this pedagogical advantage of pantomime:

> When the tribe of tragic poets had been confined [to the schools]...some god out of pity for the ignorance of the masses, introduced the dance instead, as a way to teach the multitude about the deeds of the old, with the result that now even a goldsmith can come off not half badly in an argument with someone from the academy concerning the house of Priam and Laius (Leyerle 2001, 27).

Though perhaps tinged with a subtle ambiguity bordering on sarcasm, Libanius' remarks express a certain spirit of equality behind such widespread though superficial dissemination of popular knowledge. Theatre was a site for a collective transformation and subjectification. This was made evident most conspicuously by its political function of being an integral part of such a socio-economic practice as that of Roman *euergetism*. We know from such seminal works in this field as that of Paul Veyne[15], that in the final analysis in a society like that of Rome where exchange of gifts and the value attached to such an gift-economy was a crucial socio-political operation, *euergetism* was simply "private liberality for public benefit" (Veyne, *Bread and Circuses* 1990, 10). The construction of theatres and the arrangement of theatrical shows as part of public festivals were in turn part of such civic benefit. Therefore it is interesting to approach the question of theatre in Roman society from the point of view of its political function. According to Veyne, the practice of *euergetism* as part of public service or liturgy was curiously informed by a series of overlapping contradictions. Being a civic duty, the individual, almost always the elite wealthy citizen belonging to the senatorial or equestrian class but also at times the notables who made up the municipal nobility, had to lavishly expend for public benefit like the construction of a public bath or the building of an amphitheatre or organizing a public festival like the Saturnalia. But this civic responsibility, as Veyne points out, was at times a voluntary participation on part of the notables, where the *euergesiai* were provided by certain internal moral exigencies. While at other times the responsibility was morally or even legally obligatory, for example, when one of them was elected to a public 'honour' like that of a municipal magistracy. This oscillation between the voluntary and mandatory nature of such a liturgical practice corresponded to the opposing but surely overlapping presence of a political culture of competition and collective participation on the one hand, while on the other hand, the personal sentiments of moral debt to the society and a spirit of self-sacrifice.

In a society where the political primacy of the cult of the monarchy was curiously juxtaposed with the emperor's public display of power and munificence and his private cultivation of an ethical life which would give him the moral strength to perform his duties, the relation between the public and private was complex to say the least. But this relativization of the contradiction between the public and private is not merely restricted to a tension between the idea of a public *persona* which bears down upon oneself with the weight of a mask that one has to maintain socially and even legally and a private *persona* so to speak, a mask which is like a prosthesis and which like ones clothing is both a style and a way of protecting the body from the outside. Similarly, the ethical persona, constructed in the leisure of a private life is both a cultivation of the self and a process of stylizing the soul but it also protects the soul from the violent clamour of an outside world. In this sense it serves as a mask which helps the face to withdraw into itself while disavowing and thereby protecting it from the vicissitudes of an outside world.

When it comes to the problem of theatre this relation between the public and private does not always take the form of such a synthetic-dissociation where *at times* private pursuits of ethical substance delineates possible lines of flight from the din of public power. In the case of theatre, more often than not collective imagination and personal glory go together to re-vitalize the machines of power. For example, Veyne informs us that one of the crucial features of such public benefit was to get rid of all forms of discrimination when it came to enjoying the fruits of such benefits. As Veyne writes, "If people have to fight to get a seat on the tiers of an amphitheatre which is too small, that means the *euergetes* has not done all he should have: the consumption of these benefits by each individual should not entail a diminutive consumption by others" (Ibid., n.d., 12). Clearly a gesture[16] of equality informs the congregation of bodies in a theatre, bodies which collectively participate in enjoying a common pleasure and are equally transformed by collectively re-producing its popular subjectivity. But such a gesture of equality is not antithetical to the individual gesture of seeking personal glory and magnificence from the point of view of re-articulating the burden of subjectivity. Therefore, the patron by the same gesture re-creates the aura and magnificence of his public persona while re-affirming his status and power in the socio-political hierarchy. This image of theatre which re-constituted the public as a single spectacular body which in a sense both reflected and was being reflected by the brilliance and magnificence of the patron's *persona* could not be better summed up than Chrysostom. Leyerle cites from one of his sermons:

> The theatre is full, and all the people sitting right up to the top, present a brilliant spectacle composed of so many faces that even the roof and the undergirding rafters are largely obscured by bodies. Neither roof tiles nor stone seats are visible, but as far as the eye can see human faces and bodies. In the sight of all these people enters the man who has gathered them together out of the love of honour (*philotimia*). Immediately they spring to their feet and raise a shout as though from a single mouth. In unison they call him "guardian" and "patron" of their common city, stretching out their hands. Then, in the midst of all these cries, they compare him to the great river, likening the mighty outpouring of his benefaction (*philotimia*) to the unstinting waters of the Nile. He is, they shout, the "Nile of Gifts". Others flattering him even more, deem this comparison–that of the Nile!–too meagre. Dismissing rivers and seas, they introduce the ocean and say that as the Ocean is in waters so is he in benefactions. In short, they leave no form of praise (*euphemia*) unsung (Leyerle 2001, 37)

Clearly the description of the collective as bodies and the collective enthusiasm they produce lead towards a rhetoric of infinitizing the situation both in terms of the endless display of bodies and faces and the ever ambitious use of metaphors to convey the magnitude of their praise. But this intensive reality of bodies and affects endowed with a spirit of infinity is immediately captured and brought back into the unified logic of a single body (that of the patron) and a single voice (that of the crowd). It is this dualist logic of the many and one[17] supposedly held in perfect balance with each other which in the final analysis sustains the sovereign logic of the eternal 'One' being played out within the boundaries of the theatre which always enframes the multiple.

Concluding Note on the First Two Sections

From our discussions in Sections one and two, we come to two general conclusions. Firstly, that whether it be in the domain of socio-cultural discourse or that of philosophy or even in the realm of socio-economic practice like that of *euergetism*, the question of power was always centred around the problem of *persona,* no matter what form it took. Secondly, the problem of persona was almost always in its concrete manifestation informed by an inherent struggle. This conflict which can almost be argued to be a constitutive feature of the politics of *persona* in Ancient Rome developed due to its dualist tendency of being conceived equally through logics of exteriority and interiority. In other words, while there was a tendency to find a suitable mode of individuation based upon external and accidental factors like one's birth status and the appropriate markers which would indicate such factors like those of wealth and magnificence, expenditure and generosity there was also a counter disposition. This counter-actualization of persona so to speak, was based on an ethical imperative of withdrawing from public gaze into oneself. Though lacking the foundational ironical moment of negation which in the Socratic tradition was fundamental to a cultivation of self based on the dialectic of knowledge and ignorance, the Roman practices of the self were nevertheless a continuation of this tradition of an ethical exigency. By the same token, those exercises which were meant to create a relation of the self to itself based on certain ethical practices and technologies of conduct also continued. This inward movement of the self under an ethical imperative confronted its outward movement flourishing under a political and economic exigency. From Foucault we have the impression that this seeming contradiction was the condition for something like a crisis of the subject where the subject invented itself in a fashion which sought a line of flight from public obligations and law.

Under these conditions we come to two incommensurable moments related to the reality of theatre and acting which pushes this contradiction to its farthest limits.

(a) The Theoretical Articulation of the Problem of Inconsistency: Speech and the Voice

The pronouncement of the low status of the actor was most clearly reflected in Roman law which branded actors as *infames*–without reputation (*fama*). It is interesting to note here that the etymological origin of term suggests 'without voice'. That this term had direct legal implications is evident from the fact that in the praetor's edict (digest 3.2.2.5) actors were categorized (along with procurers, bigamists and soldiers who had been dishonourably discharged) by the use of the term *famosus* (disgraceful,). Legally this amounted to having very limited or no rights of postulation for others, such that the right to ask the praetor to grant an action on behalf of someone else was taken away from them. In other words, the actor, whose actions did not corroborate with reality, could not stand by what he would pronounce with his voice. Because he was a dissembler, the actor's speech could not be trusted and hence he could not function as a guarantor for anyone else's actions. It was not simply that the actions enacted by the actor were false but the fact that his status as one who enacts false or fictive actions made them incapable of guaranteeing someone else's actions. The legal powerlessness of the actor was not simply related to his lack of rights (*potestas*) or having a limited set of rights (the actors were not legally categorized with the slaves though they both shared the juridical fate of being *infames*) but his incapacity to stand as guarantor for somebody else's actions. In other words, juridically, the actor was specifically marked by his incapacity to become an *auctor* according to Roman private law[18]. This was reflected in the public domain in the prohibition of actors to become magistrates. Similarly, a citizen would lose his citizenship if he married an actress and would have no rights over the property of the father (*paterfamillia*). The figure of the actor inaugurates a complex set of problems around the question of *auctoritas* and *potestas* in Roman law and the concept of persona (taken both in its specific juridical context but also in its ethical elaborations). Here the problem is not that the actor is denied the basic rights which are granted to the citizen but the impossibility of the person of the actor, or better the inadequacy of the actor's voice[19] to grant legitimacy to any actualization of juridical power[20]. It is as if that by denying the actor the authority of words (logos) the relation between man and language is violently severed. If the Western concept of man depends on the idea of an *animal rationale* that possess language which makes man a speaking animal, then the actor is the one who in a strictly juridical sense is excluded from language and therefore from logos.

Without going into a detailed discussion of the state of exception which is at the bottom of the relation between *auctoritas* and *potestas* we can, following such scholars like Agamben, allow ourselves the provisional definition that auctoritas in Roman law expressed that particular moment when in suspending the juridical order, Roman law founded itself by giving itself the validity which was neither substantive nor positive[21]. It expressed that constitutive moment at the very heart of legal power which is called a state of exception–a void point where "a human action with no relation to law stands before a norm with no relation to life" (Agamben 2005, 86). The disempowerment of the voice of the actor by denying him any power of auctoritas, albeit in private law, was an attempt to place him in a state of exception in relation to the juridical validity of words. By legally suspending his right to speech the actor in a way is exposed to (and in turn exposes) the power of law in its inaugural and constitutive moment of suspending itself by being in force. But more importantly, it expresses the particular status of the actor who being robbed of language is left only with his bare voice; a voice-without-speech which is how the actor is brought back within the domain of law, language and finally Roman society. We should not forget what Catherine Edwards reminds us Horace has to say about Roman acting which has deviated far from the Aristotelian desire of a theatre of words:

> For what voices have ever managed to rise above the din with which our theatres resound? You might imagine it was the roaring of the Garganian forests or of the Tuscan sea; such clamour accompanies the entertainment, the works of art and the foreign finery, and, when swallowed up in this, the actor sets foot on the stage, loud applause at once. 'has he said

> something already'?' 'Not a word'. 'Then why this response?' 'It's his woollen robe. Made the colour of violets by Tarentine dye' (Edwards 2002, 105)

It is not merely the loss of language that Horace' snide remark points at but the very affect that the actor somehow manages to generate without uttering a word. In the same way the actor's speech being paradigmatically false and hence without any juridical power would still be envied for its freedom and licence to speak. We can risk a hypothesis here that this juridical denial of language does not leave the actor only with his voice but on the contrary the actor whose profession it is to speak on the Roman stage (of course among other things like dance and mime given the nature of Roman spectacle), somehow manages to maintain himself in the place of language. In other words, lending his voice to words not his own and also externalising this act by being an actor he exposes the relation in which language always already anticipates man. Language which by its originary signifying function always stands before man, anticipating him and throwing him into history and tradition is interrupted and burst open by the actor. The actor in exposing language's performativity or its taking place on the stage stands at the very threshold where his voice both articulates language but also disarticulates it as a dissembler. It gives him the freedom to come to language freely, a language which is truly and intrinsically his own. It is on stage that man comes face to face with the absence of his voice, man who is an animal without a voice. It is on stage that man as a speaking animal becomes truly free in coming to language and speaking words which in their total lack of *dignitas* is proper to him alone[22]. From the point of view of language, by disempowering the voice of the actor in Roman law and making him into a figure of a 'bare voice' we find a way of capturing this paradox of acting within the significatory norms of language which precedes and anticipates man as his destiny. By the same token it also tries to integrate the actor–whose public and private life have entered a zone of absolute indistinction[23]–into the juridico-political sphere, at least theoretically, by categorizing him as a marginal figure without *dignitas*.

(b) The Practical (Dis)Articulation of the Problem of Inconsistency: Mask and the Face

The relation between the face and mask is the essential content of the problem of persona which we have tried to elaborate till now. The constitution of one's political persona is determined by the ambiguity of projecting it outside on to the external world of wealth and status defined by munificence but also through a certain withdrawal within oneself. This retreat within the self expressed the ethical imperative of creating an authentic role of an ethical life defined by a cultivation of the self which widened the scope of a philosophical way of life through constantly examining oneself and following conducts of behaviour and techniques of existence. The political function of such a cult of the self was to give the one who would govern the necessary ethical substance to perform the role of a 'life in politics'. The exercise of political power was determined by certain principles whose source remained to a large extent ethical in nature. Because the manner in which the authority to govern others was dependent on the wisdom manifest "in the interplay of equilibria and transactions"(Foucault 1990), Foucault reminds us that "the art of governing oneself becomes a crucial political factor"(Ibid., n.d., 89). Therefore, it was not one's status and external factors which were constitutive of one's *persona*. More and more it was not the qualification of a status but the modality of a rational being which came to determine relations between the governors and the governed. The primacy of the use of the theatrical metaphor of 'role' has to be understood in this ethical context of an internal relation of the soul to itself as much as the role presented by status and wealth. The ethical imperative of playing one's role authentically according to the principles of reason no matter what part one is assigned is well illustrated by Epictetus, as Hans Von Balthazar[24] cites him:

> Regard yourself as an actor in a play. The poet gives you your part and you must play it, whether it is short or long. If he wants you to play a beggar, act the part skilfully. Do the same if you are to play a cripple, a ruler or a private person. Your task is only to play well the part you have been given: the choosing of it belongs to someone else. (Balthasar 1988, 141)

Epictetus' words echo the stoic indifference to worldly status and glory as much as the ethical imperative of distinguishing what is within the domain of human freedom and what is outside the reach of his choice. This distinction is a crucial exercise and part of the stoic technologies of the self which further anticipates the stoic distance from the clamour of life in spite of participating in it. Marcus Aurelius best represents this dissociative logic of the self which, while participating in life, has to find a possible line of flight which is its final exercise of freedom. Again, Balthazar cites Aurelius as comparing life to the theatre-"An empty pageant; a stage play ... puppets jerking on their strings–that is life. In the midst of it all you must take your stand, good temperedly and without disdain, yet always aware that a man's worth is no greater than the worth of his ambitions" (Ibid., n.d., 143). Needless to say, that Aurelius does not consider a life more worthy which follows worldly ambitions of glory and munificence than the one which can lead an ethical existence.

The projection of the self outside into the material world of munificence to define identity according to one's status and the elements which make it visible through a culture of display remains one side of the problem of persona. To put on this external mask was to make oneself as much adequate as possible to a culture of display through signs pertaining to physical bearing, clothing and accommodation, gestures of generosity and magnificence. But at the same time the cult of monarchy also had to take into consideration the problem of the emperor's virtue, practised in his private life, his ability to control his passions which stands as a guarantee of his ability to limit the exercise of his political power. It is this play of forces involved in the projection, on to the stage of civic power, of the persona of the emperor which is equally supposed to protect him by making him withdraw into himself in order to gain access to his ethical substance and thus maintain that perfect equilibrium between participation and dissociation. This is what Marcus Aurelius points towards when he warns of the danger of being Caesarized, "see to it that you do not become Caesarized, or dyed with that colouring" (Foucault 1990, 90)

The ensuing crisis when this equilibrium is disturbed is described by Tacitus when he writes of the culminating disorder which followed when during the games of 65 CE, Nero himself appeared as an actor wearing a mask resembling himself. Edwards cites from Suetonius:

> He also wore a mask and sang tragedies in the character of gods and heros and even of heroines and goddesses, having the masks made so that they resembled him or else whatever woman he was in love with at the time (Edwards 2002, 135).

This gesture was a culminating point, at least symbolically where not only the problem of theatre reached its threshold but the entire culture of persona as a constitutive factor of Roman socio-political reality confronted its own aporia. Suetonius tells us that in confusion of seeing the emperor on stage in rags and bound with chains as the play required (*The Frenzy of Heracles*), a young solider unable to comprehend the dramatic conventions rushed forward to render assistance. Catherine Edwards analyses this moment as disjunctive when on one hand the sovereign power of the emperor is able to transcend social conventions which held acting as morally degrading, by coming on stage as an emperor. While on the other hand, it also illustrates, according to Blake, the failure of the sovereign to assume the arbitrariness of that power completely when he is not recognized as an emperor playing the role of an actor but as the emperor whose political and social position is incommensurable with his condition even on stage. However, it is perhaps more revelatory of the Roman situation than Edwards would have it because it exposes the constitutive aporia of all sovereign power. Perhaps it is impossible for the emperor to play the 'role' of an emperor on stage precisely because he is not naturally a figure of power but someone who has to constantly *play the role of power* in being an emperor. What Nero wanted to achieve was the impossible gesture of not simply be the emperor in assuming his role absolutely and arbitrarily on the political stage by putting that very enactment of power on display on the theatrical stage. In this sense he tried to destroy all distance of the self with itself when it assumes a role–be that of external magnificence or the internal role of an ethical subject. He wanted to naturalize the *persona*[25] of the emperor not by claiming any doctrine of natural (or even divine) origin of sovereignty but by denaturalizing power and transforming it into the 'innocence' of a play of power. It is perhaps this gesture which is captured in Nero's desire to make the mask the face itself; the mask which would offer protection in Roman society (as we saw before) to those actors who had the privileged right in their life outside the stage to continue the function of being respectable citizens and subjects of sovereignty. In the hands of the tyrant this mask became the very tool to expose the degraded but absolute authority of sovereign power. Nero through this gesture presented a site–the theatrical stage–where the theatre of sovereignty was exposed to its double; where the high born natural face of power corresponded with the degraded and anonymous face of the actor; an actor who captures the aporia of *persona* (which as we saw comes from the Greek word *prosopon* meaning mask and face) in presenting to us his mask which is also his face.

Section III

Metaphor

In order to approach the problem of "inconsistency" of theatre from the other point of view, namely the Christian perspective, we need to be aware of its double binding. From the early Christian fathers, probably starting from Tertullian, we find a tendency of aligning the pagan attitude towards theatre with the very nature of theatre itself. Both were taken to be deceptive and inconsistent. The Christians argued that while Roman society apparently glorified theatre as an integral part of their civic life they secretly persecuted actors which in turn reflected the reality of theatre as a place of deception and illusion. This double binding of the meaning of theatre was further displaced to exemplify the inherent ontological contradiction of pagan society as such. The Christian judgement against theatre was constructed through this constant displacement of the meaning of theatre which always stood for something else. As we shall try to elaborate, it is our hypothesis that this particular meaning which is attributed to the *reality of theatre* is related to the specific Christian obligation for truth. This obligation for truth was not only related to the obligation to hold true certain propositions which constitute a dogma, or the obligation to hold certain books as the permanent source of truth or even to obey decisions of certain authorities in matters of truth and make manifest such obedience. There was also the obligation to search and discover the truth about oneself so that a perspective can be gained about the self so that one can distinguish virtue from vice within oneself in order to exalt the former and eliminate the latter. It is our contention that the type of writings that one finds devoted exclusively to the problem of theatre and other spectacles or even those where the theme of theatre comes up repeatedly, all display a style of interrogation which corresponds to the Christian obligation of interrogating the truth about the self. This interrogative style of approaching the problem of theatre was something quite unique to the Christian practices which could be divided into two forms. These texts display methods of interrogating theatrical reality in order to recognize and make manifest the truth about its worldly and idolatrous nature in order to abandon or renounce such sinful practice. At the same time, there is also an attempt to think about the *very movement of thinking behind such spectacles* in an effort to understand the nature of the very thought of theatre. This contemplative gesture which is intimately related to the problem of confession, we would argue, becomes the pre-condition of assigning meaning to theatre as a playground of the devil because of its very deceptive nature. Ironically, at the same time, it was this contemplative tendency, where the object of interrogation is not the materiality of theatre but the very thought or logic of theatre, which produces what would later be called a theatre of life and the divine theatre. This metaphorization of the meaning of theatre where it comes to stand for a theatre of the world (*theatrum mundi*) could not have been possible without the confessional character of the Christian discourse around theatre. These are motifs to which we will return in our coming chapters. Here we would like to inaugurate our examination of the Christian problem of theatre through an analysis of John Chrysostom's idea of theatre.

Unlike many of his contemporaries, John Chrysostom not only condemns theatre for being idolatrous but also for having more nefarious and secret ways to ensnare the soul. Theatre represents everything that tricks man to perform sin through deception. Therefore, when he analyses the pagan statuary to discover greed which lurks behind such idolatrous practice, the presence of theatre continues to loom in the significatory horizon. Chrysostom writes,

> Just as the Greek diligently cares for the statue of his god, so you entrust your gold to doors and bolts, furnishing it with a small coffer instead of a temple, and storing it in vessels of silver.
>
> You protest that you do not bow down in worship as he does to the statue of his god? But you do show complete devotion to it. Just as the Greek would gladly give up his eyes and his life rather than give up the statue of his god, so to those who love gold would do.
>
> "But I do not bow down in worship to gold," someone will object. To which I reply that neither does the Greek worship the statue, but rather its indwelling spirit. In the same way you bow down in worship, if not to gold, then to the spirit that ceases upon your soul at the sight and desire for gold. (Leyerle 2001)[26]

Here gold not only corresponds to the pagan statue but it also displaces the literal significance of the statue, de-centring it from its material reality to the spirit which lurks behind the matter. "Neither does the Greek worship the statue but rather its indwelling spirit." Simultaneously, the meaning of gold is displaced from its denotative function of what 'gold' is, to the desire for gold which displaces and saturates the signification. So idolatry is not simply compared to greed, but greed becomes the spirit of idolatry, the meaning which lurks in the dark backstage, so to speak, or better, greed is the 'true' face hiding behind the mask of idolatry like idolatry is the 'true' meaning concealed behind theatre. But this is merely the beginning of this story of displacements. The desire for wealth which constitutes the meaning of greed is expressed by Chrysostom in a series of explicitly sexual metaphors. In likening covetousness to prostitution, Chrysostom not only underlines the nature of one type of sin leading to another but also unravels the nature of sin in general which never acts by itself but through the dissimulation of a secret operation which works its way behind the curtain or under the mask. Like the pleasure of sexual gratification which conceals the hateful intent of the female sex, who engages in the sexual act only to deceive man in order to enslave him and thereby robbing him of his 'natural' sexual superiority. Similarly, avarice is never the simple desire for money in itself but the desire for wealth which masks a more insidious desire for power. Therefore, while on the one hand, Chrysostom writes:

> And just as harlots belong to whoever gives them gold–even a slave or freedman or a gladiator or anyone at all, if he can meet her price...[so rich men] for the sake of gold...associate with anyone shamelessly. (Ibid., n.d., 47)[27]

While on the other hand he writes:

> At first, there was no gold, nor was anyone infatuated with it. But if you like, I will tell you how this evil was introduced: each person by envying the other brought on this disease, and once having caught it, inflamed even those who had no desire [for it]. For when they saw beautiful houses, extensive fields, herds of slaves, silver vessels, and a vast heap of clothes, they were willing to do anything to be preeminent. (Ibid., n.d., 48)[28]

Two things become clear through this passage. It is never the thing in itself that one desires. Rather one desires that which is behind the thing, concealed by the apparent illusion of the thing itself, which merely signifies this desire for something else. In this case, it is the desire for worldly glory which prowls behind the desire for wealth. Secondly, even this desire for pre-eminence which displaces the meaning of greed is further displaced by envy which is the source of glory. Such envy is generated by the feeling of a lack, or the absence of something which man longs to possess. Envy is the quintessential situation of desire which is constituted through a lack. "Money is just a word for desire itself." (Ibid., n.d., 48) While desire itself is nothing but the force which pulls the soul towards something which it does not possess–"Beautiful houses, extensive fields, herds of slaves..." In other words, worldly glory is nothing other than the shameless actualizations of desire itself. As Blake Leyerle reminds us, 'Homily after homily (Chrysostom) insists that nothing so insists people to desire riches as fondness for glory' (Ibid., n.d., 48).

Clearly, here the theme of worldly glory is related to a set of classical significations pointing to the historical reality of his (Chrysostom's) time. This is the liturgical world of Rome which is typified by such terms like *philotimia*, *megalopsychia*, etc. As we discussed before, all these terms are related to certain specific practices of Roman society linked to the pursuit of public recognition, praise and honour sought through lavish personal expenditure and display of wealth. In the late 4th century, such civic practices as that of *euergetism* was part of a broader socio-political tendency based on *display* of individual status which determined public participation and fulfilment of certain voluntary and involuntary civic duties. Behind such liturgical practices of financing construction of temples, amphitheatres, public baths and organizing festivals, was the idea of *philotimia.* The conscious attempt at conspicuous display governed by a desire for seeking social and political power was identical with the individual pursuit of 'vainglory'. This is what John Chrysostom (like many of his generation of Christian fathers) attacks through his indictment of greed and avarice. However, it is interesting to discern the role of theatre in such an accusatory religio-political discourse. It is not merely the spectacular side of this reality which made theatre an appropriate paradigm to capture this culture of display. In calling "their utter ruin, delightful" (Ibid., n.d., 48)[29] these vainglorious men, according to Chrysostom, were unable to see the truth behind the illusion, mistaking their pursuit of reputation as happiness while such actions enslaved them, making them guilty before God; exactly like sexual gratification blinded them to the truth of its sinful nature. (Ibid., n.d.) The fragility of the spectacular reality of the time is also encapsulated by the metaphor of theatre to define reality. This fragility is exposed when the deception is recognized and the inconsistency of the world is accounted for. Leyerle cites from one of Chrysostom's homilies:

> As long as those entertained are still sitting, the masks are valid; but when evening comes and the theatre is dispersed and everyone goes home, the masks are cast down and the man who is a king inside the theatre is discovered to be a coppersmith outside. The masks are thrown, deceptions depart, and truth is revealed...Thus it is also in life and especially at its end. Our circumstances are a theatre, our business acting; wealth and poverty, ruling and being ruled, and all such likewise. When this day is thrown away and night comes...when the theatre is dispersed and the masks cast down, and each person and his works is examined–not each person with his honour, not each person with his power–but each person with his works...Then it emerges who is rich and who poor.(Ibid., n.d., 52)

Finally, with this metaphor of a theatre of life, we have arrived at a perfect circularity of a process of signification around the question of theatre through a series of displacements. Theatre, whose true meaning resides in idolatry leads back to greed leading further back to vainglory (*philotimia*), an empty form of worldly glory which dissimulates the reality of the human condition; the human condition which is identical to theatre in posing to be that which it is not, in being deceptive. The meaning of theatre is given within a semantic field saturated by a series of displacements or postponements of signification. This act of postponing the meaning of theatre does not exempt theatre from being judged. On the contrary, in this process of displacement of meaning of theatre resides the very condition for the judgement passed on theatre. In perfect circularity of this displacement which returns the meaning of theatre to itself, displaced back to the very place from where it began, theatre not only gets judged but gains the power of judgement. Now theatre can pass the judgement on reality making the whole of human existence theatrical. The metaphor of theatre as a theatre of life or a theatre of the world envelops the entirety of space, time and experience. But in pronouncing the judgement that all phenomena–an infinite number of them in space and time–are theatrical so far as they hide the single truth behind it, what is expressed is a relation between existence and an infinite order of time which is given a theologic form. We can understand the metaphorization and the indictment of theatre as a dual mode of transformation which corresponds to a judgement of knowledge which incurs an infinite debt to the Knowledge (divine knowledge) which is not known to man. A Master Signifier which is the condition behind every worldly signification which in itself is perpetually displaced making its possibility of existence essentially theatrical. A doctrine of knowledge which corresponds to a doctrine of judgement where all meaning is indebted to a final signification inscribed in an "autonomous book without our even realizing it, so that we are no longer able to pay off an account that has become infinite." (Deleuze, *Essays Critical and Clinical* 1997, 128)[30]

The metaphor of world stage and the renunciation of this world become identical with each other. Similarly, the indictment against all worldly liturgy based on individual glory corresponds to the affirmation of an infinite liturgy through this process of dispossessing the world. The indictment of public benefaction and the pursuit of worldly glory, in short the condemnation of a worldly liturgy, induces Chrysostom to dispossess theatre of its worldly meaning, emptying it of all material signification and giving it a divine disposition by re-localizing its reality and opening up its semantic borders to incorporate the entire world. Against the wealth and glory of the earthly stage, which is witnessed "by prostitutes and rabble of the theatre" (Leyerle 2001, 54), he talks of "the unsleeping Eye of God" which is the eternal audience of such a theatre of the world. The timeless and permanent glory of such a theatre is what he urges one to seek–not by moving outside oneself into the external world of munificience. But, like the woman in the Gospel story who by anointing Jesus gained the eternal glory of God through her inner disposition, Chrysostom urges his congregation to go after the true magnificence of God and seek out the authentic glory of the heavenly kind. When he writes that it is more worthwhile to seek out this glory, Chrysostom transposes the meaning of theatre from its earthly state to make it a divine affair. "Its theatre is more brilliant and its prize greater" (Ibid., n.d., 55).

However, worldly liturgy is also based on a system of debt where such a debt is circulated among "finite blocks" upon determinate territories. While such a debt marks the body directly—signs of glory and munificence which marks the external self—its circulation is always territorial: the construction of an amphitheatre for a province, the establishment of a bath for a city or organizing a festival for a municipality. The infinite liturgy stretches this territory to envelop the entire world, expanding its expanses infinitely. The infinite liturgy transforms the world into a stage, metaphorizing all significations, dispossessing all meanings of their material reference. This destitution of the world at the same time demands an infinite debt, expelling man from his territories, dispossessing him of all the meanings he could have possibly attributed to the world. Making a metaphor out of everything, metamorphosing the world into a dead metaphor behind which stands the grand metaphor of a world theatre (*theatrum mundi*). In such a 'reality' everything stands for something else, while the anonymous Book collects all dead letters in order to possess them eternally. This is the universalization of the metaphor of theatre which comes as a response to the problematization of the theatrical substance at the turn of the Christian era.

NOTES

1. Quoted from Tertullian's *De Spectaculis* (Tertullian 1931).
2. Paul Veyne, in his book *When Our World Became Christian,* argues about the transformation from the pagan world to the Christian not in terms of an ideological shift which marks the moment in Western history when religion was separated from politics, each constituting a distinct domain anticipating a secular understanding of this relation. Rather, he imagines the eruption of Christianity into history as a creative moment, which he calls a "masterpiece" embodied in the figure of the first Christian Emperor Constantine. Veyne argues that this transformation was made possible through a shift of a series of power relations which was conditioned by a new logic of divine sovereignty where

God and Caesar in being distinct were also inseparable from each other. As a result, the relation between religion and politics ceased to have the kind of external and superficial nature it had during paganism and came to be systematically theorized. We follow in Veyne's spirit that this transformation of power relations was not articulated by the development of a new ideology, which was the reason behind a new regime of power and new set of obligations and obedience. Rather we have tried to follow a line of analysis where ideology functions only through what Veyne calls phraseology, which is a sort of linguistic pragmatism that articulates already dissymmetrical positions of power translating them into a language of desire and pleasure. In other words, it seeks legitimacy through the pleasure one enjoys in obedience because he thinks that it is right to obey. In other words, such a pragmatism is governed by desire for truth. Veyne masterfully narrates the way in which, during these transformative years, a new desire for truth was being developed through and around the figure of Constantine. (Veyne 2010)

3. Following Foucault, who orients certain specific ethical practices concerning the self's relation to itself to what he calls the ethical substance which constitutes in the ancient world something like aphrodisia which combines sexual desire with pleasure and enjoyment, we have tried to imagine something like a theatrical substance which would enframe the entire reality of theatre including the actors and the audience. See Chapter I, pp. 18-20
4. See Derrida's analysis of this notion of *problema* in *Aporia* (Derrida 1993).
5. For a further elaboration of how certain Christian fathers of the patristic tradition would take up the problem of the origin of theatre using these same authors, refer to Chapter 3, section on Tertullian, pp. 46-47.
6. Speech and writing were taken to be theoretical knowledge which had the potential for greatness but which could only be concretely actualized in action.
7. *Veritatis ipsius actors* roughly translates as 'players', while *imitatores veritatis* means followers of truth.

8. For a brilliant discussion of the distinction and relation between subjectivation and subjection as a problem of the double, where the thinking folds back on itself to recreate an operation of the outside, inside thinking refer to the chapter "Foldings, or the Inside of Thought" in his book on Foucault. (Deleuze, *Foucault* 1999, 94-123)
9. In *Apology*, Socrates talks about human wisdom as against other kinds of wisdom which is extra human. He, though ironically talks of expert knowledge, particularly in the context of Evenus from Paros, who charges 500 drachmas for each sitting. Socrates claims to have no such expert knowledge about anything. For him human knowledge amounts to nothing more than the minimal and limited access to one's own ignorance. And yet, on the basis of this weak knowledge grounded on negation he empties out all worldly forms of knowledge, dissolving them in metaphors and makes an incommensurable 'leap' into the unknown. But all this happens within the self with no help from the outside. See Plato "Apology" in (Plato 1997, 83-115).
10. Giorgio Agamben in his elegant article entitled "The Face" discusses the problem of the face as the quintessential human urge to possess one's own appearance as the site of both knowledge and the struggle for truth. And yet this truth, according to him, this being manifest of appearance has nothing essential or substantive behind it but the act of manifestation itself. What the face brings into appearance is the very possibility of appearing. This is the truth of appearance, where all that remains behind the face is emptiness or a void which is its eternal condition. The groundlessness of this ground which is the face itself has to be somehow displayed as having some substance, some meaning. This is the struggle for recognition which Agamben equates with the act of taking possession or controlling appearances. Whereas the appearance of the face can only in its simulation make manifest the possibility of appearance itself, the truth of such a universal possibility is turned into a personal recognizable truth when enacted through possession. See Giorgio Agamben "The Face" in (Agamben, *Means Without Ends* 1996, 91-100)

11. Stoic ethical doctrine from which, according to De Lacy, Cicero draws his concept of the *persona* in the first book of *De Officiis* differentiates four conditions which need to be considered when we talk of personae. 1. The nature we share with all human beings. 2. Our individual natures. 3. The persona arising from circumstances which is imposed on us by chance and time and 4. Those which pertain to our choices resulting from our judgement of the kind of life we wish to live. Although two of these conditions are supposedly natural to us, the duality of the concept of *persona* as both the face which we inhabit and the mask (the Greek residue of the idea of *prosopon*) which is external to us never loses its context. Hence, though all are human as different from god or animal, that individual is good who is always true to the role he plays, no matter what the circumstances, according to rational judgement and wisdom which always guide his choices. And since he cannot be truly wise, like Socrates, he cannot truly play the role of the wise man but can nevertheless try, according to his natural capability, to be like Socrates. See (Lacy 1977)
12. Ibid., p. 609.
13. In the context of Socrates, we should not confuse the idea of private and public in the modern sense of a distinction which has juridical or even customary implication. Such a distinction could rather be compared with the Greek idea of the *oikos* and *polis,* the household and the city which also resonates in the philosophy of Cicero and the Roman distinction of private and public. But in the Socratic sense, private is the interiority of the self as against the exteriority of the world and the movement from one to the other which, on the contrary can take place anywhere, anytime, be in *oikos* or the *polis.*
14. For a short but precise schematization of the place of theatre in late antiquity refer to the chapter titled "Late Antique Theatre" in (Leyerle 2001).
15. In his book *Bread and Circuses*, Veyne traces the genealogy of this practice from the early Greek society till late antiquity. (Veyne, *Bread and Circuses* 1990). For a brief but politically innovative analysis of the consequences of Roman liturgy and its relation

to the problem of the juridical concept of persona see the section on "A New Liturgy I" in Soumyabrata Choudhury's book *Theatre Number Event.* (Choudhury 2013, 18-23)

16. For another interesting analysis of the problem of *persona* from the point of view of the gesture refer to (Choudhury 2013, 19).
17. For a remarkable analysis of the relation between the multiple and the singular and its difference from the universal and the particular see Gilles Deleuze's seminar of March 26, 1973 titled "Dualism, Monism and Multiplicities" (Desire-Pleasure-*Jouissance*). (Deleuze, Dualism, Monisim and Multiplicities 2001)
18. In the sphere of private law, *auctoritas* was that which belonged to the *auctor* which is to say the person *sui iuris* (the *paterfamilias*) who can interfere and confer legal validity on the act of a subject who as an individual is deemed legally incapable to bring an act into being. For example, the tutor makes valid through his auctoritas the action of the student like the auctoritas of the father makes legally valid the marriage of the son. See "*Auctoritas* and *Potestas.*" (Agamben 2005, 74-88)
19. Etymologically *infames* which means in Roman law "without reputation" also indicates "without voice." See (Leyerle 2001, 118)
20. The use of the term *famosus* ('disgraceful') in the praetor's edict(dig. 3.2.2.5) indicates that actors had only limited rights of postulation for others, that is to say, the right to ask the praetor to grant an action on behalf of someone else. (They are classed here with, among others, procurers, bigamists and soldiers who had been dishonourably dismissed) This restriction, though not particularly severe in itself, is an indication of the powerlessness of such persons in all legal situations where the value of one's word would be measured by the presiding magistrate. (Ibid., n.d.)
21. Agamben discusses the origin of the legal term *auctoritas* in detail from its etymological sources–lithe word is derived from the verb *augeo* which means to augment, increase or perfect acts. From there Agamben traces the legal institutions within Roman law where auctoritas shows its peculiar function of suspending the law. (Agamben, *State of Exception* 2005, 74-88)

22. Giorgio Agamben in an extraordinarily evocative essay titled "Vocation and Voice" talks of this moment when man stands at the threshold of language and nature in the very grain of his voice which is nothing but the very originary moment of speech itself. He says, "freedom is possible for speaking man only if he is able to come to terms with (*venir in chiaro*) language, and, taking hold of its origin, to find a speech that is truly and entirely his own, a speech that is human. a speech that would be his voice, as the song is the voice of the birds, chirping the voice of the cricket and braying the voice of the donkey." (Agamben, Vocation and Voice 1997)
23. It is interesting to note here that almost like a mirror image of this moment, from the Roman *princeps* onwards the sovereign possesses an auctoritas in his person so far as in his "august" life it is not possible to distinguish public and private, which makes it necessary to conceive of the king's two bodies in order to maintain the continuity of *dignitas*.
24. For perhaps one of the very few and remarkable instances of tracing back the metaphor of "world stage" back to Plato and following its destiny up to such modern playwrights like Ibsen refer to (Balthasar 1988).
25. The Latin persona which is translated as person or human being, anyone in general comes from the Greek *prosopon*. In Ancient Greece, *prosopon* was used as a technical term which was most frequently encountered in Greek theology. *Prosopon* originally means "face" or "mask" in Greek and derives from Greek theatre, where the actors on a stage wore masks to reveal their character and emotional state to the audience. Therefore the word always carries this ambiguity of being both natural and artificial to human existence. On the one hand it is something which is extraneous, like a prosthesis covering the face, sheltering it and disavowing it at the same time. But it is also that which it covers and protects, namely the face. The mask which protects the face from the outside world but by the same token carries its secret. But the secret of the mask is always already offered to the world as a secret thereby annulling itself as a secret. Therefore the mask also projects the face on to the stage, freezing upon a single emotion or

a single character or better an emotion which undisputably helps us recognize the identity of the character. In Rome, persona was formalized in a figure of law which brought it very close to the idea of another Latin term *figura* derived from *fingere* meaning form or contour but also to contrive or simulate.

26. Originally cited from John Chrysostom's *Hom. in. Jo.* 65.3 [PG 59.364].
27. Originally cited from John Chrysostom's *Hom. in. Heb.* 15.3 [PG 63.120- 21].
28. Originally cited from John Chrysostom's *Hom. in. Jo.* 65.3 [PG 59.364].
29. Originally cited from John Chrysostom's *Hom. in. Matt.* 20.5 [PG 57.293-94].
30. For a brilliant discussion on the difference between a doctrine of judgment based on a creditor-debtor relation and a system of cruelty which replaces such an oppressive system by an affirmative idea of the "body without organs" which can never be reduced to subjectivism see the essay "To have done with Judgment" in (Deleuze, *Essays Critical and Clinical* 1997).

Part 2

The Problem Made Possible

Chapter 3

"How Vast the Spectacle that Day, and How Wide!"[1]: The Treatment of Theatre in Early Christianity

Section I

The Idea of Spectacle Introduced as a Problem

Desire

One of the earliest references to the theatre image in Christianity occurs in St. Paul when in the first letter to the Corinthians he speaks of the sufferings of the apostles for the Christian community such that the community is nourished in their suffering. Paul writes "For I think that god hath set forth us the apostles last, as it were approved to death. For we are made a spectacle unto the world, and to angles, and to men". (1 Corinthians 4:9). The reference to this spectacular suffering of the apostles comes in the wake of a much longer Judaic tradition of identifying suffering with spectacle. We have references from the Old Testament where bodily suffering, particularly punitive or redemptive suffering, is often declared as a spectacle which ought to be enjoyed by the righteous and his chosen ones. The idea where the redeemed would enjoy the torments of the damned becomes increasingly recurring in late Jewish literature too. For instance, in the concluding part of the Book of Isaiah we have the spectacle outside the gates of the eschatological city, of those thrown into Gehenna for eternity for rebeling against god. "Therefore thus said the lord god, behold, my servants shall eat and you shall be hungry, Behold my servants shall drink, but ye shall be thirsty, Behold my servants shall rejoice, but you shall be ashamed" (Isaiah 65:13). This ultimate spectacle would be an inversion of all worldly situations, of all worldly spectacles. "They will provide a spectacle for the righteous and his chosen ones; the later will rejoice over them because the anger of the Lord of spirits rests upon them." (Balthasar 1988, p 152)This image of the arena in Enoch 9-12 captures the eschatological situation of reversal of fortunes, where the spectator of worldly spectacles, of the circus, of the theatres and of the gladiatorial arenas where the faithful suffer pain, are tortured and executed (both Christians and Jews) would become the very object of a divine spectacle. This theatrical image of a divine spectacle, a reciprocal equivalent of all earthly spectacles would continue to inform the discourses around theatre throughout the patristic tradition right up to the commentaries of the great scholastics.

But the Pauline remark is not merely a sign for a divine spectacle. To become a spectacle to the world and to angles and men is not just a reciprocal reversal of the spectacular image. Right before the line, we have Paul remarking,

> For who maketh thee differ from another? And what hast thou that thou hadst not received? *Now if thou didst, why does thou glory*, as if though had not receive it? Now ye are full, now ye are rich, ye have reigned as kings without us and I would to God ye did reign, that we also might reign with ye (1 Corinthians 4:7).

The spectacle of suffering to which the apostles are to be subjected is a calling which would unify the community who are now divided by their individual glory. And what is the source of this earthly glory which is the cause of the division? At the beginning of the text Paul writes, "For the Jews require a sign, and the Greeks seek after wisdom: but we preach Christ crucified, unto the Jews a stumbling block, and unto the Greeks foolishness" (1 Corinthians 1:22). So the glory which they claim as their own in case of the Greeks comes as wisdom; it is as Stanislaw Breton indicates, specified by the verb "to search". It is expressed in their attitude of search under the principle of reason. But it is nonetheless the condition for an earthly glory which comes as pride and obscures the true vision, the true spectacle of the glory of Christ crucified.

Similarly for the Jews, the source of their glory is the arbitrary proclamation of the signs which are marvels to which they lay claim. As Breton observes, "marvels that manifest an admirable and incomprehensible power that erupts, in a sudden burst, to upset our calculations and disconcert our wisdom" (Breton 2002, p. 5). Hence if the Greek glory comes from their principle of reason, then the Jews draw their glory from a principle of arbitrary sovereignty that one does not seek but declare as a sign of an absolute other. Hence in the Judaic tradition, the reversal of the worldly spectacle cannot but be a divine spectacle, not of this world but of the divine order which *anticipates* the inversion of the worldly order. Hence all worldly spectacle of suffering proclaims the miraculous sign that their pain will become pleasure after the Last Judgement when all that will remain is the glory of God

> Rejoice ye with Jerusalem.
> And be glad with her, all ye that love her:
> Rejoice for joy with her, all ye that mourn for her:
> That ye may suck, and be satisfied with the breast of her consolations: that ye may milk out,
> And be delighted with the abundance of her glory (Isaiah 66:10,11)

In both these cases, that of the Greeks and of the Jews, we find an idea of a spectacle which is implicitly but nonetheless structurally coincidental with desire. In the former case the worldly eminence and pride sought through wisdom comes at the price of desire for wisdom whose object nevertheless eludes the subject. The *logon didonai* (to realize, to give reasons) will always reach the threshold of knowledge and hence would be sustained by only its desire for an ultimate transcendental object outside the domain of human reason. Hence Paul says in the beginning "not with wisdom of words, lest the Cross of Christ should be made of no effect". Similarly in the case of the Jews the claim of the arbitrary sign of the sovereign comes as an exceptional object which lies beyond the world. In the lines from Isaiah it almost comes as the oedipal desire for the mother–"as one whom his mother comforteth, so will I comfort you" (Isaiah 66:13)–which is forever out of reach in the immanent order. This desire for satisfaction which can only be anticipated and never realized is juxtaposed with the arbitrary sovereign voice of the father–"For behold, the Lord will come with fire" (Isaiah 66:15). The injunction from above would resolve all mortal crises and all worldly failure would be turned into success like all spectacles of suffering would be transformed into signs of joy because an arbitrary meaning would be attached to the failure, transforming it into success. This arbitrary sign would transform the emptiness of suffering into the fulfilment of an anticipated pleasure and resolve the crisis of not having any meaning by explaining the spectacle as a sign which seems empty now but will be fulfilled eventually on the other side. A marvellous sign thus enters the world to produce a subject so far as one can ask "who did this?" Or better, how to make meaning of this adversity or failure, in other words this negativity or lack? The sign carries the worldly lack to the divine order of fulfilment, through which it can fulfil itself and thereby give it an identity. The sign arbitrarily bridges the gap between the immanent worldly order and the transcendent divine order. The exceptional response which the sign represents makes meaning by inverting the lack into plenitude and hence failure into success and pain into pleasure. The inversion of all worldly spectacles at the time of final judgement carries this logic of a desire-lack through inversion of images of failure-success.

The Idea of Spectacle Elaborated

Suspension

Against both these attitudes which correspond to two modes of this spectacular desire, Paul speaks of a glory in the spectacle of suffering to which men and angles are witnesses. A spectacle "unto the world" is therefore also a spectacle which unfolds in the world. But it is a spectacle which remains seemingly ambiguous, caught between two points of views. Paul writes, "We are made a spectacle unto the world, and to angels, and to men" talking of the suffering of the apostles for the Christian community. This is immediately followed by a set of contradictory images, "we are fools for Christ's sake, but ye are wise in Christ. We are weak, but ye are strong; ye are honourable, but we are despised" (1 Corinthians 4:10). Clearly it is not an actual state of affairs that Paul is describing, but a spectacle which sustains the ambiguity of all appearances. We know that Paul had already talked of the folly of the cross which sustains the true meaning of its logos. "The Logos of the Cross, for those who are lost is folly, but for those who are saved, for us, it is the power of god" (Breton 2002, p. 4). It is not the word of wisdom but the logos of that which suspends wisdom and power. Hence Paul writes, "But god hath chosen the foolish things of the world to confound the wise; and God hath chosen the weak things of the world to confound the things which are mighty" (1 Corinthians 1:27). The principle of inversion here is not something governed by a logic of desire and hence *anticipated* but by a logic of suspension which provokes the ambiguity of the spectacle of suffering mentioned before. Paul continues, "And base things of the world and things which are despised, hath God chosen yea, and things which are not, to bring to naught things that are." (1 Corinthians 1:28). So instead of the distinction between the Greeks and the Jews–which in a sense perfectly captured the problem of difference in Antiquity–based on different objects of desire creating the same logic of identity Paul introduces something else to unify the Christian community. Not a formal ontological distinction between that which is not (*me onta*) and that which is (*ta onta*) but rather a strategic deployment of one to suspend the other. As a result the Christian community is created against the glory of all flesh; "that no flesh should glory in his presence" (1 Corinthians 1:29), by a dissolution of the old distinction between the Jews and the Greeks. Paul writes, "but we preach Christ crucified, unto the Jews a stumbling block, and unto the Greeks foolishness" (1 Corinthians 1:23). As Breton correctly observes that the new collective that Paul envisages, an ensemble which comes together under the sign of contradiction, the *Logos* of the *Stauros* has nothing to do with a social abstraction or a category of persons conceived through differences subsumed by a concept of identity. It is rather the spectacle of bringing into the world something through a peculiar suspension of "that which is" by that "which is not". Hence, and here again we follow Breton, it is a question of "death of evidence" for a true beginning. The words of Paul which makes sense of the problem of spectacle cannot be separated from this logic of suspension: The dissolution of all worldly categories to identify bodies, such that a new body might come into being through a lingusitic operation which is something akin to a performative utterance.

When in the early 1960s J.L. Austin's book *How To Do Things with Words* (1962) came out, it gave a new trajectory to a long debate within language philosophy and among linguists as how to develop a relation between language and the world, between words and facts. What Austin proposed through the performative speech acts was path breaking so far as it proposed a linguistic utterance which was not only related to a fact but was simultaneously and immediately a fact in itself. Here language is seen not simply from the point of view of constative or meaningful utterances but from the point of view of efficacy or performative utterances. But as Giorgio Agamben has shown, this performative operation cannot take place without the suspension of the normal denotative function of language. The performative verb (like 'I promise') is inevitably constructed by a *dictum* which in itself is a normal statement, a constative utterance which has to be attached to the performative verb without which it remains empty and without effect. (Hence 'I promise' would only have value so far as it is attached to the *dictum*–for example–'that tomorrow it is going to rain'). So we see that the performative verb which in itself is empty and without value is made effective only when attached to a denotative utterance whose denotation it suspends, making it empty in turn.

Thus the foolish things of the world would not simply confound the wise and the weak would not only confound the mighty by inverting the given order but the performative gesture of this utterance would make the world shine in the reflected glory of god because as Paul writes this suspension of the worldly glory is replaced by the glory of God. Hence the performative utterance of the suspension of all worldly glory of wisdom and might is immediately followed by the spectacle of the glory of the Lord. "He that glorieth, let him glory in the Lord" (1 Corinthian 1:31).

From the point of view of glory, the performative utterance functions like an optical contraption. Like a mirror it displaces the object from its actual field, suspending that field and displacing it into somewhere else, a non-denotative field of pure reflection, of only surfaces and immediate realities. But such surfaces can only emerge at the expense of depth which is suspended or perhaps better kept at a perpetual abeyance. The profundity of the world gives up its depth at the foot of the cross, such that all depth of wisdom becomes the folly of surfaces, and all folly carries within it the displaced and suspended profundity of its hitherto reality in order to effectuate the coming together of a new body, the Christian body under the sign of the Cross. The logos of the cross is thus a performative utterance par excellence which is not the wisdom of word but the reflected glory of the kingdom of God. Hence Paul can write, "For the kingdom of God is not in word but in power" (1 Corinthians 4:21). Now we see the expressivity of the "Logos of the Cross" emerging not merely as denotative of a particular discourse but as efficacy which not only takes the place of the former but effectuates a new beginning based solely upon the condition of displacement. The logos of the cross is not simply a negation of the flesh, but the creation of an immaculate body which shines in the reflected light of the lord.

From Spectacle to Glory: Continuation of the Pauline Logic

The use of the theatrical image of spectacle in the Pauline context is thus inextricably linked with the problem of glory. The ambiguity of the point of view of this spectacle is something the ancient world had not known. To become a spectacle to the world is thus distinct from the idea of the suffering philosopher who becomes a spectacle to the gods and men as proposed by Epictetus. Now it is no longer the question of "the true philosopher who offers a spectacle, particularly in misfortune, to delight both men and gods" (Blumenberg, 1997, p. 153) as Epictetus observes in his *Diatribes*.

To become a spectacle in this sense presupposes a spectator-god whose indifference to the affairs of life anticipates *distance.* It is this distance which becomes the principle under which the philosopher can master the empty suffering of the world in order to overcome the emptiness of the world stage. In his suffering, the philosopher is uplifted and displayed to the gods, who though invisible are watching. But by the same gesture, or rather as a consequence of this suffering which the philosopher masters, he himself is placed beside the gods gaze, as the transcendental spectator. By this double movement, the philosopher not only offers a spectacle of his own suffering in the face of gods but himself occupies a position next to the gods. As a man who has overcome and hence distanced himself from the tumultuous sea of life[2], he is no longer a mere mortal but a sage, a transcendental spectator who delights in his own indifference. Hans Blumenberg has noted that the pleasure or delight of this transcendental spectator is not a sadistic pleasure of seeing someone else suffer. It is the joy of realizing the safety of one's own solid ground which is distant from the sea of suffering that the world entails. Blumenberg observes:

> Clearly, the pleasantness that is said to characterize this sight is not a result of seeing someone else suffer but of enjoying the safety of one's own standpoint. It has nothing to do with a relationship among men, between those who suffer and those who do not; it has rather to do with the relationship between philosophers and reality; it has to do with the advantage gained through Epicurus' philosophy, the possession of an inviolable, solid ground for one's view of the world. Even the spectator of mighty battles who is not threatened by the perils of war has to be aware of the difference between the need for happiness and the ruthless caprice of physical reality. Only the observer who is secured by philosophy can blunt this difference into a distance. It is the sage–or at least the man who is prepared for the natural process and the business of the world by the *doctrina sapientum*– who both carries theory ideal of classical Greek philosophy, figured by the spectator, through to its end and contradicts it on a decisive point. (Blumenberg, 1997, p. 26)

The contradiction of the spectator who is operating between two orders–between being a transcendental spectator whose gaze comes as result of self-consciousness which nonetheless is caught in the immanent world order–finally finds its expression in the paradoxical rift between being and praxis, between transcendence and immanence that in a sense Christianity properly inaugurates. But before we enter the complex domain of this fracture let us remember that though part of the same problem, the Pauline concept of the spectacle rather than apparently solving the paradox of the abyss that separates transcendence and immanence, *uses* it in order to imagine a new body which is that of the messianic community.

As we can clearly understand the spectacle of which Paul talks of is a far cry from this notion of the transcendental spectator who through wisdom acquires or possesses a firm ground in order to delight in his distance from the world. In Paul we do not have any simple opposition between possession and privation where one is separated from the other to be reversed in a future situation. Every possession is a privation and every privation is a true possession because the spectator is not the transcendental spectator, but a spectator of mirror images. It is here that the Pauline idea of glory becomes so important to understand the metaphor of the spectacle that in a sense inaugurates the problem of theatre in Christianity.

Paul begins his meditation on glory in the second letter to the Corinthians by critiquing the glory of the letter (law) as the ministration of death. When Paul writes, "who also hath made us able ministers of the new testament, not of the letter, but of the spirit; for the letter killeth but the spirit givieth life" (2 Corinthians 3:6). We need to understand 'letter' here not merely as law which administers death but also as the sign of the arbitrary sovereignty, the marvellous nature of power which the Jews according to Paul lay claim to, as we discussed before. Thus we see an inaugural critique of this sovereign glory of law that 'killeth' when Paul discards the Judaic idea of *kabodh* which illuminates Mosses' face after he receives the tablets of law from God. Against this provisional glory–which was "to be done away" with but which nonetheless had to be placed under a veil (*kalymma*) because the children of Israel could not look at Moses' face touched by the glory of god directly–Paul announces the infinite glory of the Messiah which he brings as a result of the "ministration of redemption". This incomparable glory is not that of death but of life which shines like a mirror reflecting but also radiating the glory of god. This unveiling of all secret source of power and glory coincides with the coming together of the messianic community which is illuminated by a universal light in which all becomes mirror images of each other. Hence Paul writes, "But we all, with open face beholding as in glass the glory of the Lord, are changed into the same image from glory to glory, even as by the spirit of the Lord (2 Corinthians 3:18). As Agamben points out that in Hebrews 1:3 we hear the echo of this same operation when the Son becomes *apaugasma* in the sense of being *reflection and radiation simultaneously.* In the case of Paul, Agamben explains:

> The optical phenomenology of glory unfolds in the following way: God, "the father of glory" (Ephesians 1:17), radiates his glory onto the face of Christ who reflects it and radiates it in turn like a mirror on to the members of the messianic community. The celebrated eschatological verse 1 Corinthians 13:12 should be read in this light: the glory that we now see enigmatically in a mirror, we will go on to see face-to-face. In the present we await the "glorious appearing" (Titus 2:13) in the same way as all that which is created impatiently waits to be "delivered from the bondage of corruption into the glorious liberty of the children of god" (Agamben 2011, p. 204).

Now it is true that Agamben specifies the messianic nature of this idea of glory which emphasizes on radiation rather than a reciprocal doctrine of glory. This makes Paul's use of the theatrical image of spectacle both central but also distinct from the doctrine of glory in later Christian writings. But in order to properly understand the implication of this set of theatrical and optical images–spectacle-glory, reflection-radiation–we need to understand that they are related not simply to an idea of being as appearance, where the world is transformed into a constellation of mirrors which reflects each other so far as they reflect the glory of god such that what is left in the immanent order are only surfaces. What is also imperative is to grant these surfaces an ethical reality which cannot be avoided at any cost. The celebrated verse of 1 Corinthians 13:12 mentioned above–"For now we see through a glass darkly: but then face to face, now I know in part, but then shall I know even as also I am known"–is immediately followed by the line "And now abideth faith, hope, charity, these three, but the greatest of these is charity" (1 Corinthians 13:13). The importance of charity in Paul cannot be confused with the later idea of charity, particularly starting from Augustine which is related to a Christian idea of love.[3] In introducing the idea of charity as the greatest of all ethical imperatives, Paul at the same time warns us of the "glory of the flesh". Thus Pauline idea of charity cannot be derived from the prevalent notions of public expenditure or philanthropic activities. Hence we see in Paul a call for charity as praxis which is outside the antiquarian idea of *euergetism* which is related to personal glory or *megalopsychia* (greatness of the soul). But at the same time it is an activity, a praxis *in* the world, a world which is however seen through the 'optical phenomenology' of mirrors and glasses. We see here an effort to bring praxis together with the idea of appearances. As we know according to Paul partial knowledge will be fulfilled, faith will become knowledge and hope will turn into certainty with the *parousia*. Faith and hope announces the paradoxical eschatological relation between the immanent order of the world and the transcendent order of god's true glory. But the two quintessentially theatrical elements, appearance and praxis, spectacular glory and charity as praxis seem to correspond to each other in Paul because they remain inherently of the immanent order. It perhaps opens up a new paradox in Paul which is akin to a paradox immanent to theatre. The world is on the one hand made into an image, an appearance, on the surface of a mirror but on the other hand, it is also real so far as the practice of charity is a real praxis and is given the highest importance. It is praxis in its true Aristotelian sense because it does not seek any *telos* or end or fulfilment. Hence unlike the Judaic idea of martyrdom and suffering which is related to a sacrificial logic of *telos*, charity is a pure praxis of messianic life. It is completely enclosed in itself and is hence *without any principle outside itself.* To that extent charity is always without an *arche* which is outside itself. Charity like theatre is fundamentally an anarchic activity. And while charity gets attached to ethics and thus loses its fundamental anarchic nature, so does theatre get attached to aesthetics and lose its anarchic heart. In charity, one only reflects the glorious kindness of God without claiming anything in return. Charity can never operate in this sense as an acclamatory gesture, and yet it is also an anarchic gesture of pure praxis. Hence we can understand the suffering of the apostles for the messianic community as nothing but an act of charity which corresponds neither to the antiquarian idea of a glory of the flesh nor a Judaic idea of martyrdom. So while Agamben points to the idea of glory in Paul as radiation and not as a paradoxical reciprocity of glory and glorification which keeps it outside the economic paradigm of the trinity in its absolute declaration of the messianic redemption, we have tried to show that this idea of a messianic life is nonetheless a life of glory and praxis which are brought together in the idea of spectacle and charity but which nevertheless traverses a different paradoxical path which is equally anarchic.

Glory as Acclamation: A Political Question

When Hans Von Balthasar identified this Pauline idea of the spectacle as part of an acclamatory legacy of spectacular suffering and martyrdom dating back to the Judaic tradition, he might not have given this particular line in Paul its distinct status which it deserved and which we have briefly tried to elaborate till now. But undoubtedly, Balthasar was correct in pointing out the relation between the theatrical image of suffering in both Christianity and Judaism to public acclamations. As we have tried to show in the previous chapter the relation between the discourse around theatre and the Roman idea of *euergetism* was fundamentally informed by an idea of public acclamation and glorification. That the use of the theatrical image in Christianity would be linked to the idea of acclamation hence should not come as a surprise. The Roman practice of euergetism becomes the site where theatre and glory come together to perform a public function which is essentially political. But even in Christianity, which would officially ban theatrical shows by the time of Justinian, it is interesting to see that some of the earliest use of the theatrical image is implicitly linked to the problem of glory and power. This not only anticipates the later emergence of theatre from the Christian liturgical practices which were, as we shall see later inherently doxological practices to exercise power through the doctrine of glory. These early uses of the theatrical images, particularly that of the public spectacle of suffering in relation to the Judeo- Christian concept of glory identifies the problem of theatre as a quintessentially political problem.

To understand the problem of glory as a political problem within Christianity, Agamben offers a juxtaposed reading of Eric Peterson's dissertation of 1926 titled *Heis Theos* and Carl Schmitt's 1927 article "Referendum and Petition for a Referendum" where Schmitt refers to Peterson's thesis. Although in his 1935 monograph *Monotheism as a Political Problem,* Peterson had vehemently argued against any possibility for a Christian political theology, he nevertheless continued to propose the 'public' and 'political' nature of the Church in its participation in the celestial city through liturgies. Quoting Peterson from another of his short texts from 1935 on angels, Agamben points out this connection between the acclamatory and liturgical aspect of the Church and the Kingdom of God. "The development of the Church", Agamben quotes from Peterson, "leads from the earthly to the celestial Jerusalem, from the city of the Jews to that of the angels and saints" (Agamben, 2011, p. 114). Now the liturgical route that Agamben identifies in Peterson's thesis which connects the 'public' nature of the Church to the "citizens of heaven" stems from his earlier understanding of the acclamatory nature of doxological practices of Christian liturgies. In his dissertation Peterson argues that the formulae of *Heis theos* should not be seen as a profession of faith but rather as an acclamation whose roots extend to imperial acclamatory and ceremonial practices of power. If one understand acclamation as an exhortation of victory or of praise shouted by the crowd which was an integral part of the public domain in Roman antiquity–where public gathering in theatre and circuses served the political function of acclamation through applause or waving of handkerchiefs not only to athletes and actors but to magistrates of the Roman Republic or to the Emperor–then we begin to understand the political function of the Christian liturgies. It is this public function of the acclamations that–following Peterson, Agamben argues–becomes informed by juridical value. The politico-religious character of such practices when imbued with juridical value not only articulates the inherent relation between law and liturgy but "expresses, in the form of acclamation, the people's *consensus*" (Agamben, 2011, p. 170) [4]. It is here that we see the acclamatory function of glory which spills over and extends its religio-political boundary to enter the profane order of the 'people' and its political function in modern democracy.

"Just as for Peterson the acclamations and liturgical doxologies express the juridical and public character of the Christian people (*laos*)," writes Agamben, "so for Schmitt the acclamation is the pure and immediate expression of the people as constituent democratic power" (Agamben, 2011, p. 171). As distinct from the power exercised under the prescribed form determined by the constitution, this constituent power (*pouvoir constituent*) has an immediate force of constituting the people *as people* through something like consensus. This effect of a pure or direct democracy is in contrast to the liberal democratic practice of the secret ballot. Agamben identifies the theologio-political source of Schmitt's analysis of referendum as popular decision and the constituent power of direct democracy in Peterson's thesis of the political nature of Christian acclamatory practices. Agamben quotes Schmitt's text:

> This scientific discovery of the acclamation is the starting point for an explanation of the procedure of direct or pure democracy. One must not ignore the fact that, whenever there is public opinion as social reality and not merely as a political pretext, in all the decisive moments in which the

> political meaning of a people can be affirmed, there first appear acclamations of approval or refusal that are independent of the voting procedure, because through such a procedure their genuineness could be threatened, insofar as the immediacy of the people united, which defines this acclamation, is annulled by the isolation of the single voter and by the secrecy of the ballot. (Agamben, 2011, p. 172)

If, as Schmitt argues, acclamation remains the "eternal phenomenon of all political communities" (Ibid., p. 172) then the political function of the constituent power of the Christian people (*laos*) becomes evident. This is already affirmed by Peterson's thesis of the politico-religious nature of the church when he wrote that the relation between the celestial *polis* and the earthly *Ekklesia* remains political which is maintained through worship. As he remarked, "It is a case of the politico-religious concept or, in other words, of the concept of order of a celestial hierarchy that the worship of the Church issues in. This is further confirmation of our thesis that Christian worship has an originary relation to the political sphere" (Ibid., p. 145).[5]

Two Preliminary Hypotheses

We find here an articulation of our first hypothesis: the relation between power and glory becomes the turning point of the conflict between the Church and the theatre as two conflicting sites of acclamations where two constituent powers fought a glorious battle against each other in an effort to constitute two separate bodies of people. It is from this perspective that we need to analyse not only the ideological attack against theatre by the church fathers but also the competitive representative practices of the patristic tradition, as we shall see later.

From this we can form our second hypothesis based on the following problematization: the obstacle posed by the cultural practice of theatre (and other such performative spectacles with definite 'public' and 'political' functions in imperial Rome) results in the development of a set of practical solutions–by the early fathers and continuing later–behind which we find a general form of problematization. The nature of this problem which elicits a number of responses, sometimes contradictory, revolves around the question of glory and the function of spectacle. The problem of theatre in Christianity is related to this general problematization of the spectacle and glory. This effort to problematize was informed not only by a desire to manifest the difficulties of existent spectacular practices but create the conditions where the given state of affairs could be transformed into a question mark. To understand this inaugural moment of Christianity as a point of problematization of theatre could thus be articulated in the following fashion: the *problem of theatre* appears at the point on the existent cultural surface, where certain forms (spectacular/performative) were held in particular relation with certain forces (the political function these forms served). It is at this point something intervened in order to put these relations to question. This point where the given set of relations were put to question generated a diverse set of responses concerning the nature and function of spectacle which continued to produce contradictory arguments and points of dispute throughout the history of Christianity. But such responses could not have been possible without this surface of cultural practices being transformed into a field of problematization. Regarding the question of theatre, what Michel Foucault calls "the specific work of thought" (Foucault, *Ethics: Subjectivity and Truth*, 1997, p. 118), was no longer ethical in nature but a religious question (though with definite ethical implications) while simultaneously, related to the understanding of earthly and divine glory. It is only through an analysis of the problem of glory within Christian discursive practices that we can understand its relation not only to obvious spectacular and ritual practices like liturgy but to certain implicit theatrical images like that of the "world stage".

Here we can propose our second hypothesis: the new meaning ascribed to the theatrical image of "world stage" in Christianity as representing the hierarchic articulation of the celestial order which we find during the Renaissance, for example in the writings of Guillio Cammilio, can be traced back to its liturgical sources retracing its steps back through the mystery and miracle plays to this defining moment of relating the earthly power of the Church to the divine power of the Kingdom of God through worship and hence glory. But for an elaboration of this second hypothesis we need to further examine the nexus between worship and the maintenance of the celestial order of hierarchy or, in other words, between glory and *oikonomia*.

Glorious Reciprocity: A Theological Question

While we have tried briefly to understand the peculiar nature of this relation between power and glory and its relation to theatre in Roman antiquity in the previous section, we now need to briefly examine the singular nature of the *problem* of glory within Christianity.

We know that the Septuagint translates *kabodh*–the Hebraic term which announces in the old testament the eschatological meaning of the full glory of God–as *doxa* which goes on to become the technical term used in the new testament for glory. In the rabbinical Judaism *Kabodh* which is related to *Shekinah* literally meaning the residence or abode of God signified an element external to God, something that made him appear or come to presence. It is this external meaning of the term which would be drastically altered in Christianity making it something internal to the Trinitarian logic. To make *doxa* coincide with the Trinitarian logic was to make it correspond to the mystery of the Trinitarian economy. Now we know that from Paul to the early fathers, particularly Tertullian and Hippolytus, the meaning of the term *oikonomia* goes through a major change. Whereas Paul's doctrine was seen as the "economy of the mystery"–where oikonomia was understood as the fiduciary activity or obligatory task that the faithful has received of announcing the coming of the Messiah where Paul is given the work of revealing what was a mystery to the world–with the early patristic tradition particularly from Tertullian was seen as the "mystery of the economy" designating the technico-religious concept of the Trinitarian expression of divine life. Hence was introduced not only the aporetic relation between being and praxis but more precisely between the economy of salvation seen as the divine praxis and the economy of trinity understood as an ontological expression. Between the two was a distinction that existed only because they were inseparable. It is this aporetic understanding of economic theology based upon the Trinitarian logic which constitutes the nexus between *doxa* and *oikonomia*, between glory and economy which finally becomes the condition on which the problem of theatre in Christianity would keep oscillating between its liturgical form and its okionomic content. Starting with John we have the Trinitarian logic of glory articulated in the reciprocal glorification of the Father and Son. "Father, the hour is come; glorify thy son, that thy Son also may glorify thee [...] I have glorified thee on earth: I have finished the work which though gavest me to do. And now, O Father, glorify thou me with thine own self with the glory which I had with thee before the world was" (John 17:1-5). This reciprocal expression of glory will open the circularity of the argument about the work of salvation accomplished by Jesus on earth as the glorification of father which is to say the economy of glory which perfectly coincides with the glory emanated by God through which the son is glorified, which is to say the Trinitarian glory residing in the being of god. This symmetrical nature of the argument is summed up by Agamben "...all economy must become glory and all glory become economy (Agamben, 2011, p. 210). The political implication of this becomes evident in the idea of the profane order of glory, or glorification which becomes an attribute not of Government (the glory of economy of salvation) but of the sovereign order of the Kingdom (the glory of the economy of the trinity) just like all the doxa refers finally not to the government but the Kingdom of God which the Governmental machine nevertheless articulates. The governmental machine thus expresses the dialectics between the economic order of a management of the glory and the glorious (liturgical) articulation of the very mystery of the economy. "Government glorifies the Kingdom, and the kingdom glorifies Government. But the centre of the machine is empty, and glory is nothing but the splendor that emanates from this emptiness, the inexhaustible *kabodh* that at once reveals and veils the central vacuity of the machine" (Agamben, 2011, p. 211).

Now this paradox consists of the objective glory of God which is eternally self identical and remains completely exclusive to him and can neither be increased nor reduced. The subjective glory as glorification which is a *demand* of this very glory that all creatures *are indebted to* becomes the condition for the impossible task of glorification defined by theology, as the constant effort to subjectively glorify something whose glory can never be affected, either increased or decrease. On the contrary this infinite objective glory becomes the condition of possibility of all worldy acts of glorification, of being subjectively indebted to an obligation to glorify through external acts. This paradox sustains the logic of the expansion of the Church in later years continually expanding its reach; moving, on the one hand, to seek out new terrains to bring under this expansive logic of glorification while at the same time moving into the most intimate micro-practices of life, and not simply obvious ceremonial/liturgical praise of hymn. All this work presupposed by the transcendent glory of god which cannot transform and hence the work always remain incomplete, indebted to the fundamental lack in the system.

Origen explains this aporetic principle of glory through a theory of knowledge which becomes rather interesting when contrasted to the idea of glory as *kleos* in ancient Greece which was attached to the domain of words and "that which is heard" as Agamben points out. This meant that for the ancients glory was related to the particular domain of intuitive knowledge which was the prerogative of the poets as Plato points out in *Ion*. But in Origen, Agamben notes, glory comes as the divine self-knowledge (*autosophia*). Origen writes:

> If, from the corporeal standpoint, a divine epiphany is produced under the tent and in the temple and on the face of Moses after he spoke with God, from the analogical point of view one could speak of the "vision of the Glory of God", that which is known and seen in God with an entirely purified intellect. The intellect that has been purified and has overcome all material things so as to carefully contemplate God, becomes divine through that which it contemplates. One can say that that is

> what glorification of the face of him who has contemplated God consists in. (Agamben, 2011, p. 206)[6]

Thus we can understand that for Origen the question of glorification which he relates to the domain of knowledge follows the same structural logic of glory and glorification. The completely selfenclosed self-knowledge of God which nonetheless becomes the condition for the possibility of the contemplative subject to produce any individual statement of knowledge. The individual intellect assumes its individuality so far as it can overcome all other elements which obscures its vision, the material things which he has to question or doubt such that he can participate in the divine enunciation of an absolute knowledge which glorifies the face of man at the moment of divine epiphany. Through a leap the individual subject who puts everything in the material world under the paranoiac lens of doubt, who sees everywhere elements filled with impurities, recuperates what he has lost in relation to material knowledge in the divine certitude of gods knowledge of himself. This split between the subject of a worldly knowledge who nevertheless is always participating *in* some transcendental *autosophia* is a type of thinking which is perhaps the true legacy of 'Western thought'. In Christianity we see this dualism being played out between immanence and transcendence in many forms, the split between being and praxis being one of them. The split becomes even more evident when we consider further Origen's writing about the reciprocal glorification of father and son conceived in terms of knowledge. He writes:

> Thus, knowing the Father, the Son has been glorified through his very knowledge, which is the greatest good and leads to perfect knowledge since it is that with which the Son knows the Father. I believe, however, that he has been glorified by his knowledge, since it is in this way that he comes to know himself [...] All this glory, through which the Son of man is glorified, was glorified by a gift of the Father. And of all the elements that lead to the full glory of man, the principal is God as he is not glorified simply because he is known *by* the Son, but is glorified *in* his Son. (Agamben, 2011, p. 207)[7].

From the theological perspective, we see here in the circularity of the argument of reciprocal glory, presupposing the self-knowledge of God which produces glory *in* the Son and not by the Son, what Agamben remarks as the perfect coincidence of the "economy of passion" with the "economy of revelation" . In other words, we see in identical terms the economy of salvation and the economy of trinity in this circularity of glory and glorification. But we also see here in the economy of passion a principle of knowledge which situates individual subjective knowledge (in the form of statement, and what is the passion of Christ if not a 'statement' in the world) in the split between the individual and that which individualizes. To be glorified in the Son means that the individuality of the Son who knows, always already carries within itself the principle of individuation which is that of the Father. In this way it is not simply a question of the Trinitarian doctrine of One substance expressed in three modalities but a split subject, who is always a subject of statement and a subject of enunciation. This problem of individuation or the production of subjectivity which Deleuze shows in Descartes *cogito* is already anticipated in the Trinitarian logic of knowledge.

As we can now understand this relation between knowledge and glory in Christian theology is quite different from the way the Ancients interpreted glory not as *doxa* but as *kleos* which was related to the domain of words and "that which is heard". To that extent this glory was not identical to divine self-knowledge but to the glorification generated out of the special activity of the poets. Of course, the skill of the poets was possible because of divine cooperation of the muses but it was not any form of skill (*techne*) which would lead to knowledge either as its result or even any form of knowledge which was self-evident within the skill. As Plato argued in Ion which we have tried to show in the first chapter, this skill was not of the order of knowledge, in so far as knowledge was self-individuating because the skill of the rhapsode (and by extension the poet) lead to false knowledge or imitation. Hence though, as Agamben argues that in the Homeric world, glory was exclusively the work of man and hence glorification, a different route was conceived to subject it to an idea of government. But interestingly, the nature of the relation which connected the glorification of the poets to the domain of governmentality was determined by a logic of desire. If the acts of the poets were glorifying acts per excellence, then they were also pleasure producing actions. In a number of texts most importantly *Laws*, Plato conceives of a conceptual framework to govern this production of pleasure by the poets (which included a large variety of figures from the tragedian and the rhapsode to the musician and the dancer) under the axiomatic principle of truth, through what he calls governors of Dionysius. These aged men of Dionysius, would have the experience and the skill to *minimally* participate in such acts but would nonetheless set the standard for these glorifying acts according to a principle of harmony and good judgment informed by reason and finally truth. They would see to it that in these acts of glorification no such pleasure is produced which would disturb the natural ordering of society, by say mixing melodies and gestures suitable of women with words for free men. But if we investigate further, as we have tried to do in the first chapter, we see that this government of pleasure could only be instituted under the sign of an original principle of Truth. This platonic idea of Truth in itself which was the condition of all earthly knowledge and yet no earthly knowledge could exhaust it was something that the acts of poets glorified in the final instant. But according to Plato, the poets glorify this truth, which is none other than the divine order, not through the mediation of knowledge but directly through divine inspiration. The domain of poetic glorification does not pass through the dialectics of knowledge to arrive at the gates of truth[8] but somehow manages to represent the inherent glory of truth through something like imitation. But such acts of glorification would only be possible if there was some inherent glory to truth, a glory exclusive to the concept of the Idea itself which dazes ones vision when one arrives out of the cave into the realm of truth and which one can only bring back into the worldly domain as mere reflection. Hence the source of the poetic glorification remains, even in Plato an exclusive glory of truth, whose dazzling spectacle can only be represented and hence glorified in return either through the mediated knowledge of dialectic or directly through poetic intuition but always incompletely.

The Glorious Machine: The Desiring Machine

Now we can better express the entire glorious machine as a desiring machine which presupposes a lack, which constantly articulates the provisional and provincial acts of knowledge, of satisfaction, of pleasure, of glorification only to be made incomplete in the process. When understood in terms of desire[9], every act of glorification seems akin to every act of desire which produces a discharge, in the form of pleasure and satisfaction. But like every discharge, instead of saturating and exhausting desire would only add to its continuum, thereby reactivating the desiring machine, every act of glorification contributes to the transcendental glory of God in so far as it re-affirms its infinite glory negatively by contributing nothing to it. As an eternal Other and an original lack the Father always produces the condition for seeking more and more glorification, more and more pleasure, such that being and praxis, transcendence and immanence would always be separated only to be reconciled. The only way for this split to be joined is through repetition, but such repetition is always without substance like all ceremonial repetition because at the very core of this repetition is an emptiness which can never be filled up. Therefore, glorification has to be re-enacted, the process starts again to produce the same (non)effect ritually and perpetually and the desiring machine continues to produce more desire, effectuate more glory. The revolving desiring machine thus produces through the desire-lack compound, the glorious emptiness of all glory which the *oikonomia* seeks to manage and maintain through providence. The early use of the theatrical image of spectacle is thus not only related to the theological domain of the problem of glory, but as we can understand from our discussion, is already related to the existential domain of producing a particular form of subjectivity, a split between this world and the next. A number of terms, world stage, theatre of the world, scene of life, theatre of life are all related in this sense to a number of concepts namely that of praxis, appearance, spectacle, order, oikonomia, being, harmony, truth. But we find the use of these theatrical terms always in the disjunctive synthesis between two concepts. Thus spectacle appears in the inseparable facture between being and praxis, theatre appears at the aporetic relation between being and appearance. Similarly, the earliest idea of 'world theatre' in Christianity appears at the split between the ordering of the world through divine providence and the condition of that order which resides in the divine will which is inseparable from the divine substance and yet they must be seen as different from each other.

Metaphor: Theatre and Economy

It is in the writings of Clement of Alexandria that we see the use of the term 'drama' used to describe the redemptive history of mankind. In *Protreptikos*, Clement writes:

> Without divine providence the Lord would not have been able to complete such a gigantic task in such a short time; on account of his external appearance he was despised, but because of what he achieved he was worshipped...For neither did the message meet with disbelief when his coming was first announced, nor did he remain unknown when he adopted the human mask and clothed himself in flesh in order to perform the drama of mankind's redemption. For he was a genuine combatant striving with his creature (Balthasar, 1988, p. 95).

The use of the metaphor of theatre to describe the Christological event here is interesting for a number of reason. The introduction of the question of providence in Christian theology is a singular moment, attributed to Clement of Alexandria which in a sense inaugurates the relation between Christian theology and history, through the insertion of the concept of *oikonomia*. As we have already discussed above, the beginning of the theological-economic paradigm witnesses a shift from the economy of the mystery, a general use of oikonomia as something like a fiduciary activity in Paul to the treatment of the Trinitarian logic of oikonomia as a mystery in itself, starting with Tertullian and Hypollitus. This shift not only elaborates a fracture in the understanding of the economy of trinity as distinct from the economy of salvation, a rift which simultaneously announced the inseparability of being and action, but with the introduction of the problem of providence, oikonomia became indistinguishable with the question of providence (*pronia*). With providence, God's voluntary act of creating the world separated it from a pagan idea of fate, which was determined as an external force following some unchangeable necessity like it does for the stoics. But with providence, the question of free will was introduced into the Christian imagination only to be subsumed by the paradox of 'divine plan' which ought to remain a mystery. The following lines from Origen clearly express the paradox of providence as something which is free and necessary, proclaiming free action and divine logos at the same time. Origen writes:

> We think that god, parent of all things, in providing for the salvation of his entire creation through the unspeakable plan of his logos and wisdom, has so ordered everything that each spirit or soul, or whatever else rational existences ought to be called, should not be compelled by force against its free choice to any action except that to which the motions of their wills would work suitable and usefully together to produce the harmony of the single world. (Agamben, 2011, p. 46)

In other words, providence defines that particular movement of God's creation which being an absolutely free act is the only standard of freedom available to the 'free' Christian subject who are obliged to be free as part of the únspeakable' 'and mysterious plan of divine logos. It is this 'mystery of freedom' which is on the one hand actualized by the economic and governmental logic of the Church, while on the other hand, it has to be vehemently followed by orienting one's will to the divine will which would be argued as the only act of freedom available to the Christian subject, all other acts being governed by conditions of forceful external necessity imposed by the devil[10]. This imperative of freedom would lead to subjective practices which would produce the confessional paradigm of Christianity. In fact the subjective aspect of divine providence realized through the economic paradigm becomes evident in Clement when we read certain sections of his masterpiece *Stromata*, where he uses oikonomia not only to propose a management of the house but of the soul itself which is perfectly mirrored in the entire universe. From an economy which regulates the flow of the mother's milk , an "economy of milk" Clement smoothly moves to the "economy of the savior" whose authenticity is guaranteed by providence. This mirroring of the individual and the world is a singular logic of not only the economic paradigm that Clement is trying to articulate through a concept of providence. This reflection of the macrocosm in the microcosm is the inherent idea behind the metaphor of 'theatrum mundi' which will flourish during the Renaissance. In Clement we perhaps see if not the earliest then at least the most articulate expression of this mirror effect which also indicated the close relation of the use of the economic metaphor and the metaphor of theatre.

But if we go back to our earlier citation from *Protreptikos*, we see the relation between the economic metaphor and the theatre take a new meaning under the concept of providence. Clement argues here that the drama of salvation, which seems to have the characteristics of theatre where the true divine nature of the lord was hidden behind his human face and his mortal flesh was like the costume worn by an actor, could only sustain its truth through something like the divine providence. Providence becomes the guarantor of the authenticity of the economy of salvation which corresponds to a drama. The economy of salvation corresponds to a theatre whose content maybe the history of redemption but it is a content whose authenticity is not self evident without divine providence. We need to understand here that Clement's entire project was to prevent the "economy of salvation" from being called a myth or an allegory. He remarks that it is quite possible to interpret the incarnation of the Son of the Creator, the becoming flesh of the Son of God in the womb of a virgin as a parable. All such actions might "appear indeed as a parable to those who know not the truth". One can easily see where this apprehension was generated when one turns to the theatres of contemporary antiquity particularly in such urban centres like Alexandria. It would not be perhaps absurd to speculate that the danger of the 'vain fables' portrayed in the 'theatres' was lurking behind his intention to distinguish 'the economy of salvation' not as a fable, a "story about gods" but a 'historical fact'. He writes at the very beginning of *Stromata,* Book I, Chapter XI, "the philosophy that is in accordance with divine tradition establishes and confirms providence, which, being done away with, the economy of the savior appears to be a myth" (Agamben, 2011, p. 47). We see here a slight inflection of the providence factor. It is not simply providence but the interpretation of it by a divine philosophy which would guarantee the non-mythic character of the drama of the economy of salvation. A divine philosophy which would not only act as a guarantor of the truth of providence which is not self-evident or immediate in the economy but which can be made immediate and truthful only through the immediacy of interpretation. We will deviate from Agamben here who understands in this move a clear distinction of Christian theology from pagan mythology and "theology". Agamben writes, "If we do not understand the very close connection that links oikonomia with providence, it is not possible to measure the novelty of Christian theology with regard to pagan mythology and "theology"" (Agamben, 2011, p. 47). While we are indebted to his scholarship which provides us the historical tools to establish this relationship between oikonomia and providence, we would like to argue that the problem needs to be perhaps understood from the point of view of the relation between theatre and philosophy whose history we have tried to reproduce schematically in the previous chapters. The clear correspondence of the economic metaphor to the theatrical metaphor in understanding the problem of salvation along with the fact that what Clement seeks here is a certain regime of truth, a certain legitimacy to a phenomenon which is ridiculously close to a fabulous structure seems to direct us to another direction. As we have seen in our earlier chapters, the fundamental relation between theatre and philosophy was determined by a certain interpretative force of philosophy to produce *a regime of truth* which could not only govern theatre but determine what myths to keep and what to discard according to principles belonging to different traditions from the history of philosophy. We saw this logic quite evidently functioning in Plato in his relation to the legitimacy of the poets.

We would argue that the immediacy of the oikonomia as the activity of self-revelation, in other words, providence could only take place in Clement through this interpretative force of philosophy to manifest the truth, a certain performative glory of philosophy, in this case a divine philosophy to manifest the truth. This force to legitimize has nothing to do with the actual interpretative content of the philosophy or for that matter any exegesis. Our investigation leads us to believe that in case of the ancients the performative glory of truth, or following Foucault one could say an alethurgic glory which was the exclusive domain of philosophy, was in constant tension with another domain of production of glory which was that of theatre. In case of Christianity, both the harangue against theatre and the paradoxical use of the theatrical image indicates its consciousness of the glorificatory logic of theatre. But now this glory of theatre and its efficacy (even as a metaphor) had to be both unleashed and simultaneously brought under the control of an alethurgic glory which was divine.

The problem arises when ever theatre seeks to pursue its own glory and no longer remains a glorificatory medium. Since Plato the effort has been to control this glory and efficacy of theatre and transform it into glorificatory machines. Aristotle tried to do this internally, through the production of a theory of theatre around katharsis, *which would make the inherent and autonomous glory of theatre docile by rendering it impotent. The entire notion of reducing theatre to its dramatic text, wherein lies its meaning and principle could be explained through this logic of governing the inherent anarchic economy of theatre expressed in its performative glory. Like today's economy which has no principle but is purely localized into micro-administrative functions and which seeks its legitimacy outside itself in some sovereign glory, only to dissimulate its inherent glory because in itself it is always already sovereign, similarly, theatre for a long time sought its glory outside itself, in philosophy, in theology, in the dramatic text or the critics column, which ever were deemed sovereign. But this was only an act of dissimulation of the inherent glory, an anarchic glory of theatre itself, which is its spectacular reality but which can only take place within the economy of theatre, the economy of the stage which is nothing but the micro-management of a multiplicity.*

Firstly, we can trace back to Clement of Alexandria the earliest effort within Christianity to give a historical content to the theme of a 'world stage' by comparing the economy of redemption to a drama. However, as it happens in the latter half of the Middle Ages, Providence not only provides the historical content for the miracle and mystery plays but also sees to it that such forms of representation are in concordance with exegetical practices. The idea of a *theatrum mundi* thus becomes available for a Christian interpretation in these plays. In other words, the idea of a theatre of the world as the history of redemption becomes the actual content for certain Christian theatrical performances.

Secondly, the question of providence inaugurates the problem of a providential government of the world based on the hierarchic arrangement of the first and second causes. The first cause coincides with divine providence according to which the world remains fixed and unchangeable in concordance with the highest good. It is made to stand as something unique and separate from the second cause which corresponds to nature and according to which the world governs itself by creating natural hierarchies or orders. But at the same time the first cause (*regimen dei* or *causae primae*) 'entails the articulation' of the second causes (*regimen intelligentiae* or *causae secundae*), the different hierarchies and particular orders of the world. This provides us with the *model* of the expression of general and special providence (*providential generalis* and *providential specialis*) on which depends what Thomas Aquinas in *Summa Theologiae* would call *De gubernatione mundi* or the government of the world.

> From every cause there results some sort of order in its effects. In consequence there are as many orders as there are causes, with one order contained under another, even as one cause is subordinated to another in such a way that the higher cause is not subject to the lower, but the way round. There is a clear example in human affairs; the domestic order depends on the father of the family, that order in turn is subordinated to the municipal order deriving from the city's ruler; the municipal order comes under the regimen of the king, who is the source of order in the whole realm. (Agamben, 2011, p. 97)[11]

This model of the government of the world based upon a providential logic of general and particular providence becomes the basis for the model for a 'theatrum mundi' which, for example, we find in the theatrical model developed by Giulio Camillo during the Renaissance. That the problem of providence provides the key for both the economic model of the *gubernatione mundi* and the theatrical model of *theatrum mundi* comes as no surprise when we begin to investigate the relation between the theatrical image and the economic image, particularly starting from Clement of Alexandria, as we have been trying to do here.

Thirdly through the problem of divine providence and its relation to the economy of redemption Clement also provides the logic of a fracture between transcendence and immanence which never the less remains inseparable. This becomes the basis for his idea of a microcosm (man) being reflected in the macrocosm of the universe. This would serve as a central theme for the imagination of *theatrum mundi* both as a theological metaphor and later its real historical uses during renaissance in the plays of Shakespeare and Calderon.

Hence in Clement we find a paradigm of the perfect point of coincidence between the historical problem of theatre and the use of the theatrical image for theological purposes such that one opens the ground for the other.

Section II

Further Elaborations of the Problem of Spectacle

Actor and Spectator: Between and Beyond

When we juxtapose the two meanings of the theatrical image that we have come across so far–the spectacle of suffering in Paul and the Drama of redemption in Clement of Alexandria–we have a curious circularity which comes across as a 'seeming paradox'. In Paul, when he talks of becoming a 'spectacle unto the world' he insinuates a process where man is both the participant and the audience of this spectacle. We have tried to analyse this paradox earlier through the Pauline idea of the glory mirroring each other, moving from glory to glory where one is made the actor and the spectator of the same spectacle, different from an earlier understanding of becoming a spectacle only in the eyes of the unaffected divine spectator and his next of kin: the ancient sage. However this idea of a divine spectator who watches the drama of the world theatre unfolding under his indifferent gaze is not completely lost in the Christian writings of the patristic tradition. Continuing the Pauline tradition of viewing the suffering of the martyrs as a spectacular reality, many Christian apologist from the second half of the second century would produce a body of matrylogical work where the problem of the gaze begins to be treated as a central problem. Particularly in view of the pagan culture of spectacles (gladiatorial contests, chariot races, theatre, circus, etc), the Christian appropriation of the logic of the spectacles had to clearly defined and distinguished from their Roman precedence. The metaphor of a world spectacle, which pre-figures the Christian notion of a *theatrum mundi*–finds itself caught in this complex matrix of relation of at least two traditions: An earlier idea of a spectacle of the world where man is only an actor of world spectacle unfolding under an indifferent divine gaze which sometimes could be identified with the quasi-divine gaze of the philosopher sage.

Secondly, a paradoxical idea of the world as stage where men are both actors and spectators at the same time. However this later idea is further complicated by two ways of viewing the world. Firstly, from the point of view of the ignorant and the unfaithful who in their desire for lustful spectacles were no different from those who performed them. This argument would further elaborate that in so far as one does not have access to the true meaning of the spectacles of the world one is implicated in it; the ordinary spectator caught in the superficial exteriority of the spectacle is as much a participant as the performer. Hence the second century apologists would defend themselves against being called murderers and cannibals by arguing the preposterousness of such condemnation on the basis of Christian deploration of all kinds of violence including capital punishments. Thus, Athenagoras of Athens emphasizes Christian opposition to violence by arguing that how can they commit murders, when they cannot even watch murders, including capital punishment in the amphitheatres–unlike their pagan counterpart? He says, "For when they [the slaves of Christians] know that we cannot endure even to see a man put to death, though justly, who of them can accuse us of murder or cannibalism?...We, deeming that to see a man put to death is much the same as killing him, have abjured such spectacles." (Castelli, 2004, p. 112)

As Christians, Athenagoras argues that even to witness such acts of violence corresponds to nothing less than committing them. Theophilus of Antioch, peer and fellow apologist of Athenagoras, defending Christians against charges of incest and cannibalism notes, "When we are forbidden even to witness gladiatorial shows lest we should become participants and accomplices in murders" (Ibid.) This becoming participant-of-the-spectator is expanded to cover all forms of spectacles by Theophilus which is based on a logic of efficacy which physically affects the spectator implicating them more and more into the performances. Hence while talking about the dangers of other such spectacles (including theatre), Theophilus observes, "And we are not allowed to witness other spectacles, lest our eyes and ears should be defiled" (Ibid.). The efficacy of these spectacles lies at a physical level allowing the spectator not only to be solicited by them but be transformed physically into something impure on which desire can easily inscribe itself . This capture by desire, which happens progressively after the transformation by the spectacle, is one of the key aspects of these arguments. Clement of Alexandria expresses it quite clearly by the third century in his *Pedagogue* when he writes, "These assemblies, indeed, are full of confusion and iniquity; and these pretexts for assembling are the cause of disorder–men and women assembling promiscuously for the sight of one another. In this respect the assembly has already shown itself bad: for when the eye is lascivious, the desires grow warm; and the eyes that are accustomed to look impudently at one's neighbours during the leisure granted to them, inflame the amatory desire" (Ibid.) It is obvious that what Clement finds impure is not merely the optical nature of the spectacles but the form of "promiscuous" congregation. But this coming together of bodies of men and women in a disorderly and unjust fashion is sustained by a spectatorial logic. Only here the spectator is not simply turned towards the stage where the spectacle unfolds, but towards each other such that they become a spectacle unto themselves. In an inverse and pejorative sense, Clement is arguing that in the places of such assemblies, these bodies become spectacles to each other. Paul argues that in their suffering the 'fathers' of the Christian community become a spectacle unto the world, of men and angels alike. But unlike such suffering spectacle which brings order to the Christian communities here a mirror opposite is imagined. However, it is not only the spectator-participant boundary which is blurred in such 'iniquitous' assemblies. The transformation of singular naturally categorized bodies of men and women into an impure admixture of bodies without order, a promiscuously assembled congregational body is nevertheless one aspect of the impurity logic. Clearly the distinction between the spectator and spectacle is replaced by a dichotomy between purity and impurity. But the space of theatre and other spectacles are seen to be places of transformation of pure, marked and categorized bodies into impure, heterogeneous mixtures which nevertheless do not cease to be spectacular. They even contribute to the desire to consume visually not that which unfolds on stage but each other. The logic of spectacle is thus expanded to replace the boundary between the spectacle and the spectator to encircle the whole space of the assembled multitude. While this transformation from the pure to impure happens at a physical–optical–level one becomes more vulnerable to be captured by evil desires. In almost a medical mode of thinking, Clement lays out the progressive decline of the moral health of the assembled body. The 'unnatural' mixing up of categories leading to a general impurity of the assembled body which is sustained by a transformative logic through the optical organs which become more susceptible to lascivious desire which then spread to the whole assembled body. "Where the eye is lascivious, the desire grows warm". But most importantly, this entire process of transformation is presented as an altogether different spectacle, a spectacle of evil which only the faithful Christian, illuminated by the truth can discern. The logic of the spectacle which lies beneath the worldly spectacle is revealed to be nothing but evil. "In this respect the assembly has already shown itself bad". But to whom has it shown itself to be evil? Clearly not the spectator who participates in such spectacles. Clearly another spectator is imagined who can decipher the inner spectacle of evil of the world spectacles. This individual who has access to a knowledge which ordinary men/women do not have is the Christian subject who has the prudence, foresight but most importantly faith to–what one hundred years later John Chrysostom would call–practice "fasting of the eyes" such when it comes to worldly spectacles he will not be tempted. But rather than *first* having the knowledge of what is the true meaning of these spectacles one has to first "let the eyes fast" (Ibid., p. 116). The practice of abstinence will lead to the knowledge and hence illumination. We shall try to develop the implication of this process later.

This argument is expanded to cover all activities whose true nature is not revealed to men without the proper knowledge, a knowledge which can come only through faith. Here the circularity of the spectacular logic again resurfaces. The world is conceived as a stage where spectacles unfold whose true meaning is not revealed to ordinary men who only witness the exteriority of the spectacles and become implicated in them because of their lack of knowledge. It is because one has no access to the truth hiding behind such spectacles that one in a sense cannot separate oneself from that which is false and that which has the value of truth. The suffering of the Christian martyrs is a paradigmatic case in this sense. The suffering of the martyr in the arena of the amphitheatre is a spectacle to both the pagan and the Christian but in two completely different senses. The pagan spectator is as much implicated in the murder as the executioner just like the spectator of the theatre is as much a figure of lust as the characters who he watches on stage engaging in lustful activities.

But the Christian subject knows the hidden inversion of meaning lurking behind that of the spectacle. He knows that what seems as suffering is actually a joy when looked at through heavenly eyes. That while seeming to be defeated, this moment of martyrdom is actually a moment of victory. Hence Minucious Felix, again a second century apologist who also happened to be a lawyer in his rhetorical treatise *Octavius* writes about the pleasure God derives from the spectacle of martyrdom:

> How beautiful is the spectacle to God when a Christian does battle with pain; when he is drawn up against threats, and punishments and tortures; when mocking the noise of death, he treads underfoot the horror of the executioner; when he raises up his liberty against kings and princes, and yields to God alone, whose he is; when triumphant and victorious, he tramples upon the very man who has pronounced sentence against him. (Castelli, 2004, p. 120)

As Elizabeth Castelli has argued that Minucious' primary objective here is to show the difference between being and appearance, the quintessential philosophical problem regarding theatre. But what we also witness here is a divine vision which not only enjoys a certain spectacle of the world but is the very condition for the inversion of its worldly meaning. We now have the logic of the inversion of the meaning of worldly spectacle of suffering, the secret meaning which resides behind the shroud of its appearance as corresponding to a divine vision which looks down upon the world. The idea of a divine being that looks down at the theatre of the world is undoubtedly implicit in this version. But the ambiguity of this divine vision becomes evident when we consider Origen in his *Exhortations to Martyrdom* when he writes, "Thus the whole world and all the angels, right and left, and all human beings, those from god's measure and those from the rest, listen to us contesting the contest concerning Christianity" (Ibid., p. 121). Exactly like Paul, we have the metaphorical use of the theatrical image of the dramatic conflict at a cosmic level standing for the historical struggle of Christianity. Again exactly like Paul, we have here the angels from heaven and the human beings all constituting the cosmic audience but no mention of a divine spectator. The cosmic audience nevertheless constitutes a historical reality whose actors and spectators correspond to each other in so far as they are all creatures of God–"God's measure"–and not the creator. Between the divine spectator of the world theatre and the spectators of the world theatre who are the witness of their own spectacle we have the spectatorial ambiguity which sustains the disjunctive synthesis of the divine theatre and a theatre of the world. At the same time we have the ambiguity of the Christian subject who in belonging to God has access to its truth but who nevertheless can only effectuate this truth through the profession of faith and not through direct knowledge. In addition to which it is a faith which is, as we shall see in a while, constantly under threat from the 'other' to which theatre belongs,

Enframing: A Historical Problem

This long detour leads us to the second idea of the figure of the spectator who in having access to truth can not only distant himself from the falsity of the world stage but who resembles God in belonging to this truth. But it is only a resemblance, a mirror image of the actual truth which only belongs to God. But that does not prevent him from establishing a relation to this truth, whose manifestation can only be possible through this subjective relation. In the light of this truth he is illuminated as the very object of that truth[12]. But he himself is not the source of this light which always comes from elsewhere. The spectator constitutes himself as the Christian subject who separates himself from the world stage as a spectator who knows that what is happening onstage is illusory while its true meaning lies somewhere else. But although now there exists a boundary between the spectacle and the spectator, between that which is illusory and that which is non-illusionary, between the darkness which resides at the heart of the spectacle and the light that illuminates the heart of the spectator, they both constitute a space which is bounded by the walls of finitude. In Paul, as we have seen both, the spectator and the spectacle is swept up in a series of optical metaphors where they become identical to each other in being all mirror images of each other. In the later uses of the metaphor of the world stage, the theatrical logic of a separation between the theatre and the audience would function together with the expansion of this boundary to cover the entire theatre space making the world into a world theatre. This inherent ambiguity based upon a complex relation between the spectacle and the spectator which is simultaneously separated and connected forms the 'encircled' space of a world theatre.

Of course we need to understand that in Paul, like in later martyrological texts, the use of the suffering image, as Balthazar points out, is related to a certain idea of constituting the 'community'. But while in Paul there is a strong sense of sarcasm in depicting the 'fathers" of the community as being made a spectacle of suffering while the rest are made to prosper [Already you are filled! Already you have become rich! (1 Corintianns 4:8,10)] there is nothing obligatory about this suffering for the community. Unlike later ascetic practices, where suffering is made mandatory held under a mimetic logic of Christ's suffering, in Paul, as in early martyrological texts there is a strong sense of heroic suffering at play. It consolidates the group making it into a community, where the suffering overflows into the community, which allows its "father" to suffer for it. Hence Paul's description is also objective and not merely (subjectively) sarcastic because he is describing here the constitution of a community, the way a community "encloses"[13] itself. But it does not enclose itself in terms of finding a shared suffering but rather en-frames itself by being both the theatre and the audience to this spectacular suffering. It is in this sense that Paul uses the theatrical image.

In Clement of Alexandria the paradox of 'world stage' comes in a somewhat different way when he compares the redemptive history of man to a drama and yet wants to preserve its historical reality. Here the paradox comes in view of the *fabulous* nature of all theatre as being unreal. However Clement uses the symbolic nature of theatre to emphasize its fabulatory *tendency* which is made true with providence. In the case of Clement the theatrical image functions quite differently but as we shall see the internal theatrical structure of creating an enclosure remains the same. What the metaphor of drama connotes is the universal history of redemption whose author and director remains a divine will but which nonetheless conditions all earthly wills to participate in it. In *Stromata*, Clement had already written that the truly wise man is he who "faultlessly plays the role God has given him in the drama of life; for he knows what he has to do and to suffer" (Balthasar, 1988, p. 156). Thus the drama of the world finds an echo in the drama of existence and the theatre of the world starts corresponding to the theatre of life. Hence we find a re-articulation of the ancient problem of the 'world stage' metaphor: the tension between the 'I' and the role, between the divine will and the personal will, between the being of the actor and the persona of the actor, which more often than not becomes indiscernible from each other. With Clement and the introduction of a providential logic we see the collective (communitarian) understanding of the theatrical image, confined to the idea of a 'community' in Paul, shifting (perhaps for the first time) to accommodate the universal idea of a world drama. While at the same time the metaphor becomes the basis for the imagination of a Christian subject who becomes more and more individualized and granulated through the development of various methods and practices to help perform the 'role' one has to play in this drama as perfectly as possible. The theological doctrine of world history creating an objective juridico-political regime which starts to perfectly reflect the subjective domain of truth acts. The macrocosm and the microcosm reflecting each other and creating an enclosure which no longer frames the boundaries of a community but defines the threshold of the world. But the internal logic remains the same which is that of énclosing' which brings this very close to the theatrical logic. In the case of Clement this logic comes in the form of the following problem: whether the drama of the world–which in a way is related to the divine theatre (of creation) through providence–is truly a symbolic representation of the divine reality or is providence something which is merely historical and worldly? Then the question arises are all histories necessarily 'real' or is it that all other histories have been illusionary except the Christian one which through providence is rendered real? Clearly the pagan history is deemed as something fabulous analogous to its myth and legends. This will culminate in Augustine for whom the struggle between the two principles of world history, the City of God and the secular state (Roman/pagan state) provides the model for the struggle between the Church and the theatre.

But we see that for Clement this history would have been a fiction if not for providence. Providence is what keeps the fine balance between drama and history by supposedly letting the symbolic reality of a divine nature enter the historical reality of the world. But at the same time by the same gesture he creates a curious threshold between fact and fiction, between history and myth when he uses the theatrical image. The real-history of redemption looks at the fabulous and mythical history of the pagans like the audience looks at the spectacle unfolding on stage. And like in all spectacular realities of theatre there is a *double* reversal even here. On the one hand, there is a reversal of the gaze where the spectator finds his gaze returning to himself from the threshold of the stage, identifying the objects on stage as the fabulous 'other' to his/her real self, the edge of the stage acting as the very boundary wall against which the gaze bounces back. But at the same time the stage always solicits, always tempts the spectator to keep looking. And in this temptation we find another reversal, where it seems as if a part of the gaze disengages from the subject and attaches itself to the object, reversing its role, such that we find now a new threshold being created not between the audience and the actors at the edge of the stage but between that which is visible on stage and that which is invisible off stage which is akin to the invisible fourth wall so famous among theatre actors. This new threshold operates from the point of view of the object on stage, which was till now the object of gaze and now has become the subject of the gaze from whose point of view the visible stage is only separated from that invisible space beyond the stage, the unsaid, unseen, void of the offstage. Hence a new threshold is created between the visible stage and that which is the invisible off stage. It seems that in Clement (and so many others of that time) the drama of redemption is not merely historical praxis but a praxis which is constantly solicited by the poiesis of the pagan world against which it seeks to establish itself. It is as if the pagan world of fabulation, a veritable world of theatre and spectacle is looked upon and rejected as the other and yet this world of fabulation never ceases to solicit Christian history. But in this relation to the fabulous world of theatre, the 'real' world of Christian history had to imagine a way to transgress it. Not merely to reject theatre, but transgress the space of theatre through the creation of an invisible, impossible space beyond under whose sign the drama of the world could be deciphered and destroyed at the same time. A destructive analysis produced by the ultimate desire for an original lack which could not only dissolve all earthly temptations like that of theatre but re-conceptualize the world from another perspective, so that the drama of existence no longer remains a fable but becomes a real history.

It is clear that what we are dealing with here are two principles of history, one that is deemed deceptive and fabulous and the other which is accepted as real. Of course this problem of two principles of history is most systematically proposed by Augustine which we will be dealing with in some detail in the next chapter. Suffice it to say here, in a condensed fashion that what Augustine tried to evolve was a theory of history which in the final analysis was based on a principle of desire which sought to distinguish two categories of love. The love of the world which functioned under the principle of *civitus terrena* and the love of the kingdom of god which functioned under the principle of *civitus dei*. The two produced two different sets of actions, which according to Augustine lead to either destruction and death or redemption and life. Ironically the operational structure of the two forms of love was identical to each other. Desire always sought its object outside itself in order to complete that which it lacked or in other words that which it did not possess and wanted to—this mode of thinking obviously betrays Augustine's Platonic influence. The key difference between the two kinds of love was that while both functioned in terms of a lack which sought to fulfil itself but which it could never do permanently because of man's mortality, earthly love got attached to objects in which it sought a mediation to approach this lack. Hence you have a structure of desire based on pleasure and satisfaction, where every act of pleasure produces temporary satisfaction through an immediate discharge which could only contribute to the original lack produced by desire. Hence one would go on loving one thing or the other in this world in the false hope of fulfilment and ultimate possession. But as each object perishes the desire is displaced to something else. Augustine proposed theatre as the perfect example of this worldly desire (*cupiditas*) which he pronounced as desire for the sake of nothing but desire itself.

Against this principle of worldly desire he declared the concept of *caritas,* a desire whose object remains radically outside the mortal domain of the *civitas terra* and hence the only true object of love, because here the desire would actually be fulfilled and the lack would be transformed into satisfaction with *parousia* when the *civitas terrena* would be transformed into *civitas dei.* This redemptive view of history proposed a form of life which ought to be spent in pursuit of this true desire and authentic love. Nevertheless for man, in the reality of history, mortality stands in the way of realizing even this desire which can only come as hope and never as certainty. These two operations correspond to each other so far as in the former the lack is constantly sought to be mediated through objects of representation while in the latter there is a demand to constitute representation under the condition of this lack. This desire-lack structure of *caritas* and the pleasure-satisfaction structure of *cupiditas* not only creates the two principles of history but as we have tried to show before in a different context *correspond* to each other so that they always contribute to the split of the subject between the subject of statement determined by worldly objects and a subject of enunciation determined by some transcendental lack. But it is always under the obligatory shadow of this transcendental Master-Signifier which remains empty that one produces judgment on to the world as subject of statements.

In the long history of the patristic tradition whenever we have encountered admonitions against theatre, particularly in the second century apologists, the problem of theatre as a site of deception has inevitably come up; along with the moral denunciation of theatre which has an even longer tradition leading back to Roman moralists. But what is unique about the Christian admonitions is that this admonition of theatre is informed by rigorous analysis of the deceptive nature of the theatrical operation which then serves as a metaphor for the entirety of the Roman culture. To be more precise, life itself is compared to the theatrical act of deception which has to be cautiously analysed and demasked so that its true meaning is reached which is already a meaning lying outside life in the domain of a divine logic which is beyond human reach and remains an invisible space. So what we are dealing with here are three spaces instead of two (of worldly illusion and divine reality) which are interconnected and separated at the same time. A conjunctive-disjunctive relation creates these three spaces, two of which are held in complement to each other while a third supplementary space is imagined, disjoined and yet functioning as the basis for an enclosed theatre of the world with its actors and audience. So first we have the deceptive space of the theatrical reality corresponding to the pagan history which the Christian subject witnesses but only as an audience because providence provides the dividing line, the 'edge of the stage', one might say, which serves as the boundary between the false and the true. But the Christian can identify the deception, the fabrication of the theatre, or even be suspicious of it only from the place which lies outside the stage. That is to say only when he has renounced his pagan life, when he has separated himself from that life of sin and has assumed the role of a spectator. It is then that he can truly see the illusion of the world stage as illusion. Only then can he become suspicious and start exploring the deception of this illusionary theatrical culture of the pagans. But the true meaning of fabrication comes from the place outside the stage because the stage is where the fabrication presents its enigma, where its plots unfold. But the condition for its existence lies elsewhere, where the plotting can be recognized, the falsity of the fabrication identified. But this is not simply the gaze of the audience whose natural capacity for recognizing falsity helps him to discover the truth. The Christian audience can, at best, recognize himself as the 'other' of this theatrical world. But it is only under the divine sign of truth, to which he is related by a complex process, that the Christian subject can become a spectator to this fabrication. This is the idea of a truth which is not exactly a substance but which determines the falsity in all fabrication, the plotting behind all plots. In other words, what we are encountering here is the concept of truth which gives falsity its value to be false. But in itself it remains empty which is to say without light or perhaps more appropriately too much light which is blinding. Let us remember the blinding glory of god that burns Moses' face. A blinding light which makes it impossible to see, making an invisible, unspoken void of its source which corresponds to that invisible space offstage, a third space, an impossible frontier, a radically uncrossable limit. It is because of this impossible limit which cannot be transgressed that the boundary of the stage is set where the actor and the audience are separated by that which gives fabrication its value of falsity while giving reality its value of truth. What Andre Green so appropriately sums up as the function of this invisible third space in theatre corresponding to the problem of 'enclosure' and can now be related to the idea of a 'world stage' which we have tried to discuss before. The theatre of the world functions as this enclosed space combining the spectator and the actor, the theatre and the audience, such that the boundary between fabrication and facticity, between myth and history is extended to become the theatrical space of a theatre of the world. Andre Green writes:

> The space of the stage is the space of the plot, the enigma, the secret; the space offstage is that of manipulation, suspicion, plotting. However, this space is circumscribable, since it is confined within the walls of the great chamber that is the theatre. [...] Thus the limit formed by the edge of the stage is extended to the limits of the space of the stage, this space offering itself as one to be transgressed, passed beyond, through its link with the invisible space offstage. (Green, 1997, p. 139)

It is this extension of the boundary that separates theatrical fabrication from spectatorial discernment, expanding and encircling both the actor and spectator into a theatrical cocoon which is now separated from a (*Other*) third space by an impossible threshold. It is in this transposition of the boundary, the displacement of the threshold that produces both the actor and the audience such that we find an access to a third space which becomes the condition of possibility of all boundaries, all thresholds. But this third space is evoked, an invisible space, an impossible threshold which cannot be transgressed but which produces the secret logic of displacement in the metaphor (*metaphora* as transposition, displacement) of the world stage. The theatrical metaphor rather than seeking the edge of the world stage whose beyond it could have clearly marked by separating itself from a divine theatre never speaks in terms of two theatres, a worldly and a divine in the texts in which it is passingly or obliquely mentioned in these early years of Christianity. The theatrical metaphor comes only as a worldly category because theatre, no matter how you see it, cannot but be immanent to the world. Rather than dividing and separating two distinct topologies, of a world stage and a divine stage, the theatrical metaphor constantly expands and folds back at the same time to include both the spectacle and the spectator of this world theatre. Only do we find ambiguous reference to a divine audience who is a spectator so far as he is also an actor through providence but the substance of whose being is different just like the being of the actor is different from the character he plays. The 'truth' of the human being is different from the role he plays. But in spite of the complex ambiguity that informs the use of this theatrical metaphor, we understand how deeply it is related to the contemporary reaction against theatre at the time. It is because the concept of theatre is caught in the middle of this series of ambiguities, but primarily between the affirmative use of the metaphor of theatre and a negative meaning ascribed to the 'real' practice of theatre that it becomes so difficult to trace its genealogy within Christianity back to these formative years of its theological development.

Section III

The Problem Reintroduced Through a Reading of Tertullian's *De Spectaculis*

Point of Departure: Defraction of *Metanoia*

It is in the ascetic treatise *De Spectaculis* (On the Spectacles) written somewhere between 173-202 AD by Tertullian that we find one of the earliest and most sustained discourses around the problem of public spectacles in Christianity. It is in this text, as we shall try to illustrate, that the response against theatre and the prohibition of visiting any site of spectacle no longer remains a mere pedagogic necessity but becomes a dogma. Which also leads us to speculate that though there had been frequent mention of the problem of spectacles in general in many other texts of this time, particularly in the works of the apologists of the second century who were trying to defend the pedagogical legitimacy of Christianity by producing a body of theological work against the imperial culture of the pagans, it is in this text of Tertullian that we find an exclusive treatment of the problem of the spectacles. The exclusivity that the spectacles receive in this text seems to coincide with a particular dogmatic turn of Christianity which had a number of historical reasons like the rise of internal conflicts within Christianity, particularly with different versions of Gnosticism. Be that as it may, the reason why this text is deemed as an ascetic treatise rather than a pedagogical text dealing with the problem of theatre needs to be examined in the very beginning. During this time we have another text composed by Clement of Alexandria, in the second half of the second century, titled *The Paedagogus* (The Instructor), which also contains reference to the problem of spectacles. But as we had tried to explain before, in this text the emphasis is primarily on the impossibility of Christian pedagogy (the instruction given by and through Christ) to provide any justification to visit the public spectacles. Through optical terms of analysis the text charts out the path which–under the supervision of the Word–would lead the individual to truth. Clement remarks in Chapter III of Book I of *The Paedagogus*:

> For, wandering in life as in deep darkness, we need a guide that cannot stumble or stray; and our guide is the best, not blind, as the Scripture says, "leading the blind into pits." But the Word is keen-sighted, and scans the recesses of the heart. As, then, that is not light which enlightens not, nor motion that moves not, nor loving which loves not, so neither is that good which profits not, nor guides to salvation. (Castelli, 2004)

The response against theatre as a place or an assembly of impurity where bodies and visions of men and women mingle with each other[14] has to be seen in the backdrop of this pedagogic path of coming to light where the pedagogue (the instructor) leads the soul to light avoiding all paths which would lead to darkness like that of the path leading to the spectacles. This pedagogic function which is inscribed in the injunction against going to the spectacles is thus closely related to the period of preparation leading to baptism which in Clement is understood as a period of teaching.

Michel Foucault in his Lectures at College de France (1979-80) titled the *Government of the Living* while tracing the genealogy of the modern subject of knowledge as the subject of truth marks this moment at the end of the second century as witnessing a certain shift. This shift he argues comes in how the Western imagination constituted its subject as both a subject and an object of knowledge which would finally lead to the confessional subject. Foucault argues that it is during these years, at the threshold of the second and third century, that the Christian relation between the subject and truth–or more precisely the relation of subject to truth where the subject of knowledge does not merely come to truth but offers its own self as an object of knowledge to be worked upon and transformed into something akin to truth–witnesses a mutation. It is during this period that what Foucault calls the two poles of the Christian *regime of truth*–the acts of truth as acts of faith and the particular truth procedures which considers the self as its object of knowledge to be examined, interrogated and purified, in other words, the confessional pole–undergoes a diremption.

The moment of subjectification which was till now dependent on a classical idea of *metanoia* is now transformed into the problem of a 'discipline of repentance' (*paenitentiae disciplina*). The Latin term *paenitentia* (repentance) which was faithful to its Greek origin in *metanoia* in the first two centuries of Christian usage now undergoes a change. In classical Greek and Hellenistic texts *metanoia* was understood as a transformation of the soul when it comes to the light of truth. It corresponded to the moment of purification when the soul, attracted by the light of truth turns on itself, or better pivots on itself to turn away from what it had been looking at till then–the material world of appearances, impurities, shadows and ignorance. This turning of the soul on itself *coincided* with the turning of the soul away from the impure world of ignorance and falsity, the world down below, towards the pure light of truth. Foucault writes in this regard:

> ... the soul can thus direct itself towards the light, a light that provides it with the spectacle of what until then was hidden from it and enables it at the same time to fully know itself, since now it will be permeated by light. And this illumination that offers it all that is visible in the invisible, that makes the invisible visible, this moment of light that entirely permeates it and makes it transparent to itself, is also of course, what will purify it, in as much as impurity is shadow, the taint, the stain. This roughly was what *metanoia* was in the pagan texts of the Hellenistic period, and also in the texts of the second Christian century (Foucault, *On the Government of the Living: Lectures at College de France* (1979-80), 2014, p. 127)

Clearly the pedagogic preparation for baptism in Clement's texts corresponded to this idea of a *metanoic* transformation through an act of faith like baptism. Here pedagogy provided the gradual movement towards the path of knowledge and truth such that the subject of knowledge, who is indoctrinated with the rules of Christian life, would move from "teaching to teaching" to a final enactment of faith, a profession of faith as a truth act which constitutes the logic of baptism. It is in this complex field of pedagogical practices leading to a truth act that we must situate the problem of spectacles in Clement. As we have tried to show before, Clement understands the spectacles as a site of unjust exchange of gazes whose mixture produces impurity which block or obstructs the subject to turn on oneself from the world below to emerge in the illumination of the true world above. The problem of spectacle is thus, at least in Clement of Alexandria, imagined as an obstruction to *metanoia*. It is a blockage in the pedagogic path to truth which has to be avoided. In this path towards truth which constitutes the preparation for baptism, what is required is the progressive accumulation of knowledge such that the subject can be initiated into the act of truth which nevertheless is an act of purification assured by God. The access to truth through the act of faith is here organically connected to the progressive constitution of the subject of knowledge which would culminate in the act of purification leading to truth. If we map this movement from pedagogy to purification we find that it is always truth which leads to purification. To follow Foucault's schema, what is imagined is a continuous progression towards the dramatic ascent towards truth. Belief followed by the profession of belief leading to illumination which spatially performs a movement along an ascending line. So it is inadequate to simply pose the problem of theatre as a moral problem in these early texts of Christianity like it is facile to argue that Clement of Alexandria's tests were merely moral texts. They were above all pedagogic texts following a long tradition of pedagogic texts related to ethical problem of a transformation of the self from impure to pure. But this transformation was always coincidental with the subject's access to truth. To analyse the problem of theatre from this pedagogic point of view is to follow a path which was set many centuries before in Ancient Greece with Plato, which we have tried to study before in our first chapter, where the problem of theatre was first conceived as a pedagogical problem. Since the moment of purification and the moment of access to truth (the discovery of truth) coincide with each other in *metanoia*, the subject's preparation to emerge as a subject of knowledge through accumulation of knowledge-content of the self and the world becomes so important in understanding the problem of theatre even during the early years of Christianity. What had not arrived in the scene was the prohibition of theatre on exclusive moral grounds of discipline. In other words, the problem of the spectacle had not yet become a problem of sin.

From Pedagogy to Perversion

Tertullian, on the other hand, addresses the question of the spectacles in a significantly different fashion. At the very beginning of his treatise Tertullian writes, "The conditions of faith, the reason inherent in truth, the law of our discipline, which along with all the other errors of the world, takes from us also the pleasure of the public shows" (Tertullian, 1931). Though Tertullian proposes a rejection of public spectacles on grounds of faith, truth and discipline, the way the treatise develops its argument points towards a different method of thinking. Firstly in the very beginning it is made clear that the treatise is meant as a preparatory text for both those who are about to convert and, interestingly even for those who have already converted—"what these are (public shows) I would have you learn, O servants of God, you who are even making your approach to God, and you too I would have rethink it all, who have witnessed and borne your testimony that you have already made your approach". Immediately we see an apparent ambiguity which was not present in someone like Clement between those who are preparing their approach to God and those who have already made that approach. This ambiguity marks a shift in the logic of baptism which is no longer seen as the ultimate moment of transformation from impurity to purity such that a perfect being of truth would emerge whose all past sins are redeemed but also, and more importantly, who, now belonging to god, cannot accumulate more sins. It is this idea of sin conceived as the 'fall from truth' which can be regained through something like *metanoia* which undergoes a change in Tertullian. Now we have the idea of an original sin which like an original stain cannot permanently and assuredly go away. We shall try to develop this point in relation to the spectacles in a while. Suffice it to say here that what is evident from this line is that the preparation to approach god is now extended to cover both who are formally preparing for baptism and those who have been baptised. To that extent one could argue that Tertullian is saying that one never belongs to god, because one never truly ceases to approach God in one's lifetime. Hence one is constantly making that approach, irrespective of whether he/she has been baptised or not. This shift in the understanding of the nature of transformation in baptism is intimately related to Tertullian's idea of original sin which will have immense implication in his response against the spectacles.

Secondly, though he assumes to tell us the logic behind the prohibition to visit public shows from three perspectives–that is from the point of view of faith, truth and discipline–we find that almost the entire text orients itself towards an investigative methodology which seeks out the relation between the spectacles and idolatry. The reason for this is explicitly proposed by Tertullian a few pages into the text. He writes in Book IV:

> But lest anyone suppose us to be quibbling I will turn to authority, the initial and primary authority of our "seal". When we enter the water and profess the Christian faith in the terms prescribed by its law, we profess with our mouths that we have renounced the devil, his pomp and his angels. What shall we call the chief and outstanding matter, in which the devil and his pomps and his angels are recognised, rather than idolatry? From which every unclean and evil spirit, I may say but no more of that. So if it shall be established that the whole equipment of the public shows is idolatry pure and simple, we have an indubitable decision laid down in advance, that this profession of renunciation made in baptism touches the public shows too, since they being idolatry belong to the devil, his pomp and his angels. (Tertullian, 1931, p. 243)

Methodologically speaking, the entire text of *De Spectaculis* moves towards an examination of the "whole equipment of the public shows" so that one can recognize the shadow of the devil lurking behind its idolatrous purpose. Dogmatic to its core the treatise looks more like a conceptual manual to help the soul prepare for a test of truth rather than a discovery of truth. The subject through the methodological processes elaborated in the text can recognize the truth behind the public spectacles such that this will help him recognize within himself/herself the truth of all truths, the eternal truth which leads to eternal life. But paradoxically this eternal truth has to precede the discovered truth of the spectacles, thereby functioning as the guarantor for the meanings attributed to individual spectacles. Hence one has to already believe in the truth of baptism even before he/she is transformed through baptism so that he/she can implement the prohibition and the renunciation of the spectacles on grounds of idolatry. The text functions as an ascetic treatise for the preparation of baptism so far as the renunciation of the public shows is seen as a test which is authenticated by the truth that the self comes to know within oneself even before one has actually been baptised. In other words the test is a purificatory gesture in itself through which one has to pass in order to demonstrate to oneself and others that one is worthy enough to apply for the eternal truth to be gained through baptism. This perfectly corresponds to Tertullian's claim that one does not get purified in baptism, but one arrives at baptism already purified. In *De paenitentia*, speaking of baptism Tertullian writes "We are not bathed in the baptismal water in order to be purified, but we are bathed in the baptismal water because we are purified". (Foucault, *On the Government of the Living: Lectures at College de france* (1979-80), 2014, p. 117). Thus we see that the three point of views of faith, truth and discipline are distributed in an asymmetrical fashion in the text where truth and discipline or knowledge and subject are coupled on one side while faith remains a kind of presupposition but paradoxically a presupposition towards which the text moves. The truth of the public shows which the subject has to discover for himself so that he can pass the text of renouncing them is already given as an act of faith functioning as a truth act. The text thus provides the set of techniques necessary to hasten the process of recognition of the truth behind the spectacles so that the subject who experiences them can have access to this knowledge which will help him renounce them. But such a renunciation is only possible through an assurance of the truth which the subject does not have at the time of renunciation and *will* gain through his profession of faith[15]. This coincidence of the presence of truth which guarantees an act of renunciation which is a form of transformation (purification) in itself and the future possibility of gaining the same truth through an act of purification (baptism) is the inherent problem which the treatise represents. So the text is conceived as a path at the beginning and end of which stands the same truth while in between we have a process of 'rational' recognition and identification of 'truths' about the spectacles which are all accumulated and gathered to produce the truth which the subject would have of oneself: The soul would discover that the experience of the spectacles is in the final analysis idolatrous and hence work of the devil. In other words, the experience of the truth of the public shows will emerge as a lie forged by the devil.

In order to produce this effect, Tertullian adopts a number of methodological strategies like using particular examples as paradigms for general principles, categorizing his analysis into different discursive domains like that of history, language, architecture, topology and finally aesthetics. But all this is pivoted on the fundamental intellectual task of recognizing the spectacles as acts of an original sin behind which lurks the shadowy presence of the fallen angel. At the very beginning of the text, Tertullian warns of the insidious nature of pleasure which can distort representation to present evil as something good. He says, "For such is the force of pleasure that it can prolong ignorance to give it its chance, and pervert knowledge to cloak itself" (Tertullian, 1931, p. 231). Now the nature of this transformation of knowledge into ignorance by cloaking or masking a thing and presenting it as something else is the act of perversion dear to both theatre and Satan.

Variations on the Original Sin

As we know, Tertullian is to be credited to have invented the idea of original sin so far as he provided a systematic concept of the heredity and transmission of sin. The contemporary ideas regarding evil within Christianity had two main trajectories. To take sin as a fall from an original moment of truth which had to be regained and sin as a blotch or stain which had to be erased. Tertullian's theory of the transmission of sin through seed was thus built on existent ideas of transmission through the seed which was quite common in Antiquity like in Democritus. Here the seed, literally the semen was seen as the element of hereditary transmission through a splitting of the body. So not only is there a feminine doubling of the body during childbirth but a symmetrical masculine doubling during ejaculation. It is this idea that Tertullian adopts to develop his theory arguing that there are two seeds, a bodily seed and a spiritual seed, a seed of the body and a corporeal seed of the soul, which is to say a seed of the body of the soul as distinct from the seed of the body of the body, so to speak. Being intricately entwined and dependent upon each other, the tainting of one of them stains the other, transferring impurity of body to soul, since the first moment of the original sin. According to this theory of transmission, one does not accumulate sin but is sinful from the very moment of birth which is the consequence of an originary sinful act. Hence the metaphor of the child becomes crucial, whose nature is sinful, which has to be transformed through conscious acts of purification into the maturity of goodness. The transmission of the seed thus not only transmits sin but brings about a perversion of nature. It is here that we find a relation of the heredity of sin to something like perversion because it is not simply a question of contagion but also a problem of corruption of nature to produce something like "another nature". Elisabeth Roudinesco has pointed out the primacy of the meaning of perversion in the Middle Ages as something which constitutes "upsetting the natural order of the world converting men to vice" (Roudinesco, 2009, p. 2) and which always presupposes a divine authority. Perversion, was thus a form of transgression of natural law authorized by a divine sovereignty challenging the very order of the natural world which is created by god. This coupling of perversion and divine sovereignty is what is implied in Tertullian's idea of perversion. Unable to decide between a dualist (Gnostic?) idea of evil which has substance all to itself against an essential good and the idea of evil as fault (Plato) of forgetfulness, Tertullian seeks out a middle way to define evil as perversion which he defines as a sort of transformation of the nature of the self into (an)other nature without thereby producing a new substance or a new nature. As Foucault points out, "There is, as it were, within one and the same nature, a passage from one nature to another, that is to say a passage from one to the other within in the same nature" (Foucault, *On the Government of the Living: Lectures at College de France* (1979-80), 2014, p. 123). The idea of perversion unfolds as a self-othering within the self, a movement of the self within itself such that a natural threshold is transgressed to produce a perverted self. It is akin to a distorted reflection on the surface of a mirror which is nevertheless conjoined to the original, pure image of sovereign self, through the logic of that very act of transgression. This is something which is truly inventive about the relation between a theory of hereditary sin and the idea of sin as perversion.

Transmission

In *De Spectaculis*, we find this relation clearly demonstrated in Tertullian's idea of the spectacles perpetuating the sin of idolatry and the argument against the heathens regarding the impossibility of god's creation which they (the heathens) argued cannot produce evil. As we noted before, the entire text of *De Spectaculis* turns on the hermeneutic desire to find the origin of all spectacles in idolatry. While idolatry itself is seen as a form of perversion or corruption of god's creation where the devil lurks behind the materiality of the idol. The material, of which the idol is made, be it gold, silver or wood is thus put to use by demons so that they can mask their true motives of destruction of humanity. In order to implement this theory, Tertullian meticulously categorizes five or six aspects from which he is going to approach this problem of idolatry. He writes:

> We will therefore cite the origins of one set of spectacles and another–showing how they were cradled in the world; next in order, the titles they bear, the names to wit by which they are called, next again their equipments, and the superstitions they serve, thereafter the places and to what presiding spirits they are dedicated and then the arts employed and their reputed authors. (Tertullian, 1931, p. 243)

History, language, architecture, topology and finally aesthetics; these are the discursive field which he narrows down to investigate one and only one problem. How in each of these domains, the spectacles find their originary logic in idolatry and how such knowledge is distorted and masked to produce the semblance of a harmless, 'good' culture of pleasure. For example, he traces the origin of the Roman games to the Lydians, a much prevalent idea among the antiquarian historians. However Tertullian disregards

Varro's semantic interpretation of *ludii* from *ludus* meaning play (in Varro, if we are to belive Tertullian, it means to "run hither and thither"). Tertullian writes that the "verbal issue does not matter when the real issue is idolatry" because *ludii* are so called from the Lydians who were the original performers, (here Tertullian claims to follow the lost Greek historian, Timaeus) the Romans brought from Etruria along with the name and the time. Lydians (who interestingly are said to have migrated from Asia) according to Tertullian share a clear aural correspondence to Liberalia, the name given to the games which also happen to correspond to Father Liber (Bacchus). Irrespective of the actual historical validity of this argument, which is not our concern here, we can clearly see the methodology employed here. A transmission of the idolatrous origin of the games is seamlessly construed aurally. Lydians-ludii-liber makes a logic of transmission possible exclusively on phonic terms. The semantic consistency is completely disregarded as with the case with Varro. Tertullian himself writes, "For since in a general way the games were called Liberalia, the sound of the name clearly signified the honour of Father Liber (Bacchus)" (p. 245). It is this sensory transmission of an original moment of staining which is prevalent in all the discursive fields enumerated above. Again in case of the equipment used in the circus, Tertullian argues that it is not a question of an excess of display of statuettes or images or cars or chariots or thrones or robes. For Tertullian the display of equipment is not related to illustration of excess which was one of the key problems among antiquarian moralists against spectacles. For Tertullian, however, *pomp* does not connote voluminous excess but is almost literally interpreted as succession or procession leading back to some beginning point. "The pomp (procession) comes first and shows in itself to whom it belongs" (p. 249). It is a linear chain leading back to its idolatrous and tainted origin. The procession itself, through its linearity, metaphorically indicates the hereditary transmission of an originary idolatrous moment of the game. Pomp as procession becomes the metaphor for the transmission of the sin of idolatry. He clearly expresses this hereditary logic of transmission a few lines later. "If less elaboration is bestowed on it all in the provinces, where there is less to spend, still all the shows of the circus everywhere must be attributed to their origin, must be examined at their source. For the little rivulet from its spring, the tiny shoot from its first leaf, has in it the nature of its origin" (p. 251). The examination of the origin is necessary because it is the nature of evil to hide its source, to mask it and present it as something else. This is the deceit which permeates the logic of all spectacles even architecturally. So citing Plutarch's *Life of Romulus*, Tertullian seeks to expose the hidden meaning of circus which is dedicated to Consus (the god of counsel, also the name of Neptune) when he writes, "There is still an underground altar, dedicated to that Consus, in the Circus, at the first turning point" (p. 247). It is the omnipresence of the devil and his fallen angels which the Christian subject has to constantly be aware of. He has to examine every space, every nook and corner of the world not merely from the objective perspective of identifying them as subjects of knowledge but situating themselves in these real spaces in order to examine their own selves as objects of knowledge. Hence to the question whether it is allowed to visit the circus at some other time when there is no performance Tertullian argues that there are no laws laid down vis-a-vis places and one can even visit a temple devoted to the heathen gods provided there is sufficient cause which is unconnected with the business or character of the place. He says:

> The whole world is filled with Satan and his angels. Yet not because we are in the world, do we fall from God, but only if in some way we meddle with the sins of the world. Thus if, as a sacrificer and worshipper, I enter the Capitol or the temple of Serapis, I shall fall from God–just as I should if a spectator in circus or theatre. Places do not of themselves defile us, but the things done in the places, by which even the places themselves are defiled. We are defiled by the defiled (p. 255)

Transmission and Perversion

The evil is attributed not essentially to bodies (unlike the Gnostics who in their dualist logic conceived of any material body as itself evil) but to what Tertullian would call the abuse of bodies. It is through this logic of the use and abuse of bodies that Tertullian would provide an argument against the heathen criticism of the Christian prohibition of spectacles. The pagan argument was that Christians renounce the pleasure of the spectacles because they despise life itself being 'a race of men ever ready for death'. Further the heathens would re-articulate a Christian argument to their advantage by saying that how can the Christians denounce the public shows when they themselves argue that all things being created by God and given to man are essentially good including the things which go to make the public shows. Since everything from the stones of the amphitheatre to the voice of the singers are all God's own, how can they be hostile or alien to God? To this problem Tertullian argues that because we have only partial knowledge of God through natural law and not through right of sonship, (which only the Son has) we are not aware of not only his presence but that of his rival powers who challenge God's creation by abusing the things which have been given to us by divine creation for use.

> They are also unaware of the rival powers that confront God for the abuse of what divine creation has given for use. For where your knowledge of God is defective, you can neither know His mind nor His adversary. We have not then merely to consider by whom all things are created, but also by whom they are perverted. For in that way it will appear for what use they were created, if it once appear for what use they were not. There is a great difference between the corrupted and the uncorrupted because there is a great difference between the Creator and the perverter. (p. 235)

We see a number of interesting arguments being condensed in this precise response to the heathen question of the goodness of all creation. Firstly, God has a dual function of creating and using the world he has created for good. While Satan can only abuse or counter-use God's creation but not counter-create. Hence there is an ontological difference between God and Satan who being a fallen angel finds his condition of existence in God. Hence Satan can only pervert, which is to say abuse, God's creation which God had meant to use. So between creation and use of the world there is something like a distinction or difference, a crevice so to speak through which perversion appears in the form of abuse. So if use of a body is an action which is willed by God, abuse is a moment of assertion of an autonomous will, external to God's will. Devil is the name given to this act of autonomous willing outside the will of God. Hence perversion is a form of othering of the self when it can no longer make its will coincide with the will of God such that there is a modal transformation of nature without a new nature being created. Abuse is thus a new use of the body outside the governance of the divine will, an incorporeal transformation of the body without creating a new body. But more interestingly, Tertullian says that we are not only not aware of the being of God but also unaware of his will or mind. Hence we do not know how he wants a body to be used and how he wants it not to be used. We can only know this through its opposite that is through the abuse. ("For in that way it will appear for what use they were created, if it once appears for what use they were not"). But interestingly, we are also told that we are not aware even of the will of Satan because being God's adversary his mind is also beyond our reach. Then how do we come to know if something is abused or used with an intention outside the will of God?

If the will of God can only be known through the opposition set between the use and abuse of bodies then such an opposition is inaugurated through the creation of an inaugural "No" to an 'other' which is created by the force of this negation. The will of Satan which perverts all use of bodies produced through divine creation, transforming them into abuse, is as much outside knowledge as the divine will to use bodies. But by forcing an originary 'no' to the abuse of the world which is otherwise unknown, it not only makes it known but forces it into being. In other words, one *creates the very moment of abuse itself by simply recognizing it as such* which is otherwise presumed to be beyond knowledge hence beyond judgement. And because it is only through evil that good can be known hence God comes as a by product of the creative appearance of evil through bodies which are abused It is this will to negation which Nietzsche would claim to be the original creative but weak force of the Christian in his concept of *ressentiment*, who can only think of the use of a body as an afterthought to an inaugural abuse. Hence it is perhaps difficult to separate the problem of use from the question of subject. In other words the subject, who is actually produced *a posterior* to an inaugural decision to say no, transforms the creative force of this inaugural weakness which can only say no to the world into a choice between yes and no, between the subject's freedom to use or abuse.

Hence Elisabeth Roudinesco can argue that every form of perversion reinforces the presence of a sovereign law (sovereign good) to which it is inextricably tied which explains why abjection and sublimation formed a causal chain during the Middle Ages in medieval practices of mortification. Of course because it is always produced as an originary force of negation, it would sometimes become difficult to appropriate it into a logic of divine sublimation produced as an afterthought. The force of weakness or the power of powerlessness, however one might think of it, would be too much to be sublated and transformed into an oppositional logic of beautiful sublimation. This problem of the original force of impurity of the body which has to be purified and resurrected becomes interesting when we consider the question of women martyrs. In case of women the body was already seen as tainted and abused because of its 'natural' function of procreation, menstruation, childbirth, etc. Hence she had to be imagined already as a purified object whose transformation from impurity to purity through martyrdom had to be preceded by already possessing the pure body of the virgin. The abusive body of the female sex had to be first imagined as the pure virginal body which would symbolically erase its sexual difference thus making it pure so that it can be ready for the ultimate purification through martyrdom into the immaculate body of the solider of Christ. Here the inaugural negation which creates the abusive body of the female sex has to go through a double bind of symbolic purification in order to be imagined as a sublime body. Again the problem of mysticism, in the late Middle Ages, with their ordeal involving the body creating the kind of otherness through an inaugural rejection and abuse of the body extended to its maximal degree became a huge point of contention in the history of Christianity. Roudinesco remarks about the creation of this absolute place of negativity which the Mystics created for themselves to achieve salvation thus, "That unknowable place is bound up with initiation. Its place is therefore an elsewhere, and its sign is an anti-society. To put it another way, we define as mystical 'that which departs from normal or ordinary paths, that which is not inscribed within the unity of a faith or a religious reference, and which is marginal to a society that is becoming secularized and to an emerging knowledge of scientific objects' (Certeau 1978:522)" (Roudinesco, 2009)

Transmission, Perversion and Habitation

Coming back to our text and the problem of transmission of the evil of idolatry, Tertullian repeatedly points out that it is not the places themselves but their abuse which defile them. Evil can be transmitted to others if they are not careful enough. There is a sense of fear or anxiety regarding the public shows as a perpetual threat which can corrupt the soul anytime. Hence we have to be constantly reminded "who they are to whom places of this sort are dedicated to" (p. 255) because our only weapon against the danger of defilement is our will which has to recognize the danger at every step in order to struggle against it. Foucault has pointed out this aspect of the sin in Tertullian, where it is seen not merely as a perversion or a change of our nature which paradoxically remains the same and becomes other simultaneously. For Tertullian sin is also the way the other has entered your soul and has taken possession of a part of it. Unlike the earlier idea of sin as fall which leads back to the Gnostics and neo-Platonists where the soul having lost his seat beside God and fallen into evil matter, struggles to ascend back to its former place of purity, Tertullian sees evil as something which resides within the soul, hides in its dark corners; an other which has taken possession of the self and is within the self. This other is the devil. Hence in *De Spectaculis*, Tertullian talks of the inherent violence of all spectacles which constitutes an affective chain within the soul of pleasure leading to eagerness, leading to rivalry which finally leads to "madness, bile, anger, pain and all the things that follow from them" (p. 271). But the source of this progression from pleasure to madness is nothing but a *lapse*. He says, "No one ever comes to pleasure without some feeling, no one has this feeling without some lapse, and the lapses actually contribute to the feeling". It is this lapse, this temporary suspension of not only judgement but also memory which is not only the work of the devil but the very 'church' within which Satan reigns and exercises his power. Hence Tertullian writes immediately following these lines that the source of the feeling leading to madness is thus a hollowing out of thinking which corresponds to a temporary suspension of rationality, an "empty-mindedness" such that the self is free to transform itself into something alien. Perversion as a modal transformation which brings about a change in the body without producing a new body can thus take place in this time of lapse producing madness and the frenzy of the soul[16]. Through the theory of lapse we see in Tertullian a re-working of the idea of enframing where the performers and the audience are brought together under a common logic of desire as a lapse leading to pleasure and frenzy. "If thou saw a thief, says the scripture, thou didst consent with him". (p. 271) The struggle against the devil is the struggle against the ubiquitous power of this desire which splits the self into the part which is God's creation to be used and that which belongs to the devil and is abused. "Still we are separated from them in all that is worldly. For the world is God's; what is worldly is the devil's" (p. 271). This separation of the world from the worldly has to be a constant exercise of the self on itself where the worldly elements have to be recognized and rejected which is never an easy task because firstly it is always hidden, masked and secondly it is everywhere. Therefore the danger, the peril of the "worldly" and by extension the idolatrous danger of the public shows can present itself anywhere. The entire world is filled with Satan and by extension the whole world is deceptive. Hence we see that the world unlike a neo-Platonist and Gnostic tradition of dualism is not seen as illusory but very real, in fact too real to be just disregarded. It has to be explored, examined and deciphered like the self so that the world of divine use might be separated from the world abuse of Satan. Hence the self becomes a kind of reflection of the world and worldly both of which has to be examined and recognized for what they are so that one can separate what belongs to God from what belongs to the devil.

The Paradox of Deception

Hence citing Corinthians, Tertullian says, "'Not that an idol is anything'," says the apostle but what they do, 'they do in honour of demons' who plant themselves in the consecrated images of—whatever they are, dead men or as they think, gods" (Ibid.). This deceptive quality of idolatry becomes most prominently embodied in the theatrical shows as against all other public spectacles. Along "with those features of the stage peculiarly and especially its own, that effeminancy of gesture and posture" (p. 259), the stage is also particularly perilous because it misleads one into idolatry. Therefore apart from these forms of impurities of gender bending and perversions of one's natural disposition, theatre provokes idolatry in a more insidious and surreptitious fashions by pretending to be art whose authors are glorified in the theatre. Tertullian urges his readers to be suspect of all such arts "whose authors they must execrate in their very names" (p. 261) because all such names are deceitful. What lies beneath such names is akin to what lies behind the mask of the actor in the theatre: the other of what is presented to the world. It is as if unknown to the unsuspecting and ignorant spectator, the ground beneath his/her feet is displaced as he/she no longer finds himself/herself in a theatre but in the church of Satan, glorifying in the name of those alien deities, the demons who have usurped the names of all the authors. Though the arts (particularly the tragedies and the comedies but also the pantomime, and the mime) are authored by men, but they come as gifts from the devil who presents men with such gifts so that they (men) can glorify the names of deities behind which lurks demons. It is through this deceptive process that they manage to persuade naive ignorant men to glorify the name of the unclean one. Hence Tertullian notes, "nor would they have given the arts to the world at that time through the agency of any other men that those by whose names and images and legends they determined they would negotiate the trick of their own consecration." (p. 261) The deception and masking performed on the stage is replicated and repeated off stage in the very institution of theatre and all such arts in the name of such false deities. We see here the problem of theatre articulated, probably for the first time, not merely as imitation which is illusory (which is how the Platonic world would view theatre) but theatre is argued to be a place of deception par excellence, intimate to the devil. Theatre and the arts are not questioned simply on the basis of their ontological inferiority as part of a differential economy of judgement prevalent in the Classical and Hellenist period. It is now seen as a struggle between truth and falsity with its necessary moral consequences. Theatre (and the arts in general) ceases to be simply illusory. Illusion gains a certain reality so to speak as the work of the devil. Now we have entered the heart of the paradox of evil embodied in theatre which Augustine would theorize later. The proof of the devil as embodied in theatre is that it deceives. Hence though illusory or rather because of it theatre is harmful and to that extent it is real. In other words, theatre being the art of appearance *par excellence* is essentially ambiguous which provides the very certainty of its evil. Hence, firstly, the experience of theatre is a real threat to the self which has to first recognize the deceptive reality of theatre which seduces and tempts under false names. Secondly, the self has to free itself from any attachment to such experience not because it is an illusion, on the contrary because it is too real. The renunciation of all spectacles (but particularly theatre) is based on this idea that the more one wants to renounce them the more one has to bring the truth of these public shows to light. It is only through such an operation of examination and scrutiny that one will realize that what is actually at stake in these spectacles is not merely a question of pleasure but a deeper and nefarious motive of the devil to consecrate his name by wearing the mask of false deities. All such acts of counter-glorification which has the danger of establishing an 'other' economy of vice have to be renounced.

The Trial of the World

But even when the renunciation of theatre moves from a pedagogic necessity to a question of ascetic practice of self-purification, it cannot bypass the imagination of a world spectacle. In Tertullian this comes in the form of a world tribunal. Against certain apologists of public shows–who argue that God, being the omnipresent spectator of the spectacle of the world, looks down even upon these worldly spectacles without getting defiled so it cannot possibly pollute man to view them–Tertullian responds with the precision of a jurist. He argues that the comparison between the spectatorial position of God and the spectators of such defiling and sinful acts as those of the worldly spectacles is ludicrous. Because God views the world with a divine detachment which is impossible for man to imitate because he is already implied in the world's sins even if he is only a viewer. To be implied in the evil of worldly spectacles even as a passive observer is already made clear, as we have tried to elaborate earlier, through something like an 'enframing' of the performer-spectator as being equally culpable. Now Tertullian builds upon this logic by imagining human reality as something like a world tribunal where man must always play the part of a defendant who is on trial hence always under the 'panoptic' vision of a divine judge. Tertullian writes:

> Would that God looked on at no sins of men, that we might all escape judgement! But God looks on at brigandage, God looks at cheating, adultery, fraud, idolatry, yes, and the spectacles, too. And that is why we will not look at them, that we may not be seen by Him who looks on at everything. Man! You are putting defendant and judge on one level!–the defendant who is a defendant because he is seen, the judge who because he sees is judge. (p. 281)

Man has to constantly feel the gaze of God upon himself in everything he does even when he seems hidden, even in the most intimate moments of his actions and even thoughts. Hence he has to put himself on trial constantly so that he might come out purified and worthy of the truth of God. The 'self' which is on perpetual trial is the self which is always seen, always exposed to the divine gaze. But the preparatory exercise for the self to undergo the final transformation and come to the light of God is the obligation of man to present his own self on the stage of this world tribunal so that he can witness himself being judged. So in this imagination of a world tribunal man is both the defendant and the witness. In Tertullian the imagination of a world stage becomes that of a courthouse drama.

Blushing or Becoming Red? On the Question of Shame

But to become witness to one's own trial is also to bear witness to the dissolution of that part of oneself which is held in sin. It is here that Tertullian introduces the idea of shame and the ambiguity of its appearance in the public spectacles particularly in that of theatre. On the one hand, Tertullian denounces the theatre for being a place without shame. "Fifth acted out by the buffoon playing the woman, banishing all sense of sex and shame, so that they blush more readily at home than on the stage" (p. 275). But for this very reason of being a place without shame, to participate in the theatre is a shameful act. Hence talking about the women on stage he observes, "Those women themselves, who have murdered their own shame shudder (you can see it in their gestures) to find themselves in the light and before the populace, and blush once in the year" (p. 275). What is this blush which comes through murdering all sense of shame?

In a small piece titled "Antithetical Meaning of Primal Words," Sigmund Freud compares the ambiguity of negation in dreams where contraries are always represented in a fashion where it becomes impossible to distinguish them such that they form combinatory unities. This "preference for combining contraries into unities" (Freud, 1957) where their remains no valid way of determining clearly if an element admits of its opposite is something which Freud compares to certain words which would occur mostly in archaic languages. For example, in Latin the word 'sacer' means both sacred and accursed. Following the analysis of the famous German philologist Karl Abel, Freud explains that it is because our thinking functions through comparisons which in this case means through an oppositional mode that these words would carry their inverse meaning with them. So they would not only signify themselves but the very oppositional basis of their existence. But since language does not merely express thoughts but also communicates there has to be some kind of anchorage of the sense in which it is used in a line. So in case of these languages, particularly in the written form this was done by something like a determinative sign, placed immediately after the alphabetical ones, which would assign the particular usage of the meaning in that sentence[17]. We can perhaps explain the problem of shame as that kind of a primal expression which always carries within itself its opposite which is the condition of its possibility of existence. According to this line of thinking the blush is nothing but the determinative sign which anchors the expression to its positive and affirmative pole. The woman who blushes on stage being without shame is ashamed of the very fact of her being without shame. The stage being a place of ambiguity of appearance and reality is made 'real' whose (im)moral value is affirmed through the 'determinative' gesture of the blush. However this kind of oppositional mode of thinking in case of morality is something which has a particular historical genealogy in Christianity. Michel Foucault in a short article titled "Sexuality and Solitude" while talking of the relation between subjectivity and truth, particularly the shift in the techniques of the self from the Greco-Roman to the Christian period proposes a unique aspect of Christian morality. Analysing the fourteenth book of Augustine's *City of God*, Foucault shows how with Augustine, the question of sexual morality was no longer a problem of a differential logic of power where the normative discourse was set around the differential position of the subject in the social hierarchy which would determine for him what kinds of sexual acts are admissible and which types are prohibited. But in Christianity, starting with Augustine, it was the sexual act itself which was described in its horrific and graphic details as the immoral act par excellence. But in spite of such horrific physical detail of the sexual act, Augustine admits that there might have been sexual relation in paradise before the fall but such acts were completely controlled by Adam whose body was in complete obedience to his soul and will which was in harmony with the will of God. But when he sought the autonomy of his own will that is with the original sin of disobedience, Adam lost control of his body which was rendered upon him by God as punishment. Hence while in paradise the sexual act was completely in Adam's control like the sowing of seeds, it was in his control because his body obeyed his command like the finger obeys the command of the one who gestures. But with the fall, Adam lost the ontological support for his will and hence his body or rather parts of his body revolted in disobedience. The epileptic nature of orgasm is the very idea of such a body which is no longer in control of one's will. As Foucault remarkably notes, "Sex in erection is the image of man revolted against God" (Foucault, *Ethics: Subjectivity and Truth*, 1997, p. 181). Hence Adam's famous gesture of hiding his genitals in shame is not because he wants to deny their presence but because he wants to dissimulate the fact that they have become autonomous, moving by themselves without his consent. Shame is what hides and reveals the possibility of a body thinking for itself beyond good and evil in the innocence of its own becoming. The shameful blush is the remainder which reminds the self that it has lost its place by the side of a sovereign will where the body remained under the obedience of the self. And by that very gesture it seeks to capture the body in its shameful moment of a bare life. To witness oneself at the very moment of one's de-subjectification, the way Agamben conceives of shame thus cannot escape the problem of a sovereign capture of the body by the very gesture which reminds one of its loss. The shameful blush is nothing but this 'becoming red' of the cheeks which is the expression of creation. It is the redness of the fever of becoming, the symptom of the body creating itself through its own thinking in the act of lovemaking or in the passionate outburst of an actor on stage. These figures witness the moment of dissolution of their subjectivities in order to constitute themselves. They create themselves as thinking bodies revolting against the sovereign will of the constituted self. Hence their redness is nothing but the sign which indicates the temperature of their becoming. Shame is the cunning which tries to veil the tremendous force of their creation making an active force into a reactive one binding it to the ambiguity of active and reactive. Tertullian testifies to this cunning deployment of the problem of shame by making theatre both a place of shamelessness and shamefulness. In the final analysis he tries to capture the image of theatre as the place where man revolts against God by producing an alternative economy of thinking and affects by calling it a place of unreason–a place of madness. Here Tertullian employs an ingenious way of connecting the loss of self-control to the idea of perversity as self-othering. He writes about the words uttered and the gestures made by the spectators thus, "Next taunts or mutual abuse without any warrant of hate, and applause, unsupported by affection. What of their own are they going to achieve who act there in that way–when they are not their own? Unless it be merely the loss of self-control"? (Tertullian, 1931, p. 283) So the gestures and words of the spectators are not merely beyond their self-control but by losing self-control they become someone else, (an)other, which is inconsistent with their self. Thus if Tertullian calls this a form of madness or a lack of rational thinking a loss of one's self-will then paradoxically he also calls it a form of perversion, a willful transgression of the natural low. In other words, there is a form of inconsistency introduced in the self which behaves in two completely different ways under these circumstances. Hence he remarks, "So it comes about that a man who will scarcely lift his tunic in public for the necessities of nature, will take it off in the circus in such a way as to make a full display of himself before all" (p. 283). And it is as an extension of this argument that we find the reason behind the famous Christian denunciation of Roman culture for its hypocrisy and perversity–Romans who would glorify theatre but denounce the actors, promote the spectacles but not even grant citizenship to the majority of performers. That which for the Romans was part of a differential logic of morality based on social hierarchy, for Tertullian becomes an inherent logic perversity[18].

Fabulation: The Final Spectacle

However in the end, the renunciation of the pleasure of spectacles is seen not merely as a preparatory exercise of purity where the self is to be brought under the scrutiny of its own knowledge. Like a guide book, Tertullian's text does not merely provide us the origin of each spectacle with its accompanying nature of evil which is to be renounced. Despite the horrific image painted of such a 'spectacular reality' it becomes the point of departure for another vision equally spectacular in its coming into being: the day of final judgement. If for Tertullian there is no "greater pleasure than the disdain of all pleasure" (p. 296) then the realization of this pleasure, its point of discharge is constructed in the spectacular fabulation of this day of final reckoning[19].

> ...Yes, and there are still to come other spectacles–that last, that eternal day of Judgement, that day which the Gentiles never believed would come, that day they laughed at, when this old world and all its generations shall be consumed in one fire. How vast the spectacle that day, and how wide! ...Those sages, too, the philosophers blushing before their disciples as they blaze together...And, then, the poets trembling before the judgement-seat, not of Rhadamanthus, not of Minos, but of Christ whom they never looked to see! And then there will be the tragic actors to be heard, more vocal in their own tragedy; and the players to be seen, lither of limb by far in the fire; than then the charioteer to watch, red all over in the wheel of flame...Such sights, such exultation,–what praetor consul, quaestor, priest, will ever give you of his bounty? And yet all these, in some sort, are ours, pictured through faith in the imagination of the spirit. But what are those things which eye hath not seen nor ear heard, nor ever entered into the heart of man? I believe, things of greater joy than circus, theatre or amphitheatre, or any stadium. (pp. 297-301)

If there was an effort to separate the Christian subject from the fabulatory and idolatrous world of pagan reality, then such an effort produced what Elizabeth Castelli calls the 'counter-script' of Roman performativity. Analysing a number of martyrological texts from the early centuries of Christianity, Castelli argues that though a strong polemics against spectacles existed among early church fathers, there was an equally conspicuous appropriation of antiquarian spectacular tradition by these early Christian writers. This spectacular tendency becomes more and more visible as the martyrological texts distance themselves from actual historical reality of the vents of martyrdom. The work of memory, she argues, informs these texts with an increasing fabulatory and performative elements which come in many forms. In such texts like *Passion of Perpetua and Felictas* and others, the counter narrative not only attempts to take control of the performance by assigning characters more freedom to act on their own, putting the control of the spectacle in the hands of the Christian 'performers'. We shall come back to this question of freedom of the 'Christian subject' in a while. They finally, as with time the collective of Christians consolidated itself, tried to produce a recognizable interpretative framework. One of the key aspects of this work of memory on the texts was to produce more and more visceral and spectacular descriptions of the executions, the gratuitousness of the acts of violence themselves which paradoxically contributed to produce more meaning. The more gratuitous and spectacular the descriptions of the executions the more they added to the inner meaning of Christian resilience, heroic courage and faith. Simultaneously the fabulatory nature of the text was also intensified for the production of the 'truth' of Christian liturgy as against the falsity of the pagan rituals. Castelli notes:

> The move becomes increasingly important over time as the memory work of martyrology becomes ever more distant from its historical anchoring. The performance is detached from the arena as an historical setting and begins to travel more freely in the imagination of later readers and hearers. The spectacle of Christian suffering becomes, in the commemorative repetitions in the liturgy and devotional texts, its own genre of performance. (Castelli, 2004, p. 124)

What we find in the Tertullian text is perhaps the earliest example of all these tendencies coming together which can be summed up in three steps.

(a) An inaugural negative reaction against the spectacles which becomes the basis to search for a performative language to express their true nature.
(b) This performative utterance against the theatre serves as the ground for an inverse gesture of creating a spectacular vocabulary of their own. Such a vocabulary is fundamentally dependent on an intellectualization or metaphorization of such a reality, transposing or better inversing it into the world of a spectacular fabulation.
(c) The possibility for such performative thinking would start to actualize itself through the liturgical practices as Christianity consolidated itself over the centuries.

Some Concluding Remarks on Methodology: Towards a Critical Evaluation of a World Historical Revenge

Towards the end of his first essay in *The Genealogy of Morals*, titled 'Good and Evil, Good and Bad', Nietzsche cites the above passage from Tertullian, to establish his argument of what constitutes heavenly 'bliss' for Christianity. Nietzsche concludes that what consists of this happiness is a pleasure built upon a logic of recompense. Nietzsche argues that what lies behind Tertullian's advice against the "cruel voluptuousness of the public spectacles" (Nietzsche, 1994, p. 30) is the will of the powerless to fabricate as a compensation for their earthly weakness an ideal space of power. This desire to be powerful one day is manifested in their fabrication of "the kingdom of God" behind which lies the force of their hatred. Immediately before citing this example from Tertullian, Nietzsche quotes a famous comment by Thomas Aquinas, "The blessed in the heavenly kingdom will see the torment of the damned so that they may even more thoroughly enjoy their blessedness." (p. 29). The force which fuels what he calls the "phantasmagoria" of a Christian paradise is a hatred whose logic he had painstakingly tried to develop in the preceding pages. Firstly he recognizes this attempt as an intellectual effort which comes as the product of an originary revenge on 'life'. It is what he calls a "fabrication of ideals" concocted by the "intelligence of priestly revenge" (p. 17). So it is a fabrication, a product of imagination but more importantly it is the expression of an essence which is primarily intellectual. In fact Nietzsche argues that cleverness is the very condition of existence of this type of men. But behind the creative imagination of such intellect lies a politics of revenge which is not merely psychological superiority but historical advantage. But what constitutes this politics of revenge and how does it manifest intellectually? It is here that we have to understand the genius of Nietzsche who, as Deleuze remarked, introduces the concept of value and sense to Western philosophy. In other words, Nietzsche discovered, perhaps for the first time in Western philosophy, that behind the sense of meaning is the power of values. Sense is always to be seen as the capture of a thing, or a phenomenon by a force which appropriates it making it into a sign so that nothing remains outside it. This force which comes as a symptom through the sign operates creating and recreating relations between bodies in history which are nothing but a "variation of senses" (Deleuze, 1983, p. 3) which expresses these relations of forces. Sometimes values are transformed to create new values thus bringing about a process of revaluation through the operation of forces which are contingent to history. Thus thinking might come as judgment, but in the final analysis it is the product of a creative force which always affirms. We will come back to this point. Since value is always presupposed by perspectives of appraisal, to evaluate is not merely to create values but to express modes of existence of the one who evaluates or judges. The principle on the basis of which the value is created is drawn from the mode of being of the one who evaluates. Evaluation is the process both critical and creative through which values derive their valuation. In other words, high and low, noble and bad are not given values but differential elements in a process which tries to determine the value of values. To analyse and discover the problem of values, which is the task of philosophy, is to engage in the task of finding the value of values. Critical philosophy moves towards an analysis of modes of existence or processes of evaluation so that all things can be referred back to their origin which is to say the inaugural moment of the valuation of values. This in a nutshell is the task of genealogy.

According to this line of thinking, the Christian tradition, and even before that the Judaic tradition brings about a re-valuation of an earlier classical value ascribed to the question of morality. The Christian morality (also Judaic) which Nietzsche identifies as slave morality conditioned by an essential powerlessness brings about a "revolt" in the form of a reaction to the active mode of expression of classical morality which evaluated through a differential logic of high and low, or good or bad.. This transformation takes place when in an original moment of hatred which is nothing but an affective moment of *ressentiment*, the self creates something like an outside, an other which is external to itself and to which it can now say 'no'. Nietzsche writes:

> The beginning of the slaves' revolt in morality occurs when in ressentiment itself turns creative and gives birth to values: the ressentiment of those beings who, denied the proper response of action, compensate for it only with *imaginary revenge.* Whereas all noble morality grows out of a triumphant saying 'yes' to itself, slave morality says 'no' on principle to everything that is 'outside', 'other', 'non-self': And this 'no' is its creative deed. This reversal of the evaluating glance–this essential orientation to the outside instead of back onto itself–is a feature of ressentiment: in order to come about, slave morality first has to have an opposing, external world, it needs, physiologically speaking, external stimuli in order to act at all–its action is basically a reaction. (Nietzsche, 1994, p. 20)

For Nietzsche history is nothing but the flow of these active and reactive forces which creates and recreates values. In case of Christianity what they replace is an active force of creating values. In this form of evaluation the self turned onto itself in its saying 'yes' to itself creating a form of morality which was governed by an inaugural affirmation. This affirmation not only was the condition of their thinking and making sense of the world but an affirmation which was determined by a logic of power over oneself, a mastery of the self as Foucault would demonstrate through his genealogical analysis of Greco-Roman ethics. Hence the relation of this inaugural moment of affirmation which was the creation of their value of good to that of bad was not oppositional. Rather there was a sympathetic relation with the bad, the unhappy, and the unfortunate. It is from the "pathos of distance" that one assessed the 'bad' as something towards which 'good' was, to a large extent, *indifferent*. Hence the relation between the good and bad was never a relation of destructive hatred or negative rejection. The sphere of the bad was something he was not familiar with or even if he managed to have some distorted idea about it, such distortion was always informed by some form of pathos. Hence the bad were also pitiable, unhappy. The affirmation was never lost even where the bad was named as *contemptuous*. He says, "This is a legacy of the old, nobler, aristocratic method of valuation that does not deny itself even in contempt" (Ibid., p. 21). This was the original differential logic of the creation of values of good and bad according to Nietzsche.

But Christian ressentiment has no sympathy for the bad. Here it is a question of an originary negation which becomes the condition for existence. It is a question of negating the outside such that the self can be created. The non-self towards which the self is oriented but only through its denial, the outside which has to be hated and rejected is as much a creative act as the affirmation of the self in case of the nobler valuation. However in case of *ressentiment* because the inaugural creative act is a negation, affirmation in the form of happiness can only be produced *artificially* which is to say intellectually. This intellectuality which creates the "effigy" of a world of heavenly bliss is determined by the powerless affect of hatred, the reactive force of ressentiment. From this point of view we can not only understand Nietzsche's use of the particular theatrical image in Tertullian as an example of Christian intellectuality but find a comprehensive framework of understanding the nature of Christian thinking of the problem of theatre. Tertullian's vision of the spectacle of final judgment, the metaphorical phantasmagoric and inverted theatrical re-enactment of all earthly spectacles can be seen as the product of an intellect, an artificial and intellectual rendition of the actuality of theatre which is abhorred and negated. But it is nevertheless a *creation* of an idea of theatre, a creation of what Nietzsche calls the powerless–the product of a will towards powerlessness. If we follow this line of thinking by Nietzsche, we come to the inevitable conclusion that what Christianity succeeds in doing is taming the 'nobler' idea of theatre through the reactive force of *ressentiment*, making it into an "instrument of culture". Nietzsche observes, "one would undoubtedly have to view all instinctive reaction and instinctive ressentiment, by means of which the noble races and their ideals were finally wrecked and overpowered, as the actual instruments of culture" (p. 24).

As there is a difference between the contempt of theatre as a lower form of imitation that we find in Plato and the hatred of theatre in Tertullian as an evil enemy, there is also a distinction that we need to maintain between the logic of governing theatre through a management of pleasure and the transformation of theatre into an instrument of culture through intellectualization which we first find in Christianity. And the result of this mode of separating the affective function of theatre from the intellectual process was to introduce the problem of *depth as opposition* (for example, opposition between true and false, text and performance, even ritual and theatre). This opposition as depth in the idea of theatre replaces 'the distance of pathos'–a differential logic–which was a classical mode of evaluating theatre on the basis of a lower or higher intensity of pleasure according to which it would be judged as good or bad. As we have tried to explore in the first chapter, Plato's idea of theatre in *Laws*, as a place where pleasure should be governed according to a logic of harmony and order could be interpreted in this light as an attempt to evaluate theatre as a place which ought to produce moderate and orderly pleasure oriented towards the 'good'. This was the pedagogic function of theatre which Plato imagined which could not have been possible if theatre was conceived as a perversion. Even in Roman antiquity the problem of theatre as the problem of *persona* expressed the problem of a differential logic of hierarchy of modes of existence. With Christianity, the introduction of the logic of perversion made theatre an 'evil enemy' opposed to the 'good' but at the same time this hatred helped to create an idea of theatre as a place of depth, where it was assumed that behind every deceit there was a truth, behind every trickery there was an intention, behind every mask there was a face. The metaphor of theatre as 'world stage' carried this logic of depth as opposition by juxtaposing the 'illusion' of a theatre of the world to the 'real of a divine theatre'. Moreover as an intellectual version of the reality of theatre, the 'love' for the 'world stage' metaphor in theological texts could only be built on the hatred of the real theatre. In other words, the reactive force of ressentiment created the singular Christian meaning of theatre in terms of its intellectual and metaphorical value based on the evil value attached to its historical reality. An intellectual and artificial 'yes' to the metaphorical use of the theatrical image could only be possible on the basis of an original 'no' to the historical reality of theatre.

However, we should not confuse this negation as the negation internal to judgment, which from a dialectical perspective is seen as the very beginning of thought. Ressentiment though no doubt gives rise to thinking should not be seen as the movement from the affective to the intellectual where "the intellectual function is separated from the affective process"[20] so that the intellectual can grasp the affective and make sense of it. In fact the orientation to an outside which the self creates and the utterance of the 'no' are simultaneous to each other such that one does not create the other through an original negation but the negation itself is the very act of creation. In other words, the very phenomenon of oppositional logic according to which ressentiment describes its relation to the world nevertheless is the creation of a reactive force–a 'powerless' force. What we need to understand about Nietzsche's idea of *ressentiment* is that it is only *one* symptom in a constellation through which a force can appropriate a thing and make it into a symptom. Ressentiment is one such singular moment when the self is so absolutely consumed by hatred and denial that this reactive force also creates the very mode of oppositional thinking which is essential to the powerless. Hence Nietzsche would argue that like the strong cannot but be strong because it is the very essence of their *mode of existence,* so the weak are irremediably powerless.

But while the noble in their will to power affirm the very mode of existence which is their 'life' and in doing so affirms a differential logic of thinking, the weak can only affirm their weakness. But it is the very essence of this mode of existence that it creates depth in thinking by artificially grafting a cause to life which is nothing but the symptom/sign of a particular force. Ressentiment thus succeeds in producing a subject by artificially transforming a quantum of force, will, action into an agency, the will to choose. This will to choose between good and evil, this freedom to manifest strength or weakness introduces artificially a 'being' behind deed, separating the person and the action. But as Nietzsche never forgets to remind us such misconstrued notion of agency is nothing but a pure invention symptomatic of a particular mode of existence which is informed with ressentiment. There is no substratum behind action and the effect it produces because causality is only an afterthought typical to a weak mode of thinking and existence. With ressentiment arrives causality and the oppositional relation between cause and effect which even scientific thinking cannot abandon. Deception through which depth is introduced in thinking of the weak is always self-deception in the beginning which tries to transform an inaugural utterance of 'no' into the artificial self-affirmation through freedom. Hence Nietzsche would remark that Christian intellectualism is the type of artificiality which transforms a mode of existence into an accomplishment, or in other words a will to power into a supposed choice of existence of a subject. This is the essence of powerlessness, its true effect which is a self-consuming hatred, creating an oppositional logic of thinking. But it is all the same a *creation* of a negativity and not the re-affirmation of an existent negativity. What Nietzsche seems to teach us is that there is also something like a will to powerlessness creating oppositional, if not dialectical, thinking which is just one variation among a multiplicity of ways in which forces apply themselves to bodies to create thought. The symptom of the Christian mode of thinking around theatre is informed by a logic of opposition transforming a previous differential logic of understanding theatre as action and effect into an oppositional relation between cause and effect. This mode of thinking about theatre would have enormous consequence in Western history becoming a dominant method of understanding theatre in its various aspects. Through our investigation in this chapter we have tried to provide something like (an)archaeology of that originary moment of transformation of the problem of theatre when the reactive force of culture came to delimit the active force of creation by an act of world historical revenge.

NOTES

1. Quoted from Tertullian's *De Spectaculis* (Tertullian, 1931).
2. The metaphor of the tumultuous sea which always carries the possibility of shipwreck and the safety and solidity of the ground from where the spectator observes the arbitrariness of the waves is a recurrent theme defining existence in Western metaphysics which is closely related to another metaphor which is that of theatre, where the tragedy of life is played by the actors while the audience watches the unfolding of this existential drama not as a participant but as an external observer. Both these metaphors, that of the sea and that of the theatre correspond to each other in many aspects, from the arbitrariness of the events at sea and the drama that unfolds on stage, to the dangers of the players concerned to the debate regarding the nature of involvement of the spectator. See (Blumenberg, 1997)
3. The Augustinian idea of charity or charitas is fundamentally related to Augustine's meditations on love and the two forms it takes. That of worldly love or *cupititas* and of heavenly love or *charitas.* Though pursuing different objects, a worldly object in the former and a heavenly object in the latter, both *cupiditas* and *charitas* had the same structure of desire which is to want something outside the self. The problem and the challenge was to orient this desire to its right object which was that of God which could never be found in the world. But in Augustine *charitas* had this fundamental structure of desire which sought to somehow produce an impossible relation between immanence and transcendence . The Pauline idea of charity does not follow an

effort to suture the break between transcendence and immanence but a new paradox of something like a reality of appearance.

4. Agamben cites this from Peterson's 1926 dissertation *Heis Theos.*
5. Cited by Agamben from Peterson's work. It is necessary to point out here the cruciality of a singular debate which spanned over 30 years between two Catholics and its relevance to any argument regarding the theological origins of sovereignty and a philosophy of history. This debate which took place between Eric Peterson and Carl Schmitt was informed as much by common presuppositions as by long periods of silence. In his famous essay "Monotheism as a Political Problem," Peterson came to his famous conclusion that a Christian political theology was a "theological impossibility". As an oblique but obvious critique of Schmitt's thesis that modern secular politics founds itself on political theology, Peterson's detailed analysis of a history of the development of the power of the church in the West ironically leads us to the same theological problem of a deferred *eschaton* as does Schmitt's thesis. But while Schmitt identifies the nature and identity of the *katechon*, the power that defers Christ's Second Coming (and the realization of the *eschaton*) in the empire of the Church, Peterson identifies it in the reluctance of the Jews, being the chosen people to convert. Agamben re-imagines the famous Schmitt-Peterson debate in terms of his thesis on *Oikonomia* and its relation to the concept of the *katechon*. See (Agamben, 2011)
6. As cited by Agamben from Origen's *Commentaire*, pp. 333-335.
7. Ibid., p. 343.
8. Though this arrival, as Kierkegaard points out is only a forced or axiomatic affirmation of the idea in Plato, who unlike Hegel could not arrive at the Truth through the internal movement of dialect. Unlike Hegel's triadic dialectical model of thesis-antithesis-synthesis, the cruder Socratic model of thesis-antithesis allowed Plato to enforce the concept of the Idea only externally like an axiom. But for Socrates the forms of knowledge, through dialect lets one arrive only at the threshold of truth negatively. This is the famous Socratic ironic knowledge epitomized in the Socratic phrase "to know that one does not know." (Kierkegaard, 1989)

9. In the works of St. Augustine, the problem of love having the structure of desire would at every step correspond to the problem of glorification according to the logic we are trying to understand here.
10. Foucault shows in his reading of the problem of libido in Augustine, how the phenomenon of sexual stimulation was taken to be an act against the free will of an individual who only can will good imitating God's will, when parts of his/her body starts to function against or in spite of his/her will–like in the case of erection in men. This loss of control of one's own body, which starts to function on its own, or better which starts to function under the will of the devil was taken as a state of unfreedom. Hence sexuality was now conceived not simply in terms of a collective morality but something related to the individualized subject through the concept of freedom and in the final analysis through providence.
11. Cited from Thomas Aquinas' *Summa Theologiae*, I, q. 105, a. 6.
12. We shall return to this problem of truth where the subject himself/herself is made into an object of truth, what Foucault would call reflexive truth acts and it relation to the problem of theatre in more detail in a while in our analysis of Tertullian's text.
13. We shall elaborate this term, which we have borrowed from Derrida in the context of theatre in a later footnote.
14. As mentioned before Clement's remarks in *The Paedagogus*, "These assemblies, indeed, are full of confusion and iniquity; and these pretexts for assembling are the cause of disorder–men and women assembling promiscuously for the sight of one another. In this respect the assembly has already shown itself bad: for when the eye is lascivious, the desires grow warm; and the eyes that are accustomed to look impudently at one's neighbours during the leisure granted to them, inflame the amatory desire" (Castelli, 2004)
15. Foucault in his lectures at College de France brilliantly analyses this moment in Tertullian as the earliest recoded testimony to a shift in the very nature of the regime of truth that Christianity as a religion of salvation eventually becomes. Foucault argues that what we witness in Tertullian is diffraction in the movement of

metanoia which was earlier seen as the moment where the subject discovered the truth and the truth within himself simultaneously. Now we have two levels. One the truth one gains access through an incorporeal transformation like baptism, but then there is another truth that of the movement itself, the preparation for baptism which also brings about an incorporeal transformation but a transformation which is never complete, never fulfilled. Here in the movement of the soul towards truth, constantly struggling against evil, trying to free himself from the clutches of the devil, preparing and training himself to defeat the unclean one. This struggle, this constantly deferred moment of a transformation is the truth of the soul which has to be manifested before God. So the movement of the subject towards truth can thus be schematized as the desire of truth *for* the soul which *in* order to become truth in the soul has to first manifest the truth *of* the soul. This is what Foucault argues underlies the meaning of repentance. (Foucault, *On the Government of the Living: Lectures at College de France* (1979-80), 2014)

16. Later Augustine would take up this theme of the evil of public shows as producing a "lapse" in his *Confessions* in the story of his friend Alypius who though reluctant to go to the shows initially was solicited by the frenzy of the spectacles.
17. Freud explains from Abel's thesis "if the Egyptian word "*ken*" is to mean "strong", its sound which written alphabetically, is followed by the picture of an upright armed man; if the same word has to express "weak", the letters which represent the sound are followed by the picture of a squatting, limp figure." (Freud, 1957)
18. On one and the same account they glorify them and they degrade and diminish them; yes, further, they openly condemn them to disgrace and civil degradation; they keep them religiously excluded from council chamber, rostrum, senate, knighthood, and every other kind of office and a good many distinctions. The perversity of it! (Tertullian, 1931, p. 285)
19. The full citation from *De Spectaculis*, Book XXX: "But what a spectacle is already at hand, the return of the Lord, now no object of doubt, now exalted, now triumphant! What exultation

will that be of the angels, what glory of the saints as they rise again! What the reign of righteous thereafter! What a city, the New Jerusalem! Yes, and there are still to come other spectacles–that last, that eternal day of Judgement, that day which the Gentiles never believed would come, that day they laughed at, when this old world and all its generations shall be consumed in one fire. How vast the spectacle that day, and how wide! What sight shall wake my wonder, what my laughter, my joy and exultation? As I see those kings, those great kings welcomed (we are told) in heaven, along with Jove, along with those who told of their ascent, groaning in the depths of darkness! And the magistrates who persecuted the name of Jesus, liquefying in fiercer flames than they kindled in their rage against the Christians! Those sages, too, the philosophers blushing before their disciples as they blaze together, the disciples whom they taught that God was concerned with nothing, that men have no souls at all, or that what souls they have shall never return to their former bodies! And, then, the poets trembling before the judgement-seat, not of Rhadamanthus, not of Minos, but of Christ whom they never looked to see! And then there will be the tragic actors to be heard, more vocal in their own tragedy; and the players to be seen, lither of limb by far in the fire; than then the charioteer to watch, red all over in the wheel of flame ; and next, the athletes to be gazed upon, not in their gymnasiums but hurled in the fire–unless it be that not even then would I wish to see them, in my desire rather to turn an insatiable gaze on them who vented their rage, and fury on the Lord. "This is he," I shall say, "son of the carpenter or the harlot, the Sabbath-breaker, the Samaritan, who had a devil, This is he whom you bought from Judas; this is he who was struck with reed and fist, defiled with spittle, given gall and vinegar to drink, This is he whom the disciples secretly stole away, that it might be said he had risen–unless it was the gardener who removed him, lest his lettuces should be trampled by the throng of visitors!" Such sights, such exultation,–what praetor consul, quaestor, priest, will ever give you of his bounty? And yet all these, in some sort, are ours, pictured through faith in the imagination of the spirit. But what are those things which eye hath not seen nor ear heard, nor ever entered into the heart of man? I believe, things of greater joy than circus, theatre or amphitheatre, or any stadium." (Tertullian, 1931, pp. 297-301)

20. Jean Hyppolite cites this line from Freud's *verneinung.* In his analysis of the text Hyppolite traces the difference between something like an original negation which is condition for judgment and hence internal to judgment and something like an idea of negation which is more like an attitude of negation resembling a kind of adjudication. Hyppolite argues that the movement from the primal affective relation to the intellectual affirmation is not merely a pure dialectical movement where in the acceptance of what is repressed the affective is not lost but preserved as a negation in the intellect which is thereby constituted and affirmed as a negation of negation. Hyppolite following Lacan problematizes this clean dialectical movement arguing that the primal affective relation cannot be seen as purely psychological but always already embedded in history. It is this historicity of the affective which resists all attempts to think of intelligence as completely detached from the affective in order to grasp it. Hence intellectual denial does not destroy the affective but carries it within itself by the creation of something like a symbol of negation. This condition of possibility of thinking as judgment which always comes through constituting a symbol of negation would be an interesting way to treat the problem of theatre in early Christianity where the metaphor of world stage might perhaps be seen as the symbolic negation of all worldly spectacles. However, Christian consciousness in its denial of the pleasure of the stage doest not destroy it but only manages to accept it through an act of repression which continues to oscillate back and forth between a religious consciousness and an aesthetic unconscious. (Lacan, 1991, pp. 52-61)

CHAPTER 4

"You Touched Me, and I am Set on Fire to Attain the Peace which is Yours."[1] Variations on Certain Theatrical Readings of Augustine

Section I

What is a Reading and What is An Aporia?

Criminality

Perhaps there is no such thing as an innocent reading of Saint Augustine. Every reading of Augustine is always already a trespassing–a crossing of legitimate boundaries set by other writers, by other readers; whether it is Marion, Derrida, Lyotard, Arendt, Heidegger or even Augustine himself. For what is his *Confessions* if not the reading of Augustine by Augustine? By the same logic every reading of Augustine is also a transgression because it inevitably crosses the limits laid down by the previous reading. An illegitimate overstepping of the rules and norms of previous readings is inscribed in every reading *as such*. So, echoing Althusser, one could say that every reading of Augustine is a guilty reading. But while Althusser, in *Reading Marx*, sought the "justified crime" (Althusser 2013) of reading scientifically we will try not to get entangled in the duality between scientificity and ideology. The criminality that Althusser sought was to take him beyond the innocence of an immediate reading, which is to say a reading that would not merely uncover the essence of things in the transparency of their 'concrete' existence. Althusser's scepticism makes him suspicious of all such innocent readings leading back to "religious fantasies of epiphany and parousia" (Ibid., n.d., 16). In short, Althusser sought a criminality of reading which would not be resolved by the fetishistic expression of a totalizing theory of history. It is against such a Hegelian concept of the whole as a spiritual totality that he sought a scientifically guilty reading, which ought to be structural. A structural reading which would constantly expose its own de-centering and distance when–instead of discovering its manifest truth–it is taken back to that "structure of structures" (Ibid., n.d., 17): history. It is in the precarity of the historical singularity that Althusser sought the true criminality and the genuine meaning of reading.

Now, we could have followed this path if we wanted to track the problem of theatre in the precarity of historical singularities. This is what we have in a certain way tried to do in the previous chapters. We have sought to understand the problem of theatre, problem understood here in the sum total of its Greek sense of *problema* signifying both protection and projection[2], both related in some sense to the idea of boundaries or thresholds. We have till now sought to understand the problem of theatre at such historical thresholds, or historical moments of crossing-over. We have seen, as in the last chapter, that at the threshold separating the pagan world from the Christian, theatre comes up as a problem precisely in this sense–where, on the one hand, it was protected through the creation of a metaphorical substitute or a figurative prosthesis, so that the idea of theatre is given shelter in such figurative use. Theatre becomes a secret or dissimulation of something unavowable. On the other hand, theatre is projected as something to be accomplished somewhere else, something to be completed elsewhere, which is to become the place of Christian liturgy. Thus the precarity of history becomes the condition for the possibility of theatre to emerge as a problem at a certain threshold which also allows a transformative passage. A discontinuity is woven into the series of discontinuities, which goes on to make the precariousness of history into a "structure of structures". But it is when we try to enter Augustine from this perspective that we encounter something like an aporia.

Metaphorization

It is probably true that scholars like Jonas Barish have a tendency to reduce the nuanced rigour of Augustine when it comes to the question of theatre. We witness such hasty conclusions when Barish seemingly identifies what he calls a "residual manichaeism" in Augustine's response against theatre. (Barish 1981, 54-55) However it would not be absurd to argue that Augustine undoubtedly chides theatre for a number of reasons in many of his texts. We might disagree about the nature and intensity of Augustine's anti-theatrical prejudice, but his discussions on the subject reflect a near universal suspicion of theatre prevalent among early Christian fathers. One could even identify a general dialectical tendency which informs this suspicion of theatre. While *City of God* offers a denunciation of theatre from the point of view of a cultural dialectic, *Confessions* approaches the problem of theatre from the perspective of an intimate dialectic of the self. But it is in some of his early dialogues–*On the Teacher* and *Soliloquies*–but also such later works like *On Christian Doctrine*, that we find a more detached critique of theatre coming out of a dialectic of truth. Donnalee Dox in her *Idea of the Theatre in Latin Christian Thought* sums it up well when she contends that the Augustinian response to theatre stems from three perspectives 1) moral: "theatrical shows encourage bad behaviour" (lust, pride, etc.) 2) religious: "theatre is rooted in pagan religion (idolatry, illicit sacrifice, etc.) 3) philosophical: "theatrical representation interferes with Christians' ability to know God" (Dox 2004, 12). It is from this third perspective that Augustine stands unique in the patristic tradition regarding the discourse of theatre.

Augustine, as Dox argues, extends this argument of an epistemological inadequacy for a Christian world view–which appears in the most systematic fashion in his *On the Christian Doctrine*, as a theory of signs. Theatre here presents the curious problem of producing signs which are of the category *ignota signa* (signs whose meanings are unknown), which seek out their meaning in and through the performance. This makes performance, according to Augustine, always already incomplete, and it needs human conventions and institutions, in other words, specific cultural conditions to produce meaning. Hence he writes:

> If the signs made by actors while dancing were naturally meaningful, rather than meaningful as a result of human institution and agreement, an announcer would not have indicated to the Carthaginians, as each actor danced, what the dance meant, as he did in earlier days...It is quite credible, for even now if a person unfamiliar with these frivolities goes to the theatre his rapt attention to them is pointless unless someone tells him what the movements mean (Ibid., n.d., 25)

Not being what he calls *propia signa*, theatre exposes the arbitrariness of the relation between the signifier and the signified which is only produced by the authority of conventions. Though he does not extend this relational logic conditioned by arbitrariness and disjunction to the very heart of language and representation as such, it remains Augustine's genius to have identified the basic structural condition of a disjunctive logic which informs the semiotics of theatre.

However, such precise structuralist analysis prevents Augustine from allowing theatrical representation to have the capacity to carry the value of Christian truth. Truth, which needs a consistent theory of signs as *propria signa*, which, though relational, is nevertheless in complete agreement with the things they signify, and in the final analysis corresponds to the immediacy between the Word and Flesh. Similarly, Augustine would criticize the signifying potential of theatrical representation, while at the same time acknowledging it in such texts like *On the Teacher* and *Soliloquies.* Investigating the nature of similitude and the structure of resemblance that theatre generates, Augustine offers another ingenious critique on the semiotics of theatre. As Donnalee Dox points out, here Augustine is motivated by the desire to acquire "a method for discerning truth from the phenomenal world, including human-made representation" (Ibid., n.d., 27). When Augustine provides a precise definition of falsity–"we call that false which tends to be something and is not" (Ibid., n.d., 27)–we might safely assume that he is providing the ground work for a much more complex understanding of truth based on relational and formal logic. So he would argue that there are two kinds of resemblances both of which produce falsity but their relation to truth are structurally different. So there are jest, poetry, etc., which produce signs which tend towards the thing they represent, which is to say, tend towards the truth but are themselves false. Then there is stage acting which tends towards false representation but is not itself false. When a stage actor like Roscius[3] portrays the character of Priam, as a man and a tragedian he is true to what he does (as an actor he acts), while what he produces as a result of such acting–the character of Priam–is definitely false. To be not true in one respect while not being false from another point of view makes theatre an inherently incomplete form of expression. Lacking the uniformity of truth it is denounced by Augustine as being grounded in false knowledge. The problem of falsity is also the primary reason for Augustine's denunciation of metaphors which he argues is the usurpation of the proper by the improper[4]. From the point of view of their semiotic structure, metaphor and theatre are mirror images of each other, which become all the more complicated when we find Augustine's writing not only filled with the use of theatrical metaphors but, in certain works like *Soliloquies*, the work's own theatricality that can very well serve as a 'figure' of theatre.

This relationship between metaphorization and theatricality in Augustine is explored by Michael Foley in many of his writings. We will indicate a set of tendencies that Foley identifies as theatrical in Augustine's writings, which also testify to a process of metaphorization of the carnal reality of theatre that is at work in such texts of Augustine as *Soliloquies*, *On the Christian Doctrine* and *Confessions.* In his essay "A Spectacle to the World: The Theatrical Meaning of St. Augustine's Soliloquies", Foley tries to highlight the theatrical disposition of the Bishop of Hippo from at least two perspectives. Firstly, he tries to identify a certain implicit sympathy for theatre which Augustine, according to Foley, betrays at various moments while discussing the subject. But what is much more interesting and relevant for our purpose is the metaphorical use of theatre that Foley discerns in *Soliloquies*. Within the intense brevity of a single paragraph from the text we find the most prominent use of the theatrical metaphor, which also clarifies the very meaning of the neologism *Soliloquies* that Augustine, in a sense, invents anticipating the very essence of modern tragedy leading up to Shakespeare[5]. Augustine writes:

> It's ridiculous for you to be ashamed, as if we hadn't chosen for this very reason the sort of discussion which, because we are speaking with ourselves alone, I want to be called and written down as the *Soliloquies*. This is certainly a new name and perhaps an unrefined one at that, but it is sufficiently suitable for indicating the gist of what we are doing. In fact since there is no better way of seeking the truth than by questioning and answering, and since hardly anyone can be found who isn't ashamed of being refuted in a disputation (and for that reason it is almost always the case that the matter under discussion, one that's off to a good start, is booed off the stage by the rowdy hullabaloo of stubbornness, and all the while souls are being ripped apart mostly out of sight but sometimes out in the open)–I most calmly, in my opinion and agreeable decided to seek the truth with God's assistance by means of being questioned by my very self and giving answers to myself. Consequently if at any time you have rashly tied yourself up in knots, there is nothing to fear in returning to them and loosening them; for otherwise one could never get out of them. (Foley, A Spectacle to the World: The Theatrical Meaning of St. Augustine's Soliloquies 2014, 250)

There is of course a certain dialectic at work here concerning the human desire for truth and the inability of mankind to know the truth about themselves, which we will try to examine for ourselves in a while. Suffice it to say here that Foley identifies in this desire for knowledge, which ironically leads to a concealment of truth or what he calls "the paradoxical desire for self-concealment and self exaltation" (Ibid., n.d., 251), something akin to the Platonic idea of *thumos*.[6] Foley contends that theatre becomes a metaphor for this thumotic sin which Reason outlines for Augustine in this inner dialogue. Obviously this is nothing new to Christian writings of the time. What Foley points to here is the metaphorical use of theatre to indicate something akin to the sin of vainglory or pride, which for many of the early church fathers was a common tendency. John Chrysostom's writings, for example, are charged with such accusatory use of the theatrical metaphor particularly in relation to the sin of vainglory. What is interesting about Foley's argument is that he contends that the very structure of soliloquies as an inner monologue of self with itself is externalized and dramatized as a dialogue between two characters. This corresponds to certain theatrical practices of the time where a single actor uses a single but asymmetrical mask to indicate two different moods (Quintilian, for example, talks of actors using such masks where one side would have a raised eyebrow connoting a jovial mood, while the other side would have a lowered eyebrow indicating anger). There might also have been cases of a single actor portraying two different *personae* using two alternative masks, particularly in pantomime. Whatever might be the case, Foley uses the adjective *bifrons* (two-faced) to characterize the essential theatricality of *Soliloquies*. Foley extends his argument further by contending that such theatricality allows Augustine to develop a veritable therapeutic theatre because, in the final analysis, what *Soliloquies* tries to achieve is to heal the soul, which disperses itself through pride and vainglory. To find a cure to the theatrics of life that would un-tie the knots that suffocate the spirit by returning to the problem and approaching it with reason. Thus, instead of using the theatrical metaphor to indicate the thumotic sin in order to dissolve it, according to Foley, we find a replacement of one kind of use of the theatre metaphor with another. He writes, "Given the doubly theatrical nature of the Soliloquies, then, when Reason recommends soliloquizing as a solution to the destructive theatricality of life, he is not so much rejecting all theatricality per se as he is recommending as substitution of one kind of theatre for another" (Ibid., n.d., 256). It is in this second sense that we need to understand the use of the metaphor of *theatrum mundus* in Augustine. In Sermon 178, Augustine narrates an anecdote of the poor Christian usher who found a bag of gold coins and returned it to its owner without accepting any reward. The owner is indignant at not being able to show his gratitude, and refuses to accept his own money, whereupon the Christian distributes it among the poor. Augustine summarizes the situation as one where each was trying to be honourable in his own way in the eyes of God by declaring–*theatrum mundus spectator deus* (the world is a theatre and God is the audience). According to Foley, the Augustinian use of this already famous metaphor offers an alternative to a life of vainglory that constitutes the social and the political not by withdrawing from communal life, but by enacting the theatre of life as if God was the only spectator, such that there be no inconsistency between one's inner self and its outer appearance. It is here that the passage from the objective reality of theatre to its metaphorical usage encounters something like an impossible blockage. If we remember our previous discussion, it is on the basis of an inherent inconsistency which is both epistemological and ontological that theatre is deemed inadequate for any Christian representation of truth. But here we find a use of the metaphor of theatre (*theatrum mundi*) whose cathartic quality manifests exactly in curing the very inconsistencies of the self's relation to its truth.

The cathartic value ascribed to the metaphor of *theatrum mundi* from this line of argument seems to abolish the very meaning of theatre as a place of inconsistent truth. This cannot be simply discarded as coincidence, because the processes of metaphorization in Augustine can be argued to be conditioned by an inaugural paradox from another perspective. For example, the process of metaphorization evident in Augustine's *Confessions* can be argued, as Foley has tried to do in another essay, as re-producing something like a sacramental topography. The arrangements of the books in *Confessions* can be demonstrated to be metaphorical counterparts to certain specific liturgical practices starting from catechumenal practices before baptism like *scrutinium* (scrutiny) or *redditio symboli* (returning to the creed or reciting the creed from memory) or the so-called Liturgy of the Words[7]. Foley inexhaustibly demonstrates how the books use such practices metaphorically to constitute a liturgical topography. But again when he tries to explain how from Book X onwards the metaphors change to indicate the liturgical practice of Eucharist he confronts something like an aporia. It is because Book X primarily deals with memory, where Augustine argues that the past is made present only in memory, Foley can argue that it corresponds to the commemorative function of the Eucharist. However, as he indicates in *The City of God*, the Eucharist is conditioned by a fundamental paradox where the Church remembers and repeats in the sacrifice of the altar the singular and unrepeatable Passion, in which Christ offers up to God the whole communion of saints by "having them in mind" (Foley, The Sacramental Topography of the Confessions 2005, 47). Similarly as we shall see in a while, the metaphorical use of memory standing for the Eucharist confronts its own paradox in forgetfulness, which in a sense is the key to a phenomenological understanding of *Confessions*. Further, when before her death Monica urges "remember me at the altar of the Lord" (Ibid., n.d., 47), the paradox of the Eucharist is again played out, where the demand to remember her at the sacrifice of the altar is determined by her desire that Christ should remember her at the sacrifice of the cross. This is not simply an anachronistic use of the metaphor of the Eucharist, but the very aporia which informs and makes impossible any metaphorical passage in Augustine, while simultaneously producing the infinite demand of metaphorization.

Dispersion

It is in Heidegger's reading of Augustine that we find a precise phenomenological summing up of the problem that theatre brings about. In his phenomenological interpretation of Book X of the *Confessions*, undertaken in a course he gave in 1921, Heidegger presents the problem of facticity or the revelation of thinking existence to itself as the fundamental course of Augustinian thinking. This facticity could lead to a "double hermeneutical possibility" (Malabou 2005), as Catherine Malabou would later argue, in order to become the condition of possibility of re-imagining life as machination. Machination has to be understood as akin to the will to bring forth the truth in terms of formulating life anew. In other words, machination is understood as the creation of life as a new efficacious moment–to machinate this effectiveness in history or make possible this 'makability'. The making of life itself out of itself such that it would correspond to the recognition of the possibility of the deployment of Dasien. We will return to this complex question of "making truth" within oneself as the confessional moment *par excellence* in Augustine. What is interesting for our purpose at hand is to extract a reading of the problem of theatre from Heidegger's reading of Augustine reading himself in *Confessions*.

Heidegger quickly moves through confession as a form of self-knowledge to the very enactment of such a reading of the self by itself. While elaborating how confession moves from a question of "what" of self-knowledge to the "how" of the being of life, Heidegger writes, "the question *where* I find God has turned into a discussion of the condition of experiencing God, and that comes to a head in the problem of what I am myself–such that in the end, the same question still stands but in a different form of enactment". (Heidegger 2010, 139) It is the search of this "how" which brings about the authentic mode of enactment of life. The path that leads to this point where one becomes a question to oneself, where the self is offered as a problem, is purely relational. As Heidegger illustrates through an analysis of the problem of memory (*memoria*) and forgetfulness (*oblivio*) in Augustine, facticity is always given as a relation. When Augustine writes of the mystery of forgetfulness, which nevertheless presents itself as forgetfulness in memory, Heidegger observes the undifferentiated presence of the *content* of a representation and the very enactment of representation of *memoria* and *oblivio*. In being absent to one's *memoria*, forgetfulness becomes something which is grasped as absence. But perhaps more importantly it is grasped as a desire for that which was once there as present to oneself and which ought to be here at one's disposal but is not. Hence, presently, as the absence of *memoria*, this being-absent is grasped. This is the enactment in its "intentional relational sense" (Heidegger 2010, 140) which articulates the entire search for the place of the self. As not-being-present, the truth of existence is offered to consciousness in confession as the facticity or the revelatory moment of facticity.

But it is this grasping of forgetfulness as the authentic form of factical life which is covered or disclosed in what Augustine would call the dispersion of life. If happy life (*beata vita*) for Augustine comprises the universal search for truth which is still unknown, then the forgetfulness of such truth can nevertheless lead to the desire for a search for that which is not completely lost. To forget entirely, (*ominio oblivisci*), not to possess the very direction of access to truth, to shut oneself completely against such truth, so that one does not even realize that it is still present in oneself in a certain relational direction is what dispersion brings about. The Augustinian notion of the *beata vita* (happy life) for Heidegger is primarily relational because it is where the mode of access or knowledge of the happy life coincides with the actual mode of having a happy life. Dispersion in a sense distorts this relation replacing it with another relational logic. So even in dispersion the desire for truth does not completely disappear but becomes perverted such that one is so absorbed in the "what" of living that one forgets "how" to live. It is this forgetting of how to grasp the forgetfulness that constitutes the condition for experiencing factical life, which is realized in dispersion. Thus dispersion is nothing but this "scattering into the many" of the self which is unable to re-collect itself. In other words, the self forgets how to move inward into itself thereby forgetting how the self is constituted at the very moment when it realizes that its source is missing from itself; that the knowledge of its source has always already been forgotten. Thus instead of loving the truth which is disclosed as an original forgetfulness, or as a primordial place where one stands in the emptiness of existence, one abandons oneself to "living", which is an absorption in factical life that is closed to itself, which is to say, it is closed to the truth of existence. Hence instead of moving towards the truth, which coincides with the truth of existence conditioned by an original nothingness, what one comes to love is the "what" of existence. Heidegger writes:

What is loved at the moment, a loving into which one grows through tradition, fashion, convenience, the anxiety of disquiet, the anxiety of suddenly standing in vacuity; precisely this becomes the "truth" itself, in and with this falling enactment. The truth and its meaning is taken even in this modification –that is one does not only retreat from the vacuity, but even more, and primarily, from the ""movement" towards it. (Ibid., n.d., 147)

Under these circumstances, in the anxiety of facing the 'real' of existence the self tries to protect itself by projecting itself into the many, which is to say it allows itself to be dispersed in to the world which it comes to love as "truth" replacing it for the real "truth".[8] In this situation the self does not want to be reminded of its disavowal of the original anxiety of the truth. "They do not want to let themselves be startled, because they are motivated–in a certain sense, genuinely, for them–to not want to be deceived" (Ibid., n.d., 148). When Augustine writes, "They do not want to be convinced that they are deceived" (148), it is this disavowal that, according to Heidegger, the self wants to protect, which leads to a condition that is primarily aesthetic. Augustine observes:

Their love of truth takes the form that they love something else and want this object of their love to be the truth; and because they do not wish to be deceived they do not wish to be persuaded that they are mistaken. And so they hate the truth for the sake of the object which they love instead of the truth. They love truth for the light it sheds, but hate it when it shows them up as being wrong... Yes indeed: the human mind, so blind and languid, shamefully and dishonourably wishes to hide, and yet does not wish anything to be concealed from itself. But it is repaid on the principle that while the human mind lies open to the truth, truth remains hidden from it. (St. Augustine, *Confessions* 1998, 200)

This love of the object instead of truth is, rather, the love of the object where the self is not implicated in a fashion where one has to be exposed to one's own judgment under the light of truth. To aestheticize in this sense is to find the place where one can enjoy in a relaxed fashion the objects of the world and allow oneself to be dispersed, without confronting the force of truth implicated in the facticity of life. To protect the self from the anxiety of its own truth, one closes the boundaries of the self by forgetting to move inside oneself. Instead one moves outside, transgressing the divine laws of truth and justice, projecting oneself onto the world in a fashion which would no longer remind one of misery, but instead can even make objects of suffering into objects of desire and enjoyment[9]. This is the aesthetic nature of all moments of dispersion. An aesthetic dispersion, under the relaxing presence of objective security, closes the self onto itself and hence also closes the self onto truth. It is the moment when the self has enframed itself by disavowing the tremendous force of standing in front of truth. However, even now the self continues to love truth more than error and thus seek happiness in the multitudinous worldly reality of life. Therefore, through dispersion one can seek happiness but only in this aesthetic fashion. Like an audience in a theatre that finds pleasure even in the tragic sequences represented on stage by making itself immune to suffering and converting it to so many objects of pleasure and love, the self also aestheticizes truth by occupying the enframed position of the aesthetically motivated theatre audience. It is an aestheticization of reality itself, which is precisely what is behind Augustine's problem with the tragic plays he experienced as a student in Carthage. As we will try to examine more elaborately later, Augustine's fundamental problem with these tragic plays is their disposition to turn misery into objects of desire which gives pleasure to the audience. Even if the audience is moved by the sufferings witnessed on stage, such pain is immediately turned into the "aesthetic" pleasure because of which "he stays riveted in his seat enjoying himself" (St. Augustine, *Confessions* 1998, 36) . The true disposition towards such "agonies and tears of life", in short, towards misery, should be endurance. Hence Augustine writes "Therefore some kind of suffering is commendable but none is lovable" (Ibid., n.d., 37). To tackle the sufferings of life is to endure them, which does not mean the difficulties should become a delight. As Heidegger never fails to indicate, the true and fundamental character in which Augustine experiences factical life is through *molestia*, the burden of life, the difficulties and suffering which can pull life down, so that the more one lives, the more is the possibility of such suffering actualized. This makes of life a *tentatio* (*which* is to be understood both as temptation and trial), but it also calls for life to be concerned of itself. This according to Heidegger is the fundamental structure of the relation of life to itself which is "enactmentally" experienced as facticity. Therefore this sliding down by the weight of life, captured in the sense of *defluxus* or dispersion, also produces what, following Augustine, Heidegger would call *the curare* (being concerned), which together would make the structure of *molestia*. This in turn would become the character of factical life, the authentic 'How' of life itself. We see in *molestia* a kind of disjunctive synthesis of two opposing drives or forces: one pulling outwards, which is that of dispersion (*defluxus* and its different avatars like *tentatio*, *concupiscentia*, *voluptas*), and one pulling inwards, which is that of concern (*curare* and its different modalities like *contentia* or continence, and *tolerari* or endurance). It is in this play of centripetal and centrifugal forces that life is held together and given to itself as the 'How' of authentic life.

However, as Derrida would later remark, in hinging this argument on *molestia*, which, in turn, produces facticity as revelation (akin to *aletheia*), the burden of the theoretical dimension of truth is never taken away. By the same token, such a moment of life revealing itself to itself is always already subsumed by a constative utterance where something is recognized as what it is. Such a reading of Augustine does not produce the transformative possibility or the lightness of reading that is perhaps the secret beauty of Augustine.

Poetics

Eugene Vance, on the other hand, offers an immensely erudite and equally interesting reading of Augustine in his essay, "Augustine's *Confessions* and the Poetics of Law" (Vance 1986). What is truly interesting, particularly for our purpose, is that the essay is entirely devoted to illustrating the transformative possibilities that are present in the very enactment of reading itself, and the sense it generates within Augustine's text. As we noted above, certain scholars, like Michael Foley, have pursued a line of argument regarding Augustine's treatment of the problem of theatre from the point of view of his use of the theatrical metaphor. However, Vance provides a general thesis on metaphorization in Augustine on the basis of a transformative possibility of law. In a fashion worthy of his brilliance, Vance is able to show that this transformation in the idea of law in Augustine, which is expressed in the metaphorical use of certain terms, is inextricably related to the question of language and reading. Vance provides a series of transformations that, he argues, are at the heart of *Confessions*: the transformation of the Judaic law of the letter to the Christian law of the spirit, as reflected in the transformation of the use of the term circumcision, which singularly evokes the image of Judaic law. Thus Augustine writes, as Vance points out, "From all temerity and all lying circumcise my lip, both my interior and my exterior lips. May your Scriptures be my chaste delights"[10] (Vance 1986, 6). The imperative of the letter of law is transported into the figurative domain of the spirit. Circumcision either becomes the Pauline "circumcision of the heart" or, more uniquely to Augustine, language opens a new relationship with law beyond the literal or constative relation, while the metaphor of lips replaces that of phallus as the primary symbol of Law. But Vance goes even further to demonstrate how such transformation which is of theological and juridical interest is again reflected in the very content and form of the book *Confessions*. Thus the narration of Augustine's past events–the confession of events–is 'abruptly' discarded to move into an analysis of the Scriptures, particularly that of Genesis by Book XI of *Confessions*. But even before that, Book X, which perhaps remains the most analysed Book[11] of *Confessions*, had already transformed the *narratio* of events of his own life to the *enarration* of the Law of nature and memory. But what is most interesting for our purpose is the transformation of the performative act of reading that, Vance argues, moves from a reading that engenders the Law of Sin to a reading which is the demand and fulfilment of the Divine Law. From the temporal language which ensnares Augustine into the labyrinth of law, desire and death[12] to the language "without the syllables of time" which comes through the gift of grace, Vance meticulously tracks this passage from the literal to the figurative. This is finally reflected in the transformation from the temporal dimension of language to the "firmament of transparent writing" (Vance 1986, 31), which allows man to intuitively understand and contemplate the universe through something like an immediate intellection. Hence, in the grief of his friend's death, Augustine transposes the mortality of the flesh to the transience of words themselves, understanding the ontological status of verbal signs which, because of their impermanence, can only be used and not enjoyed. Vance cites Augustine from *Confessions*:

> They rise and they set, and by rising, as it were, they begin to be. They increase, so as to become perfect, and when once made perfect, they grow old and die... See too how our speech is accomplished by significant sounds. There would be no complete speech unless each word departs, when all its parts have been uttered, so that it may be followed by another. For all these things let my soul praise you O God, creator of all things, but let it not be caught tight in them by the love that comes from the body's senses (Ibid., n.d., 19).

It is the becoming of existence surrounded by the boundaries of mortality that is reflected in the becoming of language–which not only temporalize language, making it an inadequate medium to access the eternal knowledge of Truth, but this language also pulls Augustine into the violence of law and the death, which is the essence of all temporal law. Whether it is the violence inflicted upon him as a child by his teachers while he struggled with the labour of learning the laws of grammar and eloquence, or the internal violence of conflict of his two wills (a spiritual and other worldly will which wants to pull him upwards into the *firmament* of unknown knowledge, and a carnal and worldly will which pulls him downwards into the *figments* and images of the material world) which he confronts before his conversion–in both the cases, as Vance argues, there is always the element of transgression which exposes "the single violence of death in language" (Ibid., n.d., 25).

This alienation in language and law which death brings about, or put inversely, death that is the consequence of law and language is extended to the eloquence of rhetoric and the labours of logic. While the sin of vainglory and pride constantly accompanies eloquence, logic leads the mind to dialectical phantasms that are inferior to the power of the mind itself, which is capable of thinking them in the first place–a power which, being comparable to God's power of creation, can come only as a gift from God.

It is against such eloquence of rhetoric and labour of logic, which bears the cursed fruit of Adam's sin translated into the labours of mankind in the created word, that Augustine seeks the immediacy of a language which stutters and babbles but is able to express the Word made incarnate in the Flesh. Freeing himself from a carnal language and the dead letter of law, Augustine can now offer in a language of praise that babbles, his brightness, his riches and his health onto God.[13] This language which stutters and babbles also makes possible a transition of knowledge from the events of his erstwhile life that he offers as so many sacrifices in his confessions to the re-creation of a new life which is cosmic in the immediacy of its intuitive knowledge[14]. Vance remarks, "The passage from autobiography to exegesis is the passage beyond 'the book of the life of each man', as Augustine calls the process of self-recollection to the Book of God" (Ibid., n.d., 28). This passage from the book of life to the Book of God can be read as a figurative passage from the metaphor of carnal life or better the theatre of life to a divine theatre. The passage reflects a movement from one kind of reading of carnal language carrying the burden of law, desire and finally death to a kind of intellectual knowledge and "transparent writing" which does not unfold in temporal sequence and is not dispersed by the equivocity of signification but is encountered as the face of the Word. This is the kind of celestial reading at the heart of the idea of reading as *lectio*, which is freely willed in delight and not imposed as a labour for the punishment of sin. The condition of possibility of *Confessions* rests upon a reading which is not toiling, a reading which is without difficulty, simple and joyous. But, at the same time, a reading that makes possible the event of reading itself, as it comes as the gift of grace. Reading as encounter, which counter-actualizes (as we shall see later) any possibility of representation because it is outside the normal understanding of temporality as a linear progression. In its moment of pure intellection it overcomes not only any dialectics of representation and constative theories of truth, but also the authority of performative generation of truth effects through eloquence. As Vance concludes, "If Augustine's own story is good (and he thought at the end of his life that it *was*), it is not because he was its author, nor because it was written under God's Authority; rather, it is God's gift, as is the Sabbath reserved for those who do not turn away from God and from his book" (Ibid., n.d., 32). A language and a reading that does not offer any passage from the world of sensual reality to the realm of abstract significance because it never trespasses boundaries to become transgressive and get caught in the grid of law, desire and death. Rather, a language which supports a pure encounter that can only be intuitive, but which is also the work of thinking. Being infinitely rapid and absolutely immediate, this reading would only be made possible by the help of a memory that can survey all the works of the world in infinite speed to produce a simultaneous condition, where the present is infinitely broken into past and future[15]. As we shall see later, only under such a condition of a broken present can the gift of reading befall as an encounter and make possible these lines from *Confessions*, "They always behold your face, and without any syllables of time, they read upon it what your eternal will decrees" (Ibid., n.d., 32). Vance emphasizes on finding a concept of reading within *Confessions* that is without such "syllables of time", and a self that is becoming-universal. It is the metaphorical passage from the narration of autobiographical events in the early books to the exegetical demand of a cosmic scale which Vance calls a "hermeneutical performance" starting from Book XI. However such a transformation stills depends on finding a poetics of law. Like the classical understanding of Aristotelian poetics, which depends on finding a *telos* to the activity whose sole function is to lead up to that moment of transformation of means to an end, Vance also seems to allude to a certain reading of Augustine which would search for such a teleological passage. To move from the snares of temporal law, inscribed into an idea of reading, to the idea of a divine law that frees reading of its temporality and death is to signify Christ as the quintessential figure of mediation. Vance analyses Christ in terms of the mediatory significance gained in Augustine rather than as another moment of encounter with the Christ-event, through which the grace of God is actualized. In the final analysis, to search for a poetics of law in confession does imply a sacrifice of law through confession, law which is already understood as sacrifice and death. As the essence of poetics rests upon the catharsis of desire, so does the significance of Christ in Augustine seem to produce a cathartic figure–Christ, whose presence would turn the failure of his neo-platonic quest to climb the steps of knowledge into the success of gaining an access to the knowledge of his inner self–this is how Vance envisions it. Knowledge of the external world (the essence of Augustine's neo-platonic quest according to Vance), embedded in representation and a temporality of language, is also marked by law and death, in other words, a mimetic knowledge of the world based on a logic of sacrifice[16]. Alternately the movement within oneself, inaugurated by the mediating figure of Christ comes at the expense of sacrificing this very notion of sacrifice and law. This brings us back to the problem of a figurative sublation of sacrifice, with which Vance's entire approach to confession begins, with an interpretation of the Pauline notion of "circumcision of the heart" as the figurative or metaphorical use of the logic of Judaic law of sacrifice. To search for the poetics of law in *Confessions* therefore makes possible this metaphorical passage into a divine reading.

Aporia

But what we need to search for is a reading of Augustine which is not merely a trespass or a transgression or even the problematic of a passage but an aporia. An aporetic reading, which is to say, a reading which is always already guilty of its incompleteness; a reading which is constantly reminded of its failure to cross its own boundaries by the same borders which it cannot pass by itself; a reading which is haunted by the impossibility of its passage into any meaningful significance. It is a generative guilt handed down in the incompleteness of every reading, but, at the same time, it makes all such reading equal insofar as they are all incomplete. But only rarely in such readings do we find a recognition of their own guilt, an admittance of their own incompleteness. It is those other "guilty" readings which offer us the infinite demand of reading itself; the absolute demand of making sense of that which is without sense. In other words, what we require is a reading which constantly demands of us the crossing of such an impassable passage, of passing from non-sense to sense. But such a demand cannot come under the subjective mastery of the one who reads, of the philosopher-master who has the capacity to walk across the border into the realm of significance. Such impassability becomes passable only when the impossibility of the passage from non-sense to sense "comes to pass". It is something like the gift of reading his own self which Augustine receives from God through grace; a reading which comes as an infinite demand to recognize his own powerlessness to make sense of his life without grace. When Augustine writes that he has become a question to himself it is not in the sense of a problem which can be overcome by himself, but precisely in this sense of an aporia which can only befall us; like a riddle we encounter on our way much like Oedipus encountered the sphinx. And like the Sphinx, such an encounter demands of us something which is less of a solution and more like a password–a secret code which hides behind ordinary expressions or an unreadable sentence, which when read opens a passage in the heart of the impassable making it passable in some sense. But such a reading can only come as the infinite demand of something we encounter or something which befalls us. We cannot reduce such a reading to the overcoming of a problem, either historical or philosophical. When Jean-Luc Marion remarks about the impossibility of avoiding Augustine because of his historical and philosophical/theological importance, but also points towards the absolute inaccessibility of Augustine from any such historical, philosophical or theological perspective he has exactly the aporia of Saint Augustine in mind[17]. So we have to seek another form of guilt in our reading of Augustine, which has to do with an infinite forgiveness because it is practically unreadable. Because the trace of the singularity of the event of reading will always be dispersed in the multiplicity of the readings, we must ask for forgiveness as we seek out such a guilty reading. It is against such dispersion that one has to seek forgiveness because all reading is guilty of being incomplete as a result of such dispersion. At the same time reading cannot but be such dispersion, such proliferation into endless signifiers. By the same token, it is the primary hypothesis for this chapter that any such incompleteness, which is constitutive of every reading, also makes it theatrical. Towards understanding such a theatrical reading of Augustine, we will begin our search keeping in mind that precious Augustinian lesson that every search for the unknown is already known insofar as it knows that there is something, albeit unknown, to search for.

Section II

A Possible Reading of Augustine from a "Classical" Perspective of Theatricality

It is our first hypothesis that Hannah Arendt's reading of Augustine can be interpreted from a certain theatrical point of view. This theatricality which Hannah Arendt discovers in Augustinian thought could be characterized by the canonical figure of a classical reading of theatre by philosophy. By classical we mean an interpretation of theatre by philosophy where truth is seen as external to the art of theatre, though its externality is deemed to be innocent. This innocence is rendered possible by giving imitation an ontological structure which is independent of truth; which is to say that artistic imitation by itself cannot produce simulations of truth. The function of imitation is primarily practical; it produces certain therapeutic passions so that they can be dissolved and the subject who projects these passions and desires can deposit the same in order to overcome and be cured of them. Hence instead of simulations of truth what imitation produces is catharsis, which is nothing but a transference–generation of passions and desires only to overcome them so the subject can enjoy the beneficial effects of regaining his/her previous state. But though this is an isolated operation where only the self is involved, like in any act of transference, Aristotle, in *Politics*, talks of cathartic music[18] as that basic form of music that produces catharsis *for all*. This notion of equality is based on a negative logic, because what is common to all is not merely the production of desires but also their dissolution. In other words, the descent into desire and passion culminates in the eradication of the same so that the subject is now ready for ascendancy depending on his or her capacity. Thus, in case of music for example, the subject can enjoy higher forms of pleasure, like intellectual satisfaction, in other sorts of music, dependent on his or her social, cultural and intellectual position. But what everybody undergoes is the minimum cathartic enjoyment of music so that they are made capable of such social, political and intellectual ascendancy. Hence though imitation is rendered external to truth or free of simulation in terms of its ontological function, theatre nevertheless generates equality through imaginary verisimilitudes. Therefore the essence of theatre is generative rather that imitative. At the same time, the space of theatre is imagined through the production and circulation of desire such that a libidinal economy best characterizes the theatrical reality. Though, as an assemblage, theatre is seen as an imaginary arrangement of multiplicity, it nevertheless constitutes the spectator as subject by becoming his/her object of desire while itself coming into being and disappearing. In other words, in its very becoming, theatre captures the spectator and constitutes him/her into a subject of desire who is simultaneously cured of his/her desires by transferring them onto the other scene. It is our hypothesis that Arendt's analysis of Augustinian philosophy, particularly Augustine's idea of love is fraught with such a theatrical understanding. Arendt seizes Augustinian philosophy in a fashion that exposes these characteristics of imitation/generation, transference and equality on the one hand, and an economy of desire on the other, which is mediated through law such that a classical figure of theatricality is unravelled.

We know it is Arendt who first identifies the structure of love, in Augustine as craving or desire (*appetites*) in her brilliant dissertation

Love and St. Augustine (Arendt 1996). Arendt argues here that it is this expression of love as desire which sets Augustine apart from someone like St. Paul, in whose thought love also occupies a central place[19]. This structure of love as desire in Augustine signifies a singular mode of human existence, which demands that there be an object of love outside the lover who or which, depending on the circumstances, is none other than his beloved. Thus love as desire always seeks its fulfilment outside the self which loves. This is the terrible isolation of the lover who stands in separation from the object of his love. In order to end this separation or alienation one must find the fulfilment of one's desire and this becomes the true meaning of enjoyment in Augustine. Enjoyment is nothing other than the termination of love in finding its fulfilment. It is the resting place of love where the restlessness of desire finds its peace. "You touched me and I am set on fire to attain the peace which is yours" (St. Augustine, *Confessions* 1998, 201) writes Augustine. It is this state of perfect respite, when the lover belongs to the beloved, that he calls happiness. Hence there can be no happiness without enjoyment–that is, without possessing your object of love. Hence his remark: "No one is happy who does not enjoy what he loves. Even those who love things they should not love, think themselves happy not because they love but because they enjoy"[20] (Arendt 1996, 19). Because of man's mortality he can enjoy nothing of this world because every object of love in this world is corrupted by man's own impermanence. However this corruptibility does not negate his search for happiness, but only distorts it. While what he seeks is outside him, the condition for this search remains caught in the subjective domain of personal happiness. And the final nature of that happiness is immortality. But the impossibility of possessing such happiness forces his personal zeal to be happy–which conditions all his acts of love–to transfer the corruptibility of his own life into the world in the false hope of enduring. Such is the despair of this love of the world which inevitably meets its dissolution. There is then a certain subjective constitution of the world through this desire, which Augustine calls *cupiditas*. Thus *cupiditas* is not simply the love of the world which is perishable, but more significantly, it is the constitution of the world as a perishable thing by the lover of the world who wants to cling to something more permanent than himself in order to forget his own mortality. Augustine writes, "For we call 'world' not only this fabric which God made, heaven and earth....but the inhabitants of the world are also called the 'world'... especially all the lovers of the world are called the world"[21] (Arendt 1996, 15). Against this mundane love which clings to, and by that very gesture constitutes the world, which is called *cupiditas*, the right object of love ought to be that which is incorruptible and eternal, that which is not corrupted by the passage of time as is the present moment, and is thus projected into an absolute future. In other words, only God can be the true object of enjoyment. This love is what he calls *caritas* "the root of all evil is *cupiditas*, the root of all good is *caritas*"[22] (Arendt 1996, 17). Love as *caritas* orients one to the source of his/her existence. In having God as the object of desire, man establishes a relation to his creator. Thus a creature-creator relation is established where the creature learns through love–which is to say, by orienting his desire to the source of his being–the true origin of his being. The creator, which comes before the creature, is identified as the true 'before', the eternity which encompasses the temporality of man, or the Being which encircles and is also the source of all becoming. But because God had also created the world into which man is born, the world also precedes man thereby creating the confusion of a false 'before'. To love the world instead of God, which is to say, to love creation over the creator is to love the false 'before' instead of the original 'before' which coincides with the very being of God. To slide from the creator to creation constitutes the original moment of sin. In other words, to desire the world instead of God constitutes a descent which corresponds to what Augustine calls dispersion of the soul, which prevents one from recollecting the true before. In dispersion, one not only desires the world but one desires it so that one could transfer the anxiety of mortality, which is to say, overcome the fear of death, by aligning oneself to something which he/she thinks to be more permanent that himself/herself. But this desire is never fulfilled because either death wrenches him/her away from his/her object of desire or the object perishes, in which case desire finds a new object to love. This is what Augustine calls the dispersion of the soul which, Arendt argues, moves from one object of desire to the other, being scattered and multiplied in the process. *Cupiditas* is thus a form of desire that puts the self in relation to a temporary enjoyment, which takes the shape of mortality (or better death!). Worldly desire can only lead to such temporary discharge which becomes the condition of the possibility of renewed desire, but whose hidden condition remains a fundamental lack.

To move from *cupiditas* to *caritas* is thus not merely to orient one's will to the correct object of desire, but to overcome the suffering of worldly desire plagued by fear, in desiring God who is eternal and hence permanent. But even here, the object of desire remains outside the self, while desire maintains its structure as craving (*appetitus*). Therefore exactly like *cupiditas*, even in *caritas* death remains the unsurpassable bridge which separates man from his object of desire. The peace of consuming one's desire, in other words, the tranquillity of satisfaction which forever eluded *cupiditas* is also unavailable to *caritas*. Augustine's famous lines from *Confessions* echoes this restlessness of desire, "You touched me, and I am set on fire to attain the peace which is yours." (St. Augustine, *Confessions* 1998, 201)

What has changed in the movement from *cupiditas* to *caritas* is not the self's relation to a fundamental lack, which remains the structure of desire in both cases, but rather the presentation of this structure. In case of *caritas*, love as craving is not presented as a pleasure-discharge compound which hides or better represses a desire-lack relation as happens in case of *cupiditas*. In the case of *caritas* the desire-lack compound is exposed or discovered as the true essence of man's existence, which is to say, it is recognized as such. It is this recognition of the repressed that differentiates *caritas* from *cupiditas*. And in this recognition not only the anxiety of worldly desires, but the desire of the world itself is both recognized and seemingly overcome. This 'overcoming' of worldly desires makes a desert of the world by loving that which is outside this world. At the same time, according to Arendt, to move from *cupiditas* to *caritas* in Augustine also means to move from the dispersed external reality of the world into the concentrated reality of the inner self *(homo interim)*–a gesture which we discussed before as the concern (*cura*) for the self. Arendt's analysis of the concept of love as craving in Augustine not only discovers an economy of desire, which is at play here, but also gives a cathartic dimension to the idea of concern in Augustine. To put it succinctly, the implication of Arendt's interpretation leads us to identify the Augustinian idea of concern to the psychoanalytic idea of cure. What is made available through this movement from *cupiditas* to *caritas* is the knowledge of death as also the possibility of a beginning. In relating oneself to one's creator as the true 'before' one simultaneously realizes the 'after' of death as a return to this original before. The 'after' of death would thus repeat the 'before' of man's true origin only if he orients his desire to an object that is not only unavailable for satisfaction, but this impossibility of satisfaction is recognized by the self as the knowledge of a fundamental lack that informs love as *appetitus* (craving). Recognition-Return-Repetition is the progressive logic through which transference is achieved, which relieves the subject by turning the misery of the world into mercy. At the same time it opens up the other scene, that is, the unconscious is made available as the divine scene, the site of the Real that makes the world available as an imaginary arrangement from a divine perspective. This world of temporality, of impermanence comes into being and then disappears but not before the gaze of the subject is fixed onto it as the object-cause of desire which constitutes the subject as the subject of *cupiditas*. To be cured of *cupiditas* is to re-cognize the world from the point of view of *caritas*, to recognize the world from the point of view of the other scene–the unconscious.

Now imitation, in this schema of things plays a complex but crucial role. As a basic ontological structure, imitation determines all the actions and movements of life. Man can relate to his "before" only through imitation. As a consciously adopted way of life, imitation is the only mode through which life finds it possible to relate itself to its source, even when it is the wrong source. Even when one falls into the ways of sin, it is according to Augustine, as Arendt never fails to articulate, nothing but imitation. Hence Arendt cites from *Confessions*, Book II, "All who have withdrawn from you and boast of themselves against You imitate You perversely. But even in thus imitating You they demonstrate that You are the Creator of the whole nature". Perversion is thus nothing but an imitation of God without acknowledging the dependency that any such imitation entails on that which it imitates. In other words perversion is the distortion of imitation without the explicit knowledge of imitation itself. Hence, in pride, which is the vice of all vices, man presumes himself to be a creator. He imagines that through his human endeavors he is setting up a world which he loves and which he seemingly creates through such love. "The lover of the world is also the world" (Arendt 1996, 25). So while perversity is sometimes seen as a movement towards nothingness, it never becomes nothingness because it always maintains its imitative structure, albeit without any explicit knowledge of its model. As we shall see later in the chapter, law in the final analysis means nothing but the knowledge that it provides of the imitative structure of being, though negatively. It succeeds in doing this by pointing to the limitation of all human imitation, and thus providing man with the knowledge of what is the true object of imitation. In other words, law provides the knowledge of the gap that separates the being of man from his actions. Perversion is when this gap is dissimulated while man presumes himself to be equal to God by imagining his action to coincide with his being. But in all these cases imitation remains the basic ontological structure which governs human conduct. However, at the same time, Arendt is carefully precise in pointing out that, in itself, imitation is neutral not belonging to either right or wrong. Imitation is rendered harmless in this schema of thinking because it is set free from whatever orients it to whatever end. In other words, though there is always a will which orients imitation to either a life of righteousness or a life of vice, intrinsically imitation is not linked with will. Hence Arendt writes:

> As an ontological structure, imitation is independent of man's attitude towards it, and it leaves man in his inherent freedom

> as long as this function (which he is himself) has not been expressly taken up by him, through not subjecting himself to its judgment on the right or wrong of his actions. Within imitation he is free, though only for himself and not for God. As the determinant of all man's actions and omissions, God cannot even be discovered as long as man leaves imitation objective, that is, as long as he does not expressly take up imitation and thereby once more seal his dependence on something outside him. (Arendt 1996, 79)

To take up imitation "expressly" is to fulfil the demands of law which operates within the self through conscience. The demand inherent to being, that which comes as law is the recognition of the insufficiency of the imitative structure of being to accomplish the demand of fulfilling the law. This in turn means the inability of man to completely relate himself to his true source–to fulfil the demand of desire (caritas) and belong to God. So when the law says "though shall not covet" it not only brings to man the knowledge of the world as the wrong object of love (as desire, *appetitus*), but by orienting him to his otherworldly desire makes man aware of the impossibility of attaining any such object. In desiring something otherworldly man's situation does not change because man still belongs to the world and is *of* the world. Expressed differently, law not only demands that man makes the world into a desert by orienting his desire to an other, it also relentlessly reminds him of his inability to fulfil this very demand by making him recognize his place in the order of things. This is the double binding of law, which constantly reminds man of his mortality by making him take up the question of imitation (conduct) explicitly.

So imitation itself does not bring positive knowledge of the dependency of man on being as eternity. This explicit knowledge comes as man turns towards his being by way of *caritas.* Imitation in itself does not reveal explicitly the incapacity of man to belong to God. It merely articulates the inherent demand of effecting a relation to being. In other words, through imitation, man searches for his being but the knowledge of his incapacity to find it is not present inside the structure of imitation. What comes forth through imitation is only this desire of law. On the other hand, law ("thou shall not covet"), which comes through conscience, is also the consummation of evil because it wrenches man away from his habit. In Augustine as Arendt shows, it is habit which sustains evil rather than passions, which makes him argue that "humankind's inclination to value its sins is not so much due to passion itself as to habit"[23] (Arendt 1996, 83). Habit creates the blockage necessary to pull man back into the world by obscuring his vision of the transience of life, creating a secondary absolute. Here imitation sustains habit which detracts man from his view of death by making man turn to the wrong 'before'–the 'before' of the world instead of the 'before' of the creator. Hence Arendt remarks, "habit is the eternal yesterday and has no future. Its tomorrow is identical with today."[24] (Arendt 1996, 83). Thus man is dragged into a cycle of pleasure and discharge without ever letting him recognize the truth repressed behind such desire. Habit binds man to his wrong past by willing against his will. "The law of sin is the violence of habit by which even the unwilling mind is dragged down and held, as it deserves to be, since by its own choice it slipped into habit" (St. Augustine 1991, 141). By creating something like second nature, habit tries to dissimulate the real source of being by turning man's gaze back into the world, which he then starts claiming to be his source. The conflict that habit generates of two wills–a carnal and a spiritual, an old will which returns man to the world and a new one which tries to detach him from the world by turning him to God–is finally resolved by the force of law, which brings forth the knowledge of this wrong turn of desire. Law, which gives the knowledge of sin, tells man that though the world antedates him, it is not the true object of his desire. Habit, which hides the transience of his life, and tells man to believe in his perpetuity by orienting him to the wrong before, is destroyed by the demand of law which commands man to abandon the world for the love of God. Law, in this sense, commands him to see the truth behind such a false cycle of pleasure and discharge by demanding the recognition of divine substance, the true 'before', which is the only object man ought to love and desire. When man turns to his true before, death is no longer dissimulated but recognized as the limit of his desire. The desire of the divine substance is immediately realized as an impossibility when man re-cognizes death as the punishment for his original sin, which prevents him from enjoying God as substance. Because God cannot be enjoyed as the substance, because death sits between desire and its satisfaction as the impassable passage, God comes as the lack which man not only seeks as a possibility, but actualizes through his conscience. Hence conscience brings man in the presence of God (*coram Deo*) by concretely realizing through his actions the command "thou shall not covet". The original source of this law remains a lack hence it is always already presented as a demand which man is incapable of fulfilling. As an infinite debt which, in spite of all his actions, man is never able to re-pay, law comes as a demand within imitation (imitation through which man conducts himself in the world and performs his actions) which makes man realize the true status of his desire. If as Augustine writes, "they imitated by loving" they also recognize the limits of imitation through such love as craving (*appetitus*). In other words, the impossibility of enjoyment of the Other comes as the law as demand that cannot be fulfilled. Man confronts law to remind himself of this explicit inability to fulfill law. Law becomes the demand within imitation which makes man realize the status of his desire. If he imitates by loving, then man also recognizes the limits of such love by imitation through law.

However, Arendt argues that for Augustine law also indicates the knowledge of death not merely as a natural phenomenon, but death as punishment for the original transgression. Insofar as all of mankind 'historically' generates out of Adam, everybody is assimilated within the purview of law as mortal beings. The recognition of this equality is the condition of possibility for grace. Therefore the eternal limit of this assimilation by law opens up the possibility of equality. The love of one's neighbour which constitutes the society of faithful takes place under the commandment of self-denial. To love one's neighbour as oneself has to be interpreted as the love with which man comes to God in *caritas*. The terrible isolation that *caritas* demands is not destroyed but preserved in the love of one's neighbour because the commandment of self-denial exposes man to the imperative that he should love his neighbour like he loves God. In gaining himself back through love (*caritas*) man also learns to love his neighbour in the self-denying image of his love for God. Man learns to love his neighbour in his createdness and not through creaturely love. This is the indirect path of loving one's neighbour, who he loves in loving God. This is the great albeit indirect equalizing capacity of *caritas*. In denying the other creaturely love, one penetrates the worldly elements to love the other in his real being. Thus the other is not loved in his mortality but in his being forever, his very 'whence' because loving one's neighbour is merely an occasion to love God, who is the source of all being. But this love cannot just come as law because law only makes intelligible the impossibility of such love. One loves only under the grace of God which is not dependent of the will of man. The concrete realization of the community can only take place after the historical reality of Christ's resurrection. However, the redemption promised by Christ is not only for the sinners but redemption for all. If Christ remains the historical point of realization of grace, and thus the community of the faithful, then such reality rests constitutively on the overcoming of the negative 'historical' reality of the fall through its recognition. In other words, the condition of possibility of grace rests on the recognition of the principle of generative equality unleashed by original sin. As we discussed before this recognition occurs through law and conscience. But if law, as we saw, is the knowledge of the impossibility of its fulfilment, then this inherent lack has to be historically made *effective.* If the grace of God through Christ's suffering redeems not an individual sinner but the whole world then such transformation overturns an already existent community to deliver it to a community of the faithful. However *civitas-terrena* or man-made world is not arbitrarily founded or dissolved. In the last section of her thesis Arendt argues precisely on this point. She argues that, for Augustine, the transformation from *Civitas Terrena* to *Civitas Dei* is a transformation of a historical principle of generation to another historical principle of redemptive love. This generative principle based upon the 'historical fact'[25] of Adam's descent in God's plan alone makes possible the reality of Christ's redemption.

But this reality also founds a definite and obligatory equality among men who actualize their equality by interdependence and an economy of exchange. Hence imitation of each other in the *civitas terrena* is based on belief (*credere*), originally founded upon and historically fixed in their common descent from Adam and in a kinship which is beyond simple imitation. Hence Arendt would write "Each individual already belongs to Adam (that is, to the human race) by generation, not by imitation. The possibility of imitation, and thereby of freely choosing the grace of God did not exist until Christ revealed this grace to all people through his historic soujourn on earth" (Arendt 1996, 102).[26] Therefore the function of law is to bring the knowledge of this generative equality based on a common fate. But the knowledge of the equality of the human race in view of man's original sin and his mortality as the definitive punishment for it, on the one hand, isolates him in his faith and abandonment of the world. At the same time, it re-constitutes the social through neighbourly love. Such an idea of the social does not rest on a generative principle of equality, but on the free choice of *caritas* as love of the neighbour, which is, ironically[27], not possible without grace. The indirectness of neighbourly love that is revealed through redemption, at the same time, reveals the generative principle of the human condition of equality. So, imitation, which is how neighbourly love actualizes itself at the moment of grace, also unfolds as law which helps man to recognize the impossibility of its own fulfilment and thus also the generative principle constitutive of human equality. In other words, the moment of grace actualized concretely in Christ also reveals to man the knowledge of his common origin in Adam and thus his equality. This becomes the condition for his love of the neighbour, which is always indirect because it is in the image of his love of God, which in turn is inherently incomplete because of his descent from Adam. To put it succinctly, a moment of revelation becomes the ground for a principle of equality based on love which is actualized by imitation. But for Arendt this moment of revelation which ushers in a new principle of equality based on free choice is not possible without the generative principle of equality which is already historically determined. Here revelation at the moment of grace is only the transference or the sublation determined by the recognition and negation of worldly sins. Hence the new principle of equality ushered in by neighbourly love is only possible on the negative presupposition of the principle of generative equality.

The presupposition of a negative principle of generation for grace to arrive, or in other words, the recognition of the gap that separates man from God through his fall, becomes the condition for its own overcoming. The relation between fall and grace is thus captured in a dialectical movement where the recognition of the fall brings about the overcoming of its negativity, thereby negating the negation and bringing man to truth. But what Arendt's classical method seems not to identify is the paradoxical nature of the Augustinian idea of grace made possible through confession. The paradox of confession as "*qui facit veritatem venit ad lucem*", meaning to make truth inside oneself to get access to the light.[28] But at the same time this making of truth is not possible without being already under the light of grace[29]. In Arendt we find a dialectical resolution, which forces this paradox to take up the semblance of consistency by dissimulating the simultaneous appearance of truth and grace by showing that one leads to the other. Such a dissimulation leading to a continuous movement from truth to grace based on a dialectical logic of sublimation, in the final analysis gives way to the presence of the subject–the subject of law who actualizes law, not *externally* under the force of a juridical command, but through the *internal* demand of conscience. But conscience, which abandons man before God, is only actualized by turning man's weakness in the face of law into the power that he gains by conscientiously following the law and thus speaking on its behalf. In other words, a legal subject is pre-supposed, who accepts the conventions and conditions as the demand of his being. He accepts such demands because the inherent incompleteness of his being can either lead him to dissipation and dispersion, caught in the cycle of pleasure and discharge, or function as the subject of an original lack (an Other), abandoning oneself to the demand it generates and which he can never fulfil. But ironically this limit situation gives him the power to constitute himself as the subject of law–or better a consciousness with a conscience. The brute force of a transcendental law (as the Lack/Other) is thus mediated only through the production of a conscious subject *with* conscience. It is through this constitution of a subject *with* conscience–where conscience is seen as an attribute of the subject–that we are re-introduced to the logic of capacity. Only those who have the capacity to possess a conscience are worthy of grace. If grace is the moment where the subject becomes indebted infinitely to God in order to constitute a community of the faithful based on the equal indebtedness of all who are touched by it, then such indebtedness is only made possible by conscience, which is nothing but the capacity to be in debt.

From the above discussion we can reinterpret Augustine's argument in *Confessions* about tragedy from a new perspective. In Book 2 of *Confessions*, Augustine argues that "tears and agonies" can be objects of love because misery is the condition for mercy. But theatre (tragedies) offers no such transformative possibilities because it offers such misery for worldly pleasure. Theatre, in being caught in the economy of worldly desire (cupiditas), cannot transform misery into mercy, throwing man back into the circuitous path of pleasure and discharge. The imitation of theatre fails to produce an explicit knowledge about the function of imitation and the structure of desire in the life of man. It merely catches man in his habit, bringing him back to the world, making him believe that he is "of the world", which is to say "after the world". Thus distracting man and detracting from his genuine object of love, habit blinds his view and makes man, by his own will, love and take pride in his own creations rather than in his createdness. Hence, while talking of mercy a few lines later, Augustine writes:

> This feeling (mercy) flows from the stream of friendship, but where does it go? Where does it flow to? Why does it run down into the torrent of boiling pitch, the monstrous heats of black

> desire into which it is transformed? From a heavenly serenity it is altered by its own consent into something twisted and distorted. (St. Augustine, *Confessions* 1998, 36)

Clearly theatrical imitation does not lead to a genuine recognition of misery as objects of love (as *caritas*), which would transform it onto the "heavenly serenity" of mercy. What takes place is another sort of transformation, which is a perverse transformation, insofar as perversion is the transgression of some form of natural law. This other transformation makes such an object of misery into an object of pleasure (cupiditas) by the operation of one's own will. ["Nothing makes the mind give way to desire except its own will and free choice" (Arendt 1996, 81)]. In view of our analysis of Arendt's interpretation of Augustine, and the previous discussion on how such an interpretation would accommodate Augustine's views on the problem of pleasure and pain in relation to theatre, we can risk the hypothesis: the theatricality that Arendt discovered in Augustine, which is cathartic and classical in nature, denounces actually existing theatre of his time precisely (and not without irony) on its incapacity to produce an effect which would be cathartic in nature. In other words, Christianity, from this perspective, rejected theatre because it was not theatrical enough to accommodate the kind of incorporeal transformation of the self that was required at the time. For Augustine, Arendt would perhaps argue that such a transformation, which constitutes the self and the social in a twofold fashion, could only be sought through love. We need not forget that one of the very few times when Augustine comments on the pedagogical advantages of learning from theatre, it` comes in *On Christian Doctrine* precisely on this point. Here Augustine praises theatre or rather the ability of theatre to draw a crowd who gather together in their common love for an actor. This capacity of theatre to constitute a collective, to produce a congregation by finding a common in an indirect fashion is something akin to Christianity albeit in a much lesser magnitude. Augustine writes:

> For in theatres, dens of iniquity though they be, if a man is fond of a particular actor, and enjoys his art as a great or even as the very greatest good, he is fond of all who join with

> him in admiration of his favourite, not for their own sakes, but for the sake of him whom they admire in common; and the more fervent he is in his admiration, the more he works in every way he can to secure new admirers for him and the more anxious he becomes to show him to others; and if he find anyone comparatively indifferent, he does all he can to excite his interest by urging his favourites' merit...If this be so, what does it become us to do who live in the fellowship of the love of God. (St. Augustine, *On Christian Doctrine* 2009)

Here theatre is envisaged as a place of congregation where the collective bond is not created by the self coming in proximity with the other directly[30], but through the shared experience of an affect produced by the actor. That which brings the crowd together is only an indirect realization of that affect, which is experienced by all equally. This reflects Arendt's interpretation of the Augustinian idea of the social based on neighbourly love. As we tried to show earlier, this idea of the social, propelled by love of the neighbour always sets up a relation of the self to the other (a relation of neighbourly love) indirectly under the command of an absolute Other. It is the self's love of God (the absolute Other) which comes as a command to love one's neighbour. In other words, only in loving God can one love one's neighbour, to constitute something like the new social under a new principle of equality based on choice. But this new principle is made possible only through the recognition of an earlier principle of generative equality, which was the moment of constitution of the social before grace. The recognition of this generative principle is the recognition of death as the punishment for the original sin. Grace from this point of view becomes the dialectical overcoming of death, which nevertheless continues to preserve death negatively. In order for death to die, man needs the redemptive moment of grace, which is historically made possible through Christ. Thus we see that the only time Augustine praises theatre is when he compares the power of theatre to produce congregations based on equality through an implicit idea of transference and catharsis. The theatrical metaphor of equality is used only to magnify the significance of religious equality which indirectly brings men together as loving neighbours in their common love for God which is the basis for a Christian congregation. The theatrical metaphor of equality thus achieves its religious meaning by dialectically translating and overcoming its sinful past and inhabiting the purified domain of religious use. The meaning of theatre itself undergoes the theatrical operation of catharsis to emerge as something that retains its significatory power but is purified of its dangerous affective realities.

Section III

Preparatory Remarks on Another Possible Reading of Augustine

(a) Point of Departure: The Concept of Use Introduced Through the Problem of Theatre

Endurance Contra Enjoyment

In Book 3 of *Confessions* Augustine terms theatre that "amazing folly" (St. Augustine, *Confessions* 1998, 36) that turns pain itself into pleasure. This is the very source of Augustine's problem with theatre in this book. As an actual cultural practice that he witnessed as a student in Carthage, theatre unfolds in the book both as the real crisis of a life of flesh that he formerly lived as a student but also, and more interestingly, as the sign of that very life which he has now abandoned. As a problem of a form of life, theatre, or more particularly tragedy, with which he is concerned in *Confessions*, poses the singular problem of producing pleasure in the spectator through eliciting pain. He writes, "I was captivated by theatrical shows. They were full of representations of my own miseries and fuelled my fire. Why is it that a person wishes to experience suffering by watching grievous and tragic events which he himself would not wish to endure? Nevertheless he wants to suffer the pain given by being a spectator of these sufferings, and the pain itself is his pleasure." (Ibid., n.d., 36) These remarks succinctly sum up the whole of Augustine's peculiar problem with tragic plays. For the spectator, like he himself was, when he is moved by the tragic scenes, he does not *endure* the pain himself but is only a passive receptor of the pain whose outcome is active enjoyment. So the pain itself becomes the object of enjoyment. In other words, the pleasure derived from pain makes pain an object of enjoyment and thus an object of love. This relation between enjoyment and love runs through the entire body of Augustine's work. Enjoyment or pleasure leads to happiness. So enjoyment is also indicative of good, or rather, pleasure is in itself good. And one craves or desires for that which is good. This is also what love is. But true enjoyment cannot be transient. True pleasure has to be permanent. The object of desire thus cannot perish. Otherwise one is thrown back into the world of fear or sadness where happiness of experiencing pleasure will always be complemented by either the fear of losing the object of pleasure or the sadness of having lost it. Thus death always corrupts love when the object of love is not God. Because only God is the incorruptible who can truly be enjoyed eternally. Everything else has to lead to this enjoyment, which is the only true and eternal object of desire. Thus we have the concept of *use* (St. Augustine, *On Christine Doctrine* 2009, 3) in Augustine where the world is divided into things which are either used or enjoyed. Thus everything in the world has to be used to attain the only true object of pleasure, which is truth in God. Theatre poses a particularly interesting problem in this schema of things.

Pain and Use

Firstly in the tragic plays, pain itself becomes the object of pleasure. Thus he writes, "tears and agonies, therefore are the objects of love" (St. Augustine, *Confessions* 1998, 36). One feels compassion which is severed from a misery which ought to be endured. Thus when one sees misery unfolding on stage, a misery which is imaginary, one does not endure that misery in order to feel mercy. This is antithetical to the suffering of Christ, which he endured on the cross to abandon it for the glory of resurrection. The suffering of flesh which Christ endured is paradigmatic of the suffering of the Christian life where pain is not loved for its own sake but used in order to abandon it for love of God. Suffering can only be an object of love in its *use* to achieve the ultimate object of love, which is truth in God. Thus the world, which is the source of all pain, has to be used so that it can be abandoned in order to realize the true object of pleasure. In this light we should see the seemingly contradictory statements of Augustine in *Confessions*, where he writes, "At times, therefore, suffering can be proper objects of love" (Ibid., n.d.), which is followed in the very next paragraph with these words, "Therefore some kind of suffering is commendable but none is lovable" (Ibid., n.d., 37). That suffering can be an object of love is possible when it is not enjoyed in itself, but which in its retreat opens the way for the true enjoyment of the truth in God. This is why suffering in itself is never lovable. Thus pain in itself is not pleasure but it can be the condition for the possibility of pleasure. "You fashion pain to be a lesson." (Ibid., n.d., 25). This lesson is thus always a lesson in endurance. Endurance is distinct from enjoyment. In endurance there is always an element of use of the pain for the sake of something else. Endurance thus marks a capacity for reaching a goal which is outside that which is endured. In other words, endurance is never an end in itself, it always opens the way for one to reach divine bliss. One endures in order to overcome that which is endured, making endurance a condition for the possibility of a transformation.

Theatre and the Desire of Death

In the case of tragedy, Augustine sees a foreclosure of this possibility of transforming the world into a condition for the possibility of truth to arrive, because theatre itself poses to be the finality of its own possibility. Theatre thus refuses to die in transforming death itself into desire. For Augustine, in the world of flesh, which is a life without life, death becomes the condition of possibility of true life and the desired object of pleasure. As he writes, "You bring death upon us so that we should not die apart from you" (Ibid., n.d.). Not to live apart from God is also to realize the true object of desire in God. But here theatre actualizes death itself as enjoyment, thus foreclosing the future possibility of a true realization of any such life. In *Confessions*, more than being a false representation, theatre's, or specifically tragedy's, problem is its truth effect. Through their representation of pain on stage, tragic plays generate agony and despair in the spectator as the possibility of a life of flesh which cannot be redeemed through its abandonment. On the contrary, it presents for Augustine a false redemption through actualizing simultaneous pleasure. In presenting pain itself as pleasure, tragic theatre exhausts the potential of the world to be transformed into a condition for the possibility of redemption. Tragedy befriends the world with its false tears in its fornication against God. This befriending is the 'internal enemy' of the true life of spirit which always expresses itself through a gesture of withdrawal. Theatre was a product of the world of flesh, an exclusively human artifact and necessarily transient. In this sense also theatre is paradigmatic of a life marked by death in Augustine's schema of things. Nonetheless it insists on its presence by making this world available for pleasure through pure means. This paradox of, both, being an exclusive product of the world of flesh which makes it desperately transient, and yet refusing to be dissolved for a higher end, denying itself its due termination by constantly producing pleasure out of death, makes theatre occupy the ironical place of being a sign that refuses to function as a sign. This is the crisis which the real of theatre poses in Augustine.

Retreat of Death

How can this 'unjust love' for theatre be transformed into the sweet and good love of a life of the spirit devoted to the supreme truth? It can only be good if it is related to God. But then how can a life which is marked by the unjust abandonment of God be returned to Him who is the source of all justice? This is the movement which *Confessions* seeks to achieve. Let us recall the lines, "I intend to remind myself of my past foulness and carnal corruptions, not because I love them but so that I may love you my God". (Ibid n.d., 25). The unjust love that is marked by death, or more precisely, the love which is nothing but the desire of death, has to be transformed into the love of life. As Augustine writes, "You seek the happy life in the region of death; it is not there, how can there be happy life where there is not even life?" (Ibid., n.d., 64). So the problem of *Confessions* starts to take shape. How can life in its carnal corruption which ceases to be life and appears as death be returned to the bliss of a true life? Memory becomes the very ground of this transformation. But this transformation is not simply a return to a life lost after the fall, which can now be retrieved. Rather, it effectively produces the possibility of a radically new life. The descent of man is not merely lamented but joyously lamented for necessarily producing the condition for a new ascent. A condition for a new beginning, which is not to retrace the steps back, an impossible task because of the inevitability of the descent. To return in Augustine is never to return to the same place which is forever lost, but to seek a new beginning on the ground of this loss. Thus, he writes in one of the most enigmatic passages in *Confessions*, "Surely after the descent of life, you cannot fail to ascend and live? But where will you ascend when you are 'set on high and have put your mouth in heaven? Come down so that you can ascend, and make your ascent to God" (Ibid., n.d.). Here, there is already the possibility of a new return which is made inevitable by the descent of man. The fall of man already announced the possibility of resurrection. The 'return to our heart which the confession declares is never the general return of a community or a race. It is the highly granulated and singular return of the one who confesses of his faith in Christ, "who is gone from our sight so that we should 'return to our heart'" (Ibid., n.d.).

In Christ, death is abandoned for life. This is the function of endurance. Not just an overcoming of death through resurrection, but the destitution of death itself. In being abandoned *to* death, Christ abandons death itself for life. To endure death is to make death inoperative. This is perhaps how the following line from *Confessions* needs to be interpreted: "He who for us is life itself descended here and endured our death and slew it by the abundance of his life" (Ibid., n.d.). This is the movement that Augustine wants to re-enact through confession; where the life of corruption marked by death has to be overcome by rendering death inoperative. There has to be a sort of death of death itself. As he writes, "Lest I die, let me die so that I may see it." (Ibid., n.d., 5). But how to achieve this death of death itself through the act of confession? Or in other words, how to render death inoperative so that death itself produces the ground for the possibility of a new life? Here we confront the concept of love again in Augustine. For the love of God is the very condition for rendering death inoperative. So that one may enjoy the true object of pleasure, everything else has to be used. For the sake of the ultimate object of enjoyment, the world is made available for use which also renders the corruptibility of the world inoperative. This inoperation is only an effect of *use*, where one uses the world through its abandonment. Thus the mortal world is overcome through a gesture of abandoning it, by not enjoying the world but using it.

Memory and Sign: from Use to Abandonment

Let us address this problem through the specific theme of theatre which we have chosen. In making theatre an example of the life he formerly led as a student, a carnal life marked by decay and corruption, he exposes this life to the judgment of the Almighty. But how can such an exposure take place? Preciously by recalling that very life which is done, not in pleasure, but in the hope of attaining eternal bliss. Thus, memory, in its act of recollection, does not merely recall past events but transforms them into things which stand for other things. This relationship between memory and use needs to be elaborated. Augustine conceives of memory both as an active moment of recollection which is present to itself through itself–and hence is a real process and can bring about actual transformations–and as the storehouse of worldly objects, whereby they are grasped through the senses and kept as images to be gathered and recollected for a future use. In case of affects, memory stores the emotions and passions that the mind experiences at any particular moment as meaningful images but is itself not affected by them. Hence Augustine calls memory "the stomach of the mind" (Ibid., n.d., 191), where food for thought is stored in its sweetness and bitterness. But the stomach itself is unable to taste them. Thus one can recollect the memory of a past sadness or fear without getting sad or scared in the present. This translation of the world of flesh into thought-images makes the world available in its absence. In absenting itself from the world, memory, through images, stands for the world and retreats from the world at the same time. Thus memory offers the world for use. The real of theatre did not allow this retreat to be possible because it created signs which were available, not for use, but pleasure in themselves. It thus had to be translated and transformed through memory into signs functioning as use.

The material reality of theatre, then, stands for the life of flesh Augustine formerly led as a student. Thus the material reality of theatre is transformed into a sign of the life of corruption, which Augustine now offers as sacrifice to the Lord. In Augustine, a sign is always a thing which stands for another thing, and is always available for being used, not for its own end, but for something else. Here theatre is such a thing–used as a sign for a life emptied of all life, a life marked by death and corruption, or more interestingly in case of theatre, a life dedicated to the enjoyment of death. Thus, this life, in becoming a sign, stands for the hope of being sacrificed so that the true object of desire, the incorruptible love of God, is realized. In making the real of theatre available as a sign, Augustine overcomes the place where death is enjoyed by abandoning it for a place where life is enjoyed. But this can only be possible if theatre, as a sign, uses death as a condition for the possibility for this hope of life to emerge. Thus using the world as a sign is also making the world available as a ground for the possibility of redemption. Just as, in Augustine, the punishment of the disordered mind is its own disorder, which in being a punishment becomes the condition for order to arrive. Or for that matter, hunger for carnal pleasure always remains insatiable. This inability to find satisfaction is the very misery of the life of flesh that forces one to seek more misery in the form of more carnal enjoyment. The act of confession turns this life of corruption into a life of endurance, thus becoming the condition for the fulfilment of the spiritual hunger. These are parallel movements of discordant themes in Augustine's *Confessions*, connected (Ibid., n.d.) (Ibid., n.d.) by the single thread of an act, a gesture where all these instances of worldly things are transformed into signs of a corrupt life to be sacrificed. The same movement is found vis-à-vis law, which we cannot fully develop here, where transgression and law are reciprocally related through pleasure. The act of transgression is related to the desire to transgress, which is the outcome of prohibition. But again, through the use of transgression (and in turn law) as a sign of illicit desire, desire, as produced by transgression, is abandoned for justice. In other words, law is rendered inoperative by making desire for transgression invalid.

Confessions, through its gesture of transforming every element of enjoyment into things to be used, make this world available for a radical transformation. In order to find stability and rest in God, the confessional soul is eternally restless. This restlessness is finally the effect that Augustine seems to generate by making the world available for use. Once the world is exposed as the very ground for the possibility of grace to befall, this ground, by that same gesture, loses all grounding. It is caught in the fever that is nothing but the hope of being converted into something new. This is the restlessness of the world which silently and secretly screams between the lines of *Confessions* tearing it apart into a thousand fragments going in different directions, only to be gathered again under a light which is utterly different from all our kinds of light.

(b) Point of Elaboration: A Reading of Augustine's *Confessions* as a Text of Desire

Desire and Signs

In the middle of *Confessions* while talking about his meeting with Vindicianus the astrologer, Augustine writes, "This instruction, either by him or through him, you (God) gave me. The doubt which you imprinted in my memory I was later to follow up with a personal investigation." (Ibid., n.d., 56). It is this desire to search for meaning which seems to give a very different unity to this work, which is distinct from the unity sought by the harmony of parts in service of the whole. If the whole of *Confessions* is a kind of search for truth, then this search is not determined by the final recognition of a single truth, which happens at some definite point in the text. Rather, the truth of God seems to have been broken into an infinite number of pieces which is diffused and scattered all over the text. Here interpretation is nothing if not a constant and agonizing effort to gather and collect all the pieces together to give it a final and conclusive form. In other words, even formally, the text seems to be a metaphor for Augustine's life, whose multiple forms he now tries to investigate through the interpretation of various signs, be they signs of love, signs of knowledge or even trivial everyday signs of worldliness. Augustine observes, "... this is mind, this is I myself. What then am I, my God? What is my nature? It is characterized by diversity, by life of many forms, utterly immeasurable". Of course, it is the nature of this truth that it almost always eludes him. It is *in* the failure of interpretation that he has to hold himself together. Thus, while trying to investigate the problem of forgetfulness and its relation to memory, he notes "I at least, Lord, have difficulty at this point, and I find my own self hard to grasp. I have become for myself a soil which is a cause of difficulty and much sweat". However, the determining force of this passage through various failures of interpretation is his burning desire to search for the truth, rather than that truth itself. "May I know you, who know me. May I 'know as I also am known'." However what seems to be the condition for this search is not the truth in God but rather the *desire* for this truth. In other words, the love of God urges him forward in the path of knowing God. Of course, it is the nature of this love, as desire or craving (*appetites*), to seek fulfilment in the object of love, which is the trinity of God for Augustine. But the search would always end in failure because of man's (Ibid., n.d.) mortality. So while death becomes the great obstacle to the fulfilment of desire, it is also the condition for desire to exist in the first place. Because life finds its termination in death, life desires to seek its meaning elsewhere, outside the temporality that is its condition. But since fulfilment always ends in failure and frustration, what keeps life on its path is not the object of desire, but desire itself, as it passes through innumerable elements and signs, whose meanings are sometime completely hidden, sometimes partially given and at times almost seem to be illuminated. Even from the point of view of the present state of confession, which comes after his conversion, this desire remains still unquenched; it is not yet fulfilled in the enjoyment of its object, which is God himself. Thus the truth of God still eludes him and hence his desire still remains alive. It is this secret unfolding of desire that envelops the entirety of *Confessions*. It is not a desire which finds fulfilment and content (in both senses of the term) in the tranquillity of truth. Rather, in its effort to seek its content, desire seems to constantly fail and invigorate the search simultaneously. Take, for example, the case of curiosity, which is nothing other than a desire for knowledge. The worldly signs of everyday life make Augustine curious even after he has willed to give in to the demands of truth in God. He writes:

> When I am sitting at home, a lizard catching flies or a spider entrapping them as they rush into its web often fascinates me. The problem is not made any different by the fact that the animals are small. The sight leads me on to praise you, the marvellous Creator and orderer of all things: but that was not how my attention first began. It is one thing to rise rapidly, another thing not to fall. My life is full of such lapses and my one hope is in your great mercy. (Ibid., n.d., 213)

Although it seems that the meaning of the worldly sign that he interprets according to the demands of recognition of a whole (which is God the creator) solves the problem by creating a perfect harmony between the sign and its meaning, it is yet insufficient because it produces an incommensurability between the sign and its recognition. Because it is not the recognition that determines the desire for seeking interpretation, but an encounter with a worldly sign which activates desire. Thus desire always begins from an encounter and produces an incommensurable gap between what activates it and what can terminate it. So, in spite of recognition, which ought to have quenched desire, it remains alive in other lapses, in other encounters. In fact, it is this structure of desire, which is always in excess to recognition, that characterizes the entire search for God as creator. As Augustine writes, "You were radiant and resplendent, you put to flight my blindness, you were fragrant, and I drew in my breath and now pant after you. I tasted you, and I felt but hunger and thirst for you. You touched me, and I am set on fire to attain the peace which is yours."

It is this subterranean life of hunger which conditions Augustine's present life of serene interpretation of his past. It is in this violent need for peace that Augustine finds a meaning of a truly religious life. A religious life is, then, not a life which gets captured in law through the recognition of truth, but rather a life which, in passing through desire, realizes itself in encounters with violent signs of the world. These signs demand to be interpreted, that is, to be identified with their meanings in order to grasp their essence in thought. This is the web of desire that the soul passes through, in which the soul transcends itself, which is also a sort of realization of this desire. The act of transcendence resurrects the soul at the level of essence. It is in this interpretation of the world in order to find a singular essence, an essence which is nothing but a viewpoint of this world, that the soul finally transcends, not the world, but itself, and becomes witness to the creation of a new world within this world. The purpose of desire is to dematerialize the world so that it emanates signs–signs which become more and more transparent, and finally identify with a spiritual meaning in order to create essence, which in turn would create life anew. This is the movement of desire in Augustine. It not only gives an individual a unique viewpoint to the world, but also individualizes through accessing the pure faculty of thinking by providing food for thought. This is the world of confession where everything can become a sign and hence a food for thought. The structure of love as desire in Augustine, which remains the same for both worldly love (expressed in *Cupiditas*) and the love of God (expressed in *Caritas*), responds to this demand of sustaining (Ibid., n.d.) oneself in thought in a world which has become absolutely alien. The structure of love remains as desire, not because of any inadequacy of reason, but because in the absence of redemption–which can only come at the end of time–it is desire which activates thought, even the thought of God. In the temporal world of becoming, where death alienates man, not only from the world, but also from his own being that resides in God, it is love characterized as desire which can create a condition of sustaining thought as such.

If desire is the gathering force of the search for truth in Augustine, then let us now inquire into some of the key concerns which the search unfolds. This we will try to do through an investigation of two sets of concepts in Augustine–that of Memory-Time and Desire-Imitation.

Memory-Time

The search for truth, in Augustine does not start at the level of the world. It begins at the level of the soul. As he says, "I had become to myself a vast problem". It is the search for a resolution of this problem of the self, and not collecting proofs for the guarantee of an already recognized truth, which seems to give a certain unity to the text.

So we need to ask ourselves what inaugurates this search. Is it a will towards knowledge and a given necessity of logos which comes through a force of law and demands recognition, a recognition that would in turn guarantee its permanence? No, it seems the other way round. What inaugurates the search is not determined by any pre-existing method, where the mind, under the dictates of reason, embarks on collecting proofs for what it already knows, what it already has given to itself by law and faith. Rather it is the necessity of an absolutely sudden encounter, a contingent happening in the world, which, in a way, inaugurates the search. It is the moment of his first encounter with death in the form of the demise of a friend. It is the demand of this encounter that creates the necessity for the search of the meaning of his being. Although, from the point of view of the present moment of confession, the moment which Augustine now inhabits and from where he looks back at his life, the singularity of the moment in his past is already gathered in other singular moments even prior to this, which makes him question himself. In the case of his encounter with *Vindicianus*, the astrologer, or his encounter with theatre in Carthage, or his encounter with the Manichees–these are separate moments, fragmented pieces of time from his past, which forced him to question his self. In other words, they are occasions which necessitated an interpretation of the meanings they held in the form of violent signs. The gift of thought, then, arrives only after, and not before, a violent encounter with a sign. There cannot be recognition of the gift but only a gathering which re-collects in thinking. Now that Augustine sits and contemplates in tranquillity, within his life of religion, he can, through the use of memory, gather these signs of violence and search for their true meaning that always escaped him earlier. Although, now, as then, the desire for the search is always there.

So we might propose that, in Augustine, intelligence or thought always comes after an encounter with a violent sign oriented to it by its demand of explication and development. Here the interpreter is not acted upon by any law of universal recognition but rather functions according to the constraints of a localized encounter. But such a hypothesis naturally leads us to the question of what re-collection is in Augustine. What is the role of memory in this process of recollection and what is the nature of this operation in itself? Recollection, in Augustine, is very different from our understanding of voluntary memory. Voluntary memory always proceeds through resemblance. It depends for its meaning on an external object, which is the past that can be accessed by memory at the present moment. So the past remains always relative to the present in a double binding. It is the past of a "present" which is "no more", but it is also the present in regard to which it is the past. Voluntary memory cannot apprehend the past without recomposing it with different presents. And the present remains inextricably caught in conscious perception which claims that it finds the meaning of impression in the object. It is this objectivist function of voluntary memory which distinguishes it from the idea of re-collection. In recollection, one remembers not the things themselves, but their images. Although these images are emitted from things which enter the mind through the senses, once they are in the mind they suffer a curious transformation. In a way, the sensations are rendered inoperative in terms of their objectivity. The meaning of these sensations is no longer sought in the objects themselves, but they are gathered and used by the mind for its own purpose. It is the function of the mind to gather these images which it recollects from memory but use them for its own cognition. Thus Augustine writes:

> Once again they have to be brought together (cogenda) so as to be capable of being known; that means they have to be gathered (colligenda) from their dispersed state. Hence is derived the word cogitate. To bring together (cogo) and to cogitate (cogito) are words related as ago (I do) to agito (agitate) or facio (I make) to factito (I make frequently). Nevertheless the mind claims the verb cogitate for its own province. It is what is collected (that is, by force) in the mind, not elsewhere, which is strictly speaking the object of recollection (Ibid., n.d., 189)

Thus to recollect is not an objective operation, but a moment of subjective association, where the past maintains its difference with the present but is nonetheless repeated as past. This becomes clear when we consider the function of memory in recollecting past experiences or encounters generating affects. According to this line of argument, I can be far from glad in remembering myself to have been glad, and far from sad while recalling past sadness. So long as one remains in the realm of conscious perception, an image always has an external relation of contiguity with the object of perception. So, for example, if the image of a landscape makes us joyous, we seek the meaning of that joy in the landscape itself. But in case of memory in this Augustinian sense, remembering a landscape which made you happy once can make you sad now, although the image remains the same. This is because, here, the external relation of the image to the sensation in the past context gets completely absorbed and transformed into a new sensation in the mind itself. In a sense, recollection internalizes the past context which now becomes inseparable from the present sensation. So the past remains as past in the present sensation. The image of the landscape rises up in its sadness as the past, but the sensation is absolutely new. It is the sensation of sadness. The profound truth about recollection in Augustine is that here, memory is not resemblance, nor identity, which are conditions for recollection, but the difference between the present and the past that is repeated in the present. Thus the past coexists with the present as past. Hence the role of the memory is always secondary in Augustine such that it constantly provides food for thought but is always subject to the mind as such. Augustine notes, "The affections of my mind are also contained in the same memory. They are not there in the same way in which the mind itself holds them when it experiences them, but in another very different way such as that in which memory's power holds memory itself" (Ibid., n.d., 191). Memory is that which offers the mind the access to the faculty of thinking as such. To that extent it is limited to its own condition, but nonetheless constantly provides materials which the mind dematerializes in order to create the spiritual meaning of the still too material images. No wonder Augustine calls memory the stomach of the mind. So one can come to a second proposition. In Augustine to think is to create nothing but the act of thinking itself.

If recollection is an act of gathering par excellence, then Augustine introduces a double movement to this understanding in *Confessions.* What is confession if not an act of gathering all the selves that one had once lived and has now emptied of meaning, has sacrificed in an effort to transcend? But that does not prevent him from thinking of this multiplicity of selves in their pure formal logic in order to create the "view point valid for all associations", to create a style of thinking "valid for all images of the world". Religion is the site for this style of thinking–where the self, in the process of gathering the multiplicity of selves, creates itself anew in thought. As Augustine writes, "Great is the power of memory, an awe-inspiring mystery, my God, a power of profound and infinite multiplicity. And this is mind. This is I, myself." (Ibid., n.d., 194)

What the mind gathers through memory is nothing but time. And in gathering time the mind swells up, bloating from the pressure of the ages inside. Fragments of time, broken into different sizes and shapes exert tremendous pressure onto the soul in an effort to find their lost unity. It is this swelling up of the soul with time that Augustine calls distension. "Because your mercy is more than lives, see how my life is a distension in several directions.'

Time, in Augustine, arrives out of the future and passes on to the past though a present without extension. So it "comes from what as yet does not exist, passes through that which lacks extension, and goes into that which is now non-existent" (Ibid., n.d., 232). Then how can we measure time which can only be done over some extension? This is the problem of time in Augustine which finds its expression in distension. Since we cannot measure time, neither according to the past nor the future, because both do not exist, it ought to be the present which is a measure of time. And yet the present lacks extension. So it must be somewhere else that time is measured. Time which flows from the future into the past, is thus consumed in its futurity. And while the belly of the past grows as this future passes through the present, the present itself vanishes in a flash. And yet we measure time, in long and short stretches because time's measure is the mind. Thus the future which does not exist can be consumed and the past which now has no being can grow because they are absorbed in the intensity of the presence of the mind. Augustine notes:

> For the mind expects and attends and remembers, so that what it expects passes through what has its attention to what it remembers. Who therefore can deny that the future does not exist? Yet already in the mind there is an expectation of the future. Who can deny that the past does not now exist? Yet there is still in the mind a memory of the past. None can deny that present time lacks any extension because it passes in a flash, yet attention is continuous and it is through this that what will be present progresses towards being absent (Ibid., n.d., 243)

So there is a coexistence of the past and the future as memory and expectation in the continuity of the present attention. But what characterizes the continuity of attention is the intensity of concentration. It is in the present moment of self-consciousness that vast stretches of future and past is absorbed. This makes this consciousness pregnant with the unconscious of temporality, or in other words—eternity. It is a primordial time, before time came to be deployed and developed in a series. This idea of time as distension resonates with the Neo-Platonist idea of *complication* which they used to designate the original state in the *One.* This state precedes any development or deployment or "explication" of many, and thereby affirms the unity of the multiple. It is this unconscious simultaneity of time that is transformed into successive moments of consciousness, which is always already temporal. But it is the impossible demand of tracing the unconscious of time that Augustine desires when he writes, "From such a mind nothing of the past would be hidden, nor anything of what remaining ages has in store" (Ibid., n.d., 245).Thus we realize that there is another notion of a *provisional eternity* which is not the un-changeability and stasis of "before time", but the intensity of a present state of the soul swelled up with the unconscious of temporality, where the past, present and future coexist, so that his whole existence has become time itself. But this coiling up of time within the soul as the essence of temporality also corresponds to a forgetfulness of the world. Like the lover who forgets himself in his desire for the beloved so that, although he starts with an expectation of his own happiness realized through the beloved, he ends up somewhere else. This elsewhere is a place of pure non-belonging because, in the process of desiring the world of the beloved, he forgets his own. But neither can he truly belong to this other world because his mortality will always separate him from the object of his love. Thus, he no longer loves in reference to his own self which he has emptied of all meaning. But, at the same time, neither can he belong to world of the beloved, except as exclusion. *In transit* (*transitus*) the lover truly becomes an alien in his world. Thus, the self as time, while desiring eternity, becomes forgetful of itself. Time in its desire for eternity forgets temporality. Thus Augustine writes, "Leaving behind the old days I might be gathered to follow the one, 'forgetting the past' and moving not towards those future things which are transitory but to the things which are 'before me', not stretched out in distraction but extended in reach, not by being pulled apart but by concentration". Distension is this moment of concentration which does not let the mind distract itself in objects of the world. So the mind is not dispersed but focused on its true object of love which is eternity embodied in God. The soul, which has become time itself, desires God, with whom rests eternity. This can only happen when the temporal world is forgotten and the soul is *in transit*. Of course this desire of time to belong to eternity is never fulfilled because time is defined by its own end which makes it temporal and also incommensurable with eternity.

In Augustine, the creation of the universe is held in a paradoxical relation to the creation of man. Because man is created both with and in time, from the point of view of time, man is after the world, whereas from the point of view of eternity or God, man is simultaneous with the world because God created everything simultaneously. Hence we have the creation of the universe as *principium* and that of the world of man as *initium*. It is this world of man, which is stretched in time and bordered by eternity, which will come to an end. So as we saw earlier, while the mind swells with time and becomes time itself, its desire is to find its fulfilment in the unchangeable eternity from which it is irrevocably separated. But in this state of transit what the soul truly gains is the point of view of eternity. This view point is the essence of time in eternity, which corresponds to an incommensurable gap between time and eternity. Thus this essence which conditions the viewpoint is nothing but difference itself. Not an external difference between two identifiable objects, but rather a more primordial difference internal to the human heart, which not only makes them impenetrable to each other but singularizes them as these impenetrable individuals. The viewpoint of eternity being difference itself, each subject expresses the world from a certain point of view. But being an absolutely internal difference, what it expresses is an absolutely different world. This is why one can only know the truth of confession through faith and not knowledge. "But 'love believes all things'" at least among those love has bonded to itself and made one. I, also, Lord, so make my confession to you that I may be heard by people to whom I cannot prove that my confession is true. But those whose ears are open by love believe me." Confession, being an exploration of one's soul, is thus a singular experience which can only be offered as a viewpoint to the world. But the world so expressed does not exist outside the soul. And yet it cannot be identified with the soul because it is not only individual, but it also *individualizes*. So each soul carries within it a world which is its essence. It is singularly the essence of that soul because it singularizes the soul in the first place. In a sense the soul holds the essence captive within itself. And it is through love as desire that these worlds come together. The generality of love gathers these different world-souls so that the desire for interpretation under the spiritual imperative of *Caritas* becomes our only window to these other worlds. This is the religious life par excellence. But this is also the life of art. As Marcel Proust once observed, “Only by art can we emerge from ourselves, can we know what another sees of this universe that is not the same as ours and whose landscapes would have remained as unknown to us as those that might be on the moon. Thanks to art, instead of seeing a single world, our own, we see it multiply, as many original artists as there are, so many worlds will we have at our disposal, more different from each other than those that circle in the void..” It is this artistic unconscious of religion which seems to haunt Augustine’s *Confessions*.

Imitation-Desire

In his *Commentary on Paul’s Epistle to the Galatians*, Augustine writes these enigmatic lines, “they loved by believing, they imitated by loving”. Hannah Arendt identifies imitation as a fundamental ontological structure in Augustine that determines man’s conduct, such that even its seeming desertion leads only to perversion—where the individual instead of imitating the universal Being in God, tends to stand in its place. Thereby he ceases to serve God through imitation, claiming to be at one with God. This is the definition of evil as perversion of the will in Augustine. Imitation is, then, a process through which man can be recognized in terms of whether he is in service of God or whether in trying to identify himself with God he pretends to take God’s place. This problem is analogous to the structure of logos as a relation between whole and parts, where the part always imitates the whole but cannot replace it, but serves the whole under the imperative of a law of recognition. Thus recognition always comes on the basis of an *a priori* abstract signification which is forced by law. As abstraction, this kind of signification has to be deployed by a pure force of law because it is founded solely in the mind and hence is always arbitrary. But it is the force of law as a pure form without content that makes the whole already present before it is recognizable in any of its parts. This is the work of an objectivist signification. Thus service is always related to an abstract moment of *a priori* knowledge, which would otherwise be arbitrary if not kept in its place by law. Thus imitation as the work of man in the service of God is always already recognized on the basis of an objectivist signification even before one starts to work. Perversion is when man fails to recognize the already present whole (in God as Being) and starts acting *as if* it is the whole. Once we recognize that this acting is nothing but imitation, we not only recognize perversion but again anchor becoming to Being. Because man, as a temporal creature endowed with nothing but becoming, can only imitate Being but cannot take its place. There cannot be a fragmentary becoming which is a whole in itself, in this line of thinking. In Augustine, what the recognition of evil finally points towards is that there cannot be an absolute evil. This is why evil does not exist except as a deprivation of good.

Secondly imitation, as Arendt points out is always actualized in Love. But here lies the inadequacy of understanding 'love as imitation', because–as a basic ontological structure governing the whole of life–imitation, in Augustine, is independent of man's attitude towards it. Man always has a choice of not taking imitation as objective recognition, that is, not subjecting himself to its judgment of right or wrong. In fact God cannot be discovered unless imitation is expressly taken up by the individual. Thus, within imitation, man is free although only from his own point of view. So one can imitate the wrong object and thus be perverted in the eyes of God, but not in one's own, which is what happens when one starts to imitate the creature instead of the creation. This is also why acting in the theatres is a form of perversion for Augustine. In a way, to recognize perversion is to imitate the point of view of God. But all this does not change the structure of imitation as a neutral ontological form. Like desire, which can be for the wrong object, imitation can also be directed at the wrong model. But when it is explicitly directed towards God the demand of "being as God" appears. As Arendt writes, "In performing this imitation, the reality of which is the absolute denial of the self found in the world, man comprehends his existence as the outright opposite of God, expressed in the impossibility of equality between him and God" (Arendt 1996, 84). But even this revelation becomes the source for his apprenticeship to truth, which in this 'limit case' comes through a 'betrayal'. In his utter failure to be equal to God man sustains himself in hope. This is why "the Christian creed is constituted by hope" (Ibid., n.d.). Even if love follows the structure of imitation of something outside the self, and not desire, we come back to the same moment of hope in order to sustain oneself in life and thought. This hope is nothing but the actualization of a desire which cannot find its object of enjoyment but fulfils itself in transit, always partially, always in its own movement in the world.

If hope is the only actualization of love in the world, then, in the transcending expectation of eternity, death becomes relative. Since all fear is finally the fear of losing the self in death, a freedom from this fear of loss produces a fearlessness. "The freedom of *caritas* may rise above the servitude of death." (Arendt 1996, 144) The fearlessness that sets in is always conditioned by a self-sufficiency oriented to an absolute future. The self is projected as an outside good to be sought after. This future self-sufficiency manifests itself in the world as desire. Hence, unlike the Stoics, in Augustine, the question is no longer how to come to terms with death, but with life, "For there are those who die with equanimity; but perfect are those who live with equanimity" (Ibid., n.d., 154). Love manifested as desire in *caritas* uses the signs of life, which are violent, deceptive and cruel interpreting them freely without being bound by their violence. Hence intelligence comes always after an encounter in order to make sense of it from the point of view of an essence hidden in the sign, whose extraction in thought is what we call its free use. The revelation of a primordial difference between God and man inaugurates a reign of hope which individualizes man as a Christian subject, who interprets the world in terms of the signs it emits, in accordance with a hope which is sustained by desire. This individualizing difference repeats itself anew in each man to create a mind which is always radically new. Augustine quotes from Paul, "Be not conformed to this world, but be reformed in the newness of your mind".

Now the state of the world can be deciphered from this new found viewpoint which the soul assumes. It is not only the viewpoint that the soul assumes, but it is the viewpoint which creates this soul. So we have something like an order of love in Augustine. Since existence can be divided between things which can be enjoyed for themselves, and signs which can be used for the sake of enjoyment, it is this original structure of love as desire which translates the world of temporal things (*res*) into a world of signs (*signa*). Because God is the true and only object of enjoyment and everything else stands for the sake of this enjoyment, the world ceases to stand on its own and becomes pure means. But such an end is always conditioned by a primordial difference because, in his mortality, man is incommensurably separated from this end. From this standpoint the lover approaches the world and discovers that there are certain things above him (*supra nos*), some things beside him (*iuxta nos*) and finally things beneath him (*infra nos*). It is according to this order that one needs to either love or use the world. "He lives a just and holy life who is an impartial appraiser of things, He is a person who has a well ordered love and neither loves what he ought not, nor fails to love what he should. He does not love more an object deserving only of lesser love, nor love equally what he should love either more or less, nor love either more or less what he should love equally". (Ibid., n.d., 156) The signs of love are thus arranged in a serial order and in the lover's attempt to progress in this series, he repeats himself because the structure of love remains desire, where the self tries to step out of his world in an attempt to possess something that does not belong to him. But his failure to possess his object of love does not terminate his desire. It actualizes it even more intensely as he climbs onto the next thing in the series. Finally through differences and contrasting relations introduced in the signs of love, the lover approaches the realization that the series converges ultimately upon its law, which is that of an essence capturing an original difference. This is not the law which keeps the whole and the parts together. This law of essence is rather conditioned by an original difference which never lets the part be absorbed into a whole. The fragment acts as a whole in itself that can find its unity only formally in being conditioned by an original difference. But the realization of this law only takes place when the lover has abandoned the temporal world and the signs of love they emit, no longer trying to enjoy them for their own sake but using them for the sake of something which he provisionally attains–namely, eternity. Thus, 'in transit', the lover realizes that the series of love is determined not only through repetition but through an original difference which always separates the lover from his beloved. Thus the absolute of eternity embodied in God, which is the transcendental and true object of love, is already repeated in our loves for other objects and appears as a mode of transition from one experience of love to another. The essence of this love is nothing but difference, which takes a general form in repeating itself in the progressive series that the signs of love inaugurate. At the limit of this series is the experience of a love not for a transcendental God, but a love of all humanity in their 'common' desire to attain God. Augustine writes, "Not everything which should be used should be loved, but only that which through a certain community with us is related to God". It is this love which is established in the community of those who, like myself, are "in transit" and can achieve "happiness" only in regard to God. The limit of this concept of love as desire is incarnated always in a group whose generality is determined by its nearness to the object of desire. So *nearness* is the last degree of essence as an original difference. It is in the nearness of God that one forgets the world and emerges as a subject "in transit". Although there is something tragic in each of the experiences of love repeated in the world, which inevitably end in failure, there is something comic and joyous in the repetition itself which is now transformed into free use. For when Paul says, "Yeah brother, let me have joy of thee in the Lord", Augustine comments, "Even in the immediate context to 'enjoy' is used in the sense of to 'use with delight'. For when the thing that we love is near us, it is a matter of course that it should bring delight to us" (St. Augustine, *On Christine Doctrine* 2009, 12). This is the joy one finds in hope which propels one to love one's neighbor according to oneself. The world, from the point of view of this hope, becomes a comedy whose signs are empty in themselves, standing for the truth that can only be achieved through their proper interpretation. In its vacuity and forgetfulness the world emerges as a pure means which the subject "in transit" can decipher in his nervous exaltation. The concealed affinity that brings the community of Christ together is their ability to interpret the world together, as it truly is–a world emitting empty signs, which can only be dematerialized and raised to the realm of a spiritual meaning through their common apprenticeship to truth. Augustine writes:

> But when I love you what do I love? It is not physical beauty nor temporal glory nor the brightness of light dear to earthy eyes, nor the sweet melodies of all kind of songs, nor the gentle odour of flowers and ointments and perfumes, nor manna or honey, nor limbs welcoming the embraces of the flesh, it is not these I love when I love my God. Yet there is a light I love, and a food and a kind of embrace when I love my God–a light, voice, odour, food, embrace of my inner man, where my soul is flood lit by light which space cannot contain, where there is sound that time cannot seize, where there is a perfume which no breeze disperses, where there is a taste for food no amount of eating can lessen, and where there is a bond of union that no satiety can part. This is what I love when I love my God (St. Augustine, *Confessions* 1998, 183)

It is this dematerialization of the world that love as desire initiates–a form of dematerialization that is always incarnated in substances, making them light, ductile and spiritual. To be sensitive to the signs of this dematerialized[31] world is the learning process of the apprentice, who deciphers and interprets these signs according to their essences. What sustains him in this inexhaustible and constant act of deciphering is his desire for truth which like the Promethean heat never quenches, never burns out. What gives unity to this structure is purely formal. In other words, it is a self-sustaining structure which constantly finds its expression in ever new modalities, in ever new forms of expression and styles of thinking.

A Concluding Reading of Augustine from an "Immanentist"[32] Perspective of Theatricality

The Broken Line

"Late have I loved you, beauty so old and so new: late have I loved you" (Ibid., n.d., 201).These words carry within them an ancient secret which is not exhausted in any signification. From the point of view of that secret, they are not the relived reminiscence of how one arrived at the destination or reached the place where the search is finally terminated. These words from Book X of *Confessions* belong to language insofar as they do not speak of anything; and insofar as they do not speak of anything, they do not belong to the one who speaks. One does not possess them because they do not denote anything. But the question may arise–why? Why do they not mean anything and why are they not, in the final analysis, attached to a body which speaks or even about a body about which they are spoken?

A few lines later Augustine writes, "You were fragrant, and I draw in my breath and now pant after you. I tasted you, and I feel but hunger and thirst for you. You touched me and I am set on fire to attain the peace which is yours" (Ibid., n.d.). To "pant after", to long to attain "the peace", is to move forward along a straight line towards that which has not still come or that at which you are yet to arrive. Therefore to be late is also to be early. The words express a delay, which is at the same time anticipation. The one who confesses these words maintains himself in that instant so that he can act out something which is still in the future and already in the past. It is this moment, *when* he confesses by expressing in language an expression which, denoting nothing, makes language possible. But again the question arises how? We shall return to this problem of possibility of language and the problem of truth in a while. Let us pursue further, at least for a while, the problem of time.

A divided time, a time which is always too late or too early, which belongs either to the past or to the future. A time of 'either/or' which does not merely put time out of joint by expressing this disjunction but also synthesizes it simultaneously into the moment of expression. If God is the lord of *chronos*–God is *chronos*–who grasps time as the eternal present that subsumes what to us is the past and future, then divine present is "the circle in its entirety, whereas past and future are dimensions relative to a particular segment of the circle which leave the rest outside" (Deleuze 1990, 150). Interestingly enough, this divine experience of time is opposed to the experience of time which is exclusively theatrical. The actor in this sense is always anti-God because he also experiences time in the present but his present is the instant, the most narrow, contracted moment through which he encounters eternity. It is that which divides linear temporality–temporality understood as the linear movement of a succession of 'nows'. The succession of 'nows' can never coincide with each other, thus making possible a straight line where each point or 'now' passes on to become the 'now' which is past and where the horizon of a future 'now' is always visible. The actor interrupts this temporality by dividing up this line endlessly, by breaking up each 'now; into a fractured moment–a "past-future" segment. This infinite segmentation, infinite division of the present instant into past-future, is what is common to both acting and the Augustinian notion of time as *distention*. Instead of a profound experience of the fully present which extends itself to past and future in divine time, time, in Augustine, rises up–or better–swells up in its unlimited past-future reflecting an empty present–hollowing out the present which only gives form to this void. As Deleuze says, "The Actor belongs to the Aion" (Ibid., n.d.)–so does the one who confesses, who also belongs to the straight line of Aion[33]. In this sense, for Augustine, the one who confesses always plays the role of the one who confesses. He has to be like the actor who revives his role at every instant because, like the actor, he cannot know any other life but the life of the present moment. Thus Augustine affirms, "My Lord, every day my conscience makes confession relying on the hope of Your mercy as more to be trusted than its own innocence. So what profit is there, I ask, when to human readers, by this book I confess to You who I now am, not what I once was" (St. Augustine, *Confessions* 1998, 180). But there is no character of the confessor which he can identify with. The role of the confessor is never that of a character but that of a *theme.* To play the role of the confessor is always to elaborate on the theme of forgiveness. This is the impersonality of the confessed events, the neutrality of the past remembered that can be recalled in memory without its corresponding passions–the sins of the past recognized as sins only in evoking them without passion–like so many singularities effectively liberated from the limits of individuals and persons, communicated in their neutrality. But at the same time recalling these moments in their impersonality individualizes the confessor as the confessor–like playing the role individualizes the actor as the actor. Thus while playing out the role of the confessor one acts out other roles, dividing oneself into these other roles somewhat like the present instant, which is divided up into so many fragments of past-future in the actor/confessor's experience of time. This is how the actor and the confessor both "make truth" instead of reporting.

Between the Event of Confession and the Confession of Events

The event of confession and the confession of events have this relation. Like the actor, the confessor delimits the original event, abstracting from it only its form and its contour like so many singularities floating in a void–Augustine calls memory, which is the quintessential tool of the confessor, the stomach of the mind–which constitute it. The event of confession is not the events of the past denoted but the "object-event" (Deleuze 1990) as expressed or made expressible. Because it is offered in love, which is yet to come but for which one is already late, the present of confession abolishes itself, which gives it the value of present. Confession finds it value in its own abolition, its own absence of confessing anything. This is the event structure of confession which is made possible because one can only confess that which is already known. "May I know You, who know me. May I be known as I also am known." (Ibid., n.d., 179). In negating one's past–the confession of events–nothing negative is expressed from this point of view, unlike the recognition of sin as the demand of law that we have discussed before. Rather the confessional event releases the purely expressible in its two halves. The past-future, as two halves which always lack each other, comes together as a disjunctive synthesis in the present, constituting the presentness of the event of confession–the "who I now am"–hollowing out any substance from the "I". The problem of the two halves lacking each other is paradigmatic of the relation between sin and grace as discussed before. Only on the recognition of sin can grace arrive, while, without grace, one cannot recognize one's sin. The past can only be grasped on the basis of the future–a future which will only arrive if the past is grasped. Therefore one half always exceeds the other by virtue of its deficiency, which also expresses a deficiency by virtue of an excess. If grace is an excess–a gift which befalls the faithful–then it befalls them who have confessed their sins and exposed their deficiency. But such deficiency can only be recognized by those who are "visited"[34] by excess. It is this paradoxical structure of the event of confession which empties out the "I" of any content in the expression "who I now am" voiding it out of every substance.

The actualization of the "I" as the confessional subject, which has "I" as its object of confession, can only function as long as we think of confession as performative utterance. However, as long as the confessional subject speaks performatively, he does so under certain conditions and conventions. Complying with these conventional conditions gives the subject the ability or capacity to produce the event by speaking. As Derrida so incisively points out, by becoming the master of the situation in complying with these conditions, the eventness of the confessional event is neutralized. In talking of the evental nature of confession, Derrida says, "Because I have the mastery of this situation, my very mastery is a limitation of the eventness of the event. I neutralize the eventness of the event precisely because of the performativity" (Derrida,

Composing "Circumfession" 2005, 21). It is from this point of view of performativity of the event that the subject constitutes itself. But such subjectification is only possible when one abandons oneself to the demand of law. A demand which generates the capacity to speak of the event. This forecloses the possibility of expressing your will towards that which unexpectedly befalls you. Confession in the historical sense, the sense in which Foucault examines it as a historical paradigm for the modern subject, always witnesses this foreclosure of the eventness of the event of confession by making it *a problem of will prior to the profession of faith*[35]. From this point of view, one can wills towards the knowledge of oneself during confession only by complying with certain conventions and conditions (norms and techniques). Thus only by abandoning oneself to these conventions (laws) does one paradoxically attain the capacity of exploring, discovering and expressing the truth about oneself. Confession *is* reduced to the following of certain techniques of the self such that one recognizes the self as a sinful object, which only *prepares* the self for its final transformation. In abandoning oneself to these conventions one does not attain true purification but is purified for purification, so to speak. In giving yourself up to law, you become the master of the situation insofar as you can speak of the truth about yourself, which as a master-researcher you have searched for, discovered and placed forward in front of others. Foucault's extraordinary analysis takes up this performative aspect of confession by examining precisely that line from Augustine's *Confessions* Book X which carries within itself the expressivity of the event. "Qui facit veritatem venit ad lucem" (to make truth inside oneself to get access to the light) (Foucault 2007, 171). Foucault is aware of the perfect circularity of the line. He who confesses–or makes truth within himself through confessing–comes to light. But one can only confess and thereby make truth in the light, when he has been purified by the grace of God. Foucault however treads another path–a pragmatic path of historical details to show how these two obligatory moments concerning the making of truth and the access to light become two separate and autonomous poles within the history of Christianity. We would argue at this point that the evental upsurge of confession in Augustine is precisely to keep this paradox alive. The separation of 'making truth' and 'coming to light' only forecloses the evental possibility of confession by making it performative, which, in turn, becomes constitutive of the subject. The subject who, by abandoning himself to law, gains the power to speak of the event, thereby neutralizing the aleatory condition of the event. In Augustine, however, will and power are never mediated by law because law always actualizes itself as conscience–as a demand inherent to being, which radically exposes oneself to the gap between such a demand and its fulfilment. What conscience actualizes in the self by exposing the self in the presence of God (*coram dieu*) is the incommensurability between law and its fulfilment, which in turn un-conceals the abyss separating will and power. To be abandoned to law under such circumstances expresses the powerlessness of the individual, whose weakness becomes the condition of possibility–the site–for the event to befall. Yet the site never becomes the necessary condition for the event, which maintains its absolute unpredictability.

Impersonality of Forgiveness

While Foucault, in the final analysis, shows us how this state of abandonment is forced by the cunning of history to become constitutive of the techniques of the self–which produces the Christian subject as the confessional subject, Derrida travels the other path of deconstructing the confessional subject from the point of view of the event. By comparing the singularity of the confessional moment with the powerlessness evocative of the powerlessness of the child marked by circumcision, Derrida tries to preserve the eventness of the event of confession in his concept of "Circumfession". He writes:

> The event is absolutely unpredictable, that is, beyond any performativity. That where a signature occurs. If I so much insist on circumcision in this text, it is because circumcision is precisely something which happens to a powerless child before he can speak, before he can sign, before he has a name. It is by this mark that he is inscribed in a community, whether he wants

> it or not. This happens to him and leaves a mark, a signature on his body. This happened before him, so to speak. (Derrida, Composing "Circumfession" 2005, 21)

However we have tried to travel a slightly different path of reading a certain theatricality to the event of confession by comparing it to the problem of acting. We are trying to understand this eventness as a kind of counter-actualization, like that which simmers behind every moment of acting. The disjunctive synthesis of the instant is a way of bringing in proximity, of making a convergent series of the singularity of confession and that of theatre. The theatricality of confession is not merely its performativity, as we have tried to demonstrate. It is the singular relation to truth that makes confession theatrical, so to speak. Like theatre which, as Alain Badiou would say, "makes truth" (Badiou 2013, 104) in a singular fashion, gathering different possible forms of relations to truth, so does confession "make truth" by counter-actualizing different possible forms of actualization of what we have called 'events' confessed. This is what Augustine has in mind in Book X when he talks of the power of memory, which gathers particular affect-producing events by recalling them, while simultaneously disengaging them from their corresponding affects. Confession makes truth only through this superficial method, bringing meanings out of their depths to the surface in order to make sense of them. Hence you can ask for forgiveness for acts committed which you can no longer be the subject of. In fact you can only ask for forgiveness when you are no longer the subject of that for which forgiveness is sought. As Derrida would write, "What is terrible in confession is that I am not sure that I am the one who can claim the mastery of or responsibility for what has been done, and I am not the one who can claim to be improving and to be good enough to repent" (Derrida, Composing "Circumfession" 2005, 25). The depth of meaning produced through the actualization of an event has to be brought to the surface, has to be made impersonal and pre-individual, so that it can be offered to seek forgiveness. But at the same time seeking forgiveness does not guarantee redemption. Hence, to will for forgiveness does not coincide with the power to be forgiven. It is in this powerlessness that confession carries the trace of the event. The trace of the singularity that befalls can only be universalized through such forgiveness because the moment the singularity of the event is expressed–the moment it enters language–it is available for all. It is not only my own sins for which I seek forgiveness, but for that which has scarred me always already, the wound which is before me. It is the condition of possibility for my confession in the first place, the singular trace of the event which is now made available for all. Forgiveness is the structure through which the singularity of the event of confession and its universal sense is made possible. It is this relation of a singularity which is made universal–through the disjunctive synthesis of an 'asking for forgiveness' when there is nothing to forgive–when one is not the master of one's actions for which forgiveness is sought. It is something like the disjunctive synthesis of the actions of the actor who is not the master of the actions of his character, and yet it is through him that such actions are performed.

If the event of confession coincides with the confession of events only by abolishing itself–which is to say, Augustine's confession gives itself the value of confession only by abolishing that which is confessed–then we are again in the proximity of theatre, this time from the point of view of the event. This is because the counter-actualization of theatre is precisely based on its precarious nature. The ability of theatre to be called theatre–to give itself the value of theatre on the basis of its disappearance or absence–makes theatre into a singularity. Nevertheless, such a theatrical singularity, being directed towards an audience, 'amplifies' its own event for a collective thus becoming a universal purpose. In the case of theatre this relation between its singularity and universality opens up the quasi-political dimension of theatre. In the case of confession, the relation between the singular trace of the event that is made universal in language comes to us only as a paradoxical search for an impossible forgiveness. This opens up the religious dimension of confession, where religion stands as an idea for a universal community.

"Making of Truth"

All this finally leads us to the question of truth. When we say that both theatre and confession radicalize the question of truth, we generally mean that both these modes of expression have dispensed with the theoretical constative mode of truth. At the same time, as we have tried to demonstrate, neither the singularity of theatre nor that of confession speaks performatively of truth, thereby becoming the master of truth. When Augustine in Book X of *Confessions* talks of "making truth" to "come to light", he does not have in mind the reporting of certain true facts of his past. Because confession is always to confess what is already known, there is no question of recognition at work here. By the same token, it is absolved of any representative function in its general sense. When one confesses, one confesses nothing. At the same time, one does not confess oneself. One always confesses the other, as Derrida would say. (Derrida, Composing "Circumfession" 2005) Or as Augustine would write, "May I know as I also am known" (St. Augustine, Confessions 1998, 179) . It is because confession does not speak of anything which is not already known–"Moreover, you hear nothing true from my lips which you have not first told me" (Ibid., n.d., 179)–in confessing, the self always ends up confessing the other. The taking-place of confession, which can have value only through its own effacement, relates itself to that which has taken place–the place itself–only by becoming its other. When Augustine confesses the sins of his past, it is this self which he abolishes by speaking of it. Hence confession is always the other's confession within the self which confesses. This is the reason why confession is always meaningless. Augustine does not confess because he desires to reach a reconciliation or redemption. He is always already redeemed by the grace of God actualized through Christ. Hence confession is not a process of transformation that has a *telos* or an end which produces reconciliation. In other words, confession is not therapeutic. Hence its theatricality is never cathartic. Confession therefore becomes nothing other than an esoteric speech, which brings to the surface that which sustains faith–namely, hope. As we saw before, in Augustine, will and power are separated by the abyss of mortality, which can only be overcome by the event of grace that befalls man without his willing it. But, from the point of view of man, it is hope which gives shape to the fathomless gap, the void which separates man from God. Confession is therefore the making of truth in hope, or better, making of truth as hope. It sustains man between the event which has befallen and the event to come (between the Christ-event and *parousia*). But to hope is to bear witness to that which cannot be witnessed. To remember in confession is thus akin to how Augustine speaks of the impossible function of memory when it confronts forgetfulness. "Yet in some way, though incomprehensible and inexplicable, I am certain that I remember forgetfulness itself, and yet forgetfulness destroys what we remember" (Ibid., n.d., 194). To remember forgetfulness is to remember the abolition of memory that corresponds to the taking-place of confession (like the taking-place of memory), which in its taking place abolishes the place itself–the place of confessed events (or the place of memory). At the same time, Augustine writes that if confession is about praising God, and in praising God I call upon God, then, "How shall I call upon my God, my God and Lord? Surely when I call on him, I am calling on him to come to me. But what place is there in me where my God can enter into me?" (Ibid., n.d., 3). The impossibility of the place becomes the condition of possibility of place to take place through the task of confession. For God to penetrate man or for man to be entered by God, there must first be the event of love which demands man be worthy of that which befalls him. To make truth is to make the events which befall my life mine, to become equal to them such that I can release the truth which is their eternal secret. To be resigned to the eternal truth of the event which befalls me is to carry the trace of the wound, which can turn death on itself. Augustine urges one not to hesitate "to die to death and to live to life" (Ibid., n.d., 150). There is something like the theatre and its double in the intimate impersonality of death that is the source of the double accomplishment of Augustine's confessions–its actualization and counter-actualization. Confession evokes the abyss of that present, to paraphrase Blanchot, which is emptied of its presentness, divided into the death of the past-self and the hope for an impossible future-self towards which man is not able to project himself. It is as if in death he always forfeits the power of dying, dissolving the "I" into the void, where he never ceases to die but never succeeds. This is the impossible task of making truth under the light of the event, which Augustine embarks upon.

As we have shown, making truth in confession is intimately related to the event of confession, which gives confessional truth its value outside any constative theoretical understanding of truth. It is this immanent mode of the production of truth under the demand of the event that gives confession a theatricality of its own–a theatricality which we have, following Badiou, called an immanentist theatricality. Augustine's confession, which exposes itself to so many encounters, so many historical events–amplifying and dissolving them at the same time in his intimate and singular encounter with God–must be, in the final analysis, very similar to theatre, which is endowed with an equal power of simplicity.

NOTES

1. Cited from Augustine's *Confessions* Book X (St. Augustine, *Confessions* 1998, 201)
2. For a detailed and nuanced understanding of this idea of the problem and its difference with aporia see (Derrida, *Aporias* 1993)
3. Augustine chooses here Cicero's favourite actor which is, perhaps, not arbitrary and not only shows the influence of the one on the other, but also their different approaches to the problem of acting. Cicero talks of the moral excess of the stage while appreciating its ability to convince and affect people through its spectacular nature. Cicero would argue that the rhetor should learn the skill of the actor to produce spectacular realities.
4. In Sermon 33 on Psalm 143, Augustine argues about problem of metaphor as 'usurpation' (*usurpata translation*) see (Vance 1986, 9).
5. Kierkegaard would distinguish the difference between the concept of guilt in ancient tragedy as determined by the self's relation to an objective reality resting outside himself which would be called

fate or destiny while the contradiction of a modern tragedy would be quintessentially an internal contradiction of the self with itself like the paradigmatic case of Shakespeare's Hamlet. Kierkegaard would thus identify *anxiety* as the very essence of modern tragedy, which is conditioned by the question of the self by itself. In this sense the soliloquy of Hamlet is also paradigmatic of the very problem of anxiety, which could be traced back to its Christian roots particularly to this text of Augustine. See Kierkegaard's "Ancient Tragedy's Reflection in the Modern." (Kierkegaard 1992)

6. In Plato's writings *thumos* is identified as that spirited part of the soul which is opposed to its appetitive and rational parts.
7. Book VIII seems to narrate stories from Augustine's life which mention telling of other stories. This structure Foley argues corresponds to the Liturgy of Words or Mass of the Catechumens, which also narrates stories within stories leading to the Gospel.
8. Arendt would later argue that this dispersion is a way of man's enacting the desire for immortality by deferring the question of mortality in aligning the self to the world, which he believes would outlast the self. By not only desiring the world but also deluding himself in possessing it, man seeks a happy life which constantly slips out of his grasp. See (Arendt 1996)
9. "They love it when it encounters them as glitz, in order to enjoy it aesthetically, in all convenience, just as they enjoy every glamour that, in captivating, relaxes them. But they hate it when it presses them forcefully. When it concerns them themselves, and when it shakes them up and questions their own facticity and existence, then it is better to close one's eyes just in time, in order to be enthused by the choir's litanies which one has *staged* before oneself". (Heidegger 2010)
10. Again to maintain consistency with the said author's use of these lines for his own analysis, we have cited it from the essay and not from the primary text of Confession itself.
11. As we discussed earlier, Heidegger's entire seminar was on Book X of *Confessions.*
12. Vance explores the possible relation between this trio not only from the Pauline perspective that the letter of the law kills because

law only perpetuates transgression, which is conditioned upon the very presence of temporal law. Vance explores this relation between law and death in Augustine from the point of desire and language. As Augustine notes, it is only in language that he starts identifying his objects of desire thereby bringing him within the boundaries of law and finally death.

13. "And I babbled my brightness, my riches and my health to you O Lord my God" from *Confessions,* Book IX. (Vance 1986, 26)
14. "Meanwhile I interpret the sky of sky as the intellectual sky, where it belongs to the intellect to know all at once, not in part, not in a dark manner, not through a glass, but as a whole, in plain sight, face to face, not this thing now and that thing then, but as has been said, it knows all at once, without any passage of time. By the earth invisible and without form, I understand an earth without any change of time, which change is wont to have this thing and now that". From *Confessions* Book XII. (Ibid., n.d., 32)
15. In *City of God*, Augustine writes, "'And another book was opened' it says. We must therefore understand it of a certain divine power, by which it shall be brought about that every one shall recall to memory all his own works, whether good or evil, and shall mentally survey them with a marvellous rapidity, so that this knowledge will either accuse or excuse conscience, and thus all shall be simultaneously judged. And this divine power is called a book, because in it shall read all that it causes us to remember." (Ibid., n.d., 29)
16. Phillip Lacou-Labarthe has explored this relation between mimesis and sacrifice, particularly between catharsis the essence of the tragic and its sacrificial signification. Jean Luc Nancy has brilliantly explored the problem of sacrifice, arguing for the emergence of a new notion of figurative beginning with Socrates and Christ. See (Nancy 1991)
17. The opening chapter of Jean-Luc Marion's book on Augustine *In the Self's Place: The Approach of St. Augustine* is called The Aporia of Saint Augustine where he makes this point. (Marion 2012)
18. "People prone to pity or fear or those who are generally emotional necessarily undergo the same experience as do the others to the

extent that they share in each of these emotions and for all there arise a certain *katharsis* and relief accompanied by pleasure. In a similar way, the kathartic melodies provide a harmless pleasure for all," writes Aristotle in *Politics*. For a detailed analysis on the political function of katharsis see (Ford 1995).

19. For Paul love does not unfold as desire to be consumed and hence fulfilled as enjoyment. It is faith rather than love which seeks fulfilment in Paul which is finally consumed in vision. Love rather finds its "bond of perfection" even on earth and is the only way to end man's Godforsakenness. Hence love in Paul remains more important than faith and hope because it is through caritas, that man can find the expression of his attachment to God. Here it is only love which can overcome the human condition, which transforms the lover and makes of him a person whose love does not cease in his final happiness, when he shall finally attain God in the afterlife. This love continues without cessation in the afterlife as it did on earth. This is a far cry from Augustine for whom love unfolds as desire which will find its fulfilment in the final object of enjoyment in God himself. But as this is not possible as long as man is trapped in his own mortality, this enjoyment which comes as a vision can only be attained in the afterlife when one shall behold the divine and thus consume him in his act of seeing. This enactment can only be that of vision because, for Augustine, vision remains the perfect form of possession. Unlike Paul, for whom vision is the fulfilment of belief in knowledge, Augustine expresses vision or the act of beholding as the fulfilment of desire. When seen alongside Augustine's injunction against theatre as the place where knowledge is consumed for the pleasure of knowledge itself, the above distinction resonates with the cautionary tale of a voyeuristic possession of knowledge that Augustine warns us against. See Hannah Arendt's *Love and Saint Augustine*. (1996/1929, pp. 31-32).
20. Originally quoted from Augustine's *The City of God* VIII, 8, by Hannah Arendt. It is to be noted that some of the following quotes are not taken from Augustine's original texts but from Arendt's book *Love and St. Augustine* (1996/1929). In places where

such quotes are used, the citation in the body of the text reads (Arendt 1996/1929) followed by the page number though a separate footnote identifies the original Augustine text and the page number as cited in the Arendt text. Where texts have been quoted from Hannah Arendt's own writing no such footnote has been provided.

21. Originally quoted from Augustine's *Homilies on the First Epistle of John* II, 12.
22. Originally quoted from Augustine's *Commentaries on the Psalms 90*, I, 8.
23. Originally cited by Arendt from Augustine's *Christian Doctrine.*
24. From the point of view of habit one could also interpret Augustine's response against theatre, which (for example, in *Confessions*) he denounces not only for its sinful generation of illicit passions but also for perpetuating a desire to go to the theatres and enjoy the spectacles in spite of willing against it. As happens with his friend Allypius who once drawn to the gladiatorial games found it impossible to block the contagion of pleasure and was pulled back into the crowds which he initially wanted to set himself apart from. Thus he continued to participate in this cruel enjoyment for a long time out of what can only be analysed as habit. See (St. Augustine 1991, 100, 101).
25. One should not confuse 'historical fact' with the modern scientific notion of the facticity of history but take into consideration something akin to the facticity of history from a revelatory perspective based on Christian theology. This revelatory idea of history as facticity could be compared with Heidegger's idea of facticity which plays a crucial role in his analysis of the phenomenological basis of Augustinian thinking.
26. For Augustine the idea of trust as belief is central to the idea of interdependency and the management of the world through an economy of imitation. But at the same time this idea of belief as trust (*credere*) is distinct from the idea of faith which extracts man from the world into the realm of the *Civitas Dei*. Hence Augustine writes in *Eighty-Three Different Questions*, "there are three kinds of belief. Some are always believed and never understood, such as

all history, which runs through temporal and human acts. Other must be understood to be believed, such as all human reasoning (Derrida, Aporias 1993). Thirdly there are those which are believed first and understood later, like divine matters". (Arendt 1996, 101) Again in *Faiths in Things Seen*, he writes, "if this faith in human affairs is removed, who will not mark how great will be there disorder and what dreadful confusion will follow? Therefore, when we do not believe that we cannot see, concord will perish and human society will itself not stand firm" (Ibid., n.d.). An Augustinian idea of the economy of human affairs could be analysed by juxtaposing this understanding of exchange based on belief, and desire based on a continuous variation on the principle of pleasure-discharge.

27. We need very carefully to define grace as that which reaches the level of irony at maximum in Arendt. It is through a continuous rejection of the world under a principle of negation that one is able to ascend till the limit of grace. Grace, according to Arendt, is given only as the limit of an abyss–an original separation between man and God, at whose edge he can stand through a principle of negation. Hence grace comes as the limit of reality which is based on a concept of irony at maximum and not as an event which befalls as a paradox.
28. We have used Foucault's translation of the line which occurs in Book X of Augustine's *Confessions* (Foucault 2007, 171). In the translation by Henry Chadwick which we are using as our primary text the Latin line is translated as "for he who *does* the truth come to the light" (St. Augustine, *Confessions* 1998, 179). Derrida also comes back to this line in his *Circumfession* as "making the truth" and not as doing the truth. (Derrida, Composing "Circumfession" 2005)
29. We shall elaborate on this question of the paradox in the last section of this chapter.
30. We can clearly see the difference between an Augustinian idea of the theatrical congregation used as a metaphor and the congregational 'reality' of the spectacles as place of impurity of mixed bodies, as we find in Clement of Alexandria. "These

assemblies, indeed, are full of confusion and iniquity; and these pretexts for assembling are the cause of disorder–men and women assembling promiscuously for the sight of one another. In this respect the assembly has already shown itself bad: for when the eye is lascivious, the desires grow warm; and the eyes that are accustomed to look impudently at one's neighbours during the leisure granted to them, inflame the amatory desire." See Chapter III, p. 27.

31. From this point of view of dematerialization of the world, Augustine's philosophy seems to be exactly the mirror opposite of the comic gesture as we shall see in our last chapter.
32. We borrow the term an "immanentist" from Alain Badiou's use of the word to designate a singular relation between theatre and philosophy. He writes, "I will name this relation immanentist, by which I mean the following: theatre neither has the truth standing outside of it, nor must it be content with a catharsis of passions, or of the drives, nor finally is it the absolute descended onto the scene's finitude. Theatre produces in itself a singular and irreducible effect of truth. There is such a thing as a theatre-truth, which has no other place except the scene". (Badiou 2013, 101-103) Badiou goes on to elaborate on this thesis by constructing four elemental dimensions of the theatre-truth, namely its, a) evental dimension inscribed in the relation between the theatrical text and its performance, b) its experimental dimension inscribed in its treatment of time, producing an artificial time where the instant encounters eternity, c) its quasi-political dimension which is produced through the universality of the idea by being an art form that is quintessentially public in nature. d) And finally the amplifying dimension of the theatrical truth, which elaborates its relation with history, presenting it in a fashion that is neither representational nor absolutely aesthetic devoid of politics. It is the moment where a real historical sequence would meet the artificiality of time making that sequence immortal. We have tried to read the philosophy of Augustine in order to find a movement within that philosophy that we can call theatrical from this perspective adhering to Badiou's schematization in spirit and not strictly in letter.

33. Deleuze in logic of sense distinguishes between two conducts of time. The Chronos which is continuous and circular and the Aiȯn which is the broken line of segmented time. (Deleuze 1990)
34. Derrida expresses the evental structure of the confession as a visitation which is absolutely unpredictable, as against an idea of invitation, which is determined by the intentionality of the host and thus subsumed by the mastery of the subject. See (Derrida, Composing "Circumfession" 2005)
35. Foucault identifies in confession a distinction which separates it from a simple profession of faith thereby distinguishing two poles through which the Christian subject is constituted historically: By the profession of faith which coincides with the sacramental moment, particularly of baptism, and by the making of truth which coincides with the confessional moment. Though they are intricately entangled at specific historical conjunctions they are also distinctly conceived within the history of Christianity. Foucault traces the genealogy of this separation back to the patristic fathers, particularly Tertullian. See note 15 of previous chapter.

Part 3

The Actualization of the Problem

CHAPTER 5

"The Wise Man Laughs Only with Fear and Trembling"[1]: Representation, Repetition and the Materialist Threshold of Medieval Imagination

Introduction

When Charles Baudelaire wrote his famous essay "Of the Essence of Laughter" from which the main title of our chapter is taken, he unambiguously identified the wise man as the Christian sage "who is filled with the spirit of the Lord". (Baudelaire 2006, 142). In fact Baudelaire's entire thesis on the comic is based on the fundamental historical assumption that the comic as we know it could not have been possible without Christianity. Standing at the threshold of modernity, Baudelaire looks back upon history to identify another threshold when the world not only became Christian but also comic. The poet imagines the Christian reality as a reality of thresholds and boundaries which introduces something quintessential to the Western imagination–the temptation to transgress: in other words, desire. Laughter is therefore intimately related to the ancient accident of a fall. One wonders if the fall–even the accidental fall of a man slipping on a banana peel–does not remain the very essence of the comic referring to the contingent, finite and material reality of the human condition. Baudelaire therefore argues that such a moral and physical degradation conditioned by the fall makes any notion of utopia or paradise immune to laughter. There is joy in any imagination of paradise, whether divine or earthly, based on the realization that everything is good and wholesome but there is no laughter. Whether we place it in our past or in the future, which is to say in memory or prophecy, the image of paradise, the poet argues is simple and composed but without the comic. If we stretch this argument further then we see a very interesting analogy emerging between the idea of the comic which is essentially profane and the messianic idea of profane time as the time-of-the-end-of-time. According to this messianic tradition[2], particularly evident in the writings of Paul, profane time which is stretched between the first coming (the Word made Incarnate in Christ) and the second coming (*parousia*) is nothing but the extension of a threshold between *civitas terrena* and *civitas dei*. As we know, the end of time and the salvation of mankind are announced by Christ which is to be realized in his second coming. The time of history after Christ therefore expresses *the time it takes for time to come to its end*. Our time, the time we live in, therefore does not represent anything. It is "homogeneous, empty time"[3] which nevertheless repeats the entire configuration of time in being the time it takes for itself to come to an end. Empty homogeneous time therefore represents nothing but itself, becoming the content of what it represents. From this point of view it might not be completely incorrect to argue that empty homogeneous time is essentially comic. Baudelaire might not have reached for its messianic meaning but he was well aware of the fact that it is through the concept of threshold, which Christianity introduces into history, that comedy is made possible[4]. Hence we have the poet writing about the Christian sage who is anxious about laughter, "he holds back on the brink of laughter, as though on the brink of temptation" (Ibid., n.d., 142). Baudelaire's two general propositions in the essay, firstly that the comic is fundamentally related to a question of subjectivity, an ego who feels superior to that which he finds comical and secondly that such a subject comes as a symptom of a contradiction between a degraded material world and a higher, purer world of spirit is based on this problem of the threshold. Being profoundly human and therefore Satanic, laughter is essentially contradictory, being "a sign of infinite greatness and of infinite wretchedness, infinite wretchedness in relation to the absolute being, of whom man has an inkling, infinite greatness in relation to the beasts" (Ibid., n.d., 148). The comic subject therefore always expresses a sense of movement between these two poles being caught between a force which insistently pulls him back into the material world but which cannot dissuade him from desiring the infinite universality of the absolute. Hence the poet evokes the terrible laughter of Melmoth, the man whose laughs always stand on the frontier of what we call the human and a higher life. Melmoth, in the final analysis, ends up "always believing himself to be on the point of escape from his compact with the devil, forever hoping to exchange his superhuman power (power to laugh), cause of his misfortune, for the pure and undefiled conscience of a simple soul, which he envies" (Ibid., n.d., 151).

In a brilliant move, Baudelaire introduces yet another defining threshold into the problem of laughter. That which is profoundly human is also the source of his superhuman power. In being quintessentially human because he cannot help but laugh, man acquires the power to subvert the authority of a simple conscience which is given to him to control his actions. Here another interesting relation emerges between Baudelaire's notion of the comic and Christianity. As we discussed before, in St. Augustine the concept of *libido* is related to the autonomous movement of bodily organs. Laughter, from this perspective can be seen as something akin to the phallus whose autonomous movement was regarded as a result of the Fall of Man. We know that this idea of libido challenges the divine will (reflected in the human will before the fall) by letting certain parts of the body act involuntarily on its own–for example, the erected penis which acts autonomously beyond human control. This was a consequence of Adam's desire to seek autonomous will which resulted in the loss of any ontological support for that will which in turn made certain parts of his body disobey his commands, the sexual organs being the first to rise in such disobedience. Laughter, for Baudelaire has a similar nature which is why unlike joy it cannot belong to any paradise. And as Foucault remarked that sex in erection is the very image of man revolting against God's sovereign power, so can one perhaps say that such a man is also laughing uncontrollably at his own incapacity to command his sexual organ. Baudelaire's entire modernist mentality is disposed towards a thinking of laughter from this point of view of threshold. The wise man or the Christian subject can only come to the threshold of comedy in trepidation. He observes, "the wise man is afraid to laugh, just as he is afraid of profane entertainments or concupiscence" (Ibid., n.d., 142). But at the same time he writes, "The comic can be absolute only relatively to fallen humanity" (Ibid., n.d., 152). This is perhaps where the genius of Baudelaire's analysis lies. Writing in the second half of the 19th century it is this idea of the comic as the absolute concretely realized in the materiality relative to fallen humanity which places him so close to someone like Alenka Zupancic, writing in the first decade of the 21st century but still pondering over the problem of the same comic threshold. For both Baudelaire and Zupancic, it is the subjective, the relative and the contingent which is also to say material, finite reality which holds the key to the comic. But it holds the key to laughter, according to Zupancic by seeking its own necessity and becoming an absolute in itself, like Baudelaire would talk of the grotesque as absolute comic which has no proof of being comic except for the substantiality of instantaneous laughter that it produces. We shall come back to this aspect of Zupancic's understanding of the comic as a concretely realized absolute constitutive of the subject where the subject becomes indistinguishable from substance; but that is for later. We are concerned with Baudelaire's point of view on the comic as he sits on the threshold of modernity and looks in both directions, into the past of a Christian reality which according to him gives comedy its metaphysical foundation through its conception of the fall and the ontological schism it introduces. It is because of this schism that all contradiction generative of comedy is possible.

Baudelaire notes that the object of laughter is precisely the one who is unaware of being caught in a contradiction. If the object which elicits laughter is unaware of his/her comic situation, it is because he/she is unable to *consciously* move between two extremes—the universal absolute and the finite particular. However in reality, he/she is doing nothing besides moving between these two poles inadvertently. The emperor without his clothes is the object of fun because he continues to act like a king, universal and absolute in his authority despite being exposed in his particular, contingent reality of a naked man. It is not because he is naked that we laugh but because he is unaware of the movement which he, himself, makes possible between the absolute and the relative. The spectator who is not only conscious of the comic but is aware of her own superiority to the comic object laughs because she is aware of this movement which reflects her own oscillation between wretchedness and superiority. In fact it is because of this movement between the superior and the inferior that laughter is possible in the first place. The comic object and the comic subject (spectator) are therefore on either sides of a threshold separating the conscious and the unconscious. According to Baudelaire, the modernist imperative is to bring them together in the subject of the artist who is always not only split between the conscious and the unconscious but is "an artist only on condition that he is dual and that he is ignorant of none of the phenomena of his dual nature" (Ibid., n.d., 161). Therefore if Baudelaire is to be believed, modernity lies in the very overcoming of the schism introduced through Christianity which makes comedy possible. But this overcoming is nothing other than the affirmation of this schism in the very heart of modernity through the alien figure of the artist who is its result. It is our intellectual responsibility to embark on an analysis of the modernist moment, epitomized by Baudelaire, which is sustained by the figure of the artist and the disjunctive synthesis he brings about to the ontological separation between action and Being introduced by Christianity. One may argue that this disjunctive synthesis which makes comedy possible is also responsible for the Christian discourse on the incarnation of the word into flesh. Insofar as the Word is not represented in the Flesh of Christ but made Incarnate, the absolute is made concrete in the figure of Christ. But that would also imply that it is not only Christ who died on the Cross but the transcendent God himself. Hence from a speculative dimension of Christianity, as introduced by Hegel, the death of Christ is an intrinsic moment of the Resurrection. However we cannot say that with the death of Christ, his transcendent essence is returned to the beyond from which it came. Such an idea of universality is what Hegel would call bad universal, which was the case with the Greek gods as universal power which was not limited by individual appearance. According to Hegel it is precisely because of this that such a universal was limited as it was not bounded by an idea of concrete individuality which could actualize it.

Christianity had to deal with the inconsistency of its own divine logic of the Incarnate Word because logically it would lead to the death of Christ as the death of God as Beyond. The affirmation of transcendence as real and concrete, which was the singular project of Christianity, would lead to the paradoxical distinction between Being and action which at the same time remained inseparable in the Trinitarian logic.

However this would become the veritable source for the "comedy of Christ" in its different forms which we will try to explore in our last section. But first let us see the other side of the story; of how this inconsistency was forced to dissimulate itself which gave rise to a number of controversies and strategies of controlling them. While the controversies were symptomatic of the difficulty of resolving the fundamental inconsistency of the Christian logic, the strategies adapted to resolve them bear witness not only to the dissimulation of such an inconsistency, but the appropriation and even dissemination of the ontological separation which was a product of this paradox. Therefore let us first approach the Incarnate Word which according to Baudelaire has "never laughed" because "in the eyes of Him who knows and can do all things, the comic does not exist" (Ibid., n.d., 142)

Section I

Failure of Representation and the Reinforcement of an Opposition

Representation: A Generic Use

When Michal Kobialka moves away from the particular idea of theatre in order to adopt a more general term–representation–to explore performative practices of medieval Christianity, he challenges something fundamental in theatre historiography. In the introduction to his book *This Is My Body: Representational Practices in the Early Middle Ages,* Kobialka systematically lays out the epistemological field within which such discursive elements like archival scope, performative disposition and socio-cultural conditions play out their roles, contracting or expanding their meaning and purpose to propose different theories for the development of medieval 'theatre'. Without going into the details of how Kobialka manages to deconstruct each of these theories which cover a vast methodological spectrum from philology and linguistics to anthropology and performance studies, we would like to emphasize the function of using such a general term–representation–to capture certain extremely localized and concrete fragments from a particular historical episteme. Kobialka forewarns that his intention is not to qualify or adjectivize these practices as either theatrical or dramatic–or even, one might add, performative–but rather to "view representational practices as a field of enunciative possibilities" (Kobialka 1999, 31). This field Kobialka identifies with the enunciation of a single phrase "*Hoc est corpus meum*" (This is my body). But this single phrase engenders a hermeneutic heterogeneity which problematises the entire field of medieval representation giving rise to a multiplicity of "enunciative possibilities". It is not surprising that this moment which brings together the most general idea of representation to specific practices–for example, Kobialka analyses the singular practice of monasticism as recorded in the *Regularis Concordia*–would coincide with the 'event' of incarnation. It is under the sign of the event of Incarnation–when the word was made into flesh–

that the particular representational expression "This is my body" is transformed into a generic phrase.

The paradoxical moment of Incarnation (comic) therefore provides the perfect background to see the problem of theatre within Christianity consuming itself without finding any resolution, exposing itself to the nakedness of its own complexity. We have been arguing in the previous chapters that the problem of theatre within Christianity undergoes a unique transformation when material practices of theatre (and other spectacles) are forbidden while theatricality is given a figurative or metaphorical value. This process was quite different from the metaphorical use of the theatrical image in the Greco-Roman period[5]. In other words, while the concrete existence of theatre was negated (at least theoretically) within Christianity, a theatrical essence was abstracted and preserved as a mystical substance from which the Christian subject was naturally alienated. Interestingly this state of alienation was imagined through the metaphor of a 'theatre of the world' (*theatrum mundus*) because of its deceptive connotations while the former 'pure' substance of theatre was imagined figuratively as a divine spectacle which coincided with the divine substance.

Our thesis is seemingly contradictory to Kobialka's exploration of the generic problem of representation in the early Middle Ages because our object of study is the particular problem of theatre within the whole of medieval Christianity. However, we would contend that they coincide at this very problem of Incarnation. While Kobialka tries to see in this dogmatic moment the condition of a heterogeneity which opens up early medieval Christian practices only to be forcefully closed by the 12th century, we are trying to trace the outcome of an epistemological shift which happens at the very beginning of the Christian era (metaphorization of theatre). As we have tried to argue the shift comes through a process of metaphorization which fully realizes its possibility when medieval Christian drama tries to *represent* the dogma of Incarnation. What we are trying to argue is that the problem posed by theatre and its consequent metaphorical appropriation can be identified in a number of theological discourses since the beginning of the

Christian era. However it is with the Mystery plays of the 12th-13th century and the discourse surrounding them that the problem enters a new phase. It will be our effort to show here that it is not productive to reduce the stakes of the debate by arguing whether such plays were truly theatrical or not. Disregarding the whole controversy of finding a 'true method' of searching for the origins of medieval theatre it is perhaps more fruitful to see these *plays* as concrete historical attempts to actualize the epistemological problem of theatre metaphorically. To put it otherwise these plays were as much attempts to explore the metaphor of a divine theatre as they were attempts to represent the metaphor of a theatre of the world which was carnal, transient and most importantly deceptive.

To put it more clearly, on the one hand Kobialka tries to examine, under the generic term representation, nothing but the repetition of representations generated by the failure of any homogeneous idea of representation within Christianity. On the other hand, such failure of representation becomes the ground for heterogeneous repetitions through various concrete practices. According to Kobialka, this reinforces a certain affirmation of difference which is repeated in each of these failed moments of representation. However we have tried to pursue a slightly different method of approach but which eventually coincides with Kobialka's fundamental intention. We have concentrated our efforts to examine firstly, the status of a more or less particular idea of theatre (closely associated with spectacle) and how this idea is deployed to make sense of a Christian understanding of the subject who is alienated from his/her essence. Secondly, we have tried to examine how this tragic process of metaphorization (to produce Christian subjects) was also an effort to dissimilate the paradoxical, comic understanding of Incarnation.

The ancient world saw in theatre a tragic moment when the universal could be externally repeated through imitation within the boundaries of the individual. The finite individual came to represent the universal (infinite) through the tragic but external moment of imitation. Christianity, on the other hand, produced a singularly complex situation. On the one hand, it proposed the abolition of all external relation to truth through imitation, replacing it by the idea of a beyond where 'real' truth resides. It is this beyond which comes to constitute the Christian subject as a self who does not *imitate* this universal essence but is an actual product of it. At the same time such a self is also alienated or separated from this original substance. To put it differently, imitation (man made in the image of God) as a form of representation had to constantly represent this alienation or separation of the subject from his/her own essence. By the same token one can say, representation had to constantly represent the failure of the subject to represent its essence or substance. We have been trying to argue that the metaphorization of theatre, rather than representing theatre at an ideal level, testifies to the failure of representation. Metaphorization has to be seen as tragic reinforcing of an oppositional logic between an abstract universal order and a concrete order of contingent human reality. The metaphor of a theatre of the world, as we shall see later, becomes a way of conveying the separation of such a human world with its fleeting contingent moments from a 'divine theatre' which is the invisible essence of all that exists and yet remains outside the reach of existence. Similarly the theatrical representation of medieval mystery plays would try to convey the failure of the subject to imitate his/her essence. Therefore the effort of these plays was twofold: firstly it tried to accentuate the contradiction between an imminent and a transcendent order; secondly there was an effort to gain access to the beyond–figuratively or metaphorically. In other words, Substance comes into the medieval imagination only as an alienated reality as a result of metaphorization. Moreover the discourse around these plays during that time suggest that whenever they came to be accepted and approved as possible didactic forms it was because they reinforced the oppositional distance between a divine and a human order. In other words, while for the ancients theatre represented the imitation of the universal order of gods by the human order of mortals within Christianity theatre came to represent the very failure of such imitative representation. This was the essence of its pedagogic function. Let us see how.

From Anti-Theatricality to Anti-Humanism

Jonas Barish is surprised that the 12th-13th centuries display an anomaly to his argument that anti-theatrical prejudice increases during proliferation of theatre. Though dramatic forms flourished during this time in mimetic processions, paternoster plays, para-liturgical plays, scriptural cycle plays and morality plays, gradually moving outside the church premises onto the streets, Barish observes that the responding body of "condemnatory theory" was neither prolific nor profound as compared to, say, denunciations of theatre by Church Fathers in late antiquity. Apart from the occasional episodes of condemnation of specific cases of theatrical excess or reprimanding the lower clergy for their enthusiasm and involvement in such events, the anti-theatrical writings of this period demonstrate an exceptional reticence. Barish suggests that the reason behind such acceptance must be because of the Christian origin of medieval theatrical practices as contrary to earlier prejudice against theatre which coincided with Christian hostility for an alien religion and culture.

However as we have tried to argue in previous chapters anti-theatrical prejudice neither disappeared from the horizon nor was it mollified. Moreover if we take Barish's argument about the scarcity of condemnatory theories as our point of departure, we would have to hunt for an alternative explanation of this phenomenon. It is our hypothesis that anti-theatrical prejudice was no longer determined by a relational logic external to what we call the theatrical substance. Rather the knowledge of theatre was so completely absorbed within the discourse of Christianity that by the time of the 12th-13th century any discourse on theatre was treated as an exclusively Christian problem. This is quite different from the relation of philosophy to theatre where the former wanted to govern the latter. Yet behind such desire for governmentality was an idea of mastery. Theatre though related to philosophy nevertheless enjoyed some autonomy.

The formal and juridical expulsion of Roman theatrical practices formally puts an end to any scope for doctrinal acceptance of theatre within Christianity. However, the simultaneous appropriation of theatre as a metaphor used for Christian religious purpose meant that a theatrical imagination survived at the heart of Christianity. Therefore, unlike an anti-theatrical prejudice which was external and anti-nomical (literally as the opposition of two types of 'nomos' of the world like it was in case of Christian hostility for Roman theatre) now the problem was internal to Christianity itself. It seems that Jonas Barish's theory of anti-theatrical prejudice stands challenged in this moment. Barish argues that the anti-theatrical prejudice is like a permanent kernel of distrust inherent to human imagination. It stands as a universal antithesis to what Barish calls the "theatrical" which is intrinsically human. Insofar as this anti-theatrical 'substance' is anti-human, theatre stands as a reflection of humanism. Theatre in this sense stands justified in the name of a mysterious theatrical substance which coincides with the essence of humanity. The anti-humanist logic of the anti-theatrical substance always keeps it in an oppositional position giving it its negative identity. All the various attempts to explore the different anti-theatrical qualities within diverse historical discourses by Barish can be argued to be efforts to gather examples to justify this thesis. These examples are accumulated so that they can serve to justify the presence of a universal anti-theatrical substance identical to anti-humanism in order to pose it against the humanist identity of theatre. Clearly this is not simply a problem of generalization but a question of ideology. Christianity, according to our thesis, appropriates the theatrical imagination to the extent that any anti-theatrical prejudice has to be primarily seen as a problem internal to Christianity. The anti-theatrical substance in Christianity gets entangled within a complex logic of humanity which can only find its meaning outside itself. As we discussed earlier, a major anti-theatrical moment original to the Christian imagination was to see theatre as a place of deception. But it is precisely because of this deceptive quality of theatre that it became a metaphor for the deceptive nature of material life itself. Moreover the divine essence which was the condition of possibility of this material life also came to be seen as a divine 'theatre of creation' which was outside the scope of humanity. Even if we accept that the opposition of 'theatrical' and 'anti-theatrical' corresponds to a split between 'human' and 'anti-human' or 'beyond human' we would also have to agree that Christianity maintains this split within itself. In so far as this split is not only internal but constitutive of Christianity, we might very well speculate that with Christianity anti-theatrical prejudice undergoes a significant structural shift. It can perhaps be argued that for the Ancients, particularly the Greeks, philosophy (anti-theatrical) was an other worldly experience which was held in an external relation to theatre which was viewed as essentially belonging to this world. However for the Christians both theatre and its anti-theatrical 'other' were absorbed into a single discourse which was always already split. In other words, Christianity being a discourse of alienation, theatre came to occupy a complicated reality producing its own double. Therefore we can argue that among the Greeks the problem of theatre was essentially a problem of representation and how to control it. While within Christianity the question of theatricality essentially becomes a problem of truth and the failure of representation. Metaphorization of theatre coincides with this failure of representation which also opens a new understanding of the tragic.

A New Deception

As we mentioned before there is a surprising lack of anti-theatrical texts from the time when Christianity dabbled with theatre most conspicuously in the latter half of the Middle Ages. Jonas Barish argues that:

> The key to this forbearance lies of course in the fact that the theatre this time had not sprung from an alien religion, but from Christianity. It originated from the Church and it maintained close likes with the Church. It took its subject matter from the central truths of religion. It re-enacted the mysteries of the faith, it made the very alters its stage, and it involved the massive participation of the clergy. (Barish 1981, 67)

Obviously the cultural and religious distance which informed the discourse around theatre in the early years of Christianity was no longer there. That distance had already been forcefully abolished by the renunciation of all forms of theatrical practices reminiscent of its pagan origin. The tortured debate around the truth and falsity of theatre was no longer superimposed onto the truth and falsity of an alien race. By the time the discourse of theatre again emerges the world had become Christian, so to speak. Therefore as Soumyabrata Choudhury so perceptively remarks, "the stake of truth was invested in the authority of the *one* Christian body on earth–the church–and its protection" (Choudhury 2013, 25). However though the playground had changed the fundamental elements of the game had not. It was still a game of truth and falsity which surrounded the question of theatre. But unlike its Greek and Roman precedence the condition of possibility of this game of truth was no longer determined by mimetic representation. The new game would be played under the Christian axiom of truth which is indivisible and yet individualised and not open to any mimetic representation. This is why we are arguing that it would not be correct to assume that there was a decrease of anti-theatrical prejudice in this period. However because the problem of theatre is completely absorbed within the single discourse of Christian truth, anti-theatricality has to be seen from the point of view of a general problem of representation.

It is in a treatise on Anti-Christ by Gerhoh of Reichersberg, a German theologian of the 12th century that we find a clear indication of emergence of a new ambiguity between truth and falsity surrounding the question of the relation between the church and theatre. He writes in one of his chapters that those who use a church for representing the deeds of Anti-Christ or the rage of Herod are themselves guilty of the vices of the personages portrayed...they don't, as is their intention lie in their playing, but exhibit the truth" (Barish 1981, 67). We already have a precedence of this line of argument in Tertullian who implicates the performers and the audience of bearing the 'truth' of the same idolatrous lie of the pagan myths. The only significant difference in this case is that, unlike pagan theatre in these Christian plays, if we accept the truth of the vices we would also logically have to accept the portrayal of Christ and other virtuous characters as part of the single Christian truth. In short, theatre has to be given the phenomenological status of an experience. In other words, theatre could no longer be seen as an allegorical or metaphorical interpretation of a Christian truth which can be regulated and codified through symbolic conventions and institutional authority but a direct and immediate experience of the Christian truth.

Here perhaps lies the source of the conflict between an allegorical and a phenomenological position of looking at representation which makes possible a whole body of debates and controversies surrounding the problem of theatricality in the Middle Ages.[6] Symptomatic of this ambivalence is a treatise on miracle plays entitled *A Treatise of Miraclis Pleying,* perhaps the chief anti-theatrical document from the 14th century of possible lollard inspiration. Written in the form of sermon it displays what Barish calls "a valuable glimpse of what one may assume to have been a vigorous minority opinion during the growing years of the Wycliffite movement" (Ibid., n.d., 67-68). The primary accent of such anti-theatrical prejudice seems to be on the concept of 'play'. Tertullian, or for that matter, Augustine refused theatre on the basis of its deceptive form which was metaphorically used to understand the falsity of pagan culture and religion including its mythology which was the content of these plays. For these early Church Fathers, in the discourse against theatre, form and content perfectly reflected each other contributing to the logic of its falsity. For the 14th century preacher however this was not possible because the content of these plays was Christian par excellence and could not be part of a simple dualist game of true and false. However the value attributed to the form of theatre had not changed and this becomes the ground of his polemics against such performative practices as the miracle plays. In an almost obsessive fashion the preacher fixes on to the word 'play' in order to condemn these forms of representation. At the heart of this assault is an understanding of play not merely as make belief or fiction but a question of wilful deception. Symptomatic of the 'Lollardy' of the treatise, as Barish suggests is the frequent use of the Scripture to justify many of his arguments particularly related to the signification attached to the term 'play'. Therefore the scene from the Old Testament where Ismael is seen by his mother, Sara, playing with his brother Issac is highlighted by the preacher as suggestive of the beguiling nature of play. He suggests that it is through playing that the plot to "deprive Issac of his heritage" (Barish 1981, 72) was conceived by Ismael and his mother. Hence 'play' is already associated with a certain intentionality which makes its appearance very different from its reality. We have already seen how Augustine evokes the paradox of intentionality in relation to the actor who, intending to be someone else (a character) on stage, fulfils the demand of who he truly is (an actor). To be more precise, according to Augustine, the actor while intending to be false comes to truth. In the case of our preacher however the process is inverted. The intentionality of depicting the truth of Christ's passion would inevitably end up being false because of the deceptive nature of play. Play would always introduce a distance between the original event of truth and its effort to re-enter the world through its re-enactment. The phenomenological proximity envisaged by the players is a false proximity according to our preacher. The interval which separates the *experience* of these plays from the "truth" they propose to propagate is also intensified, according to him by the non-serious nature of these plays which are meant for amusement. The denunciation of theatre on the basis of the worldly pleasure it generates was nothing new to Christianity at the time. We have already discussed this in our section on Augustine. However what is interesting in this case is his discussion on laughter which he clearly associates with the bundle of signification devoted to play. Christ, he assures us, never laughed but shed his blood and tears in continual penance for our sins thereby chastising us to remember that "all our doing here should be done in penance, in disciplining our flesh" (Ibid., n.d., 68). Clearly what is at stake here is a level of experience which the theatre cannot provide according to our preacher. Not because it is allegorical or symbolic. As we shall see in a while he is quite aware of the immediacy of bodies in theatre and its efficacious power on the audience. Rather he evokes a kind of penitential discourse of the flesh as against any use of body for pleasure and amusement.

Play and the Axiomatics of Pain

Though he does not give any structural or ontological explanation to this problem of amusement we can surmise from some of his remarks that what he is primarily concerned with is the impossibility of re-enactment of the event of Christ through a medium like "play" which by definition is non-serious. As Johan Huizinga points out, non-seriousness is an important element of play. However because it does not announce any positive qualities of play, it is extraordinarily easy to refute[7]. As we move from "play which is non-serious" to "play which is not serious," we find its fictitious and deceptive nature correspond to its capacity to generate laughter and amusement. Rather than the simplistic argument that behind such logic of amusement is the puritanical dread of pleasure,[8] we would argue that the central contradiction does not revolve around pleasure which is only a by-product of the foundational dispute. The fundamental problem is to conceive of a way to access the incorporeal object of Christian truth. Whether a mode which proffers distance is capable of re-producing the 'real' of the truth of Christ or whether the only possible way to access it is through a subjective moment of incorporeal transformation. Therefore in response to such claims that the plays offer harmless recreation aimed at conversion the preacher argues that there is nothing genuinely recreational in attending plays because true recreation for a Christian consists in merciful and compassionate actions for his unfortunate neighbour. The recreation offered by the plays is a "feigned" recreation. What the plays offer is a sort of pleasure which does not immediately concern the self but a pleasure which is generated by viewing things at a distance from the self. While the 'true' pleasure for a Christian lies in compassion which introduces an immediacy of experience which is not available in the concept of a play. The falsity of pleasure is therefore not only related to the deceptive nature of play which offers worldly objects for pleasure. Laughter and amusement introduce distance at the heart of a materialist experience of flesh which ought to be endured in "fear and trembling". Amusement therefore threatens the experience of bodies and flesh outside penance which according to our preacher "'utterly reverses' the works of Christ" (Ibid., n.d., 68). Play is therefore associated not only with laughter and the distance it generates which obstructs any phenomenological experience of the "eros" of the truth of Christ but it is connected with an effect of putting the world out of joint, of upending the order of the world. But play according to our preacher does more than simply invert the world. It generates mirth which "undisposith a man to paciencie". For the preacher mirth which is integral to play is related to amusement, being distinct from any Christian idea of recreation because of its association with laughter.[9] To un-work the disposition of man, turning him away from the divine path to worldly pleasure is the function of such play, informed with laughter and amusement. Therefore laughter and play produce a turning of the self upon itself moving away from what is its true spiritual requirement. The pleasure of worldly laughter and play turns a man back on to himself because through such enactment man wants to be visible to the world and not be visible to God. Since man himself belongs to the world such a movement is necessarily a turning away from that which lies beyond him and his world, namely the divine world of spirit. Therefore to "undisposith a man" is to make him lose his orientation in the world so that he is no longer oriented to the world of spirit through the sacrifice of his flesh but rather be attached to his flesh by being distant from the truth. Only fear and trembling sustain our belief in him because it orients us towards divinity ("Godward holdith") by digging into our flesh the memory of truth while amusement and laughter fosters forgetfulness. Therefore all claims to the didactic nature of these plays are refuted by the preacher on account of the frivolous distance which sits at the heart of any phenomenological experience of such plays. The pleasure they generate are improper for any Christian pedagogic purpose because the object of such pleasure is concerned to the self immediately. A paradoxical set of movements are involved here which makes such pleasure unacceptable. Firstly such pleasure enjoyment turns man away from Christian truth which is beyond the world and the self which is part of the world. However, and this is the paradoxical second point, the only way to gain access to such otherworldly truth is to turn upon oneself and be concerned only with things which concern the self and its conscience–to provide it with spiritual nourishment and renunciation of flesh. Plays, on the other hand, divert one's concern for the self by turning the gaze on to the other (scene), which in turn, orients the gaze away from the divine world beyond and brings it back to this world.

Though fear and trembling are also 'feelings' (*sensum*)[10] related to a phenomenological experience of reality which is informed with penance and mortification of flesh, such experience also inscribes the truth upon memory. On the one hand, such penitentiary practices as mortification of flesh and other techniques of inflicting pain on one's own body must be seen as a test to remind oneself that one is worthy of the truth. To approach the truth in fear and trembling does not mean that one would gain access to such truth immediately. Rather it is an attempt to constantly remind oneself that one has a disposition towards the divine truth. The pedagogic project is naturally antithetical to our preacher's understanding of theatre because the former seeks orientation while the latter disorients. On the other hand, as scholars like Jody Enders have shown, the architecture of the body in pain was intimately related to medieval rhetorical practices where pain was associated with both the invention of truth and memory. The phenomenological experience of bodily pain would therefore create what Nietzsche would later call "one of the most enduring psychological axioms" (Nietzsche 1994, 192). Such an effort to vicariously inflict pain so that the truth of Christianity "scorches the memory" finally leads us to believe that it was not the phenomenological experience of the immediacy of bodies which would lead our preacher to denounce theatre. It was not the allegorical desire to approach the truth of Christianity through codified means and institutional norms which was the basis of his attack of miracle plays as if the plays were too immediate and sensual. We would rather argue that what was lacking in the play, according to this treatise was that impossible immediacy of the experience of truth. What the plays constantly introduced through their display of bodies and pleasure was a distance and an inability to repeat the truth. What these plays ended up repeating was a constant failure to represent the truth of the Passion. The preacher could not allow such negation to be miraculously transformed into an affirmation of truth.

When the preacher argues that painting could be a viable mode of Christian pedagogy because they can be like "books" for the unlettered, maintaining their innocence and keeping their appeal to the carnal senses to the minimum he completely rejects plays from any such visual effects of didactic nature. For him the visibility of these plays is never innocent, unlike painting, because they always proffer lies and deception. What is unacceptable for the preacher in the phenomenological experience of theatre is the fact that it contaminates the form with its content, infecting its content of Christian truth with the deceptive nature constitutive of its form. The intentionality of the painting is always consistent with what it represents while the intentionality of the actor who wants to re-enact the truth of Christ is always divided between the truth of the event and the falsity of his actions on behalf of someone else. Therefore even more than the enactment of these plays, the preacher criticizes the claim of those who see these plays to be edifying. The inconsistency between what these plays truly are (amusement) and what they claim to be (didactic) make them in the eyes of the preacher more wicked than the plays themselves. The severity of the accusation has perhaps something to do with the fact that in this case it is not only that the plays are deemed didactic, which they are not, but in this very gesture of deception—calling something that which it is not—Christian pedagogy itself becomes theatrical.

What the treatise against miracle plays finally testifies to is the nagging inconsistency inherent to all representative practices when it starts to function under the axiom of revealed truth. Theatre becomes a paradigm of the problem of representation because it ends up repeating its own configuration more than what it ought to represent. From a certain point of view theatre is unable to sacrifice its own materiality while at the same time it exposes its materiality as deception, devoid of any meaning, unable to come under the subjection of a beyond. Christianity on the other hand was looking for a consistent logic which would explain the materiality of our world as conditioned by a divine and spiritual world beyond which analogically gives this world its meaning, despite being completely separated from it. The construction of an allegorical reality of such a spiritual beyond as opposed to the violent physicality of the material world gave Christian imagination an opportunity to respond to such an inconsistency.

The Figural Interpretation of History

In the intellectual climate of the 12th century, heavily influenced by an Augustinian tradition, it is no wonder that vernacular religious theatre would pose a linguistic and metaphysical complexity which purely Latin liturgical drama seldom displayed. We can take the example of one such para-liturgical text from the mid-12th century titled *Le Mystere d'Adam* to briefly consider how language, particularly, the form of dialogue operated in service of a Christian metaphysics of dualism. This anonymous play written right before the scholastic upsurge bears testimony to an intellectual tradition devoted to the craft of theatre which is mostly neglected in traditional histories of medieval theatre. The play almost seems to be a creative 'double' of the theory of language developed by Augustine and the early church fathers. As a para-liturgical text, the play seems to embody its threshold status oscillating between Latin and vernacular French. As we shall see in a while the entire play seems to be informed with this doubling effect which precariously places it in the metaphorical position of a 'double'–a dramatic fiction of liturgical truth. But what is even more interesting is the play's internal constitution which, in deviating from its original liturgical truth, also tries to respond to the problem it generates through its very structure. By the same token it responds to the conflict between a phenomenological and an allegorical interpretation of liturgy which has been the source of a number of controversies.

We know that an Augustinian theory of language reflects the ontological status of man who is essentially a sign-maker. However God created the cosmos by an original performative utterance despite being absolutely distinct from the substance of his creation. Man who is of this created material world is made in the image of God but his spirit is alienated from God. This is why the language of man will always already be insufficient to express the *incorporeal* and uncreated God. The language of man will always carry within itself the lack of this incorporeality being always in some sense corporeal, referring either to the corporeal words or corporeal things which all belong to this world. However under the mastery of the Incorporeal One, language can create things by speaking about them which would be part of his created world. Augustine remarks, "He alone is ineffable, who spoke, and all this were made. He spoke and we were made" (Vance 1986, 190). So language is both the 'medium' of creation and the created 'thing' which gives it a singular status in Augustinian thinking as a way of accessing divine incorporeality. However language of man is the perfect medium for human beings to come into a social contract thereby giving language its horizontal axis. Therefore dialogue between men can be traced along this horizontal axis when conventional signs (*signa data*) invoke a common will to signify (*voluntas significandi*). But by the same token language becomes the instrument of subversion of *will* and the conflict generated by the imperialist desire of imposing a single linguistic will as testified by the tower of Babel. The internal dissonance of language despite its horizontal function of producing the most basic of all social contract becomes evident when we examine the Augustinian attitude towards the internal function of *how* signs operate. Here Augustine talks of the vocal sign (*vox*) which is characterised by its pure corporeality and externality and which stands as the material *signans* for the inner word or *signatum* which he also calls an inner voice (*vox interioris*). But where things become complicated and relevant for our purpose is when Augustine proposes this inner voice as also a *signans* whose truth is a incorporeal event, a flash of intuition which we cannot maintain in our memory except through *supplementation*. So *signans* (signifier) is always already supplementary to the *signatum* (signified) which is always already absent. Language therefore functions through such a process of supplementation of that which is always already absent, which is always already gone in a flash. A proliferation of these supplementary *signans* and inherent lack of the original *signatum* articulates the structure of the language of man. Therefore enunciation which is to say the passage of thought into words would always be a failure. Augustine observes, "My own discourse is almost always displeasing to me as well.... when I realize that they are inferior to my idea (notus), I become sad that my language does not suffice with regard to my mind" (Vance 1986, 192). However such failure of words to repeat thoughts is not seen as a moment of absolute negation by Augustine. It is perhaps here that we comes across the most radical and interesting interpretation of the Augustinian theory of language. Rather than being subsumed by the sadness of the impossibility of language to repeat Augustine talks of the miraculous trace (*vestigium*) it leaves:

> It leaves, in some miraculous way, however, traces (vestigial) in my memory, and these persist in my memory during the brief expression of syllables and allow us to produce those audible sounds that we call language (lingua), be it Greek, Latin, Hebrew, or some other, whether these signs are merely thought by the mind or proffered vocally. But the traces themselves are neither Latin nor Greek nor Hebrew nor are proper to any people. They are a production of the mind just as facial expression are of the body...It is certainly not possible for us to express or manifest these traces which the conception imprints in the memory to our listeners in the same way that our facial expressions are open and manifest... Thus we may imagine how different the sound of the voice is from a flash of the intellect, since it does not even resemble the impressions it leaves on memory. (Ibid., n.d., 192)

What is at stake here is the event of thought—"the flash of the intellect"—as the incorporeal object which cannot be repeated but which nevertheless leaves its trace on to language. Such a trace is nothing but the original difference of that which separates language from thinking. The difference which separates material language from the immateriality of the flash of the event of though is also constitutive of language. This difference is the very being of the trace which makes language possible. By the same logic, it is through the trace that language manages to repeat the difference which sustains it and makes it possible. The failure of representation is therefore transformed into the very affirmation of the trace of that which cannot be expressed or manifested. Under the divine mastery of the Incorporeal One, language might corporeally create things including itself. But the language of man, exposed and vulnerable as it is to divine mercy can never allow man to become its master. Whenever man has tried to become the master of his language what has followed is the fate of the tower of Babel. Rather, language carries within itself the trace of the incorporeality of the event of thinking. Of this trace he should never presume to be the master thereby enjoying verbal signs rather than using them. For Augustine verbal signs ought to be only used and not enjoyed because in the final analysis one uses language only in the name of the trace. When Augustine notes, "If it is a carnal slavery to adhere to a usefully instituted sign instead of to the thing it was designated to signify" (Ibid., n.d., 192) then it's not only the materiality of language that Augustine raises a cautious finger at. To use language is to liberate the trace of that incorporeal object from which it is eternally separated but which is constitutive of language.

To use language rather than enjoy it is also to move from the horizontal axis of language to find a vertical axis. It is the use of language for prophesy which is meant for the consolation and hope of men. Therefore prophesy is not the language of mysteries which no one understands because in it man speaks in a tongue meant for God. In prophetic language he uses his tongue to speak to men but such that it would bear the trace of that which is beyond. The language of prophesy is the true use of language because here worldly signs stand for that which is beyond. Only its trace is borne by language 'figuratively'.

Eric Auerbach has brilliantly shown how with Augustine there is a significant shift which happens in the figurative use of language. Already with Tertullian, he argues, a change in the theory of tropes and figures is distinguishable. With Tertullian's interpretation of the Old Testament, we notice that naming of certain characters offered a phenomenal prophesy or prefiguration of the Saviour to come. This unique feature of phenomenal prophesy of the Church father which Auerbach identifies leads to an emergence of a new meaning attributed to the problem of "figura" as it emerges from the Greco-Roman world. (*figura* comes from the same body of words as *fingere*, *figulus*, *fictor* and *effigies* meaning plastic forms). Tertullian however does not confine himself to a simple interpretation of the persons and events of the Old Testament as prefigurations of the New Testament and its history of salvation. He introduces an aggressive realism to this entire interpretative exercise, not only disallowing all spiritual and allegorical interpretation of the Old Testament but arguing that the prophetic figure is as much a concrete historical fact as is its fulfilment by concrete historical facts. "Christ confirming his figures" (Auerbach 1984, 30). This pattern of what Auerbach calls figure and its fulfilment informs Christian use of language from its beginning. However while Tertullian gave a concrete phenomenological and historical substance to both the figure and its fulfilment–for example, in one passage from his treatise *Adversus Marcionem*, Tertullian talks of the concrete and historical reality of Law as juxtaposed with Christ as its fulfilment (Ibid., n.d., 32)–the only spiritual function is left to the intellect which recognizes this relation between the figure and its fulfilment. In Augustine, however, things become more complicated. On the one hand, Augustine continues to attribute phenomenal reality to the figure using it as both static and dynamic forms of the body. Therefore he understood the Old Testament as phenomenal prophesy along with his colleges recognizing them as letters of Scripture in their carnal and historical reality whose hidden meaning is revealed in their Christian fulfilment. However in this interpretation of the figural dimension of the Old Testament he introduces a three stage development. As Auerbach notes, "in the confrontation of the two poles, figure and fulfilment" Augustine introduces a break. "The Law or history of the Jews as a prophetic figura for the appearance of Christ; the incarnation as fulfilment of this figura and at the same time as a new promise of the end of the world and the Last

Judgement; and finally the future occurrence of these events as ultimate fulfilment" (ibid. n.d., 41). The ultimate fulfilment being placed outside history and temporality, Augustine manages to impose a transcendental and supra-temporal meaning to concrete phenomenal history. This makes possible the concrete event to be transposed, albeit completely preserved, outside temporality and into eternity. It is this metaphorical interpretation of history based upon an arche-separation between the phenomenal figure and its allegorical fulfilment that is played out in Augustine's theory of language which in turn produces the ground for the linguistic deployment in a play like the *Le Mystere d'Adam.*

Dual Axis

Eugene Vance has noted how the entire play is structured like a "primeval metaphor" in a truly Augustinian sense who defined metaphor as the usurpation of the proper by an improper signification. The *mise en scène* of the play is an evocation of nothing less than the usurpation of paradise–the proper place for man–by a Satanic gesture. The use of bilingualism enhances this division between the proper and the improper where vernacular is used to depict the fall and the fate of man, while Latin implies the pure and proper place of paradise. However vernacular is also used as a language of prophesy, promising the spiritual future of Christ's second coming. If metaphor is the improper "usurpation" of language for Augustine, then its highest possibility lies in its figural use. Again the difference between Latin and vernacular is not only employed to identify two distinct worlds but to convey the theological meaning of *via negative* which is the condition of worldly reality. As Augustine explains elsewhere, the material order is constituted as a result of the primary denial of God, embodied in the fall. Therefore, the material order is the world of passion which is a "region of difference", a region which is not only different from God but different from itself because having its true essence in God, the condition of its possibility of existence can only be accessed *via negative.* We see this difference being played out in the opening scene when Adam and Eve stand together in front of, what Vance calls, God's *Figura*. God is depicted as a pure 'metaphor', as an 'emanation'. As the dialogue between God and Adam commences, we are made aware of the curious progression of language along a vertical axis where God in his omnipotence and omnipresence exchanges words with Adam which reflects a vertical hierarchy. Hence the sequence of speech acts before the fall corresponds to commands, reminders, consents, warnings. For example when 'Figura' instructs Adam of his creation from dust of earth, Adam consents through his confirmation "I know it very well" (Vance 1986). Before the fall the dialogue between Satan and Adam illustrate less words spoken by individualized characters than abstract images of good and evil caught in their tension. Hence here we have such declaration of Law as when Adam announces "He must be judged by law of treason who perjures himself and betrays his lord" (Ibid., n.d., 198). This sequence of dialogues however quickly changes even before the fall with the entry of both Satan and Eve on stage. With the anticipation of the fall looming, speech acts become illocutionary, and persuasive, illustrative not only of the seduction of Eve by Satan but a kind of language which starts operating along a horizontal axis among equals. As Satan opens his discourse to seduce God's Word which is always "simple and straight forward" (Anslem) it becomes adorned by similes and metaphors. The improper usurpation of signification, in other words, metaphorical use of language starts to reflect the rift Satan is going to imminently introduce into the couple (Adam and Eve) which would eventually produce the separation between Man and God. Hence Satan first tries to turn Eve away from God and her husband on to herself by comparing her beauty with worldly sensual objects, "You are frail and tender, and fresher than a rose" (Ibid., n.d., 202). Such 'usurpation' of the signification of beauty lead Satan to usurp her continuing devotion for her husband and her Creator. "The creator made a bad couple of you: you are too tender, he too hard". But all this is only possible because "Eve welcomes Satan as her interlocutor from the start" (Ibid., n.d., 201). Language follows its horizontal trajectory after the Fall, in the scenes between Abel and Cain, who are now depicted as individualized characters engaged in conversation between brothers.[11] However the horizontal axis is soon replaced by a language of prophesy, reminiscent of Augustine's figural interpretation of history. The Procession of Prophets, as Vance correctly indicates, concludes the linguist itinerary by returning to the poetics of language. But unlike the erotic courtly poetry which is implicitly denounced through Satan's use of such courtly language to seduce Eve, the new poetics which is evoked is in praise of God, a language of confession in the spirit of sacrifice. When Shadrah, Meshach, and Abednego sing from the sacrificial flames of Nebuchadnezzar's furnace, it is not the materiality of a phenomenal world which is extolled but the figurality of a world to come "There, from the burning fire, they sang out such beautiful verses that it seemed like angels from the sky" (Ibid., n.d., 207). But the most stunning example of this third movement of language comes through the appendage to the ending of the Procession of Prophets which, according to Vance, the scribe of the Tours manuscript had added as a supplement because he was doubtful of the ending.[12] Called *Quinze Signes du jugements derneir* (fifteen signs of the last judgement) this fragment functions as *supplementary* to the entire text having no direct or narrative relation to it. To that extent it is "at once the most brilliant writing in the whole play and the most autonomous from the sacred, from *auctoritas*, since it amplifies no specific biblical or liturgical text" (Ibid., n.d., 209). From our perspective we could argue that this supplementary text functions as that figural fragment which returns the text to its *here and now* from the promise of an allegorical future. Rather than the pure figural promise of a supra-temporal moment in the future, it transfers the text back to its "marvellous"[13] present by accenting on its complete separation from the transcendental journey of language.

Be that as it may, the play *Le Mystere d'Adam* testifies to a general structure of mystery plays to create perpendicular axis of two world orders. Even after liturgical drama leaves the 'Latin' church yard and starts proliferating in the 'vernacular' market square, this metaphysics of dualism is not abandoned. The use of violent realism of bodily torture and mutilation in some of these plays can be seen as rhetorical device[14] to accentuate this brutal opposition between a violent and impermanent temporal order and an eternal order of divine transcendence. Spirit and matter becomes the two great ingredients of medieval theatre whose separation is intensified in order to chastise or overcome in the promise of a redemptive future but they are never allowed to contaminate each other.

It is in the world of the comic, however, that new mixtures are concocted.

Section II

Comedy and the Limits of Materialist Imagination

A False Dualism

In a letter issued by the faculty of theology at the University of Paris on March 12, 1445 to the prelates and chapters of France, we find a reflection of medieval Christianity's general tendency towards the comic. Denouncing the abuses they associated with a certain practice called the "feast of fools" they wrote that they felt compelled "to describe how much we abhor and how much we execrate a certain kind of ritual of merriment, which is called by its organizers the Feast of Fools"[15] (Harris 2011, 1). Such "abhorrence" for merriment has been regarded as the general tendency of Christianity's response towards the comic. The denunciation of the comic has been argued to be acute than any other theatrical genres. For example, the pioneering work of E.K. Chambers, a formidable expert in the area of medieval theatre, at the turn of the 20th century saw the feast of fools as part of a folk tradition extending back to paganism rather than part of the liturgical drama emerging out of the church in the 12th century. This he argued to be a consequence of this general abhorrence towards the comic. Umberto Eco in the early 1990s in his bestseller *The Name of the Rose* affirmed this response of medieval Christianity in the fanatical monk, Jorge, he conjured up. Jorge would eventually burn down a library of a medieval monastery rather than let the second book of *Poetics*, where Aristotle had legendarily discussed comedy and laughter, come to light in a Christian world. Jorge makes it his mission of life for which he embraces 'martyrdom' to prevent the world from learning about the book. He believes laughter is Satan's invention and would destroy the very foundations of Christian order. But Eco creates another figure who represents the liberal and enlightened aspect of medieval Christianity in the figure of the Franciscan monk William of Baskerville who not only sees Christianity as a cultural and intellectual enterprise but defends laughter as a fundamental human gesture against Jorge's fanatism. As Alenka Zupancic warns us, such oppositional logic informing the concept of laughter and the comic is not only too simplistic but serves an ideological function. Eco's liberal figure who defends the comic and stands against fanaticism reflects a secular imagination of a liberal democratic culture. In fact in our late capitalist societies, to avoid any sort of dogma whether religious, intellectual or political becomes the very marker of an ideology which seeks out the distance offered by laughter. This distance Zupancic argues—following Mladen Dolar and others who have talked of the same problem with this novel—provides us with the physiological ease in which ideology can truly assert its force. Zupancic cites Dolar here:

> It is only with laughter that we become ideological subjects, withdrawn from the immediate pressure of ideological claims to a free enclave. It is only when we laugh and breathe freely that ideology truly has a hold on us—it is only here that it starts functioning fully as ideology, with the specifically ideological means which are suppose to assure our free consent and the appearance of spontaneity, eliminating the need for the non-ideological means of outside constraint. (Zupancic 2008, 4)

Comic in this sense gives the liberal subject the semblance of freedom or rather it manipulates the desire for freedom so that ideology can actualize itself through such categories like 'positive attitude', 'free will' and ironical humour. At a time when the dominant ideology has become a suspicion of all ideologies and when affirmation of freedom corresponds with a state of un-freedom it is important to understand the function of the comic within certain obvious ideological discourses like Christianity outside any simplistic oppositional logic. In any case comedy has an ideological function within Christianity which exactly corresponds with the ironical distance that laughter generates and the sense of superiority required for ideological reaffirmation of subjectivity. This is what we would call the presence of the "ridiculous" strain of the comic within Christianity. But there is yet another more radical strain of the comic within Christianity which is related to the idea of "folly". We shall come to that in a while. Let us simply rearticulate our hypothesis. It is our contention that at least two strains of the comic is made available to us from the history of Christian discourse in the Middle Ages: the "ridiculous" and the "foolish". Of course this does not exhaust in any sense the innumerable comic genres that developed in and around the church and which were deeply enmeshed in a number of folk performative traditions. Neither does it imply that these two strains were strictly distinct and never crossed paths. On the contrary, they constantly overlapped each other: for example the way feast of fools served as part of liturgical practices in the 12th-13th century as recent studies have shown[16] makes the analysis of the idea of the comic within Christianity so much more difficult during this period.

Part I: Alienation or the Ridiculous Character of Comedy

During the 4th century, John Chrysostom wrote a number of treatises against a certain "ascetic" practice prevalent among believers of his time which was termed Spiritual Marriage. Though studies in early Christianity came up with the term 'spiritual marriage' which some recent scholars have called 'pseudo-marriage', this non-legalised and non-sexualised cohabitation of Christian heterosexual couples lacks an 'positive term' which has come down to us from this period. The lack of any positive term has marked the debate around this practice since late antiquity, when late antique authors not finding any existent terminology to designate a practice of women living in this manner invented the term *subintroductae*–"females brought in surreptitiously". A translation of the Greek term *syneisakatoi* which implied "people brought into [the house] together" or more negatively "illegitimately introduced", this terminological confusion already anticipates the nature of the development of the discourse of Spiritual Marriage within Christianity as something negatively marked, identified with such meaning as 'surreptitious' or 'illegitimate'. One of the fundamental reasons for this unilateral treatment of the practice is the severe lack of writings by subjects who practised spiritual marriage. And yet the ambiguity of the terminology, as we shall see, betrayed the curious position of these couples who were both respected as genuine ascetics by society and denounced by the many of the early church fathers. Chrysostom himself calls the women "virgins" while designating the men as monks who meant to do well but were led astray by their own efforts. What was at stake was a certain idea of "liturgy" associated with the practice where men were assumed to perform a "service" as part of a "religious duty" towards weak and needy women by giving them financial and material support as dictated by the Christian doctrine of charity. It is this idea of equating such a 'form of life' as liturgical that prompts Chrysostom to use certain comic techniques, primarily borrowed from the tradition of old comedy (Aristophanes) as rhetorical devices to express his hostility towards it. What was implicit but perhaps most fundamental to the idea of spiritual marriage was an idea of friendship between the sexes beyond the gendered roles assigned to them by Christianity. It was an idea of friendship which at least to Chrysostom's philosophical mind carried the danger of corresponding to the Aristotelian theory of friendship. We shall return to this important aspect of the discourse in a while. Spiritual marriage was therefore seen as a form of life which claimed to be in the name of religious duty. Chrysostom uses the term *leitourgian* to designate chores performed by married women as well as any act of Christian love or charity but he refuses to accept this "service of women" as part of any Christian doctrine of religious duty. Therefore the main trajectory of Chrysostom's polemics against spiritual marriage is to disprove such a way of life as part of any Christian idea of religious duty. The deployment of the comic technique is therefore a rhetorical strategy to develop an argument which would create the necessary ironical distance separating such a form of life from any idea of Christian subjectivization. From the point of view of

Spiritual marriage, they were championing Jesus words promising a radically new era in which hierarchies of this world–essentially gender hierarchies–that structure and divide society are upended. These men and women were claiming to practice a way of life where men and women rejoiced in each other's "holy" company in order to concretely realise such an utopic vision of paradise on earth. What Augustine would later call "vita beata", a possibility of life which could only be truly realised in the *Civitas Dei* was something these "ascetics" claimed to have actualized within their household creating something akin to a divine "oikonomia" in so far as the economy of the trinity was sustained by a logic of equality and not hierarchy. It was such an upended world created within the general economy of this world that Chrysostom wanted to set right, which is to say turn back to its former position. If one of the fundamental function of comedy is to turn any world upside down, then its strategic use to ridicule an utopic vision can only be to turn it back to its existing status: a turning-upside down-of-that-which-is-already-upside-down, so to speak. In other words, to use comedy to bring comedy to an end where things can return to normal. It is this function of the comic that we will try to briefly analyse here.

The least that can be said about these practices was that they were rigorous enough to have found recognition even from Chrysostom. Therefore Chrysostom had to invent new ways to denounce and expose the truth about these practices besides calling them hypocritical and false at face value. For example, he could not and did not claim that the women living with the men were not biologically virgins. On the contrary their virgin status made them exceptionally susceptible to such an attack because it was argued that a virgin who could "discuss things frankly with a man, sit by him, look straight in his face, laugh in his presence" (Leyerle 2001, 87) was nothing less than a prostitute. So from a certain perspective these couples were faithful to their form of life which made them even more dangerous and harmful. Similarly the men were denounced for their absolute devotion to these women which was seen not as a form of spiritual freedom but obvious servility towards the 'weaker sex' and therefore 'unnatural' and a form of perversion. The form of life for these couples was therefore sustained by a style which was rigorous and completely self-evident. It was a style where a masculine public life characterized the females and a private feminine life characterized the males according to existent norms. But insofar as the enactment of such an upside down world was concerned it was rigorous, self-evident and therefore serious. It was this seriousness with which these couples performed their lives—a seriousness from which they could not be separated at any cost (particularly the women) under normal circumstances—which became the condition for the comic hostility ushered upon the men while simultaneously providing the reason for both tragic pity and violent animosity for the women. The comic in this context, as we shall see, was a method to separate the Christian subject from such a form of life, so that such a life could be isolated as exceptional and sustained (for men) by a ridiculous yet extremely dangerous logic of sexual desire. While for women it was sustained not by any sexual desire being themselves the objects of such desire but the tragic yet even more deadly desire for worldly glory. This process aimed at establishing an immediate connection between the biological status of their sexes and socio-cultural and religious value.

Chrysostom's use of the comic technique as a rhetorical devise to attack spiritual marriage was based on that aspect of comedy which thrives on the disengagement of the audience. Comedy, as Blake Leyrele suggests in this context, works through an implicit hostility which rather than "provoking an individual identification between spectator and actor, which leads to a sense of personal cleansing or catharsis, comedy creates a sense of solidarity among the audience by evoking communal recognition and condemnation of a dissident element" (Leyerle 2001, 106). The implicit hostility, Leyerle further argues is channelized towards a pedagogic function to "correct through degradation" (Ibid., n.d., 106). Rather than destabilizing any norms through humour, comedy in Chrysostom provides that site where the destabilizing and subversive effects of a practice could be ridiculed and neutralized at the same time. The fundamental intention of employing such a technique was to compare the essence of the practice of spiritual marriage to that of theatre, namely, deception. Chrysostom's central rhetorical motive was to persuade not only his audience but also those who participated in such practices, particularly the men, to call the bluff of spiritual marriage in order to abolish such a social malpractice and a religious sham. Comedy therefore functioned as a rhetorical technique which would ensure the revelation of the truth; a truth which was already available to the true Christian subject who practices an ethics of self-knowledge. But for common men who are carried away by the display and spectacle of these practices, Chrysostom's comic technique would provide the required objectivity offered by ironic distance to gain access to the truth behind such claims to a higher form of life. Comedy functioned here as a corrective principle as Henri Bengson would later argue.

Like many of Aristophanes' opening lines, Chrysostom begins the treatise by declaring that an extraordinary and new situation has arrived which calls for both an in-depth scrutiny and comic intervention. He remarks:

> In our ancestor's era, two justifications were given for men and women living together. The first marriage, was ancient, licit, and sensible... and the other, prostitution, ...was unjust and illegitimate. But in our time, a third way of life has been dreamed up, something new and incredible. (Ibid., n.d., 104)

Leyerle points out that the treatise remains faithful to the formal structure of old comedy and immediately follows the articulation of a "happy new idea" with an agon or debate where objections to the inaugural proposition are offered and counter-argued. True to this form, Chrysostom begins with a plea that his audience should not misjudge him if he tends to misrepresent the situation, which was a prevalent tradition to invite an audience to a comic debate in the satirical tradition of his day[17]. This was followed by an interlude, akin to what in Aristophanes' time was called parabasis, where the audience was addressed directly by the choral leader who either offered some political commentary or praised the dramatist. Similarly, Chrysostom seems to interrupt his dialogue and offer his commentary on how punishment should be in proportion to the sin committed and also accuses the men directly of being blasphemous in their practices. He then moves on, in the tradition of this genres to imagine a series of vignettes culminating in two scenarios where he compares the monk to an armed solider who leaves the battlefield to sit among womenfolk while the second conjures up the image of a lion which has been domesticated by feminine affection and reduced to a plaything.

But it is during his supposed display of humility excusing himself for any excess while inviting the readers to debate on the proposed newness of spiritual marriage that he betrays the rhetorical ploy behind using such a technique. Chrysostom pauses in the midst of any such anticipated objection to casually announce that surely pleasure must be the only persuasive reason for such a liaison to take place. Chrysostom rejects such a relationship without even mentioning any possibility of an Aristotelian logic of friendship among equals on the basis of virtue which could prompt such relation. Aristotle in his theory of friendship gives such an equality of virtue as the highest reason for friendship while pleasure or profit as the lowest, Chrysostom takes up the element of pleasuring and plays on the theme for comic ends. While the monks protest that their relation with these women are based upon an enjoyment of a pleasure based upon shared values and outlooks, Chrysostom offers a more insidious and sensual explanation. He goes on to say that the sensual pleasure of spiritual marriage is perhaps more intense than conventional marriages because of the impossibility of consummation of the marriage. Accepting the monk's argument that intercourse might very well not occur in such relation, he argues that such a state increases sexual pleasure rather than abolishing it. Deferral and displacement, according to Chrysostom is the true substance of pleasure because as he argues "even at the moment of intercourse there seems to be no pleasure, since by effecting the union, he has extinguished pleasure" (Ibid., n.d., 111). We see here the quintessentially Christian notion of concupiscence which extracts desire out of what the ancients termed *aphrodisia*—where distinctions between desire, sexual enactment, enjoyment and pleasure remained internal to the meaning. Foucault reminds us that sexuality in the Classical world would remain intricately liked with aphrodisiac which was treated as an ethical substance around which sexual norms were devised. With Christianity however, as we see from Chrysostom's explicit use of the term, pleasure comes to be exclusively identified with desire as lack or longing. This offers Chrysostom the necessary logic to give pleasure its sensual connotation thereby exposing the discrepancy between what the monks say and the truth, thereby also providing the comic substance to the scene. But such an understanding of pleasure as desire determined by lack also gives it its deceptive quality. Being able to produce and transmit itself through such a seemingly innocuous medium as that of vision, such *modus operandi* of desire had to be constantly kept under mental surveillance. It also makes desire very similar to theatre in its masking itself in something else like that of pain. This ambiguous relation between pain and pleasure not only makes desire theatrical but allows Chrysostom to imagine desire not only as sin but also as punishment for it. Leyerle points out:

> To illustrate further how proximity exacerbates desire, Chrysostom points to Adam after the Fall, who was placed by God just beyond the pale of Paradice to give him "a more constant punishment". Adam's long gaze at the paradise from which he was barred mirrors the eyes of the monks on the virgins' forbidden bodies. Only the devil, Chrysostom suggests, could stir up such an 'unnatural combination' of pleasure and pain in their souls. (Ibid., n.d., 114)

Theatre coming from the Greek *theatron*–literally meaning a place where one sees, a place *for* watching, a place *from* where one sees–truly becomes the devil's abode. The devil who is the other–the double–of God has the capacity beside God to give pleasure through pain and vice verse. It is this devilish theatricality of desire that one has to be always vigilant about by gaining knowledge about one's own self, by examining what is hidden behind things which seem innocuous or sometimes even spiritual. Such a subjective exercise or a technique of the self is determined by a method of clearing some distance within one's own self thereby having the space to turn on oneself in order to have one's own self as an object of examination. Such a technique of hermeneutics of the subject can be disseminated, as is evident from Chrysostom, as a collective pedagogy through the corrective function of the comic.

Two orders are being imagined here. An order of appearance where cohabitation between men and women is seen as a form of spiritual practice. Then Chrysostom offers another order–the order of reality where the same practice is seen to be motivated by sexual pleasure. But the nature of such pleasure is no longer identified with material intercourse between two bodies but rather in the concept of desire which is perpetuated through a logic of lack and perpetual deferral. In fact such lack is identified as the true substance of pleasure rather than actual sexual enactment. Certain physical capacity like that of visual perception is privileged over all others because of its apparent disembodied nature to be most effective in intensifying and sustaining this form of sexual pleasure. In other words, desire–as lack–functions as a disembodied sensual presence which not only corrupts morality but secretly resides as the 'material' face of reality behind the mask of spiritual illusion. Comedy therefore becomes a technique to unravel or unmask this truth at a collective level. Comedy not only exposes the discrepancy or difference of levels between what appears and what is real but finds its comic substance in such revelation of difference. It is not that comedy reveals the truth but the revelation of truth itself follows the corrective function of the comic. Therefore the revelation of difference between the two orders exposes that which is said to belong to a spiritual and universal order to actually belong to a material and subjective reality of personal desire. The comic technique lies in identifying the incommensurability between an infinite metaphysical order and a finite physical order while the later poses as the former. This not only affirms a dualist ideology of a divine reality as against a human reality but reinforces the incommensurability between the two. In the final analysis, Chrysostom uses the comic to call the bluff of something finite which poses itself to be infinite and universal. And being comic it can function as a rhetorical tool to persuade a collective who would want to be on the side of this truth. This is the pedagogic/conservative function of the comic which ridicules spiritual marriage as a form of perversion in order to conserve a dualist understanding of reality.

In a culture of display, appropriate gestures and codes of behaviour not only determine gender roles but proclaim as 'natural' sexual segregation which is conditioned by codes of conduct. Therefore reversal of gender roles, portraying masculine women participating in public life rather than occupying their own quarters was as much a source of laughter as men threatened by feminine incursion. As Chrysostom remarks "What shall we think when we enter a monk's house and see a woman's shoes hanging up, and girdles, head bands, baskets and a distaff, various items of weaving equipment, and all the other things women have, too numerous to be counted?" (Ibid., n.d., 123). Socio-cultural values attached to objects function as much as codes of conduct and not just as external determinants of gender roles but as inscriptions of power which determine and separate men and women at the very level of their being. Comedy here offers the distance required to accept such hierarchic divisions in the immediacy of their 'natural' truth. The reversal of gender roles is not the only inversion which is rendered comic. Chrysostom talks of these men in "service of women" stopping in at the silversmith's to inquire if the mistress's mirror is ready, if he has finished the urn, if he has delivered the perfume flask... and from there he runs again to the perfume maker to discuss aromatics for his mistress" (Ibid., n.d., 126). Such an essentially comic scene is based on the comic revelation of servile willingness of these men to please their mistresses while under the illusion of acting in freedom. Such loss of freedom in antiquity was not taken to be the consequence of misfortune, but of ethical negligence because freedom was seen as the natural consequence of an ethical life to be cultivated and practised. Servile will was therefore seen as the result of an ethical and subjective deficiency which lead to wilful degradation. And it is the unmasking of this same wilful degradation which was the corrective function of the comic element in this scene. Therefore what is implicit in the use of such a comic technique is a will to freedom which can come with the ironic distance comedy generates so that one can have an access to the truth. But as we see the nature of such freedom is entangled with ideological underpinnings which make it essentially masculine.

Faced with the problem of a utopic imagination of a society without gender hierarchies borrowed from the scriptures fuelling the rationale of spiritual marriage, Chrysostom comes up with a philosophical response. Chrysostom argues that such an imagination of a paradisiacal society is only figuratively possible outside the historical reality. But any attempt to realize it here and now leads to a dystopic vision of reality, turning it upside down and thereby making it comic. Rather than rejecting the longing for freedom Chrysostom deflects the collective fantasy of a hierarchyless society into a distant future as promised in the scripture. But such a promise of radical freedom and a new way of life can only be fulfilled if the norms of the day are followed and the status quo maintained. Therefore he observes that if these men abstain from such a foolish way of life which is devoted to the service of women, where the men mistake their servile will to be freedom then a time will come when "those women will admire you more, God will accept you before them, all men will crown you, and you will live a life which is full of freedom and full of delight" (Leyerle 2001, 139). Anyone who mistakes this future promise as a present reality is not only under illusion but lacks self-knowledge and lives under the inverted ethical imperative "by no means know yourself" (Ibid., n.d., 108). Their arrogance in believing in the illusion of spiritual marriage therefore confirms their status as ridiculous men who can become the object of comedy. What is interesting here is the relation of comedy to a certain idea of profane time. As Leyerle points out Chrysostom does acknowledge a relation between spiritual marriage and Christianity's promise of a new age. However "the time for this kind of a relationship is both past (belonging to the time before the Fall) and future (pertaining to the life of heaven)" (Ibid., n.d., 141). Spiritual marriage offers itself up to the comic, or in other words the comic is possible only in the interval between the Fall and Judgement Day. This reminds us of Baudelaire's remark that the comic is possible only because it functions under the condition of the absolute negativity of the fall. Fall and interval are two intrinsic elements of the comic. But such a work of the negative can also be seen from a materialist perspective not as an endless play of contradiction but as an objectification of contradiction as such.

The foundational logic behind the practice of spiritual marriage was a desire to concretely realise the utopic vision based upon the words of Jesus who declared his second coming when all hierarchies and divisions of this world will end and a life of freedom and equality between the sexes will begin like it was before the fall in the *Civitas Dei*. In other words, the actual practice of spiritual marriage as a form of life, unlike most other ascetic practices which were understood as so many tests to verify the purity (or impurity) of the Christian subject, was something akin to incarnation. While ascetic practices were mostly ways to prepare the subject–and this might last a whole lifetime–for the grace of god, to test if the subject is worthy for such grace, spiritual marriage actually assumed that such grace has already befallen them. It seems that such an idea was motivated by a more extremist disposition. In supposing that they live as equals, these men and women were not only trying to materialize in their very lives the pure disincarnate spirit, moving freely in a nomadic space which they had constructed for themselves without going anywhere, in the very centre of the household. But it was the same place which offered them a line of flight, as Deleuze would call, to the realm of the pure intellect. Therefore they would constantly talk of their philosophical friendship with each other which became the source of Chrysostom's ridicule. The material relation of their concrete forms of life incarnated the divine (absolute) reality of Civitas Dei in the Civitas Terrena. In doing so, the logic of their relation resonates with a radical understanding of the comic. Following Zupancic, we can also say that such a logic of incarnation is comedy and comedy is nothing other than such incarnation. Any logic of incarnation of a divine reality would not simply seek out the limit of physical reality, but in exposing the contradiction and impasses of such a materialist translation reveal the radical truth: that it is matter which is the very source and origin of such an absolute moment. Chrysostom it seems to us realised this potential of Spiritual Marriage while exposing the contradiction and impasse of a materialist order trying to express a divine transcendental order. To that extent Chrysostom's use of the comic was not quite different from contemporary use of comedy to show the essentially humanist disposition of our finite reality. Such comedy invites us to accept and even be consoled, as Zupancic argues, by the limits and boundaries of our finite existence because "our great narrative" seems to be finitude[18]. In both cases the emphasis is to expose, through the comic, the dual, oppositional nature of finitude and infinity. In Chrysostom however the master-signifier, so to speak, is never finitude but the divine narrative of an infinite god. Therefore when he exposes the finitude and subjective contingency of material existence it is always in the name of an infinite reality. But such an infinite order is held in the same oppositional and alienated relation to our finite human order. Hence the comic does not reveal the infinite at the heart of the finite, *Civitas Dei* incarnated within the limitations of the household through the contradictions and the impasses. The contradictions and the impasses which generate the comic are used to re-affirm the dualist logic of two separate orders. This is the conservative function of the comic in Chrysostom. The gross materialism that Chrysostom seeks to expose through the comic unravels a dualist structure of a metaphysics of infinity and a physics of finitude. This is the use of the comic to propagate a Christian view of the world as an alienated reality, which is separated from its own substance which lies elsewhere in a divine realm.

From our point of view, we can reframe this entire understanding of the comic as a problem of the metaphorization of theatre. It is evident that the way in which Chrysostom uses the comic form as a formal rhetorical device is conservative in nature. Its function was to use comedy as a corrective principle to reinforce an existent dualist understanding and thereby dissimulate a radically materialist moment of contradiction. The use of the metaphor of theatre to indicate the illusive and deceptive nature of these men and women make their household into a veritable comic stage. The men are invited to realise the true state of their existence (a reality conditioned by the Fall) through the distance provided by comic irony. They are offered an access to the 'truth' that the concrete and real practices of their lives are in fact an illusion constructed as a comedy. In other words their lives are transformed into a comic metaphor, without any substance and therefore devoid of political consequences. And it is because the excess of their actions correspond to their desire given as a continuous lack the only possible understanding of their reality can be through irony.

Again we have a case where the metaphor of theatre is used to denounce and undermine an actually existing theatrical potential. The metaphorization of theatre therefore starts to correspond with the abolition any materialist understanding of theatre. We can put it otherwise that the problem of metaphorization is similar to the problem of irony which offers the Idea only figuratively while reinforcing the concrete reality of the place of enunciation. Kierkegaard had already understood this primitive dialectical movement of the concept of irony when he proposed that the concept of irony is essentially a concept of negation. Therefore the power of irony, like in Socrates, is capable of abolishing the entirety of the sensual world in the name of the Idea which is not offered as actuality, but whose necessity is determined by the force of negation which it makes possible. Therefore Kierkegaard saw Socratic irony as a threshold concept between two orders which makes possible the destruction of the material order in the name of something which can only be accessed negatively. Something very similar is at work in our understanding of the metaphorization of theatre within Christianity. Christianity constantly negates the material reality of theatre as part of the illusive nature of worldly reality in the name of a divine order which is held in dialectical opposition to it. The only difference is that while in Socratic irony the threshold to the transcendental order is always presented through nothing other than constant affirmations of a fundamental negation, Christianity devises a more complicated plan. Therefore we have a prophetic and figurative understanding of the divine order which is given as a promise. An immaterial reality which is the essence of our being but from which we are alienated by a absolute moment of negation–the Fall–such that an idea of dualism is always already in place. Therefore here too irony is sustained by an inaugural moment of negation which is dissimulated by a existent dualist paradigm. This is also the function of metaphorization of theatre. However the impasses in the discourse of such metaphorization point to theatre as an object-cause of desire. In other words, a desire for theatre which continues to penetrate Christian discourses over the centuries as a lack which is constantly disavowed by a proliferation of theatrical metaphors. The comic metaphor therefore weaves its way into Chrysostom in an ironic fashion which following Deleuze,[19] we can say functions in a threefold way. It wrenches the individual from his immediate reality and places him face to face with an universal. The individual confronts the universality of his Fall by knowing himself which helps him transcend his particular sensible reality without offering him an actual encounter with his substance. The individual remains alienated from his substance which he can only access negatively through knowledge of the Fall. Therefore he now returns to his subject position which he has to constantly maintain ironically. Therefore irony makes possible a closure or a perfect circle which encompasses the world. The metaphor of *theatrum mundus* can therefore be also understood ironically translating the whole of material and historical reality into an image of deception. But the distance that the ironic metaphor generates is always recovered and the gap it introduces between the subject who speaks and the object which is spoken about is always overcome by a return to the subject.

Part II: Disjunction or the Humorous Aspect of Comedy

Contrary to popular belief that Christian orthodoxy was historically adverse to the comic, our previous discussion shows how Christian discourse would use the comic form for its own ideological assertion. A simple opposition between a conservative Christian position of disavowing the comic and a more progressive Christian view of humanism anticipates our own liberal democratic perspective on comedy as the quintessential expression of freedom of will which is the privilege of the free world. Such an understanding of comedy and its relation to Christianity is therefore deeply rooted in our own ideological viewpoints on freedom–of the variety offered by liberal democracy–and the distance from all ideology which is its basis. As we have tried to show comedy had clear ideological functions within Christianity where it was used as a polemical tool directed against those it found dangerous. However this is perhaps not the only approach to comedy known within Christianity. The Middle Ages particularly bear witness to a more radical and subversive strain of the comic being developed in its many forms which were all variations on the Christian idea of folly. The dissonant history of folly within Christianity in many ways starts with Paul when in his first letter to the Corinthians he talked of the "the fools in the cause of Christ" (1 Corinthian 5:10) who creatively repeated the divine ecstasy of the Cross. The idea of folly has resonated throughout the history of Christianity as so many repetitions of the Singular Passion of Christ. This in turn has given rise to a veritable tradition of expression of excess, madness and ecstasy in such varied forms as that of ascetic practices, the flagellants, the feast of fools and even moving into the profane domains of bawdy medieval farce while simultaneously influencing certain anti-clerical but learned and highly sophisticated plays of folly in the 13th-14th century.

Stanislas Breton is perhaps right to invoke the Platonic meaning of the Greek term *moria* which invokes the idea of excess or alienation to understand the question of folly. Breton reads into the Christian idea of folly a similar desire that informed Plato in such works as that of *Symposium*, *Phaedrus* and *Ion*: namely the desire for being collected from the multiplicity of the sensational world into the oneness of the Idea[20]. But such a singular movement to gain access to the "truly real" always involves an act of recollection where the past has to be remembered and therefore repeated continuously. It is because–Breton explains–they have a single idea which overwhelms them with its simplicity that they are mad. It is this interminable return to the "One" which is expressed in the desire of folly to ceaselessly repeat. Breton writes of the Fools of the Cross:

> And they turn their heads towards that "Nothingness" that their faith shows them to be "worthy of being", because it is in and by this Nothingness that they are what they are: divine human beings whose folly carries them in a "metaphor" (in the etymological sense of the word) which makes them continually "transit" towards the Crucified for it is there that their treasure and their heart repose. (Breton 2002, 32)

Two things are at least clear from this remark. The essence of the lives of these fools resides in some sort of an idea of a divine nothingness which is expressed concretely in their existence through the idea of movement. Their very lives are truly "metaphors" in so far as metaphor invokes its etymological source of the Greek *metaphora* meaning transit or transport. The fundamental question is that are they ever able to reach or better return to this originary and divine moment of the singular Passion which the Cross expresses? In other words, are they able to successfully repeat it in and through their lives? And what are the consequences of such a desire to repeat? These are some of the basic questions which we would like to explore here.

Breton of course understands this nothingness from the point of view of the death of God on the Cross. Of course there is a simple dialectical understanding of death as the negative which is negated in the death of God and the eventual Resurrection, ascent and Glory. For Breton, such a reading does not illuminate the simultaneous movement of descent and ascent implied in the Pauline understanding of the series of stages through which it is made possible: indwelling or subsistence in God, the manifestation in a human form, the obedience of the servant (Christ as *doulos*) unto death on the Cross and the eventual Resurrection, ascent and Glory. But the death of God in Christ cannot be a simple negation of negation leading back to the essence and re-affirming it, untouched by all that has passed. According to Breton, the Pauline idea of dispossession leads inevitably to an idea of kenosis where God not only empties himself into Christ at the moment of the Passion but the overcoming of death in Resurrection has to be seen from a disjunctive perspective, where the resurrected one emerges from the non-being. Nothingness gains its counterpoint in Resurrection by giving form to a void. To move towards this nothingness, in folly, is to perform the impossible task of repeating this singular moment of what Deleuze would call the "purely expressible". Through its movement that goes beyond death's negation into God, negation no longer expresses anything negative. It rather deploys into the world 'the reality' of the Cross which in its two halves expresses a lack and an excess at the same time disjunctively synthesized giving meaning to the Pauline idea of confounding the power of what is (*ta onta*) by virtue of the weakness of what is not (*me onta*). The Cross for Paul, according to Breton expresses this idea of two halves which always lacks from the other where one becomes strong (excess) by virtue of weakness (deficiency/lack), while the powerful because of its excess becomes weak and deficient. Folly carries within itself this moment of the "pure Event" becoming a "metaphor" who is always in "transit".

Alenka Zupancic offers a Hegelian understanding emphasing on the moment of Incarnation which bears a close similarity to Breton's understanding of the Pauline idea of folly. Zupancic argues that right after his discussion on comedy in the section of his *Phenomenology of Spirit* titled "Religion in the Form of Art" Hegel devises a "direct passage from comedy to the very core of Christianity" (Zupancic 2008, 39) which he discusses in the following section concentration on the problem of Incarnation. According to Hegel, as Zupancic argues, Incarnation is not a moment of the representation of the Absolute and the Universal Essence as is in case of the Greeks, imitating some concrete form in this world. Rather Incarnation is the concrete actualization of the Spirit in this world (this is the meaning of Christianity being a revealed religion) such that when it appears in our world God "literally disappears from the other world, and with it disappears this other world itself" (Ibid., n.d., 39). Therefore the death of Christ as the human self which incarnates the Essence corresponds with the death of God himself and the abolition of the Beyond as such. Otherwise, from a Hegelian perspective, we have to see Resurrection as a return of the Essence to itself, unaffected by the moment of incarnation re-establishing the Beyond like the Greek Gods could take any human appearance but return back, when the time came, to its universal divine form. Such an idea of Resurrection would be an example of what Hegel otherwise calls a "bad universality" because the limit of such universality is precisely that it is not limited enough by its concrete individualisation. Therefore as Zupancic says, "Thus, the death of Christ is first and foremost the death of God as the Beyond, and the implication of this Beyond in the concrete reality of human subjects" (Ibid., n.d., 40). Hence if the inaugural moment of Incarnation can be expressed with the simple but irreversible formulae God=Man, then the death of incarnation is not simply the abolition of a Beyond as a transcendental place. It is rather, as Zupancic in her extraordinary lucidity points out, the "affirmation of its existence as real and always concrete" (Ibid., n.d.). In other words, the Cross does not simply express the abolition of any transcendence in the death of God, but the concrete taking place of the place itself through its abolition. It is through its own abolition or absencing, that the Absolute concretely affirms itself. It is an Absolute which in concretely realising itself has been alienated from itself expressing itself in a completely empty and contingent figure. This is what makes Incarnation essentially comic.

From our point of view it also gives folly as 'metaphor' for nothingness a concrete and real existence in the different historical figures of the fool. Unlike the figurative function of metaphorization we talked of earlier.

The body therefore speaks in its superabundance that which it cannot speak of. The fool therefore, as Breton argues is the "living redeemed" who having "heard the call of Beatitudes" replaces common sense, taking its place turning reason into folly going beyond the law, not by transgressing it but by repeating it obsessively to expose its failure. Folly not only makes fun of the law but transforms it into a play beyond good and evil. But it is the body which enacts this play, transforming pain into pleasure and weakness into strength. Their bodily contortions and uncoordinated movements[21] seem not simply to replace the Spirit but repeat it obsessively such that they were entrusted to "display" rather than "demonstrate" conclusions 'as if the depth of things only opened up to a beyond or a "this side of" the noetic and rational' (Breton 2002, 33). Body carries the rigour of that single point of view–the Cross–whose spirit passes through it without ever being able to represent it. In being bodily incarnation of such a single point of view–the madness and simplicity of the one–these figures would always lack the totalizing function of the self. Therefore in the incoherent discourse it generates, folly completely dismantles everything that comes from the self.

Though Breton rejects the medieval practice of the feast of fools as possible example of his interpretation of the Pauline notion of folly he does attribute to it an exclusive theatricality. Speaking of the history of folly he writes, "I would speak here of representation, on condition that it be understood as closely as possible to the theatrical meaning"[22] (Ibid., n.d., 37). Breton attributes to the Christian idea of folly the primacy of theatricality because according to him like theatre, it is also fundamentally paradoxically structured. If Folly is nothing but the disjunctive synthesis of a lack or a void which sits at the heart of Christ's Passion which makes it impossible to represent yet demanding an excessive obsession for repetition then theatre also allows for a similar synthetic disjunction. It is in a comic understanding of what we have called the theatrical substance, that the superficial and surface nature of spectacular display comes together with the immediacy and depth of bodies. The universal normativity of the Cross is always abstract, belonging to the distant past which has to be actualized repeatedly in the immediacy of human flesh as an unlimited series of reflections of that singular image. If that calls for a theatre of cruelty with its actors having a morbid taste for blood and a perverted pleasure for suffering then there is another way of understanding theatricality.

Therefore Breton invokes two types of performance of folly: An immediate bodily expression, which he calls participatory, where the wounds of Christ are inscribed on the body as part of active mortification, and a more distant utterance where discourse is subordinated to caricature and mime. In the former case rather than puzzling over a possible causal logic which would explain such excesses[23] Breton evokes the medieval explanation of the power of imagination which had the miraculous effect of affecting the materiality of sensory organs. But whatever might be the possible reason, the theatre of the Cross would have to be played bodily, in participatory and performative sense to guarantee through the palpability of the flesh, the Word of the Cross. But it is exactly where such palpable guarantee is sought that all forms of verifications collapse and all one is left with is the empty materiality of the hollow body incapable of repeating anything but itself. It is here that Breton introduces the other dimension of the theatricality of folly as distance. This is the comic foregrounding of folly. A comedy where imitation "exaggerates features and gaits to recover by this exaggeration the internal logic of an attitude or comportment" (Ibid., n.d., 40). Exaggeration as an essential comic technique was not unknown to folly. By drastically changing the scale, magnitude, volume of a prop or character laughter could be induced. Such an idea of exaggeration need not be taken literally as a question of increase in measure but could well be a reduction or diminution of measure. For example one of the key characteristic of the Feast of Fools was the election of the boy bishop (*episcopus puerorum*). We have a description of him standing on a footstool wearing an Episcopal miter while carrying an Episcopal staff beginning vespers. Of course as Max Harris argues, there is historical evidence to argue that rather than dissimilarity, it is resemblance with the child Christ which was behind such enactments[24]. Such an argument can support Harris's thesis that the feast was not antithetical to liturgy but was an integral and creative part of it. However it cannot disavow its comic misrepresentation of the office of bishop. If we see the kind of criticism available from the 15th century onwards against the *feast of fools* or even the complaints of Innocent III in the late 12th and early 13th century the misuse or misrepresentation of the *office* would gain primacy over none other.

We would like to argue that it is not resemblance which has been the central internal logic behind the idea of folly but rather misrecognition. The problem of the boy bishop and many such examples of exaggeration which crowd the history of folly has to be seen from the essentially comic perspective of distance, But a distance, one might add which is more intimate than any form of imitation. Exaggeration works through a logic of excess which underlines the inherent lack which any representation carries in its heart. As Breton points out when the frog makes itself as large as the ox, what is at stake in this inflation is the absolute necessity of that which represents even though we have trouble acknowledging the complicity of the image with reality. In fact it is when the exaggerated object overwhelms our senses by completely and absolutely taking possession of itself that we realise the impossibility of representation. But rather than seeing it as the failure of repetition (or representation) we recognise in the failure the very distance which separates the object from the singularity of what it wants to repeat or represent. Therefore what such repetition repeats is not the thing–for example, the singularity of the Incarnate Word–but the distance or the absolute difference which becomes the condition of possibility of repetition. The comic as exaggeration is therefore not to be seen as the failure of repetition but rather as a passage. In this passage "from the necessity of what is repeated" (Zupancic 2008, 153) (for example, the norm of the Cross) to "repetition as necessity" we sense something essentially theatrical. Exaggeration as a comic technique is essentially theatrical no matter where it is deployed because here repetition does not represent anything outside itself. Like theatrical representation comic exaggeration is a form of representation which is itself the very content of what it represents. The persistent failure of representation embodied in comic exaggeration–for example, of the Cross–inevitably leads us to conclude that the only thing which repeats is the absolute distance itself which separates the Cross from the incessant, and we also add "foolish", attempts to repeat it. In other words folly is nothing other than the affirmation of this distance that separates the singularity of the Cross from all acts of representation making it a pure form of expression.

As Breton further explains to our advantage, the history of folly is insistent on a certain idea of eccentricity–a form of de-centring of the self realized in the Pauline assertion, "I have been crucified with Christ and it is no longer I who live but Christ who lives in me" (Galatians 2:20). This ecstasy or moving outside the boundaries of the self, Plato's *mania*, is also a form of being reduced to a sign–to the *eidos*–where it comes to exist in its most simple and raw state. To become the simplified sign is the foolish imperative of those who do not just constatively utter "I say to you he died with us" with the same subjective detachment with which one says "I say to you the tea is cold". "I say to you" has to be seen here, as Breton indicates as an oath, a performative utterance which becomes the condition of possibility of a new individuation, being identical to a new world, which is created through such an utterance in the midst of our own. As Breton writes "It presupposes that we have reached another space, and that even though we are in the world we are no longer of the world through the image of the Crucified who 'elevated above the earth, attracts all to himself'" (Breton 2002, 43). In dedicating their lives to the sign of the Cross, the fools take up an attitude where their words cannot be distinguished from their actions, where words are already explosions of actions making their lives a veritable theatre. As "metaphors" of a divine nothingness they circulate in our world as signs–moving, always in transit, transposing, being transposed and finally trespassing from the world where they live into the sign which looks into an abyss. To look into the abyss is therefore nothing other than the affirmation of an original difference which constitutes their beings. But Breton never fails to remind us that all this is possible as result of a judgement which "is not fixed in a consequent formula, in a "self-contained proposition" (Ibid., n.d., 43). There cannot be any idea of a proposition because the idea of a coherent self has already been dismantled in the "gesticulations of the body and the resources of the invective" (Ibid., n.d., 43) adopted by the fool. But behind such adoption is the lucidity of a judgment which forms a decision. A decision to live in Christ, live by Christ and live for Christ. It is a decision which, as the etymology of the word suggests, refers to an original cut (-cision)[25] suggesting in turn an original separation from the powers of the world carried by all that which is (*ta onta*). It is a final separation between the Cross under whose sovereign freedom the fragility of sovereign power is revealed and the institutions of this world. A cut from world sovereignty itself by recalling the fragility of power–the weakness of the strong confusing it with the strength of that which is not (*me onta*). The comic is generated as a result of this contradiction because comedy throws into relief the gap between sovereign freedom and sovereign power with its ideological representations.

The fools are therefore nomad creatures who in imitating Christ are made alien to this world because they have made a desert of this world upending its laws and customs under the singular norm of the Cross. They do not belong to this world though they are of this world. Like the nomad who is a wanderer fixed to a place to which he does not belong, these fools have been dispossessed of every home and every establishment having heard the call of Beatitude. It is while discussing this problem of exile as constitutive of being that Breton evokes the quality of a sorrow which knows no reason. On the one hand, the nothingness which is carried in the image of the Cross teaches them, "that the being of that which is, is the trace of a first distance that marks its exile from its origin" (Ibid., n.d., 45). But such an arche-seperation which constitutes their nomadic being, gives to them a sense of sorrow which is without reason, "sadness without cause"[26] as Michel de Certeau so eloquently puts it. It is not a question of a determined sorrow but what Breton calls an "ontological" sadness. The trail of a pure negativity constitutive of our being which makes all representations redundant and all repetitions impossible, the trail of this negativity coils at the heart of all their revelry. The fool is therefore drawn by the nostalgia of a paradise that pre-existed him and whose loss now seizes him constantly like the shadow which veils our world at morning as at dusk. One is reminded here of Baudelaire's words when he spoke of the Fall as the common origin of both laughter and tears as he remarked that "they are equally the children of sorrow, and they came because enervated man lacked the bodily strength to control them." (Baudelaire 2006, 143). However it is in this tragic dissonance that we find a secret nostalgia for an impossible origin; a transcendental origin from which these fools of Christ are inevitably separated but for which Bretons makes an appeal on their behalf. Such a secondary level of "sadness without cause" carries a secret appeal for an impossible transcendence which dilutes the immanent materialism of the comic introducing again a form of unconscious dualism.

What we require is rather a definite call for materialism which can affirm in a "redoubled" fashion, as Alenka Zupancic uses the term to talk of Deleuze's idea of repetition, and thereby "liberate what is always-already positive in the first level". If comic repetition always repeats the impossible, then such a repetition which repeats the very impossibility of all repetitions should not be seen as the failure of repetition and therefore identified as an absolute negativity. In his concept of repetition Deleuze offers us what Zupancic calls "another shift of perspective" where the incessant repetition, inspite of its failure, ought to be seen as an imperative for repetition itself. In other words, the comic repetition keeps repeating itself because it "cannot succeed in not being repeated" (Zupancic 2008, 155). This is not the idea of a nothingness which is negative but rather an idea of difference which is positive and which affirms itself every time it folds back onto that which it constitutes in the first place. Repetition therefore never leads to a failure of representation or a deficiency or a lack. It is already an affirmation and an excess. "A pure excessive positivity of the production of differences" (Zupancic 2008, 155). Here difference comes prior to any failure. Therefore "one does not fall into an undifferentiated ground, into a groundless depth, when one undoes the individual and the person" because humour comes before tragedy. Folly would no longer be seen from such a primarily tragic moment but as impersonal singularities where sense and non-sense no longer form oppositional co-ordinates of a world with depth. All depths rise to the surface and the skin becomes deeper than any other ground. In such a world sense and non-sense comes to coexist as a disjunctive synthesis giving rise to humour.

The Cracked "I": A Concluding Analysis of Humour

Written in the last quarter of the 13th century by Adam de la Halle, the French vernacular play *Le jeu de la feuillee* (The Play of Folly/ Bower) has remained a testimony to the enigma of the comic style that medieval Europe produced. Written in the emerging scholastic climate, the play has puzzled critics for ages generating responses which vary from calling it an improvisational curiosity written by self-indulgent students to a record of the emerging self-consciousness of the 12th century renaissance. It is however in the nature of deployment of language and the development of the dialogues that the play exposes its metaphysical complexities and–as we shall try to argue–a materialist unconscious symptomatic of the age. This learned anti-clerical play tells the story of Adam, an inhabitant of Arras who wants to renounce his marriage to Maroie and go to Paris to take up the habit of the clerk. Of course from the very beginning we find the shift in the treatment of the Adamic nostalgia for innocence (as compared to, say, a vernacular play like *Le Mystere d'Adam*) which has moved from a transcendental locus to a more terrestrial setting of a historical Adam caught in the domestic drama of the frustrated husband who wants to return to a more worthy life of the mind as a student in Paris. However it is in its use of language and the development of the dialogues that the play usurps a legitimate use of stable language mediating between the inner world of consciousness and the outer world of reality. The series of displacements that the play unleashes sweeps away any possibility of coherent function of signification which in turn destroys a dream of composite character or positive subject. What remains is a series of "shifters" testifying to all moments of usurpation of meanings crowding the play making it impossible to assign any define meaning to the text. In the beginning, as Eugene Vance points out[27], language seems to function through its principle of signification when Adam declares his decision to abandon his marriage to become a monk. The conscious self as the master of his decision seems to use language to convey his mind and thereby bridge the gap between the rational human mind and the world outside. Adam closes his opening declaration with the famous proverb, “It still appears from the pieces what the pot was” (Vance 1986, 211). And here begins all the semantic mischief. At first glance the use of the ‘pot’ metaphor at this stage seems obvious enough. Despite the fragmentation of Adam’s life because of his marriage to Maroie in Arras there seems to be definite hope of a collecting together of the shattered pieces, a gathering of the self in anticipation of a future wholeness. But given that Adam would never be able to leave Arras and his dreams would remain far from fulfilment the use of the metaphor seems to bear a foreboding of impending dissolution. But in the play such a theological tradition of using the pot metaphor to underscore the contingent and finite nature of man’s existence would undergo what we might call a ‘materialist’ dissipation. Returning many times in the course of the play, the motif would finally be used in its “stark literalness” to the effect of causing what Vance calls a “demataphorization in the course of the play” amounting to “a mise en cause of the tradition” (Ibid., n.d., 211)

As we know the metaphor of the pot standing for the self has a rich tradition within Christian theology starting from St. Paul who asks, “But who are you, a man, to answer back to God? Will what is modelled say to its moulder, ‘why have you made me thus?’” (Romans 9:20). While in *Confessions*, Augustine uses the metaphor to praise the glory of god who only has the power to collect all the pieces together though his grace “the vessels (vasa) that are filled by you do not restrict you, for even if they are shattered, you are not poured forth. When you are poured upon us, you are not cast down, but you raise us up; you are not scattered about, but you gather us up” (Ibid., n.d., 212). Like the metaphor of theatrum mundi which expressed the illusive and deceptive nature of finite existence, so does the pot metaphor talk of the finite and contingent life as part of a dualist logic which would oppose the fragmented multiplicity of the finite self to the unified divine consciousness. As we have seen before such a dualist regime would become the condition of possibility of an upward movement. As a result of a progressive metaphorization of the world all worldly multiplicities would be subsumed under the logic of a divine One. But in this anti-clerical play we find an inverse movement when the Absolute (One) comes crashing down to the worldly stage being broken into a thousand pieces like the pot which is hurled on stage by the end of the play which it is impossible to put back together. The use of the proverb of the broken pot no longer has a fixed metaphorical meaning but as Vance citing Alexander Leupin remarks "a shifter prophesying the destiny of writing playing itself out in the play" (Ibid., n.d., 212). From this perspective the entire trajectory of the play can be compared to the metaphor of the broken pot. The broken pot becomes a metaphor for the formal structure of the play which is fragment and decentred. Conversely, the play does not simply represent thc metaphor of the broken pot as part of its content, but in representing the metaphor of the broken pot it represents its own configuration. In other words with the metaphor of the broken-pot the play becomes the content of what it itself represents.

The proverb serves as a kind of formal rhetorical declaration of the end of Adam's self to form any coherent consciousness. From now onwards Adam's every attempt to gather together the broken pieces of his self would meet with failure. And it is through this failure to repeat himself coherently that the play would succeed in fascinating us with its humour. Immediately after his inaugural declaration to leave Arras, Rikeche Auris, one of the supporting characters, starts attacking Adam's decision by claiming that it is merely "big illusion" (Ibid., n.d., 212) and no good clerk has ever come out of Arras. Vance points here the curiously theological reverberation of the despair of the fallen man which the place Arras comes to represent as a place of exile betraying a longing for *parais* (paradise) which is "so close in name to, yet so distant from Paris" (Ibid., n.d., 212). Adam tries to defend his position by invoking a precedence, Rikier Amion, "a good clerk, careful with his book" (Ibid., n.d., 212). Again we confront a metaphorical shifter which is always "in transit" moving between a number of semantic fields. Therefore on the one hand the metaphor of the 'book' conjures up the wholesome totality of the Scriptures. It also reflects the relation between the conscious intelligent mind and the book which in turn reflects the relation between God and his two books of life and of Scripture[28]. Therefore the idea of "the book of life of each man" (Revelation 20:12) immediately symbolises not a certain unity and totality but also divine authority and an implicit idea of redemption. For example, in Augustine's City of God he writes:

> The book of the life of man is to show what commandments each man has done or omitted to do...we must therefore understand of it a certain divine power, by which it shall be brought that every one shall recall to memory all his own works, whether good or evil, and shall mentally survey them with a marvellous rapidity, so that this knowledge will either accuse or excuse conscience. (Ibid., n.d., 213)

Clearly such an idea of the book becomes a metaphor for the mind at the moment when it is seized by an absolute infinite and therefore divine power. However the comic moment arises when the meaning of "book" is twisted into other uncalled for shapes and making the sacred word enter the realm of the profane. Therefore the French word *livre* (book) shifts its meaning to signify "pound" whether of weight or of money when Hane le Mercier speaks the following lines:

> Yes, "for two deniers for a pound".
> I don't think he knows anything but that (Ibid., n.d., 213)

The ambiguity of speech corroding the integrity of the self reaches its optimum point when suddenly Adam's "I"–the master signifier–completely loses its authority in the middle of the play and becomes no longer the one who speaks but rather the one spoken about in the third person. We have discussed how in irony, the subject always begins and returns to the same position–"I"– because the ironic self being conditioned by an inaugural dualism is constitutively split. Therefore being divided between a subject of enunciation and a subject of statements it manages to dismantle all worldly statements yet re-affirm itself through the very act of such world destruction. The comic subjectivity however functions differently. It is constitutively in flux, always moving between multiplicities of semantic fields affirming only the possibility of language. But at the same time rather than language negating itself in order for the conscious subject to emerge, comic subjectivity emancipates a certain materiality of language, putting language to work in a completely contingent fashion. Therefore Vance writes about this play "Dialogue in the Jeu is not circular, not linear, not even zigzag, but aleatory and centrifugal. Having just compared himself to apot whose whole is still visible in its fragments, and having just proffered the book as a symbol of spiritual integrity, Adam now finds himself protesting against the scattering of his intentionality in the centrifugal language of the group" (Ibid., n.d., 214).

But it is when Adam narrates to Rikier about the illusion of *Amor*, about how he first encountered Maroie and how desire swept over him that we see the most starking difference from our earlier understanding of the comic. For Chrysostom comic becomes a technique to penetrate into the workings of pleasure and discover for the subject the nature of desire as longing in order to abdicate it. In this sense the comic is used as a rhetorical tool to persuade the subject to return to his former position of superiority but it is also used as a technique to examine the nature of pleasure, to discover its truth so that the subject can return to its former position of superiority. But in the "Play of Folly,"[29] comic deployment of language functions infinitely more subtly and, one must add, in a much more radical fashion. Adam starts to reminisce how he was ensnared not by the pleasure of flesh but the pleasure of words and the labyrinthine discourse of courtly love. He starts off with an ethical eye of repudiating all such illusion in the present but is soon entrapped by his very own description being swept over by a "desire to desire" less than halfway into his evocation of Maroie.

> Once her form was white and crimson
> Laughing, loving, and elegant of build;
> Now I see her as fat and ill-shaped,
> Sad and quarrelsome (Ibid., n.d., 217)

Even as Adam manages to finally wrench himself out of his desire which had dispossessed him of his self by invoking the current horrors of his relation to Maroie, desire had already migrated, activating in Rikker illegitimate fantasies about Maroie and prompting him to advise Adam to leave his wife to him,

> Rikker: Mister, if you left her to me, she would suit my taste very well. (Ibid., n.d., 218)

Language no longer functions to discover the truth of desire as longing or lack. Neither is it used to persuade one of the illusive and deceptive natures of all worldly desire. On the contrary, language becomes a vessel for desire which is not to say it comes to communicate or mediate desire. Language becomes the site where desire is encountered. As Vance remarks, "Indeed to declare one's desire negatively–in what we may call courtly denegation–can be erotogenic" (Ibid., n.d., 218). As we can see this is completely different from the metaphorization of desire as deceptive like theatre. In the latter case desire is negatively defined through the process of such metaphorization while in the former case once desire enters the domain of language, though it might have negative intentionality, language makes it impossible for intentionality to achieve its necessary end. To that extent language becomes the condition of possibility of the failure of consciousness. In the final analysis it is this failure of consciousness to represent itself in language which becomes the source of the truly comic. Under such conditions any idea of objective truth completely collapses. The source of the comic in the play becomes an "apt emblem of man's absurd will to construct meanings in an aleatory world" (Ibid., n.d., 220)

However the aleatory yet concrete creation of a subjective reality which makes the comic world possible does more than simply subvert the universal essence of a coherent and totalizing subject. If all subjectivity is broken into a thousand pieces in their rapid descend on to the comic stage, it is Derve, the crazy boy–the quintessential fool–who remains intact and unscathed in his non-sense. In a world where men are caught in their own deception, the fool happily declares that he is the king and where women remain a by product of men's fantasy and language he declares himself a married man. But we agree with Vance that through his madness the fool illustrates more than "the mere failure of the human will to signify" (Ibid., n.d., 221). His progressive desire to degrade language coincides with a certain emergence of a comic subjectivity where "the work of the negative", so to speak, finds its own absolute moment. A subjectivity through which the universal is not represented but is made absolutely concrete. Here the figure of the fool becomes an universal in itself by a centrifugal force attracting the absolute to itself, rendering it concrete within itself but also exposing it to its own contingency, its own localization. The fool declares himself the prince of poets who can transform words and objects through his absurd will: by adding an "l" to the word apple (*pume*) he makes the apple he is eating at Picardy into a feather (*plume*) that flies off to Paris like a mere word (abstract language). Here we should not see the two words separately but as a disjunctive synthesis of two terms which nevertheless cannot be distinguished. Like a mobius strip, '*pume-plume*' (apple-feather) are the two sides of the same surface of language on which the profound and the sublime, the abstract and the concrete collide. The finite heaviness of the apple and the infinite lightness of the feather open up a contradiction which constitutes the figure of the fool in *Jeu* as a finite figure which is nevertheless the origin of something which cannot be reduced to simple finitude. Apple undermines the lightness of feather pulling it towards itself as much as feather induces lightness into the concreteness of the apple. The frequent chivalrous abstractions of the medieval world–love, beauty, authority–are rendered empty yet concrete in the figure of the fool.

Following Hegel's idea of the comic, one can say, in the figure of the fool, *"the self is the absolute Being"* (Zupancic 2008, 28) but absolute substance in becoming a subject gets alienated from itself expressing its own fragility and emptiness. Alenka Zupancic points out how in Phenomenology of Spirit the section on Spirit is devoted to the relation between Spirit as the world and how it is held in relation to Consciousness (which itself moves from Consciousness–Self-Consciousness–Reason). The moment when Reason becomes Spirit it becomes aware of itself as its own world while simultaneous becoming aware of the world as itself. While this realization of the Spirit in the world gives it real historical shapes primarily in the form of ethical life moving from Greek (immediacy of the Spirit–ethical order) to Christian (the point of Culture when being split in two it is alienated from itself) to the moment where it becomes "certain of itself" in "Morality". But it is in the next section on Religion, according to Zupancic's brilliant reading of the text, when Spirit rather than demonstrating how it appears to itself, illustrates how it conceives of itself that things become more interesting. In other words if the section on 'Spirit' is devoted to understanding how Consciousness had to come to its own Absolute then the section on 'Religion' tries to develop the argument as to how the Absolute achieves Self-Consciousness which is to say how the absolute sees itself, rather than how it is conceived by Consciousness. As Zupancic writes, "Hegel's point is that Absolute Spirit as the product of consciousness is, precisely as this product, something real, something that has material and historical existence" (Ibid., n.d., 15). It is in this back drop that Hegel talks of epic-tragedy-comedy as the three modes of realization of the Absolute Spirit. Now if the comic is the Self made into Absolute Being which remains alienated from itself now that it has become a subject, then comedy is not simply the dismantling of all universal foundation. Comedy in destroying all formal universal assumptions exposing the "play of caprice, of chance individuality" (Ibid., n.d., 28) does not completely do away with universals but rather undergoes a radical shift of perspective. As a result, the negativity of comic structure and the contradiction to which it exposes itself becomes inscribed on to the comic structure as a universal. To use Zupancic's words, "the universal is on the side of undermining the universal" (Ibid., n.d., 28). According to such an idea of the universal at work one can distinguish between (as Zupancic invites us) false comedy and true comedy. All those comedies where in spite of the display of contradiction, the abstract universal and the concrete do not swap places but are reconfirmed in their fixed positions, being related externally by such contradiction, Zupancic calls conservative or false comedy. Our discussion of Chrysostom follows this pattern of the "conservative comedy" re-affirming the fixed position of the transcendent and the immanent order thereby introducing dualism between the two. In true comedy on the other hand, the abstract and the concrete switch place while being held together through something like a disjunctive synthesis. The figure of the 'fool' can be analysed from this perspective as the concrete realization of medieval notions/ideas of sovereignty, chivalry and courtly love. In certain French farces of the 15th-16th century we again see this tendency of disjunctive synthesis very clearly by their frequent use of a play within a play.

Before entering into the last phase of our discussion on the concept of comedy in the Middle Ages a brief but crucial terminological clarification is perhaps necessary. Although we are using the term comedy to designate the comic genre in general we are not unaware of the generic distinctions that are prevalent within medieval scholarship regarding comedy. For example, there is an entire tradition of deeply erudite and nuanced scholarship regarding the triumvirate, namely that of *sottie*, the farce and the morality plays. An entire scholarship is available on the style, nature, and historical relevance of these dramatic/literary modes arguing about possible distinctions and identities of these genres. Similarly the tradition of the *Feast of Fools* deserves a separate study from the point of view of its history and development. Our textual analysis of some of these texts is however not motivated by any such literary discourse based on the history of these comic traditions of the Middle Ages. We are more concerned with the conceptual and structural distinction of two modes of thinking the comic in the Middle Ages which we have called 'irony' and 'humour' which in turn generate two types of comic figures–the ridiculous figure and the figure of the fool. Again, even conceptually they are not exhaustive studies of the comic imagination of the Middle Ages because other forms like that of jokes and satire with their own specific structures were also available during the same period. The two distinctions we have managed to engage with (partially, one might add) also overlap each other in many instances as is evident from our discussion of the spiritual marriages. Therefore in discussing a particular text of farce from 15th century France, or as in our previous attempt to analyse a text of folly from the 13th century we have not tried to focus on its specific literary and historical signification but used them as examples to *support* our general thesis on the philosophical implications of the concept of the comic during the Middle Ages. This thesis rests on the contention that ironical comedy in the final analysis ends up producing a logic of abstract dualism between the concrete and the universal. Though having material, human and even physical aspects of things as their content such comedy ends up reinforcing the spiritual, the divine and abstract universal as the untouched and sovereign "Other". While humorous comedy produces something like a subjective universal which is not only absolute and universal but in being concretely realized in the concrete and contingent subject it is rendered empty and without any sovereign logic other than its contingent self.

The play *At Cross Purposes, or, The Farce of the Three Lovers of the Cross* is part of a rich collection of farcical texts called *Recuiel Cohen* which were written mostly during the 15th-16th centuries by a body of writers who were also producing and performing these texts and chiefly belonged to "an influential French organization of law clerks and legal apprentices known as the Basoche"[30] The play revolves around a married lady who is being pursued by three men (Martin the Bumpkin, Walter the Welshman and William the Geek) for obvious amorous purposes. The lady devises a ruse in order to dispose of them, once and for all, after accepting their money. Feigning concern about their safety on account of his jealous husband he implores them to meet her, each in a different disguise, under cover of darkness at a secret rendezvous point. Martin comes dressed as a priest, Walter as a ghostly dead man and William as a devil. Although the lady has no intention of meeting any one of them she urges them to meet here, directing each to enter the specified spot at an hour's interval for the other. Of course the only place where a priest, a dead man and a devil can be seen loitering in the dark would have to be a graveyard. The lady sets up this 'graveyard' theatre in meticulous precision even perhaps anticipating their desperate and impatient hearts would not allow them to wait and they would end up all at the same time producing a play of mistaken identities. What follows is a brilliant comic re-enactment of a play within a play when they are each frightened by the other's disguise, acting in panic which only contributes to the confusion and thereby intensifying the comic situation. What is quintessentially comic about the situation is the impossibility of these characters to enact themselves and the characters assigned to them shifting their positions continuously. For example, Martin as the priest does try to act as a priest at times while acting as himself at other times. So after Walter-as-Dead-Man gives him a chase, a terrified Martin falls on his knees in order to pray for some time so that he is delivered from evil. A priest kneeling on his knees in order to pray only re-affirms Walter's conviction of Martin's identity as a priest and he stops to watch him. Walter-as-Dead-Man's hesitation convinces Martin that his prayers might actually be working. What is essentially comic about the sequence is that the subject changes its place. Martin is no longer an actor who merely enacts the character of a priest while Walter is no longer a spectator to whom it is being represented. As Hegel had argued that in comedy the actual self of the actor coincides with what he represents (his onstage character), similarly here we find that Martin is both himself and the priest like Walter is "at home in the drama performed before him, and sees himself playing in it" (Ibid., n.d., 35). The place of the subject is therefore usurped by the split which is evoked by the coincidence of the self (actor) and his character. We see this process being repeated in the entire graveyard scenario. Consider, for example, the sequence when Walter-as-Dead-Man seeing William-as-Devil gets so scared that he decides to seek help from Martin-as Priest. Seeing Walter-as-Dead-Man approaching him, Martin gets utterly terrified and starts praying. Meanwhile, William-as-Devil thinks that Walter-as-Dead-Man is approaching towards him and he also starts praying. Here Enders adds in her stage instructions "William might think that the "priest" is praying for the "dead man" and that prayer is working". The comic confusion of this entire sequence is built upon the split through which each of the subjects—Martin-as-Priest, Walter-as-Dead-Man and William-as-Devil–relate to itself. It is as if the gap or split between the actor and character instead of collapsing, takes an object-form and is passed around throughout the play. In representing the universal essence of the "priest", "the Dead Man" and the "Devil" they end up exposing the gap which separates them from these characters which becomes the condition of possibility under which they start representing themselves. When the universal of representation starts relating to itself what is produced is the very concreteness of the represented[31]. The comic excess of this sequence depends upon the success or failure of these subjective universals (for example: Martin-as-Priest) to relate to itself and to other such subjective universals.

We cannot but emphasize this point about this scene which makes it paradigmatically comic. Here the abstract and the concrete has switched places. The scene *does not* become comic because we have the abstract idea–of priesthood, of the spectrality of the ghost or the absolute negative power of the Devil–being ridiculed and undermined by juxtaposing it with contingent human weakness which penetrates its abstract perfection in order to entertain us comically. The comic does not betray the unpredictability of a material reality in order to become comic but because it exposes the transformation of the abstract universality into a concrete contingent one thereby betraying its vacuity. The comic humour is not produced because Martin, Walter and William in their particular and unpredictable fashion expose the human limitations which come in way of representing "universal" characters. Rather what is truly humorous for us is our knowledge of the fact that though they constantly jeopardize their enactment of the universal figures because of their human limitations, they continue to affect each other concretely as a result of such abstract universals. Even though the universal–be that of priesthood or the spectrality of a dead man or the absolute nature of evil–is exposed to be empty and ridiculous, it continues to extract concrete responses. The scenario, in the backdrop of the entire play, succeeds in exposing the empty ridiculous nature of the abstract and idea of *amour* which is nevertheless made concrete and indestructible by such comic subjects who continuously return to the same ideal inspite of its vacuity. We leave the theatre with the anticipation that given the chance they would almost certainly return to the theme of *amour* not because their desire remains perpetually unfulfilled but because it is in this movement which constitutes their existence. It is in such mechanical and empty repetition that the secret essence of their being endures. On one hand this is what makes the sequence infinitely comic while one the other it is the reason why the truly comic has endured the ages while tragedy has seen its time of rise and fall. .

Finally we see the importance of ruse as an integral part of a number of medieval comedies. A good comedy to a large extent depends upon how well is it able to construct an active deception scenario within itself leading to comic effects. The graveyard scene is part of this tradition of medieval comedy to construct within its own plot another "plot" with its own characters and situation whose success or failure depends upon the skill and mastery of its director. The success of the graveyard scene can therefore be attributed to our lady, who had conceived it with meticulous details, anticipating every move before-hand making the end sequence a veritable comedy in itself–a play within a play. In fact the rest of the play seems a dress rehearsal for this final comic showdown. Though the use of ruse or trickery is always theatrical and is quite common to many medieval farce[32], this play constructs a singular ruse which takes the form of a veritable comic theatre. An interesting point emerges if we consider the graveyard sequence as something akin to a play within a play. Because it has to be acknowledged that the comic humour comes only as a result of this game which goes terribly wrong. In other words it is only because they fail to represent their respective characters that the sequence becomes comic. In this crucial respect the ruse does not merely reflect but repeats the comic configuration which is determined by the success of its failure to represent an object (for example, the structure of comic exaggeration we discussed before). In repeating the very configuration of the comic structure it gives comedy its archetypal theatricality. In the comic deployment of ruse, Comedy betrays the fact that it does not represent anything but is itself the "very content of what it represents". (Zupancic 2008, 171)

To return to our problem of comic humour as constitutive of the figure of the fool, the following is frequently proposed: the disaffectedness of the fool, the fact that he is unaffected by the reality around him offer us the essence of medieval comedy or comedy as such because it reflects the essence of comedy which inspires our non-involvement and indifference to what is going on onstage. However we would like to argue otherwise. The fool is truly comic because his impersonality is constitutive of his being, just like what we are exposed to on the comic stage is not alien to our reality but perhaps most intimate to us. It is through comedy, epitomised by the figure of the fool that we can gain access to what is our primary concern, what is most intimate and serious to us. However this is not because any other way of accessing the very core of our being would destroy us because it would expose the terrifying nothingness of our existence. Comic repetition does not expose the impossibility of representation because behind such failure lies the terrifying truth that, everything said and done, we are all reduced to nothingness and non-being. Comedy is the art of emergence of the double, that which always repeats itself suspending all meaning and signification but nevertheless inseparable from them. In so far as comedy is a form of theatre, theatre repeats itself in comedy as much as it repeats itself in tragedy. But in so far as comedy is nothing but the repetition of its own configuration, it becomes its own double. Can we then not say that being nothing other than this game of repetition, theatre finds its true double in the comic?[33]

NOTES

1. Cited from Baudelaire's famous essay "Of the Essence of Laughter, and generally of the comic in the plastic arts" (Baudelaire 2006)
2. For an evocative understanding of Paul's notion of time and its implications for a messianic understanding of history. See Agambens's *The Time that Remains*. (Agamben 2005)

3. Walter Benjamin on his "Theses on the Philosophy of History" speaks of the attributes of history, that which are identifiable historical predicates by which we measure historical progress as having one thing in common. These different attributes which makes so called progress possible are all deployed to *fill* what is their actual ground of existence–homogeneous, empty time. Messianic in inspiration such an idea of profane temporality is employed by Benjamin to discuss the concept of time and its relation to revolutionary repetition. See (Benjamin 1969, 253-264)
4. It is interesting to note that it is in Walter Benjamin that the materialism of Baudelaire and messianic transcendence finds a tortured synthesis.
5. In the Greco-Roman period the theatrical image flourished either under some foundational myth, as in the case of Plato, or under the guarantee of a philosophical principle. See Chapter One of this thesis.
6. We are concerned with a general problem of theatricality rather than the exclusive problem of theatre though we will be dealing primarily with texts which are related to the tradition of miracle and mystery plays. It is perhaps important to note here that the controversies based upon this structural problem between a phenomenological and an allegorical interpretation is not limited to these plays. In fact they constitute the central controversies around the liturgy of Eucharist as is evident from the Amalarius debate of the 9th century or the Lefranc-Berenger debate of the 11th century. For a detailed analysis of the former see (Dox 2004). However a more precise but politically significant analysis is offered by Soumyabrata Choudhury (Choudhury 2013). As for the Lefranc-Berenger debate see (Kobialka 1999).
7. In his seminal analysis of the play-element in culture Huizinga identifies non-seriousness as a salient feature of play. But he refuses to assign to it irreducibility when it comes to defining play. The opposition between play and seriousness he argues is neither fixed nor conclusive when we consider how certain modes of play are enacted with utmost seriousness while certain expressions of

non-seriousness do not correspond to the structure of play see (Huizinga 2014)

8. Jonas Barish presents this argument in order to show how the anti-theatrical prejudice is expressed through the creation of clear boundaries between God's territory and that of Devils. (Barish 1981, 68-69)
9. In fact the implicit distinction between amusement and recreation rests on the fact that pleasure leading to mirth is intricately related to laughter and the non-serious nature of action, while true Christian recreation is always serious.
10. Amalarius had used this word to define the feeling that passes through the congregation as an effect of liturgy. Agobard one of his chief detractors objected against Amalarius' use of anti-phonal singing during liturgy because he (Agobard) argued that such singing generated the 'sweet medicine' symptomatic of the tragic actors who sing with their throat and jaws rather than their heart. This was an old problem related to the nature of Church singing which had its roots going back to Augustine. What is interesting is Agobard's distinction between 'sweet' feeling generated by such singing and the feeling of fear and trembling proper to the work of Christ and the knowledge of scripture. See (Choudhury 2013) and (Dox 2004). Interestingly anti-phonal singing has also been argued by many medieval historians of theatre, like Glynne Wickham, Marius Sepet, to be one of the principal moments of origin of liturgical drama. The medieval practice of *troping* during liturgy was a direct response to diminish the sensual effect of melodic fantasy during singing. As anti-phonal singing leads to polyphony, a single syllable of a single word could be extended through melodic elaboration such that almost forty notes would be sometimes used to decorate it. This came to be known as *melismatic* chant. Such musical ornamentation had to be checked by introducing words from the scriptures and limiting such unbridled melodic expansion. This gave rise to the practice of troping, from the latin *tropus* meaning added melody which eventually evolved into a dramatic structure. (Wickham 1974, 31-34)

11. For a more detailed analysis of the Abel and Cain sequence please refer to (Vance 1986, 204).
12. For a more detailed account of the appendage see (Vance 1986).
13. Vance has identified this appendage as the most brilliant example of *merveilleux* belonging to the romance genre. (Vance 1986, 209)
14. Jody Enders has analysed in-depth the possible relation between rhetoric, theatre and torture in medieval plays. She proposes that there was a continuous reciprocity between the theatricality of torture and the use of torture in theatre which shared common rhetorical ground. Here argument that even before such theatre of cruelty there was a medieval theory of cruelty which informed the writing and staging of such drama is crucial for any understanding on this subject. (Enders 1999)
15. We shall come back to the letter and the place of Feast of Fools in the Christian imagination of the comic in a while. For summaries of the letter and a systematic collection of available material on the Feast of Fools in English see E.K. Chambers *Medieval Stage*. (Chambers 1925, 274-335)
16. Max Harris has argued that the feast of fools were part of creative efforts to make the liturgies more interesting and entertaining for the lay folks during starting from the renaissance of the 12th century and continued to be defended by chapters till the 15th century. (Harris 2011)
17. For a detailed description of this strategy see (Leyerle 2001, 110)
18. Alenka Zupancic contrast the current tendendecy informed by a culture of finitude, which she terms a metaphysics of finitude, to the radical comic imagination of a infinity from a materialist perspective which she calls a physics of infinity. See (Zupancic 2008)
19. For a fascinating analysis of the difference between the ironic, the tragic and the humorous see (Deleuze 1990, 134-141).
20. The paragraph cited by Breton from *Phaedrus* reads, "A human intelligence must be exercised according to what is called the idea, moving from multiplicity of sensations towards a unity assembled by the act of reflection. Yet this action consists in remembering of objects that our soul has seen in times past... When it regards from

above all that to which we attribute reality in our present existence, it lifts its head towards what is truly real." (Breton 2002, 1)

21. One of the chief aspects of the feast of fools was to elect subdiaconal "fools" along with their lord sometimes a boy bishop (*episcopus puerorum*) or sometimes Pope or Abbot of Fools as *dominus festi,* or the lord of revels which would parody the different liturgical offices through exaggerated bodily imitation and, what were deemed, scandalous gestures Although recent theatre historians like Max Harris has shown that the fests were never as disorderly as they have been portrayed by both church historians and early theatre historians like E.K. Chambers. Harris goes on to argue that the feast of fools played a more orderly and creative role in Church liturgies at least till the 15th century. However in spite of the chronological confusion, the response against the feast remains a prominent fact attested by many archival documents. In fact one of the main sources from which the nature of the feast has been reconstructed remain these anti-*feast of fools* clerical documents. Harris's thesis further adds to the ambiguous place of comedy within Christianity. The feast of fools perhaps worked in a more complex fashion. Instead of participating in the destabilising quality of its own humour, it seemed to have worked to re-affirm the status quo by embedding such humour into a neutralizing frame within a disinterested and separated space. Such a space of humour rather than subverting the norm could be argued to be exceptional. From such a perspective rather than subverting it reveals the true force of law attached to liturgical practices. See (Harris 2011)
22. Curiously Breton argues that such theatrical representations emphasizing on a certain dramaturgy of the body is a prerogative of the East, while talking of fools of Christ in the West to be often writers who find their mood for madness convivial to the written word. (Breton 2002, 35)
23. Roudinesco, for example, understands such practices as part of a dialectics of the abject and the sublime which motivated many medieval ascetics to practice mortification of abject flesh to overcome and sublimate into the sublime region of divine spirit. See (Roudinesco 2009)

24. According to Harris, a 1337 ordinal from Wells cathedral states explicitly that the idea of boy bishop was to signify the Child Christ, the true and eternal high priest. (Harris 2011, 136)
25. Decision, incision, precision–all these words are direct loans from French, which in turn took them from Latin. For example, "decision" comes from French "décision", which comes from Latin "decision". In Latin, all these words are related to the verb caedo ("cut").
26. Breton rightfully points out this memorable phrase from Michel de Certeau's brilliant commentary on the *Garden of Earthly Delights* of Hieronymus Bosch. See (Breton 2002) and (Certeau 1992, 49-78).
27. Our analysis of the play is primarily based on Eugene Vance's reading of the play though for a different purpose. Through his reading of the play, Vance wants to challenge an existent hermeneutic tradition which looks at language from a horizontal perspective, presupposing communication and the mediatory function of language. Through his analysis of this play Vance wants to show how the history of medieval use of language already bears traces of what Blanchot calls a "pure interval between man and man". A place where language becomes possible only through the "other", through its relationship to "otherness" where man is separated from man by an abyss which is that of difference and which makes language possible. See (Vance 1986, 184-229).
28. Vance points out this relation between God and his two books life and scriptures from Thomas Aquinas. See (Vance 1986, 213).
29. Vance offers this as an alternative title for the play *Jeu de la Feuillee* (Vance 1986, 211)
30. For a detailed introduction to the nature and history of this particular genre see Jody Enders' introduction to her own English translations of twelve of these texts from the original French version. It is important to note here that Enders' translation of the texts are very *contemporary* in the best sense of the term. It is contemporaneous to both our times and that of the plays which is a most difficult feat to achieve. To maintain this paradox at the heart of the translation by making it relevant for our times

yet maintaining its difference from the time of its composition is truly remarkable. For example in a play titled *The Farce of the Student Who Failed His Priest Exam Because He Didn't Know Who Was Buried in Grant's Tomb*, Enders translates the main title question from Groucho Marx's famous question "Who is buried under Grants Tomb?" that he famously asked one of the contestants on *You Bet Your Life*, a comic quiz show air on TV during the .... While the actual French question came from an equally celebrated epic poem or *chanson de geste* of the late Middle Ages where somebody asks, "Who is the Father of the Four Aymon Boys?"
Enders' translation is not only absolutely precise and relevant to our times but more importantly it exposes the structural logic of comedy which is what makes comedy possible rather than the choice of subjects. ((ed.) 2011)

31. It is like in Ernst Lubitsch's film *To Be or Not to Be*, we see that in the Gestapo Headquarters a door suddenly opens and somebody announces Hitler. Everybody rises from their seats and raises their hands and shouts "Heil Hitler". Hitler enters, raises his hand, and shouts "Heil Myself!" For a more detailed description of this sequence, see (Zupancic 2008, 36).
32. Take, for example, the farce *Confession Lessons, or The Farce of the Lusty Husband Who Makes His Confession to a Woman, His Neighbour, Who is Disguised as a Priest* where an unfaithful husband is tricked by his wife and her neighbour to make a true confession about his unfaithfulness to a false priest (the neighbour comes disguised as a priest) ((ed.) 2011).
33. For a brilliant and detailed analysis of the problem of double and its relation to the comic and theatre see Mladen Dolar's "The Comic Mimesis". (Dolar 2017, 570-589)

Conclusion: To Get Past the Critic…

Section I

In his *Soliloquies*, Augustine says some interesting things about theatre. Among other observations he remarks that theatre falls within that category of things that might be disposed towards false representation but are not false themselves. Taking the case of the stage actor, the Church Father argues that Roscius, a famous tragic actor of his time, is truly a man and a professional tragic actor even though his portrayal of a character (Hercules or Hecuba) is definitively false[1]. This lack of uniformity makes theatre ontologically suspect to present the Christian Idea of Truth. The comment not only anticipates the paradox of the actor by more than millennia, it reveals the complicated metaphysics of representation Christianity was evolving since its emergence in world history. Perhaps the best illustration of the Christian logic of representation was provided by the 11th century theologian Hugh of St. Victor when he wrote:

> Resemblance by equality is one thing; resemblance by imitation is another, yet another is that of contrariety. The first is proper to the son of God, for it is said that he did not consider it a theft to be God's equal. The second is proper to man, who was indeed created in God's image. The third is proper to the Devil: indeed while God is the author and the principle of good, the Devil is the author of evil by resemblance in contrariness. (Vance 1986, 202)

In this remarkably lucid and precise definition, we are informed of the entire spectrum of Christian understanding of representation. But the implications of Hugh's definition are even more complicated. After the Fall man is no longer a pure imitation of God because he has participated in resemblance in contrariness. In other words, man who was made in the image of truth through an original act of aggression against the Father participates in resemblance through contrariness. Therefore from the point of view of resemblance, after the original sin, man as imitation falls under the power of the false. This makes life nothing more than a simulation of truth–a phantasm–based upon a logic of dissimilarity[2]. Contrariness which is brought to the surface from uncertain depths makes man's position on this earth suffer from an internal imbalance because it is no longer grounded in truth. At the same time Christianity allows man an access to that primordial moment when truth was given in resemblance by imitation (before the fall) through the Passion of Christ. However the incarnation of the Word in to Flesh is only a promise of a future (the Last Judgment) when man will regain his access to truth through imitation sustained by faith in redemption. Hence we see that man occupies a curiously analogous position to the theatre actor and to the problem of comedy we have tried to develop. In some sense he is an example of a bifurcation of the problem of resemblance in so far as he is part true and part false. In so far as all life has become phantasmagoric after the fall, man can only enact his role on earth by resemblance in contrariness. But at the same time through the idea of faith and hope, the Christian subject can imagine a life resembling truth (through imitation...like it was before the fall) which is *to come.* Therefore theatre can become an apt metaphor for life *in the present* which has become phantasmagoric, ungrounded and full of contrariness. While on the other hand, theatre itself has to be denounced for being a playground of Satan himself. A place where contrariness, contradiction has gained a concrete, existence. The world is the place where subjective imitation, based upon this materiality of contradiction, becomes indistinguishable from this objective contradiction.

However the fall is also a historical moment for Christianity which was not only 'real' for Adam or Eve but for the entirety of mankind. This introduces an idea of equality via *negative* within Christianity. Mankind is equal and anonymous, negatively speaking, as an effect of the fall. Theatre shares this definition of anonymity which is evident from Augustine's declaration that the actor is true to himself only when he is not himself. A complete loss of one's identity, a slide into anonymity is the very essence of theatre which Augustine was so well aware of. It is because of this universal and phantasmagoric anonymity, which is the theatrical substance per excellence, for which it is dragged on to the tribunal of truth by philosophy or theology to be judged. Whether it's the platonic judgment which declares it a simulation–a copy of a copy, an infinitely degraded form of resemblance or the Christian judgment of rendering theatre as a metaphor of profane life which has become a resemblance in contrariness; the former providing the condition for the governing of the theatrical substance (which we examined in the first chapter) while the latter leads to a renunciation of theatre and its simultaneous use as metaphor for life (which we tried to examine in the second and third chapter). However it has been the critical effort of this thesis to clinically penetrate the cold and calculating outer shell of these judgments to find strange and insistent signs of exïstence of a curiosity for the theatrical substance. Signs of curiosity which can perhaps be termed as 'concern' for the knowledge of theatre. It is this concern and desire which articulate the relation of theatre to philosophy and theology, playing a strange and ambiguous game of hide and seek with the judgments which are passed on to theatre in the name of philosophy or theology.

In conclusion it can perhaps be argued that the renunciation of theatre by Christianity renounced its task and let itself be carried away by the metaphor. In a certain sense the metaphor of theatre seduced Christianity, distracting it from the task of absolute renunciation dislodging it off its path. This function of the metaphor can be seen from the point of view of a foundational logic. The metaphor of theatre in its circularity of meaning (for example the semantic circle we explored in Chrysostom's view of theatre at the end of our second chapter–theatre as a metaphor for vainglory which masks the abjection of life, but theatre also as a product of *euergetism* which is conditioned by vainglory in Roman society) becomes the basis for judging theatre itself whose verdict comes as the abolition of theatre. To the problem of veracity that theatre generates we have the response which comes in the form of the creation of metaphor. However the metaphorization of theatre in Christianity perfectly corresponds with this self-sufficiency of the metaphorical substance from which the judgment against theatre is extracted. The world becomes a theatrical metaphor but equally the metaphor of theatre becomes the phantasmagoric world; a world held in resemblance to the true substance but resemblance in contrariness which is free but dissimilar to the 'true substance'.

This is perhaps the singular difference of the use of the theatrical metaphor within Christianity from its preceding history. Moreover in Plato, as Deleuze points out, the foundational logic which becomes the condition for the declaration of judgment is myth. "Myth, with its always circular structure, is indeed the story of a foundation. It permits the construction of a model according to which the different pretenders (genuine copies and false simulations) can be judged" (Deleuze 1990, 255). Therefore myth is responsible for constructing the immanent model according to which "pretenders" in Plato should be evaluated as to whether they are genuine copies or imitations of the foundational model (Idea) or copies of copies which is to say simulations. Therefore the "governors of Dionysius", as Plato argues in the Laws, are to evaluate and govern not only the musicians but such simulators and degraded pretenders like the comedians and also the tragedians; but the legislative criterion according to which they are to be evaluated and judged, in the final analysis, is based on the foundational myth of Minos[3]. Interestingly, as we saw in the very beginning of our first chapter, the metaphor of theatre is evoked in the Laws to denounce the poets. Plato uses the tragic metaphor to delegitimize the tragedians. He argues that the tragedy of life is more serious than the tragedy on stage because the former copies the Idea while the latter is merely a simulation and hence should always remain inferior. In other words the metaphor of theatre is employed to create the hierarchy between copies and simulation, between true copies and false copies. Though the operation of using the metaphor of theatre to denounce theatrical practices remains similar to Christianity a crucial difference separates the use of theatrical metaphor in the two respective cases.

While in Plato, the metaphor is only a derivative of the foundational logic of *myth* which is responsible for the judgment against theatre, in Christianity it is the *metaphor itself* which becomes the phantasmagoric foundation or the model according to which judgment is passed. Rather than using the metaphor of theatre as a derivative of a foundational myth to create a hierarchy between true and false pretenders, Christianity wants to renounce pretention as such calling it theatrical. With Christianity we see a repetition of the platonic gesture of using the metaphor of theatre to denounce theatre itself but with two signification transformations. a) The metaphor of theatre is no longer a derivative of a foundational myth according to which judgment is pronounced b) the judgment against theatre is not to govern theatre according to a hierarchic logic of representation but absolute renunciation. To express it in other words, for Plato theatre is a problem to be resolved according to a dialectic of rivalry and the use of the theatrical metaphor is to be seen from this perspective. While in Christianity the problem of theatre is related to dialectic of contradiction between truth and falsity and the creation of the theatrical metaphor is related to such a dialectic.

But even within Christianity the creation of the metaphor–*via negativa*–in some sense displays a curiosity for the knowledge of theatre which can be seen as a symptom of concern for theatre. It can perhaps be argued from a psychoanalytic perspective, an effort which we have consciously avoided in this thesis, that the judgment that is passed on theatre rises from the pre-juridical moment of desire which is immediately repressed and dissimulated by the enactment of judgment. Or perhaps to make things more complicated (in the best possible sense) the inaugural moment is not to be seen as the repression of desire for theatre which is disavowed through the judgment against it. The original moment seems to a deviation, within christianity, a split which is constitutive of its treatment of theatre and its alienation in the Christian world. This split which is constitutive of the alienation of the substance seems to be the result of the fall of the first signifier. Here the fall of the first signifier or in other words the signifier *as one* seems to coincide with Fall of Man who is no longer seen as the primary signifier (resemblance in imitation) but as that which comes through its 'repression' creating a opposition (resemblance in contrariness). Therefore the Christian subject is constituted as a signifying dyad who is stuck in his fundamental either/or. The metaphor of theatre not only articulates the judgment against theatre but also enunciates the inaugural split which constitutes it as an alienated substance whose meaning resides elsewhere, in the Other. The metaphor of theatre becomes identical with the theatrical substance in their alienated status. The judgment against theatre and the desire for theatre becomes two halves of a single division. Like at the end of Sophists, Socrates' *concern for the truth* about the false pretentions of the sophists becomes indistinguishable from the falsity of the truth of the Sophists, so does the Christian concern for the falsity of theatre becomes at times indistinguishable from their concern for the theatrical. We tried to explore this in our last chapter on the controversy of the theatrical nature of the Eucharist and the para-liturgical nature of the miracle play–*Le Mystere d'Adam.*

However this metaphysical indiscernability between truth and falsity which we intermittently see being played out historically, when the truth of ritual (or philosophy) becomes indistinguishable with the deception of theatre does not take away the violence against theatre which is equally historical. The history of theatre, particularly the social history of the actors is a testimony to the violence of repression and the force of judgment and how it can smoothly move from discursive to ethical to juridical practices finally settling on the body of the actor–practices of branding actors with red hot irons continued well into the Elizabethan Renaissance.

The genealogy of such judgments and its profound relation in influencing theatre discourse and even different theories of theatre and theatricality is perhaps yet to be written. From Aristotle's idea of a citizen-critic[4] to the modern performance scholar a genealogy of the critic and its relation to the judgments against theatre needs to be constructed. A genealogy which would not only consider the function of the critic to identify and categorize theatre or performance, structurally or even on the basis of efficacy but rather a study of the complex power relations which is responsible for the production of such knowledge .Such a genealogy has to consider the *problematique* of theatre or the study of theatre as a problem whose point of departure has to be the present concern for generating a knowledge of theatre and performance based upon efficacy. The production of the theory of efficacy which delimits the boundaries of performance in order to transform it into an object of knowledge which then can be studied has to be problematized (in the complex sense of the word) from the point of view of a genealogy of the critic-subject.

Section II

The 'conflict' between performance and theatre studies seems to grow out of a deep anxiety inherent to the game of criticism. Scholars like Janelle Reinelt see a 'productive dissonance' in the intellectual *agon* generated by such discord, reshaping the contemporary contours of performance theory making it more consequential, politically one might add, to "contemporary transnational situation" (Reinelt 2002, 201). But a claim for such global 'efficacy' of a particular form of knowledge which would nevertheless, when applied, allow local struggles to proliferate does not come without a bit of irony. While both performativity and theatricality struggle for what can only be argued as global relevance, the taking place of the discourses themselves seems to be sharply divided territorially. While the discourse of performativity seems to be fundamentally an Anglo-American practice, theatricality informs the Continental intellectual sensibility in a more concrete fashion. Clearly a gap separates the nature of these discourses–both of which desire to somehow make theatre/performance into a global/universal paradigm–and their taking place, which is highly territorial. Apart from distinguishing the nature of these discourses, which Reinelt does quite successfully, one perhaps needs to trace the history of the development of these discourses themselves and what kind of knowledge regimes they produce. In spite of the complexities of the debate, which is not possible for us to go into, in detail, at this stage a basic methodological problem with far reaching political consequences needs to be at least raised. It seems this game is fundamentally played out spatially, where players are particularly concerned about broadening its discursive territory, claiming new ones, re-conquering others which they had lost to other discursive categories. For example, though performance as an inclusive term, as Richard Schechner points out, cannot be used for everything, practically any action can be studied "as performance". Our investigation into the metaphor of theatre and its universal use as an epistemological category of a theatre of the world, since Plato, makes us suspicious about the novelty of such a universal desire as that of performance studies. One perhaps needs to trace the epistemological desire for finding a fundamental structure to all actions in the cognate categories of performance, performative, performativity to a much older desire of using the metaphorical category of theatre–a theatrum mundi–to find something like universal knowledge.

However the presupposition of consciousness which performance studies always carries with itself–one only has to examine such definition of performance as that of Marvin Carlson's that is cited by Schechner in his *Performance Studies: An introduction* to accept this presupposition[5]–brings back the problem of the Subject at the very heart of this discourse. And this, in spite of the fact that the philosophic tradition which had critiqued J.L. Austin's theory of performative utterances (primarily Derrida and Deleuze) and from which performance studies openly claim to draw its critical resource, is fundamentally identified with the 'destruction' of any philosophy of the Subject. One can perhaps explain the proliferation of "performative" statements which maintains their particular identity and meaning–ritual statements, statements of play, even the performative statements of everyday practices–from the point of view of the Subject and the theory of split that it is based upon. According to this theory, any statement in the moment of its utterance, splits the Subject into the subject of statement and the subject of enunciation. From the point of view of performance theory this can be seen in the realm of specificity of the performative statement which is always particular–the context of the performative statement can be gendered, racially motivated or determined by subversive political activities. While the subject of enunciation, in the final analysis always comes back to the efficacious subject, the subject who is capable of producing and receiving affects. Following Deleuze, one can argue that this affirmation of particular subjects of statements is always related to the Subject–a universal subject of enunciation. This introduces a logic of dualism at the heart of the performative subject who is always already split between the subject of multiple statements and the singular enunciation. In spite of the cultural variations it can maintain–it must maintain–the performative subject will always affirm this structural logic of dualism where the almost paranoiac excess of performative statements is always related to the singular lack which always informs its enunciation. To search for this 'original' and 'mystical' moment of enunciation, as the *performative substance* per excellence, through the length and breadth of human history has been the prerogative of performance studies. But as Deleuze remarks "Dualism is not defined by two, dualism is defined by the employment of the one and the multiple as adjectives" (Deleuze, 2001, 99). Without ever its object being completely known performance can enforce its law which in turn can induce a proliferation of rules which are made known according to the details of its application. In his *Performance Studies: An Introduction*, Schechner writes, "Performances occur in eight sometimes separate, sometimes overlapping situations: 1) in everyday life–cooking, socializing, "just living" 2) in the arts 3) in sports and other popular entertainments 4) in business 5) in technology 6) in sex 7) in ritual–sacred and secular 8) in play".

(Schechner 2002, 31) The rules of these situations which make them performative are given simultaneously but it never exhausts the performative substance as Schechner immediately remarks, "Even this list does not exhaust the possibilities. If examined rigorously as theoretical categories, the eight situations are not commensurate". (Schechner 2002, 31)

The series of dualism that performance studies employ ("is" performance–"as" performance, efficacy-entertainment, real-fiction etc.) in order to claim their frequent coincidence, is in the final analysis adjectives which maintain an actual dualist logic of the *one and the multiple*. The political consequence of this opposition, which surreptitiously creeps into the heart of such a discourse, is fundamentally ideological. The immediacy of efficacy, the force of freedom, the proximity of the body and the localization of cultural contexts are all mediated through the intellectual distance of criticism. The obscure *object* of performance immediately produces the *critical* subject who is aware of the performativity of the entire planet and even of the whole cosmos but who can only participate in it in so far as she is conscious of her performativity. In such a world one is not always just performing, which is what we have been doing since time immemorial. Rather in this case one is necessarily conscious of one's performativity. The logic of necessary performance not only takes away any possibility of contingency from life but makes life function under the law of performance whose mystical substance seem to coincide with the transcendental and universal substance of capital. In such an era when distance towards all ideologies has become the fundamental mode of dominant ideology, a new meaning of the 'Universal' is perhaps given to the metaphor of theatrum mundi. A new mode of attaining a logic of universal knowledge, primarily through the medium of culture is at work. Performance as the new metaphor of universal knowledge is perhaps only a modified addition to the long genealogy of the metaphor of world theatre that we have tried to study, so inadequately one might add, in this thesis.

Section III

By the 16th century the desire for the construction of what Paolo Rossi calls "'pansophia' or total knowledge" had penetrated western imagination to the extent that they were trying to find the perfect structural expression of this desire through mobilizing the image of theatre. It was yet another shift in the use of the metaphor of a world theatre which was now determined by a specular logic which sought perfect correspondence between words and things and between logic and ontology. In Italy, Giulio Camillo Delminio sought to realize this desire for universal knowledge in his *L'idea del theatro* through perfecting the rhetoric art of memory giving it the image of a theatrum mundi. Camillo's notion of a theatre "in which, by means of the doctrine of places and images, we can hold in the mind and master all human concepts and all the things that are in the entire world" (Rossi 2000, 74) pushed the limits of rhetoric and the art of memory transforming it into a treatise on cosmology. His idea of the world represented as an amphitheatre with seven levels to be accessed through seven gates not only carried the mystical import of a double number symbolizing–the seven times seven–words in the Lord's prayer. His search for the "seven measures of the fabric of the celestial and inferior world in which are contained the ideas of all things celestial and inferior" (Rossi 2000, 75) was only a symptom of the specular logic of creating an architectural image of a theatre which would correspond not only to the cosmos but also stand as a metaphor for man himself. The arena in the centre of the amphitheatre was left vacant surrounded by the seven columns of creations, called Saphiroth, according to the nomenclature in the Cabala. Clearly the image of the amphitheatre was inspired by actual Roman amphitheatre as was the arrangement of the cosmos which corresponded to the hierarchical seating arrangement of ancient Rome. But Rome was a distant past whose reality was more conjured up in the imagination of Renaissance than was actually available. Sources, like the works of Vitruvius were more often ideologically interpreted. Imagination fuelled by an ideological desire to give structure to a universal spirit was dominant at the time among men of letters. Therefore

Camillo inverted the metaphorical orientation of the amphitheatre where the empty arena became focal point from where man was to observe the whole of cosmos. The universal spirit of the theatrical image of Camillo is informed by the central position occupied by man who reflects the macrocosm of the cosmos in his microcosm.

On the other hand, Robert Fludd, one of the key English philosophers of the Jacobean age shared the desire prevalent within the hermetic tradition of philosophy to which Camillo belonged to compose the encyclopedic description of the universe. To that extent he was a pivotal figure, along with John Dee to introduce and develop the idea of the macrocosm of the universe reflected within the microcosm called man. As we discussed above this encyclopedic desire to grasp a universal knowledge took the art of memory from a mere rhetorical procedure to give it its ontological status. In the microcosm volume of Fludd's *History of the Two World* we find the engraving of a stage which is labeled *TheatrumOrbi(s)*. The plan for this stage description, as scholars like Frances Yates has shown, goes on to influence the stage of the English public theatre, during the Elizabethan and Jacobean period in a major way[6]. What is evident is that the stage design serves as part of the art of memory, that Fludd discusses where natural technique which constitutes the technical history of the microcosm, (the techniques or arts used by man) as against the outer techniques which are studied in the technical history of macrocosm are brought together. The image of the theatre stage serves as an illustration of the many mnemonic techniques employed my man in order to reflect in his microcosmic status, the macrocosm. As Yates remarks:

> He (man) is a little world which is an epitome of the great world. Not only does his physical form and corporeal life repeat the elemental composition of the world of matter, his mental and spiritual life repeat the higher celestial world. The stars in their course are naturally within his mind and memory. Fludd's two type of memory systems, the *ars quadrata* and the *ars rotunda*, the first of which memorizes 'corporeal' images, the second, celestial and spiritual images express in terms of the 'square' and the 'round', the elemental and earthy, and the celestial and

starry, aspects of the macrocosm-microcosm relationship (Yates 1969, 142)

There is no shadow of a doubt as to who occupies the empty orchestra in the middle of Camillo's model of the theatre of the world–Man. But it is equally evident that the fundamental problem of the theatre of the world is that of repetition. Now the question arises: is the repetition of the macrocosm in the microcosm a repetition of the same, where in ever narrowing concentric circles the foundation of representational logic of philosophy is repeated when the infinitely great is captured and repeated in the infinitely small? Is the stage only a copy of the world insofar as it resembles the Universal Idea? In other words, does it produce an image of the world not based upon something or the other but an Idea? Does the image of a world theatre conform to the object of theatre insofar as it resembles the idea of a world internally and spiritually? Does the image of world theatre merit the quality of theatre only in so far as this theatrical quality is founded on a Universal Essence? Camillo's model seems to point at that direction. By inverting the Christian use of the metaphor of theatrum mundi, where the all seeing eye of God inaugurates a metaphysics of infinity by the unlimited vision of the divine sovereign, Camillo manages to articulate the representational logic of philosophy[7] epitomized in the philosophy of Leibniz and Hegel. The man who occupies the empty orchestra of the world theatre in Camillo's model repeats the "Same" which is now founded upon "an unconditioned principle capable of making it the ruler of the unlimited: sufficient reason." (Deleuze, *The Logic of Sense* 1990, 259). Man thus becomes the "Similar" which finds a condition to be now seen as a continuation of such an unlimited Sameness. The repetition of the sameness brings about a productive aspect to the quality of man as a bearer of the universal model. To that extent the reversing of the earlier Christian use of the metaphor of a theatrum mundi achieves nothing radically new. It reproduces the logic of representation which had sought to find its foundation in an infinite model, opening representation up to Being , beyond the highest genera (which was the Aristotelian desire) and thereby making it possible to subordinate the infinitely great and the infinitely small.

However, Fludd's model seems to enunciate something altogether different displaying symptoms of a genuine reversal of the ideological closure of the theatrum mundi metaphor. If Camillo's image of the theatre functions as a copy of the world, Robert Fludd's image seems to function as a simulacrum. First of all it is interesting to recall that though Fludd places his image of the world stage in the 'round' system, which memorizes spiritual images, he based the image upon the real public theatres of the Elizabethan and Jacobean era. Yates reproduces Fludd's definition of theatre thus:

> I call that a Theatre, in which all actions of words, of sentences, of parts of speech or subjects, are demonstrated as in a public theatre, where comedies and tragedies are enacted. (n.d. 143)

But *ars rotunda* remains a mnemonic technique based upon capturing abstract images and incorporeal substances which is appropriate of the 'round' art. So the images are not representation of material things but 'ideas' of things which are otherwise impenetrable things without corporeality like angels, demons, effigies of the stars, images of gods and goddesses, images of virtues and vices. *Ars rotunda* was preferred by those who were educated in 'astronomy' (astral magic). But Fludd himself denounces, as Yates points out, in the beginning of his memory treatise, the use of fantastic or fictitious places in the art of memory. Fludd writes "For the original act of fixing a place in memory is weaker if the foundation is fictitious, and the further it is from a foundation in truth the less fixed it is" (n.d. 148). It seems at this stage that Fludd's understanding of fantasy was based upon a strongly materialist understanding which he explicitly accepts in the following remark "Wherefore it is to be concluded that 'the operation of the fantasy begins from the real things and not from intentions, and its acts are stronger and more certain when it proceeds from reality and returns to it" (Ibid., n.d.) Here we have new understanding of the image of *theatrum mundi*. In Fludd's work the metaphor of theatre which stands for the Universal Spirit of the world seems to move in both directions. The pure disincarnate Universal Spirit does not simply come to inform and give meaning to the material and physical reality of theatre, but the physical reality of theatre seems to move into forms of the pure disincarnate intellect. This double function seems to be at work when Fludd describes how to memorize the five words *liber, exaltabat, laetus, cultellus* and *lux.* Fludd explains that in order to do this one has to imagine the sorceress Medea as making five actions corresponding to these words as she stands in front of the five doors of the stage which he had constructed out of real stage of the period. As Yates points out, this game of memory-for-words is therefore based upon the real public theatre in which comedies and tragedies (including *Medea*) were acted bringing to life the mnemonic technique of actions for words. Two separate series are working here; a series of the signifier (actions) which is of the immanent and material order and the series of the signified (words) which is of transcendent order. The totalizing or universal spirit of the signified series encounters the finite, limited series of signifying actions. The non localizable excess of the signified series meets the limited, localized and hence perpetually lacking signifiers at the point which is called theatre. Under the power of the false, the phantasmatic power of theatre makes finite and limited actions–which are themselves simulations (because they do not resemble any model but are fictions)–to rise and subjugate the universal under its power. Through this image of the theatre of the world the universal seems to have been reversed and put to work in concrete action. As against an image of the 'theatre of the world' which Camillo produced representing through the *loci* of artificial memory the eternal *loci* of the universe, Fludd, seems to develop an image of a world stage where the universal is in *action*. Shakespeare's plays performed on the stage of the Globe theatre which so frequently spoke of the world as a stage seems to be the best example of this "universal at work".

On the one hand our attempt in this research has been to trace Camillo's idea of a world theatre back to its Platonic roots of governing simulations (theatre) in the name of true models and genuine copies. It then passes through the Christian era of abolition of theatre and its corresponding effort to metaphorize theatre for its own purpose of establishing a world order in the name of an alien truth. While on the other hand we have tried to trace those moments where the binding of theatre with philosophy or theology comes loose and they seem to express a radical theatricality of their own. Finally to reach a moment where the materiality of comedy makes an exit from all such binding and unbinding to make the universal, the ultimate prerogative of both philosophy and theology, work under its supervision.

To trace the metaphors of theatres and theatres of metaphors that has been our journey; to get past the critic and encounter a few rare moments where instead of theatre becoming more worldly, the world comes to think of itself in the strange and anonymous language of theatre.

NOTES

1. For a discussion of the importance of theatre in Augustine see (Dox 2004). For a discussion of the theatricality of Augustinian thinking, particularly in his early dialogues please see (Foley 2014)
2. For a profound analysis of the difference between copies and simulations, the former informed with resemblance while the latter being dissimilar and phantasmatic in relation to the Platonic Idea which influences Western metaphysics, including Christian theology, drawing it more and more towards an idea of representation. Please see the essay "The Simulacrum and Ancient Philosophy" by Gilles Deleuze (Deleuze 1990, 253-279).
3. In *Laws* Plato argues through the Athenian Stranger that the best laws are the Cretan laws, even better than Spartan laws which was only the second best. This was because the Cretan laws was given by Minos, who was not only a son of Zeus but the only hero to be educated by Zeus. Though the Athenians regarded Minos to be savage and unjust, it was because Minos had waged victorious war against Athens. As Leo Strauss points out, "The best legislator was an enemy of Athens. The quest for the best laws seems to compel the Athenians to transcend the laws of Athens and to become the

pupils of an enemy of Athens – to act in a way which could appear to be un patriotic" (Strauss 1975, 1). The myth of Minos is not only the foundational test based upon judgements are passed and codes are elaborated for a city about to be founded, the ironical structure of the myth provides the necessary dialectics of rivalry (between Athens and Minos) which becomes the basis of *Laws*. It is not a dialectics of contradiction between a transcendental sovereign legislator and the immanent actualizations of law.

4. Andrew Ford in his essay "Katharsis: An Ancient Problem" proposes a brilliant analysis of the concept of catharsis as a theoretical tool developed by Aristotle not only to render innocuous the dangerous efficacies generated by performance but perhaps more significantly, the objective analysis of theatre was retroactively responsible to produce the significant subjective category of the citizen critic.(Ford 1995)
5. Schechner cites Marvin Carlson: "The term 'performance' has become extremely popular in recent years in a wide range of activities in the arts, in literature, and in the social sciences. As its popularity and usage has grown, so has a complex body of writing about performance, attempting to analyze and understand just what sort of human activity it is. [. . .] The recognition that our lives are structured according to repeated and socially sanctioned modes of behaviour raises the possibility that all human activity could potentially be considered as "performance," or at least all activity carried out with a consciousness of itself. [. . .] If we consider performance as an essentially contested concept, this will help us to understand the futility of seeking some overarching semantic field to cover such seemingly disparate usages as the performance of an actor, of a school child, of an automobile. 1996, *Performance: A Critical Introduction*, 4-5"(Schechner 2002, 31).
6. "The stage walls show five entrances onto the stage. Three are on ground level, consisting of a double hinges door shown half open, in the centre, flanked by two other entrances. Two upper entrances give on to a battlemented terrace which runs across the stage front on each side of acentral bay window which projects forward and

overhangs the stage. The text accompanying the engraving states that it refers to a public theatre in which comedies and tragedies are acted." (Yates 1969, 137)

7. For a profound analysis of the way representational logic comes to dominate philosophy since Plato who creates the distinction between genuine copies and false simulation and how the former represses the latter such that the only way to emancipate philosophy would be to reverse Platonism. See (Deleuze, *The Logic of Sense* 1990).

APPENDIX I

Birth of a Concept

Anup Dhar

This PhD thesis by Soumick De titled *Perversion, Pedagogy and the Comic: A Survey of the Concept of Theatre in Christian Middle Ages* (which does not restrict itself to only the Christian Middle Ages but moves genealogically and archaeologically from the Greco-Roman to the Christian, from paganism to Roman and Eucharist liturgy, making connections between and among them as also showing breaks, ruptures, cuts) is perhaps the best work I have read in recent times and in my experience as an examiner and a reader of doctoral theses in India and abroad. The work is scholarly. It is well-researched, well-referenced and is deeply philosophical; it spans a sound and grounded review of a breadth and depth of literature not usual in doctoral thesis; as also a somewhat breathtaking and original reading of such literature. The research question is set up well: "how theatre came to be an object of thinking" or "how theatre entered the Christian mind as an object of thought" "before[1] [and the before is important in this work] it became entangled in [everyday] Christian behavior and conduct"; i.e. the work is on the "pre-history" of two sets of moves within Christianity: one, when and where "actual theatrical practices were severely denounced as perversion particularly because of its deceptive qualities and finally were legally prohibited", and two, the use of theatre as a "metaphor" in sermons, homilies and other forms of Christian pedagogic literature. The work makes the most of what "Savage Freud/Psychoanalyst" Girindrasekhar Bose calls the see-saw–the double wish–between repression/prohibition/forbidding and condensed-displaced (condensed-displaced in a psychoanalytic sense) incitement; in fact, metaphorization and metaphoric cuts a la Lacan is itself a psychoanalytic subject effect. This is perhaps the moment when "theatre becomes unfamiliar or disturbing enough to enter the realm of thought". Is theatre then an experience of the Uncanny in the long duree called the Christian middle age–which from a "historical perspective" is taken by the author as a "finite discursive phenomenon"? What is presented as disjunctive synthesis or inconsistency or "constitutive paradox" in the Introduction and splitting in the Conclusion, could it also have been presented as the work of the uncanny at the core of the Christian worldview, that is taking shape and getting from in its association with theatre, in terms of what in its history is the "problem". The thesis does well to present itself as a work in the *gharana* of the "History of Problems"; where a problem is not the ground for a solution but the ground for the birth of a concept or a particular configuration or architecture of the concept; where the problem is the link that connects a concept to concrete historical difficulties; in fact, the problem provides the "general conditions of thinking" or reflecting; from which is born–not a solution–but a concept. I find this framing of the problematic and of the birth of the concept–presented as an absolute instance of a self-referential creative event which is nevertheless relative and fragmentary at the same time–amidst an extant genealogy of the concept, as also a cosmology of concepts, scholarly and fascinating. The author argues that the concept of theatre in Christianity has three components: (i) pedagogy (tied to the doctrinal), (ii) perversion (tied to praxis) and (iii) the comic (which unsettles the dialectic and possible sublation between pedagogy and perversion; which also subverts all figures of universal essence and substance). The concept is in turn related to the concept of economy, the concept of (female) sexuality (marked by the work and phantasm of deception), and the figurative imagination of the world as an illusion or what Marx calls "the delusive appearance of things". The thesis does well to set up the "problem of theatre" and the disappearance and the consequent reappearance of the theatrical metaphor in terms of the disjunctive synthesis and the paradoxical ontological split between the "divine transcendental order" and the "mortal immanent order"–where the second is a derivative or natural extension of the first. How would these "two orders of reality" and their always hierarchized relationship get reconciled in Christian theology? Would theatre and the concept of theatricality play a role? Would theatre suffer, if not socially, at least juridically? Would the concept of theatricality contribute to the thinking of Roman liturgy as also Eucharist liturgy; or would the liturgical experience contribute to the conceptualization of theatre? The thesis explores how the "force of the comic" (designated the feast of fools as against the ship of fools) comes to be the diagonal between the two orders as also between theatre as pedagogy and theatre as perversion; comic as part of a "folk tradition extending back to paganism" rather than 12th century liturgical drama. The thesis also moves from ideas of "philosophical theatre" and "theological theatre" to the relation between theatre and philosophy (as also ethics through largely late Foucault)–a relation "which is not merely [that of] a phenomenological problem but also an ethical one". The thesis thus re-thinks philosophy from theatre–philosophy dyad, and theatre from the experience-praxis dyad. The metaphorization of theatre does not lapse into just the philosophy of theatre (into what philosophy has imposed on theatre, say for example, Plato as the architect of the ontological malaise or the metaphysical degradation of theatre as a second order of imitation/translation, including the critique of theatre for eliciting passion, desire and the realm of the irrational). This, I feel, is one of the major contributions of the thesis; in that sense, the thesis is profoundly Deleuzian (and here I have a question which the author of the thesis may wish to consider while converting the thesis to a book manuscript [which the author must; this work deserves and needs to be published]: how would we make sense of the reconciliation of the Slovenian School a la Zupancic and Deleuze in the thesis; it would perhaps be better to render explicit the [non]relationship between the two theoretical frameworks in the book manuscript. The thesis manages to work its way through (not towards) what has come to be seen in Barish (1981) as the "natural content" of theatre which gets "repressed and denied" in Plato. The thesis thus works its way beyond theatrically and anti-theatricality, including the repressive hypothesis and an anti-repressive impulse to show how theatre remained as a "problem" within Christian discourse, purely at the formal level which in turn explains the frequent use of theatre as metaphor (as world stage–world stage as symbolic negation of the worldly–or where the world is the theatre and God is the audience). The thesis shows how theatre is, on the one hand, an "apt metaphor for profane life [which is "phantasmagoric, ungrounded and full of contrariness"] in the present", and on the other, a "playground for Satan"; where theatre is "ontologically suspect" with respect to the Christian "Idea of Truth"; and where theatre is being related to the Christian logic of representation: "representation by equality", by "imitation", through "contrariety". The world, on the one hand, becomes a theatrical metaphor; the metaphor of theatre, on the other, becomes the phantasmagoric world (as if the split is between theatre becoming worldly versus the coming to think of the world itself as theatre or stage). The thesis reaches the Christian Middle Ages by building on the social and juridical inconsistency in Roman liturgical practices including the "differential logic of subectivation" around the concept of deception and the metaphor of the deceptive or illusive nature of life itself. The judgment against theatre from the Greco-Roman to the Christian Middle Ages and the 'desire for theatre' becomes two unequal halves of a split subject. One half denouncing, as if, the other half. The desiring half denouncing the other half. The denouncing half (which is never half; hence part) is in turn menaced by the desiring part. The truth of the false merging into the falsity of the true; a kind of metaphorical indiscernability. The thesis also demonstrates through a close reading of Augustine's *Confessions* how the immanent mode of the production of truth under the demand of the 'event' gives confession an immanentist theatricality. It appears the thesis moves through a number of complex manoeuvers to the uncertain folds or perhaps, the multiple plateaus of a post-representationalist and materialist understanding of theatre. The contribution of the thesis is also in presencing a new meaning of the Universal–a split meaning of the universal–through the genealogy of the metaphor of world theatre/theatrum mundi (the macrocosm of the universe is reflected in/within the microcosm called human; and where world is an amphitheatre). The thesis in that sense is not just a survey of the concept of theatre. It is a survey of Christianity (in its relationship with the Greco-Roman and with paganism); it is a survey of the cusp of theology-philosophy, including philosophical universals; albeit embarked upon and accomplished in its relationship with theatre. The thesis thus manages to show how the "problem of theatre" (where theatre is itself, in itself transformative) undergoes a "unique transformation" in terms of Moebius of the (i) forbidding of material practices of theatre and (ii) metaphorization of theatrically (which is also a negation of the materiality or materialist understanding of theatre) where a theatrical essence was abstracted and preserved as a mystical (nor mythical) substance. Though the author spends a considerable part of the Conclusion on the relationship between theatre and performance (including performativity), it would perhaps have been more in tune with the thesis to have explored how the "consequences of Christianity still pervade the modern world almost giving it a quasi-universal status" (p. 3) through the apparently secular concept-metaphor of theatre. This just a suggestion for the author to consider when he converts the thesis to a book.

I shall not hesitate to urge and encourage Soumick De to take his PhD thesis to a book length publication.

I recommend the granting of the PhD degree to Soumick De after the viva voce.

I also recommend the publication of this thesis as a book.

APPENDIX II

The 'Worlding' by/of Theatre

Milind Wakankar

Soumick De's thesis has the potential to be an essential teaching-text in the TPS-SAA, to be inserted at that level at which the fundamentals of its pedagogy are to be worked out. It is a work of great learning that rigorously and painstakingly, and with the greatest passion and deliberation uncovers something like the 'primacy' of theatre in the institution of ethical substance through Greek, Roman, late ancient and medieval discourse. It achieves in a sense a restoration of what Soumick calls 'theatrical substance' to its place in the scene of alterity, at the heart of the very possibility of an ethics. Soumick is also at the same time a philosophers' philosopher, in that his writing weaves between 'primary' and 'secondary' elaborations (so to speak) of the question of theatre, between the works of Plato, Cicero, Origen, Clement, Tertullian and Augustine on the one hand, and Foucault, Loraux, Veyne, Arendt, Vance on the other. What is remarkable is the tenacity of purpose with which in a miraculous fashion Soumick succeeds in uncovering not just the subjects of the various discourses addressed to the question of the theatre; he insinuates himself into the very subject of the enunciation itself: he is at one with it; he *performs* this intimacy; the corpus of his thesis *is* the body of the actor as it exposes for a moment nothing but its 'glorious' materiality, breaking through the strictures of specularity, mimesis and auto-affectivity–bringing into view a kind of non-messianic messianicity of theatre, one that rewrites and redefines our view of the very relation between drama and the threatre, and between modernity and modernism. In the manner of Lyotard's posthumously published meditation on Augustine, Soumick provides us with the wherewithal to inhabit the very flesh of theatricality, opening philosophy, theory and conceptuality to a form of intellectual ardor and suasion that can perhaps best be described in the early German Idealist phrase as an internalization and illustration (both at once) of 'intellectual intuition.' Those deeply moving words of Augustine in his *Confessions*: 'You touched me, and I am set on fire to attain the peace that is yours'—Soumick comes soon after the posthumous Lyotard in earning the right to claim them as his own. It is fitting that in writing a thesis about the theatre he should have redefined the prescription for a dissertation: the thesis is not just 'about' theatre; it intervenes at the deepest level of the *concept* as such, there in the abyss that is also gaping hole of the tragic; it inserts itself in that original rift and dares to inaugurate a new form of conceptual elaboration. It insinuates itself in the minimal space between the face and the mask.

Much rests here on the metaphor of the theatre as the world. 'The metaphorization of the meaning of theatre where it comes to stand for a theatre of the world (*theatrum mundi*) could not have been possible without the confessional character of the Christian discourse around theatre' (112). *Metaphora,* as Soumick reminds us, entails 'transposition, displacement'—opening up the possibility of a 'third space' outside the sheer visibility of 'theatre as the world.' One the one hand, Christianity institutes a new idea of the 'world' (it is now a form of exteriority that must be relentlessly read for the secret that it keeps) by tying it to the idea of a future transfiguration of the present. On the other hand, theatre keeps within itself the possibility of a 'link with the invisible space offstage' (André Green, 155). This impossible threshold pierces through the figurality of all *figurae* (in the sense that Auerbach has taught us), introducing the temporality of a 'now-time' that is in a sense *not yet* the figure of the future. In this deferral of 'now-time,' Soumick seems to say, theatre yields the space of a temporalization that is at once radical and irreducible. This brings the question of the work of 'metaphor' in the figure of the 'world stage' to full circle: after all, 'The theatrical metaphor comes only as a worldly category because theatre, no matter how you see it, cannot but be immanent to the world' (155).

The movement from the modulation of desire in ancient Greek *ascesis*, through the theological question of 'acclamation' and 'glory' against the ambience of Roman *euergetism* (Peterson contra Schmitt), takes, us in Soumick's reckoning, to the following crucial shift in early Christian discourse: 'in the relation to the fabulous world of theatre, the 'real' world of Christian history had to imagine a way to transgress it. Not merely to reject theatre, but transgress the space of theatre through the creation of an invisible, impossible space beyond under whose sign the drama of the world could be deciphered and destroyed at the same time' (152). Using psychoanalytical vocabulary one might say that the introjection of theatre into the Real is established at this point: 'A destructive analysis produced by the ultimate desire for an original lack which could not only dissolve all earthly temptations like that of theatre but re-conceptualize the world from another perspective, so that the drama of existence no longer remains a fable but becomes a real history.' This is the segué for the extraordinary power and rhetoric of Augustine, for whom this involves a movement from 'death and destruction' to 'redemption and life' (152). I do not have the space here to recap the beautiful and soulful readings Soumick offers in Chapter Four of this Augustinian modus. It is clear from his exposition that it is in Augustine that the 'process of self-recollection to the book of God' involves the elaboration of a kind of 'transparent writing' (in Augustine's phrase) transposed from the 'theatre of life' to a 'divine theatre' (201). More tellingly, this is also the point of insertion of the problem of theatre into a new idea of 'intellectual knowledge' (202).

Once theatre is relocated in the scene of life's persistent need 'to be concerned with itself' (198) we arrive at the fullest reworking of what in Tertullian had been the problem of the 'substance of idolatry' (172). The internalization of the idea of theatre as the space where 'Illusion gains a certain reality so to speak as the work of the devil' (172) transpires in Augustine from within the terms of what one might call a process of intro-reflection, resulting in (as Soumick puts it, in a marvellous formulation) 'the transformation of theatre into an instrument of culture through intellectualization' (183). Soumick's recourse to Nietzsche at this point is appropriate. For in Augustine the process that began in Greek antiquity, which consisted of the modulation of desire and the discipline of pleasure, reaches its fullest elaboration at the intersection of *ressentiment* and idealization. In the primordial Nietzschean setting where the weak resent and hate the strong, it becomes a question of an 'inaugural... negation' (182), one that produces an a whole hermeneutics of 'depth as opposition' (Soumick's italics removed, 183).

In short, if (by Nietzsche's account) the origin of ideation (or intellectualization) and valuation (they are the same thing) is hatred, we find in theatre a kind of secondary inscription from *within ressentiment* itself, wherein 'the reactive force of culture came to delimit the active force of creation by an act of world historical revenge' (186). This opens up a vestibule between metaphorization and intellectualization, or metaphor and concept–one could well wonder if with Augustine metaphor 'is' ideation, or metaphor and concept have begin to bleed into each other. If this is true, then we might begin to see here a fresh point of departure for Soumick's interpretive ambition. For the achievement of this introjection of theatrical substance as well as its insertion into the history of the concept (the concept understood in Hegel's sense as the 'self-concept') implies that a new understanding of the relation between 'the idolatrous' and the incorporeal would have to be broached at this point. Here we are no longer in the moment of the metaphoricity of the world as a stage. We are at the point at which, arguably, the secondary re-inscription of idolatry into the concept will have taken place. Which is to say that we are now in the domain of the comic. In this specific sense, Soumick's notion of the comic works by way of the idolatrous as that which cannot be assimilated to the work of the 'metaphor of perversion' (3). The comic is best described as the very principle of this interruption of theatre as concept (in sublating metaphor as perversion). In Soumick's words, 'the comic becomes the differential point which traverses the components of the concept of theatre including itself at infinite speed' (4). This is d-riven home with extraordinary clarity in Soumick's reading of Chrysostom's critique of the cult of 'sacred marriage.' And it is in the concluding discussion of Zupançic's reading of Hegel (by way of Breton) that one gets a sense of what is at stake in the problem of the 'materiality' of the comic. The accent here is on the notion of Incarnation 'as the concrete actualization of the Spirit in this world (this is the meaning of Christianity being a revealed religion) such that when it appears in our world God "literally disappears from the other world, and with it disappears this other world itself" [Zupançic]' (Soumick, 289). Again: 'the cross does not simply express the abolition of any transcendence in the death of God, but the concrete taking place of the place itself through its abolition. It is through its own abolition or absencing, that the Absolute concretely affirms itself. It is an Absolute which in concretely realizing itself has been alienated from itself expressing itself in a completely empty and contingent figure. This is what makes Incarnation essentially comic' (290).

Here again Soumick is always a careful and sober genealogist, for whom the shifts are minimal but very significant. In Camillo there is again, in an affirmation of ideological closure, the idea of theatre as 'a copy of the world.' But in Fludd (via the uncircumventible Frances Yates) there is the notion of theatre as 'simulacrum' (320). Clearly, with Fludd the comic possibilities inherent in Incarnation have been brought to the foreground. Here at last the 'universal is in action,' prefiguring Shakespeare's Globe. Here 'instead of theatre becoming more worldly, the world comes to think of itself in the strange and anonymous language of theatre' (322). In his incredibly rich and wide-ranging account of perceptions of the theatre Soumick is drawn then to the possibility of a new history of theatricality, one that does not remain content with the story of anti-theatrical prejudice in the manner of Barish. It would seem as though at each point in this long trajectory the traces of this anti-mimetic (or anti-Platonic) are nothing if not discernible underneath the forceful discourse of a Tertullian or an Augustine. Indeed, I would go so far as to say that Soumick has helped us uncover in theatricality the ethics of a certain idolatry that persists beneath each succeeding regime of moral sanction against theatre. 'Idolatry' here is best understood in the sense of Levinas's idea of the 'face' of the Other (although Levinas himself uses the word 'idolatry' in a very different sense). The insistence of this face or idol is precisely towards its own materiality. Here 'materiality' refers us in the first instance to the centrality of 'now-time,' which is to say an idea of history that leaves aside the persistent 'figurality' of literary realism as it was signposted by Auerbach in a 'European' corpus that is at once theological and literary-historical. Indeed with Soumick we turn away from both theology and literary-history in their investment in the futurality of the future. It is a question, as I have said above, of a kind of non-messianic messianicity of the present. But Soumick also directs us to a new idea of secularity premised on the comic. In the worldliness of this world we are led away from the Heideggerian intimation that 'world *worlds*.' With Soumick we encounter a new thesis, that 'theatre *worlds*'–it does this intimately, cryptologically, from within the very workings of the concept. This 'worlding' by and of the theatre implies a daring and bold suggestion that ought to change the way we think of perception, dramaturgy as well as sexuality (with its own leanings toward the Incarnate). We must thank Soumick for restoring the inescapable temerity of the theatrical gesture and reminding us of the need to relocate theatre to its central place in a new 'science of logic,' a new conceptuality.

And it is also for this very reason that I endorse Soumick's dissertation for its inclusion in his credentials for a doctoral degree, for confirmation via viva-voce, and of course for publication without changes. Few in my estimation have so deservedly earned the title, 'Doctor of Philosophy.

Bibliography

Aeschylus. *The Oresteia: Agamemnon, The Libation Bearers, The Eumenides.* London, New York: Penguin Books, 1996.

Agamben, Giorgio. *The Kingdom and the Glory: For a Theological Geneology of Economy and Government.* Stanford, California: Stanford University Press, 2011.

___ . *Means Without Ends.* Minneapolis, London: University of Minnesota Press, 1996.

___ . *State of Exception.* Chicago, London: The University of Chicago Press, 2005.

___ . *The Sacrament of Language: An Archaeology of the Oath (Homo Sacer II, 3).* Stanford: Stanford University Press, 2011.

Alexandria, Clement cf. *The Paedagogus.* http://www.earlychristianwritings.com/text/clement-instructor-book1.html.

Althusser, Louis. *Reading Capital.* Delhi: Aakar Books, 2013.

Arendt, Hannah. *Love and Saint Augustine.* Chicago & London: The University of Chicago Press, 1996.

Artaud, Antonin. *The Theatre and its Double.* New York: Grove Press, 1958.

Auerbach, Erich. *Scenes from the Drama of European Literature.* Manchester: Manchester University Press, 1984.

Augustine, Saint. *Confessions.* New York: Oxford University Press, 1998.

___ . *On Christian Doctrine.* Mineola, New York: Dover Publications, 2009.

Augustine, St. *Confessions.* New York: Oxford University Press, 1991.

Badiou, Alain. *Rhapsody for the Theatre.* London, New York: Verso, 2013.

Balthasar, Hans Urs von. *Theo-Drama: Theological Dramatic Theory.* San Francisco: Ignatius Press, 1988.

___ . *Theo-Drama: Theological Dramatic Theory, Volume I.* San Francisco: 1988, 1988.

Barish, Jonas A. *The Antitheatrical Prejudice.* Berkeley: University of California Press, 1981.

Baudelaire, Charles. *Selected Writings on Art and Literature.* London and New York: Penguin Classics, 2006.

Blumenberg, Hans. *Shipwreck with Spectator.* Cambridge, Massachusetts: The MIT Press, 1997.

Breton, Stanislas. *The Word and the Cross.* New York: Fordham University Press, 2002.

Castelli, Elizabeth A. *Martyrdom and Memory: Early Christian Culture Making.* New York: Columbia University Press, 2004.

Choudhury, Soumyabrata. *Theatre Number Event: Three Studies on the Relationship Between Sovereignty, Power and Truth.* Shimla: Indian Institute of Advanced Studies, 2013.

Cicero. *De Natura Deorum and Academica.* Cambridge, Massachusetts: Harvard University Press, 1993.

Deleuze, Gilles. *Difference and Repetition.* London, New York: Continuum, 2005.

Deleuze, Gilles. "Dualism, Monisim and Multiplicities." *Contretemps,* 2001: 92-108.

___ . *Essays Critical and Clinical.* Minneapolis: University of Minnesota Press, 1997.

___ . *Foucault.* London: The Athlone Press, 1999.

___ . *Nietzsche and Philosophy.* London - New York: Continuum, 1983.

___ . *The Logic of Sense.* New York: Columbia University Press, 1990.

Derrida, Jacques. "Composing "Circumfession"." In *Augustine and Postmodernism: Confessions and Circumfessions*, by John D. Caputo and Michael J. Scanlon, 19-27. Bloomington and Indianpolis: Indiana University Press, 2005.

___ . *Dissemination.* London, Oxford, New York, New Delhi, Sydney: Bloomsbury, 2016.

Dolar, Mladen, "The Comic Mimesis". *Critical Inquiry* 43; 2017: 570-589.

Dox, Donnalee. *The Idea of the Theatre in Latin Christian Thought.* Ann Arbor: The University of Michigan Press, 2004.

Edwards, Catherine. *The Politics of Immorality in Ancient Rome.* Cambridge: Cambridge University Press, 2002.

Foley, Michael P. "A Spectacle to the World: The Theatrical Meaning of St. Augustine's Soliloquies." *Journal of Early Christian Studies,* Vol. 22, Number 2, 2014: 243-260.

Foley, Michael P. "The Sacramental Topography of the Confessions." *Antiphon*, 2005: 30-64.

Foucault, Michel. *Ethics: Subjectivity and Truth.* London, New York: Penguin Books, 1997.

____. *On the Government of the Living: Lectures at College de France (1979-80).* Hampshire: Palgrave Macmillan, 2014.

____. *The Care of the Self: The History of Sexuality Vol 3.* London: Penguin Books, 1990.

____. *The Politics of Truth* . Los Angeles: Semiotext(e), 2007.

____. *The Use of Pleasure: The History of Sexuality Vol 2.* London, New York: Penguin Books, 1992.

Freud, Sigmund. *Five lectures on Psycho-Analysis, Leonardo da Vinci and Other Works.* London: The Hogarth Press and the Institute of Psychoanalysis, 1957.

Green, Andre. "The Pscycho-analytic Reading of Tragedy." In *Mimesis, Masochism, & Mime*, by Timothy Murray, 136-162. Ann Arbor: The University of Michigan Press, 1997.

Harris, Max. *Sacred Folly: A New History of the Feast of Fools.* Ithaca and London: Cornell University Press, 2011.

Hegel. *Lectures on Philosophy of Religion.* Berkeley: University of California Press, 1984.

Heidegger, Martin. "Augustine and Neo-Platonism." In *The Phenomenology of Religious Life*, by Martin Heidegger, 115-230. Bloomington and Indianapolis: Indiana University Press, 2010.

Kierkegaard, Soren. *Concluding Unscientific Postscript to Philosophical Crumbs.* Cambridge, New York: Cambridge University Press, 2009.

___ . *Either/Or: A Fragment of Life.* London, New York: Penguin Books, 1992.

___ . *Fear and Trembling.* London, New York: Penguin Books, 1985.

___ . *The Concept of Irony: With Continual Reference to Socrates.* Princeton, New Jersey: Princeton University Press, 1989.

Kobialka, Michal. *This Is My Body: Representational Practices in the Early Middle Ages.* Ann Arbor: University of Michigan Press, 1999.

Kott, Jan. *The Eating of the Gods: An Interpretation of Greek Tragedy.* London: Eyre Methuen, 1970.

Leyerle, Blake. *Theatrical Shows and Ascetic Lives.* Berkeley, London, Los Angeles: University of California Press, 2001.

___ . *Theatrical Shows and Ascetic Lives: John Chroysostom's Attack on Spiritual Marriage.* Berkeley, Los Angeles, London: University of California Press, 2001.

Loraux, Nicole. *The Divided City.* New York: Zone Books, 2006.

Malabou, Catherine. "The form of "I"." In *Augustine and Postmodernism: Confessions and Circumfession*, by John D. Caputo and Michael J. Scanlon, 127-137. Bloomington and Indianapolis: Indiana University Press, 2005.

Nancy, Jean-Luc. "The Unsacrificeable." *Yale French Studies,* No 79, 1991: 20-38.

Nietzsche, Friedrich. *On the Geneaology of Morality.* Cambridge: Cambridge University Press, 1994.

P. Foley, Michael. "Cicero, Augustine and the Philosophical Roots of Cassiciacum Dialogues." *Revue des Etudes Augustiniennes, 47*, 1999.

Plato. *Early Socratic Dialogues.* London, New York: Penguin Books, 1987.

___ . *Laws.* Mineola, New York: Dover Publications, 2006.

___ . *Symposium and the Death of Socrates.* London: Wordsworth Classics, 1997.

___ . *The Republic.* London, New York: Penguin Books, 2007.

Plutarch. *Lives.* London: George Bell and Sons, 1894/2004.

Reinelt, Janelle. "The Politics of Discourse: Performitivity Meets Theatricality." *Substance,* Vol. 31, No. 2/3, 2002: 201-215.

Rossi, Paolo. *Logic and the Art of Memory: The Quest for a Universal Language.* London and New York: Continuum, 2000.

Roudinesco, Elisabeth. *Our Dark Side: A History of Perversion.* Cambridge: Polity Press, 2009.

Schechner, Richard. *Performance Studies: An Introduction.* New York: Routledge, 2002.

Schmitt, Carl. *Hamlet and Hecuba: The Erruption of Time into Play.* Corvallis: Plutarch Press, 2006.

Tertullian. *De Spectaculis.* Cambridge, Massachusetts: Harvard University Press, 1931.

Vance, Eugene. *Marvelous Signals: Poetics and Sign Theory in the Middle Ages.* Lincoln and London: University of Nebraska Press, 1986.

Veyne, Paul. *Bread and Circuses.* London, New York: Allen Lane, The Penguin Press, 1990.

Yates, Frances A. *Theatre of the World.* London: Routledge and Kegan Paul, 1969.

Zupancic, Alenka. *The Odd One In: On Comedy.* London, England: The MIT Press, 2008.

Index